German

Genealogical

Research

by

Prof. Dr. rer. nat. Dr. phil. Dr. scient.
George K. Schweitzer

with the assistance of

Anne M. Smalley, Word Processing
Katharina Hecke, Dipl. Lehrer, Language

Neustatt an der Orla
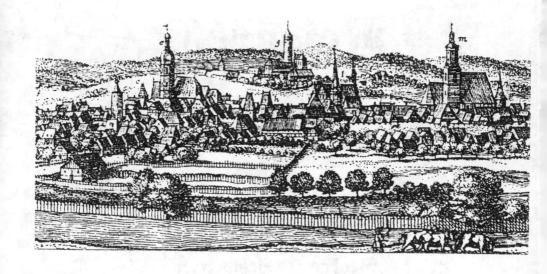

ISBN 0-913857-15-7

TABLE OF CONTENTS

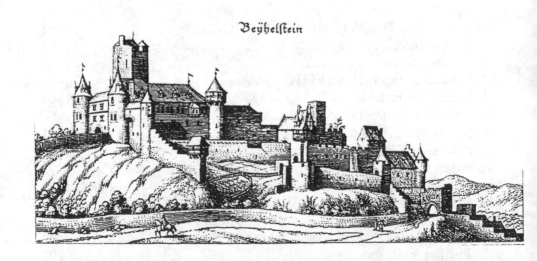

Beÿhelſtein

CHAPTER 1
(KAPITEL 1)
GERMAN BACKGROUND
(HINTERGRUNDWISSEN ÜBER DEUTSCHLAND)

1. Introduction	1. Einleitung
1. Einleitung	*1. Einleitung*

Over one-half of US citizens claim to have German ancestors, this being larger than those claiming any other ethnic ancestry. Hence, over one-half of genealogical searchers will find German forebears in their family trees. This guidebook has been compiled in order to provide these researchers with genealogically-pertinent information on (a) the geography, (b) the history, (c) the language, (d) the original records, (e) the secondary records, (f) the locations of the records in Germany, (g) research procedures in the US, and (h) research procedures in Europe for German family history research.

Present-day Germany (Bundesrepublik Deutschland or the Federal Republic of Germany) is a nation located in north central Europe, as shown by Figure 1. It is bordered on the north by the North Sea (Nordsee), Denmark (Dänemark), and the Baltic Sea (Ostsee), on the east by Poland (Polen) and Czechoslovakia (Tschechoslowakei), on the south by Austria (Österreich), Liechtenstein, and Switzerland (die Schweiz), and on the west by France (Frankreich), Luxembourg (Luxemburg), Belgium (Belgien), and the Netherlands (die Niederlande). Figure 2 displays the 16 states (Länder) of Germany (Deutschland). Notice that three of these states are constituted by large cities and their immediate surroundings: Bremen, Hamburg, and Berlin. The states (Länder) with larger areas are Schleswig-Holstein, Mecklenburg-Vorpomerania (Mecklenburg-Vorpommern), Lower Saxony (Niedersachsen), Saxony-Anhalt (Sachsen-Anhalt), Brandenburg, North Rhine-Westphalia (Nordrhein-Westfalen), Hesse (Hessen), Thuringia (Thüringen), Saxony (Sachsen), Rhineland-Palatinate (Rheinland-Pfalz), Saarland, Baden-Wuerttemberg (Baden-Württemberg), and Bavaria (Bayern).

The total population of Germany is about 79 million, with North Rhine-Westphalia (Nordrhein-Westfalen) being the most populous [17

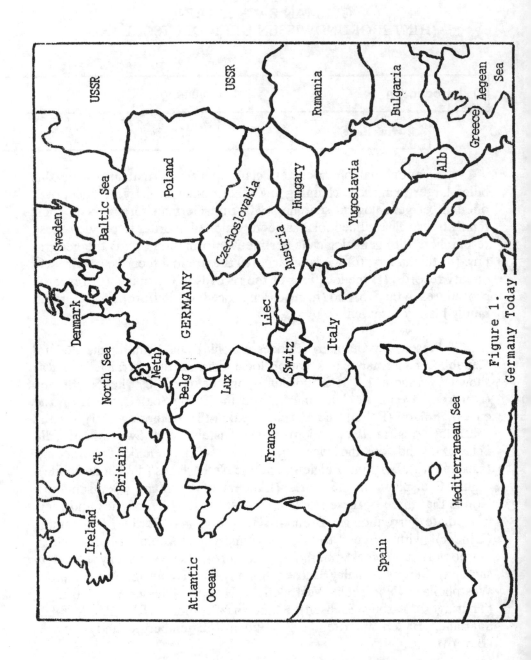

Figure 1.
Germany Today

Figure 2. Germany's States

million] state and Bremen the least [0.7 million]. The largest cities, listed in decreasing order, are Berlin [3.4 million], Hamburg [1.6], Munich (München) [1.3], Cologne (Köln) [1.0], Bremen [0.7], Essen [0.6], Frankfurt (Frankfurt) [0.6], Duesseldorf (Düsseldorf) [0.6], Stuttgart [0.6], Hannover [0.5], Nuremberg (Nürnberg) [0.5], Leipzig [0.5], Dresden [0.5], Wuppertal [0.4], Bonn [0.3], Chemnitz [0.3], Magdeburg [0.3], and Karlsruhe [0.3]. Well over 80% of Germans live in cities. The major religious faiths are Roman Catholic (katholisch) and Protestant [Lutheran-Reformed] (evangelisch). Catholics predominate in the southern and southeastern regions of Germany, with Protestants being in the majority elsewhere.

One of the major problems with German genealogical research is that there was no strongly, singly united Germany until 1871. Prior to this time, Germany was almost always a conglomeration of independent or semi-independent states (countries, principalities, duchies, domains, kingdoms, dominions, margravates) held loosely together by some common bond: religion, language, a mutual enemy, economic need, and sometimes the force of one of their number which had attained partial military domination. These states were continually splitting, coalescing, rising to power, falling from power, cooperating, warring, and rearranging. In order to make this mess manageable, it is helpful to refer to the stable, unified Germany of 1871-1914, and to use it as a standard.

2. The Germany of 1871–1914	2. Deutschland 1871–1914
2. Deutschland 1871-1914	2. Deutschland 1871-1914

In 1871, the many independent states of north-central Europe, all of which had large German-speaking populations, were united by Prussia (Preussen) through military force. The resulting German Empire (Deutsches Reich) is depicted in Figure 3, where the names of its constituent states (Länder) are given in their German forms. The English names for those which differ from the German are as follows: Bayern (Bavaria), Braunschweig (Brunswick), Elsass (Alsace), Hessen (Hesse), Hessen-Darmstadt (Hesse-Darmstadt), Königreich Sachsen (Kingdom of Saxony), Lothringen (Lorraine), Ostpreussen (East Prussia), Pfalz (Palatinate), Pommern (Pomerania), Rheinland (Rhineland), Sachsen (Saxony), Schlesien (Silesia), Westfalen (Westphalia), Westpreussen (West Prussia), and Württemberg (Wuerttemberg).

7

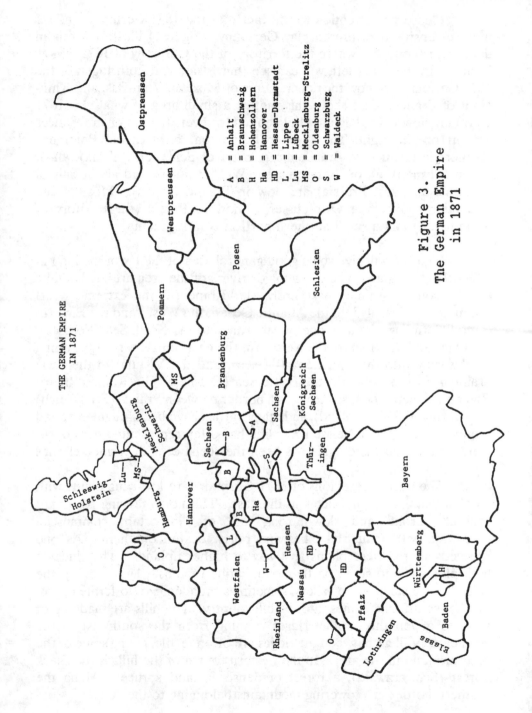

Figure 3.
The German Empire
in 1871

Please pay attention to the fact that the 1871 Germany was far more extensive than present-day Germany. Figure 4 illustrates this in detail and shows you where the territory of the Germany of 1871 is now located. In the lower left, you can see that Elsass and Lothringen of the 1871 Germany are now the departments of Moselle, Rhin-Bas, and Rhin-Haut of France. Just above this, notice a small area of what was 1871 Germany now is in Belgium (Belgien). However, the major differences are off on the right. There you will see that most of old Pommern (Pomerania), much of Brandenburg, most of Schlesien (Silesia), all of Posen (Posnan), all of Westpreussen (West Prussia), and about half of Ostpreussen (East Prussia) are now in Poland (Polen). Most of the remaining top half of Ostpreussen is now in Russia (the territory of Kaliningrad) and a small northern portion is in Lithuania.

Figure 5 will give you a good general idea of the lay of the land in 1871-1914 Germany. The seven major rivers of the area are the Danube (in the south) draining eastwardly, the Rhine (in the extreme west) draining northwardly into the Atlantic Ocean, the Weser and the Elbe (in central Germany) draining northwestwardly into the North Sea (Nordsee), the Oder and its tributary the Neisse (in the east central region) draining northwardly into the Baltic Sea (Ostsee), and the Vistula (in the east) draining northwardly into the Baltic Sea (Ostsee). The Rhine (Rhein) River has functioned historically as a border between France (Frankreich) and Germany (Deutschland), and many battles have been fought over and around it. The Oder-Neisse River line has often represented the Polish-German interface, and again has been the scene of many armed clashes.

The northern regions of 1871 Germany are low-lying plains with an abundance of inland lakes in the east. The north-flowing rivers are generally broad and slow-moving and are important commercial waterways with industrial cities and ports located on them. As one proceeds south, these plains give way to higher uplands. They include both plateaus and some partly mountainous regions. The rivers in the uplands have steep, deep valleys, sometimes broadening into fertile basins. Further south, one comes into the hill country. The hills are made up of a series of lengthy parallel ridges running from the southwest to the northeast. Valleys between the ridges are often fertile, giving some of the best farmland in the area. In the western fourth of the hills is the Black Forest (Schwarzwald), a forest of dense fir and spruce. Along the southern border are towering mountains belonging to the Alps.

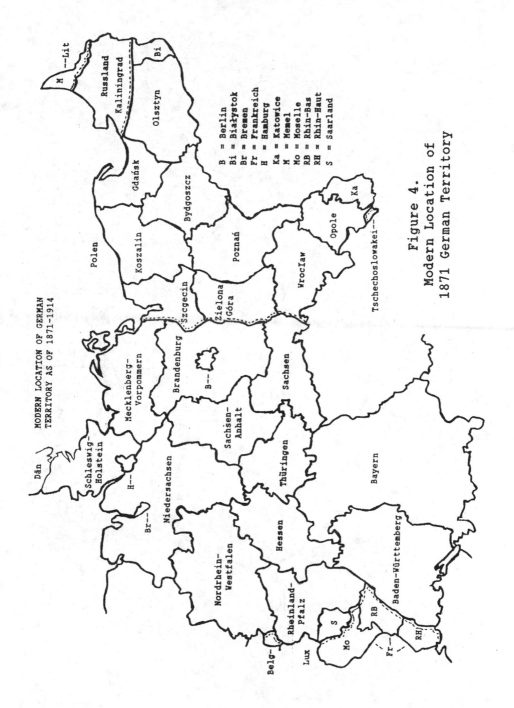

Figure 4.
Modern Location of
1871 German Territory

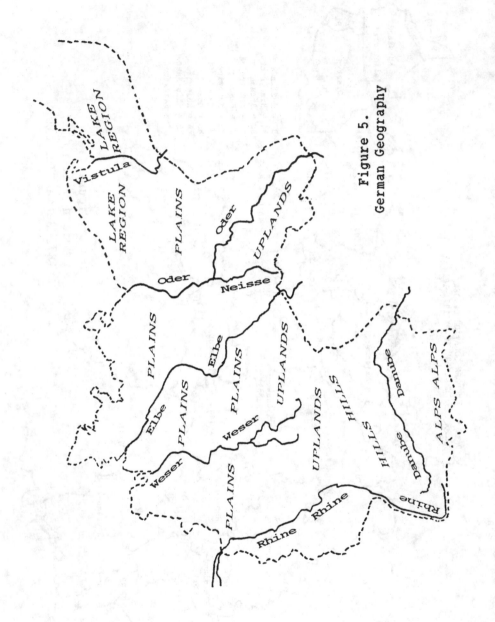

Figure 5.
German Geography

Figure 6 provides a more detailed map of 1871 German rivers. Please take note of the major rivers (Danube, Rhein, Weser, Elbe, Oder, Neisse, Vistula), and look at their numerous tributaries. These water courses and their valleys were important transportation routes during the main population movements of Germanic history. Figure 7 shows the major cities and towns of the Germany of 1871. Recall that two of them in the southwest (Strassburg, Colmar) are now in France, and many in the east (Kolberg, Stettin, Greifenberg, Schwiebus, Breslau, Posen, Oppeln, Beuthen, Bromberg and Rössel) are now in Poland. Königsberg is in the USSR, and Memel is in Lithuania. Those cities in the east have undergone name changes since they ceased to belong to 1871 Germany, so it is well to recognize that they must often be sought under their new names. This will be discussed in more detail later, because many smaller cities and towns also changed names.

3. Early Germanic History, to 481	3. Frühe germanische Geschichte bis 481
3. Frühe germanische Geschichte bis 481	*3. Frühe germanische Geschichte bis 481*

In this section, we will begin a brief history of the formation and development of Germanic peoples and governments into the unified Germany of 1871, and then into modern-day Germany. In order to understand this quite complicated series of events and the accompanying geographic changes, it is necessary that you review and frequently use the maps of 1871 Germany (Figures 3-7) and present-day Germany (Figures 1-2). Before proceeding to the detailed history, make sure that you have a good feel for the maps shown in Figures 1-7. You can assure yourself of this by looking at each map, placing your index finger on every name, and pronouncing it aloud as you do so. We will be referring to these maps repeatedly, so please don't fail to give yourself a good acquaintance with them. And remember that the Germany of 1871 functions as our standard reference Germany.

During the 100s BC, the Roman Empire had expanded north and northwest into present-day France and into the south of present-day Germany (see Figure 1). The borders of their dominion were represented by the Rhine (Rhein) and Danube (Donau) Rivers, that is, they occupied the land west of the Rhine and south of the Danube (see Figure 5). Just beyond this frontier (east of the Rhine and north of the Danube) were

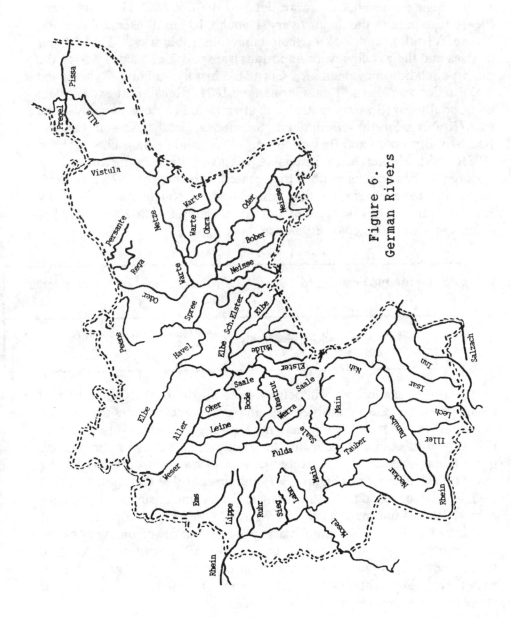

Figure 6.
German Rivers

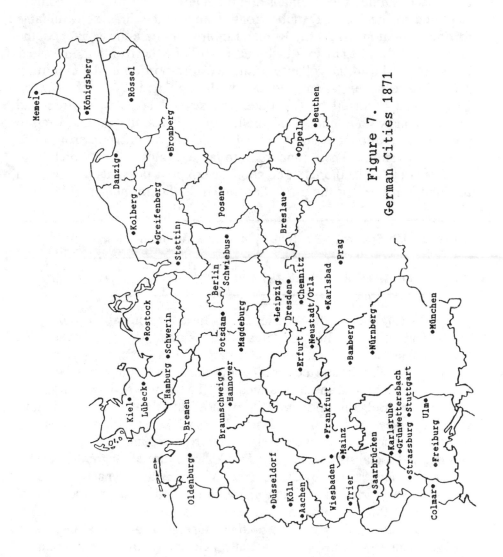

Figure 7.
German Cities 1871

numerous Germanic tribes. In 7 BC-9 AD, the Romans made several successful invasions of the tribal territories, but in 9 AD they suffered a defeat near the Weser River. Abandoning any further large-scale attempts to subdue the Germans and the many other tribes, the Romans retreated to the Rhine-Danube frontier and built a line of formidable fortifications along it. As the Roman Empire subsequently weakened, the Germanic tribes began to attack and push back the frontier until their invasions produced the collapse of the Western portion of the empire in 476. Mass tribal migrations into, out of, through, and beyond the Roman Empire had occurred by this date, and several large new tribes had formed along with a number of smaller ones. Thus, the Roman Empire was carved up into many kingdoms, which developed into numerous large and small manors. These manors were large estates of land which were ruled over by the landlords. The people were poor peasants who worked the land in return for the protection which the landowner provided.

4. The Frankish Empire, 481–919	4. Das Fränkische Reich 481–919
4. Das Fränkische Reich 481-919	*4. Das Fränkische Reich*

During the period 481-511, Clovis the Merovingian, leader of the large group called the Franks, defeated the Roman governor in the area, then subdued and unified many Germanic tribes to form the Frankish Empire. The Franks started their conquests in what is now northeastern France. They moved south into most of what is now France, north into what is now Belgium and the Netherlands, and west into what is now Germany (see Figure 1). Clovis became a Christian, sponsored missionary work among his subjects, and introduced much of Roman law, culture, and social structures. The Frankish Empire at its greatest extent under the successors to Clovis (the Merovingian Dynasty) covered territory now included in France, Belgium, and western and central Germany. In the area of Germany, the Franks exercised at least nominal control over the Rhineland Franks, the Thuringians of central Germany, the Alemanni (Swabians) of south-central Germany, and the Bavarians of south Germany (see Figure 3).

In 751, Pepin the Short took over the leadership of the Franks, ending the Merovingian Dynasty, and establishing the Carolingian Dynasty. Pepin's son Charlemagne (Karl der Grosse), who came to power in 768, extended the Frankish Empire north, east, and south. He pushed northward toward what is now Denmark, southward into Spain and Italy, and eastward in Germany to the Elbe River. The Bavarians and Carinthians in southeastern Germany were thoroughly subdued, and the Saxons in northern Germany were also conquered. Bohemia, Moravia, and Pannonia (beyond the Elbe River) were made tributaries. In short, most of Europe came under Charlemagne's sovereignty, except for Britain and much of Spain. In 800, the Pope crowned Charlemagne emperor, recognizing him as the Christian successor to the Caesars of the Roman Empire. Because of the vastness of the empire and the transportation and communication difficulties of the time, Charlemagne's control over local officials was often only minimal. Even so, his military forces kept an effective unity, and the church continued to spread and to take up land.

Upon the death of Karl der Grosse (Charlemagne) in 814, his son Louis took over. The empire began a slow disintegration, with local and regional rulers asserting themselves. Gradually the landholders and rulers began changing their feudal fiefs into hereditary estates. A commoner in these times owed allegiance to five different authorities: (1) the local or regional landholder [who was in turn under the leader of the state], (2) the leader of the state [states were now in the process of forming or had formed out of tribes], (3) the emperor, to whom the leaders of the states were responsible [sometimes loosely, other times tightly], (4) the regional archbishops and bishops, and (5) the pope. The commoner could come into conflict with any or all of these. These authorities could come into conflict with each other. And the history of the Germanic areas and peoples from this time for over 1000 years was a history of continual conflicts among all of these. The net result was to keep there from being a large strongly united German nation rather than a loose collection of small and medium-sized independent or semi-independent states. One of the important ploys of the emperors was to establish free cities whose officials reported to them only. The free cities became centers of commerce, trade, craftsmanship, wealth, and power. The practice of dividing lands by inheritance to all sons resulted in the proliferation of independent states. Bishops and abbots (leaders of monasteries) often held land, became independent rulers, and gathered great wealth. With this view of what was happening and was to continue to happen, we once again pick up the chronological stream.

When Louis died in 840, his kingdom went to his three sons. The territory of the West Franks (roughly in modern France) went to Charles, the territory of the East Franks (roughly in modern Germany) went to Louis (Ludwig), and Lothar received the emperorship and a narrow strip

of land between the two others. This land ran roughly from modern-day
Belgium and Netherlands through the Elsass-Lothringen, on down to Italy
(see Figures 1 and 3). Its central section was called Lotharingen. In 870,
the area of the newly-formed Germanic kingdom was increased by the
addition of much of Lotharingen. In 911, the last ruler of the German
branch of the Carolingean Dynasty died. By this date, five strong duchies
had formed in the Germanic region: Sachsen (Saxony), Franken
(Franconia), Bayern (Bavaria), Swabia, and Lotharingen (Lorraine). The
first four elected Conrad of Franconia king, then in 919 elected Henry of
Saxony, thus inaugurating the Sachsen (Saxon) Dynasty, which was to
prevail until 1024.

5. The Holy Roman Empire, 919–1293	5. Das Heilige Römische Reich 919–1293
5. Das Heilige Römische Reich 919-1293	5. Das Heiligen Römischen Reich 919-1293

Henry of Saxony (Sachsen), the first emperor of the Saxon
Dynasty, secured Lotharingia to his domain and raised his prestige by
leading forces which drove invading Hungarians back. His son Otto, who
came to the throne in 936, increased the power of the king over the other
rulers (dukes), dominated the church officials, used the church as his
governmental structure, established some degree of centralized government, and extended the empire further east into Slavic regions. When
Otto expanded his power into Italy, the two areas were combined in 962
when the pope crowned him as emperor of the Holy Roman Empire
which excluded France. The Saxon kings ruled until 1024 on the strength
of Otto having made the Holy Roman Empire the most powerful country
in Europe. Otto's successors became so involved with Italy that they
tended to neglect the Germanic areas, and the dukes reasserted their
independence, weakening the central authority.

In 1024, upon the death of the Saxon king, the major rulers of the
largest states elected Conrad the Salian (or Franconian) king. His son
Henry (reigned 1039-1056) promoted reform in the church which resulted
in a strong alliance of the church and the crown. The strength of the
church-emperor combination threatened the lesser rulers, some of whom
unsuccessfully rebelling. The next king in the line, also named Henry,
ruled 1056-1105, but in his reign a long power struggle between the
emperors and the papacy began. The pope turned against the growing

power of the emperor and allied himself with the dukes (the lesser rulers or princes), causing the dukes to win back the power previously taken away, thus weakening the emperor. During this time, the merchants in cities began to gain influence, which they lent to the emperor. In 1138, the first Hohenstauffen emperor came to rule, and some restoration of unity and order occurred. The second Hohenstauffen ruler was Frederick Barbarossa, who was crowned in 1155. He unsuccessfully challenged the power of the pope, whose military forces drove him out of Italy. However, when Frederick Barbarossa turned toward subduing the dukes of the Germanic areas, he was eminently successful. For the next 600 years, the Germanic area was a patchwork quilt (or jigsaw puzzle) of numerous small secular and church-owned principalities and free cities. They engaged in much warfare among themselves and against invaders, and various ones of them rose and fell as regional superpowers.

A further action of Frederick Barbarossa was to extend his territory to the east, where the Slavs were Christianized. This eastward expansion and evangelization continued for 200 years as Germans conquered, then sent in missions, then settled in the new areas. Frederick Barbarossa's successors were overwhelmed by the resurgent powers of the papal-dukes alliance and by French and English interference. This caused the Germanic region to revert once again to a multiplicity of regional principalities, rather than becoming a single, unified nation as England and France were doing. Amazingly, during this turbulence, much economic and cultural progress was achieved. Cities, trade, and commerce prospered and expanded. Toward the end of this period (1254), there were about 1600 separate principalities, cities and towns. Beginning in 1227, Prussia (Preussen) was conquered by a Germanic religious order, the Teutonic Knights, and settlers from the west came in. Between 1254 and 1273, general chaos set in, there being essentially no central authority. Warring and raiding princes terrorized the country, and lawlessness prevailed. This turmoil was to ebb and flow over the next two centuries.

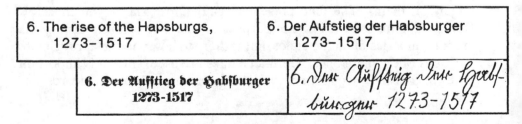

6. The rise of the Hapsburgs, 1273–1517	6. Der Aufstieg der Habsburger 1273–1517
6. Der Aufstieg der Habsburger 1273-1517	6. Der Aufstieg der Habsburger 1273-1517

In 1273, Rudolph, Count of Hapsburg (on the upper Rhine), was elected by the main Germanic princes as emperor. The general national disintegration and fragmentation continued. Rudolph added Austria, Styria, Carinthia, and Carniola to his own holdings, but exercised little power as emperor. The electors (main states) selected Adolph of Nassau to succeed Rudolph, but deposed him in 1298 because of his territorial ambitions. The next 140 years were occupied with elections of weak emperors from various states, papal interventions and conflicts, and collusion of the electors to retain their independent powers (Archbishops of Mainz, Cologne, and Trier, and rulers of Palatine, Saxony, Brandenburg, and Bohemia). During 1347-1352, the Black Death (bubonic plague) ravaged Europe, killing about a third of the population. About 1350, strong leagues (cooperatives) of towns began to form for the promotion, regulation, and protection of commerce. Powerful guilds of craftsmen were organized, and trade became broadspread and profitable. In 1409 Hus, a Bohemian professor, advocated church reform, was then excommunicated, convinced many people of his views, and was burned at the stake in 1415. This action led to a series of Hussite Wars in 1419-1436 in which Hus's followers fought Catholics. A compromise was reached in 1436. A preview of the coming Reformation had been enacted.

In 1438, Albert of Hapsburg was elected Holy Roman Emperor. For 368 years from this date, every emperor would be a member of the Hapsburg Dynasty which came to have its center in Vienna, Austria. The emperors who followed Albert added vast territories to the Hapsburg holdings. By 1500, the Hapsburgs were the dominant world power. They held all of what is now Austria, Germany, Switzerland, Czechoslovakia, Hungary, the Netherlands, Belgium, Luxembourg, and Spain, plus parts of Poland, the Ukraine, Rumania, Yugoslavia, Italy, and France. Their major competition in the Germanic region was the Hohenzollern family which ruled Brandenburg (and later Prussia). There were, therefore, two predominant powers in the Germanic area: the Hapsburgs in the south with their headquarters in Vienna, and the Hohenzollerns in the north with their headquarters in Berlin. The future of Germany was to depend largely on them. The map presented as Figure 8 shows you the Holy Roman Empire as of 1517. The purpose of the map is not to display the exact boundaries of all the states, but rather to show you the approximate locations of the main ones. German names are used, since it is important that you become acquainted with them, because German records use them.

Figure 8.
Holy Roman Empire in 1517

7. The Reformation, 1517–1648	7. Die Reformation 1517–1648
7. Die Reformation 1517-1648	*7. Die Reformation*

In 1517, Luther posted his 95 objections to abuses in the Catholic Church on the door of the church at Wittenberg. This action set in motion the Protestant Reformation. As the movement was gaining momentum among peasants, nobles, princes, and townspeople, Charles V came to the throne (1519). The German princes and the free cities saw at once that by siding with Luther they could acquire considerable advantage against the emperor and the pope. The princes were eager to take over the vast church land holdings, and the peasants hoped they would be freed from their landlords. Charles moved quickly to squelch the growing tide, and in 1521, he presided over a meeting which ordered Protestants to return to Catholicism, and ordered the arrest of Luther. Luther went into hiding, and the Protestant revolt continued at an accelerated pace. In 1524-1525, many peasants rebelled, but were promptly and brutally put down by the imperial forces. Other Protestant groups began to form, Anabaptists moving to Moravia to seek freedom. Even though Charles defeated the combined forces of Protestant princes and free cities in 1547, the Protestant pressures mounted, and Charles agreed in 1555 to permit the people of every state to adopt the religion of its ruler. In addition to Catholic and Lutheran states, Calvinism (the Reformed faith) was selected by the Palatinate in 1563, and spread into Nassau, Bremen, and Brandenburg.

A Catholic reform movement began and large areas of central Europe reverted to Catholic control. In 1563 this counter reformation mandated that all Catholic parishes begin keeping registers of christenings and marriages. For some several years, there was a temporary end to religious wars. The southern and Rhineland areas of the Holy Roman Empire (Austria, Bavaria, part of Bohemia, Rhineland) remained Catholic, but most of the rest had gone Protestant (Lutheran chiefly). Protestants also began keeping registers of vital data (christenings/births, marriages, burials/ deaths) about this time, the exact dates varying from area to area.

Lutheranism and Calvinism (particularly in the Upper Rhineland) continued to make gains in Europe, and tension between them and Catholic areas increased. In 1614, Catholic priests were ordered to start keeping death records in addition to christening and birth records.

During the 1555-1607 period of peace, the situation moved steadily toward armed conflict. Two hostile confederations, one Protestant, the other Catholic, quickly formed following a Bavarian attack on a Protestant town. In 1618, when the prince of Bohemia sought to restore Catholicism as the major religion, the nobles revolted. This action started the Thirty Years' War, which devastated the empire 1618-1648. The Thirty Years' War was actually a series of several wars in which a number of armies crossed and recrossed the Germanic areas (north to south, east to west, and back, again and again) destroying towns and cities, killing people, laying waste the countryside, raiding, marauding, and disabling commerce and transportation. Included were the armies of the Germanic Catholic League and Spain on one side, and the armies of the Germanic Protestant Union and Denmark, Sweden, and France on the other. The three latter European nations were afraid of the growing power of the Hapsburgs and also saw the opportunity to gain Germanic land.

The war ended in 1648, but the Germanic region was left in a shambles, with misery, poverty, and starvation, with about a third of its people dead, with many towns in ruins, and with essentially no political structure. The region was reduced to a loose confederation of more than 350 independent petty principalities with an overall emperor in name only. France had taken over the Alsace-Lorraine, Sweden had acquired part of Pommerania, Spain had occupied the Palatinate 1619-1648, and Switzerland and the Netherlands had gained their independence. Nearly every German city and town had been sacked and pillaged repeatedly, agriculture was destroyed, and the population was reduced from 20 to 13 million. In duration, devastation, ferocity, and violence, this war dwarfed all previous Germanic military actions. Large numbers of church records, both Catholic and Protestant, were lost during this turmoil, and record-keeping activities were repeatedly interrupted. Figure 9 shows you the major principalities of the Holy Roman Empire as of 1648. The map is not designed to portray exact boundaries, but to give you an idea of the situation and approximate locations of the main principalities. Remember that there were over 350 in all, so lots of smaller ones are not named on the map.

Figure 9. Holy Roman Empire in 1648

8. The Austrian–Prussian conflict, 1648–1789	8. Der Österreichisch–Preussische Konflikt 1648–1789
8. Der Österreichisch-Preussische Konflikt 1648-1789	*8. Der Österreichisch-Preussische Konflikt 1648-1789*

At the end of the Thirty Years' War, Germany was devastated and disorganized. The emperor could not make laws, collect taxes, or raise military. Only a complicated three-chambered legislature (Diet) made up of representatives of the highly-fragmented and independent components of the empire could do that. They usually opposed the Hapsburg emperor, constantly challenging his efforts to unite the empire. The general weakness of the Germanic area invited foreign invaders. Between 1667 and 1713, the empire was invaded several times by France which was rapidly expanding and intent on taking lands around the Rhine (Rhein) River. The territories of the Alsace (Elsass), and parts of the Palatinate (Pfalz) and the electorate of Trier were occupied by France. The Palatinate was devastated in 1674, Strasbourg (Strassburg) was taken in 1681, and further violence was brought to the Palatinate in 1688. The French did not leave the Palatinate (Pfalz) until 1697, having treated the population very harshly. Meanwhile Sweden (Schweden), took some territory in Brandenburg. During these times, in 1683, the first group of German immigrants came to the American colonies, settling in suburban Philadelphia. In 1683, the southeastern Germanic states in the Hapsburg dominion annihilated the invading Turks, then took over Hungary and much of Serbia and Wallachia. The Spanish Netherlands was also acquired, so that as of 1718, Austria (the Hapsburgs) had become very powerful. In reaction to the terrible situation of warfare, poverty, and religious suppression in the Rhineland and Palatinate, people left these areas, many coming to America beginning in 1708.

As the Hapsburgs rose to power in the south, another power began to emerge in the north, the state of Brandenburg-Prussia (Brandenburg-Preussen). In that state, the ruler began increasing his control by developing an efficient administrative bureaucracy, a central-ized tax system, and a well-trained army. King Frederick William (reigned 1713-1740) made the army into a formidable military machine of over 80,000 soldiers. In 1731, Protestants were expelled from Salzburg, a reflection of the ban against them in Austria, and some of the group went to the American colony of Georgia. Up to this time, Brandenburg-Prussia was moderately loyal to the Hapsburg emperor. When the Hapsburg emperor died, leaving only a daughter (Maria Theresa), Prussia (Preussen) in 1742 took Silesia (Schlesien) from Austria, and then the electors of the empire chose Albert of Bavaria as the next emperor. Maria Theresa rallied her possessions, defended herself as heir of the Hapsburg lands, and saw to the election of her husband as emperor. However, she did not regain Silesia. She then reorganized the Hapsburg kingdom, established a centralized government, and raised a 100,000-man army. In 1756, the Seven Years War, Austria against Prussia, broke out, and lasted until 1763. The Prussians narrowly missed defeat at the hands of Russia (Austria's ally), but emerged victorious, gaining more territory.

The influence of the Hapsburg emperor and of Austria continued a slow decline, while Prussian power was rising. In 1772, Russia, Prussia, and Austria partitioned Poland, Prussia receiving West Prussia (West Preussen) or Polish Prussia in the process. When the Austrians tried to secure Bavaria for themselves in 1777, the Prussians went to Bavaria's defense, and Austria gave up. After this, there was a period of peace, growing prosperity, industrial expansion, population increase, and enlargement of towns. The situation at this time involved two very strong major powers: the Hapsburgs of Austria (Vienna) and the Prussian Kingdom (Berlin). The rest of the Germanic region largely remained a country of petty despots who severely abused and overtaxed their subjects, and often expelled people not of the official religion. Only Württemberg and Sachsen-Weimar were exceptions. During this period, there occurred two important events with relation to emigration. The first was the invitation by the empress of Russia in 1763 for Germanic people to settle in southern Russia: west of the Volga River, around Odessa (on the Black Sea), and in central Ukrainia. The second was the participation of Hessian and other Germanic soldiers in the Revolutionary War as mercenaries of the British.

9. The French invasions, 1789–1815	9. Die Französischen Invasionen 1789–1815
9. Die Französischen Invasionen 1789-1815	9. Die Französischen Invasionen 1789-1815

The French Revolution began in 1789, and brought in an age of jingoistic patriotism accompanied by the raising of a huge army. In 1792, France declared war on Austria-Prussia, an Austrian-Prussian army invaded France, and was defeated. A second and third partition of Poland occurred in 1793 and 1795, both Prussia and Austria gaining territory. In 1793-4, the French conquered the west bank of the Rhine (Rhineland, Palatinate), and in 1798 started civil registration of births, marriages, and deaths in these areas. In 1799, a coalition (Austria, Russia, Britain) had initial success in war against France, but Austria was defeated in 1800, and the others withdrew. In 1803 Napoleon of France abolished 117 Germanic states and free cities in the western half of Germany, took land belonging to the church, and reorganized by apportioning the territories among the major Germanic states: Bavaria, Baden, and Wuerttemberg. In 1805 Austrian forces were again defeated by the French, more territory was given up, and the emperor of the Holy Roman Empire abdicated, thus dissolving the old empire. The newly constituted 167 principalities were given control of the southern and western Germanic areas, were organized into the Confederation of the Rhine, were given protection by Napoleon, and furnished the French with troops. Included in this Confederation were Mecklenburg, Hannover, Rhineland, Hessen, the Thuringen States, Saxony, Anhalt, Baden, Wuerttemberg, and Bavaria. See Figure 10 for locations, and when you do, recognize that the remainder of the territory belonged to the two largest states: Prussia in the northeast, and Austria in the southeast.

In light of the defeats of Austria, and the capture and reorganization of the western Germanic area, Prussia went to war against France in 1806. Once again France dealt them a crushing defeat. Prussia's territory west of the Elbe became a new state, Westphalia; Prussia's Polish lands became the Grand Duchy of Warsaw, and all of northern Germany was taken into the Confederation of the Rhine. French influence and control throughout the Germanic territories was strong during 1806-1813. Most of the Germanic states adopted centralized administration, abolished influence of the local estates, curtailed serfdom, moved toward religious toleration, and promoted civil rights. The degree to which these occurred varied roughly with the distance from France. Reform movements started in Austria and Prussia, both of which were somewhat independent, and Austria had raised sufficient military forces to fight Napoleon again in 1809, only to be re-defeated. They lost Salzburg and Tyrol to Bavaria. In Prussia, reform was not only military, but governmental and educational changes for the good were remarkable. In 1812, Prussia began to rally the Germanic states and their allies, and in 1813 the French were driven from Germany at the decisive battle of Leipzig. In 1814, Napolcon was again defeated in France, resulting in the restoration of the Rhineland to the German Confederation. In early 1815, Prussia was given control of

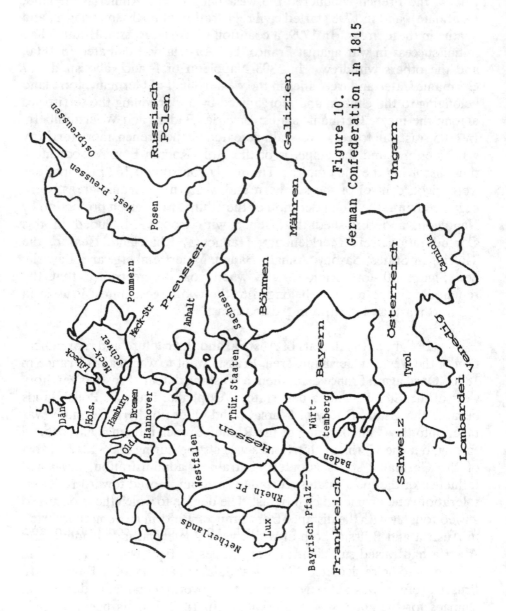

Figure 10.
German Confederation in 1815

about half of Saxony and most of the Rhineland, and later in the year Napoleon was finally defeated at Waterloo.

10. The German Confederations, 1815–1871	10. Die Deutschen Konföderationen 1815–1871

10. Die Deutſchen Konföderationen 1815-1871	*10. Die Deutſchen Konföd-rationen 1815-1871*

In 1815, thirty-nine Germanic states, now being free of the French yoke, formed a loose cooperative union called the German Confederation. This German Confederation is depicted in Figure 10. The union was loosely governed by a parliament consisting of ambassadors of the member states, and it was presided over by Austria. They awarded the Rhineland, Westphalia, and much of Saxony to Prussia. In many places sentiment was high for a unified German democracy, but the rulers were strongly opposed. With industry and transportation expanding rapidly, it was obvious that 39 German states, each with its own government, currency, taxes, laws, regulations, and tariffs, were effective barriers to commerce and social progress. Prussia began to break through these barriers in 1818, when it eliminated tariffs throughout its kingdom, and encouraged other states to follow. In 1834, Prussia established a customs union (Zollverein) and was joined by 22 other states, but Austria refused membership.

A gradually rising tide of liberalism broke out in the Germanic states in 1848 as a series of rebellions. The people were demanding abolition of feudal restrictions, greater religious toleration, governmental responsibility, and freedom of expression. In many states, reforms were made; in most states, promises were made. And a meeting of representatives of the states was held in Frankfurt. They framed a constitution, and invited the king of Prussia to head a new government. The emperor refused, and he and Austria quickly moved to suppress the Revolution of 1848 by military means. Nationalism (the quest for German unity) and liberalism (the quest for freedom) were both crushed. In 1864, when Denmark tried to assert stronger control over Schleswig, Holstein, and Lauenburg, both Prussia and Austria declared war on them. They readily took the territories, but Prussia used the question of dividing up the duchies to pick a war with Austria. When Prussia drove the Austrians out of Holstein, the Austro-Prussian War of 1866 resulted. The Austrians were defeated and were expelled from the German Confederation. The

Prussians took over northern Germany by annexation or by states joining the North German Confederation under Prussia's presidency. The southern German states (Bavaria, Wuerttemberg, Baden, Hesse-Darmstadt) were induced to sign military alliance treaties with Prussia.

As of 1868, two powerful nations dominated Europe, feared each other, coveted parts of each others lands, and were moving toward armed conflict: Prussia and France. In 1870, the Franco-Prussian war started, and the southern German states immediately joined Prussia. The German armies won decisive victories in 1870 and 1871, and France ceded the Alsace (Elsass) and part of Lorraine (Lothringen) to Germany. We say Germany, because when the southern states joined Prussia in the war, the North German Confederation became the German Empire with the emperor (Kaiser) being the King of Prussia. All of the Germanic states (except for Austria) were now parts of a united German country, nation, or empire. This Germany is the one shown in Figure 3 and in Figure 11.

11. The German Empire, 1871–1918	11. Das Deutsche Reich 1871–1918
11. Das Deutsche Reich 1871-1918	11. Das Deutsche Reich 1871-1918

The newly-formed German Empire had a pseudo-democratic parliament, but actual power rested with the emperor (Kaiser) and his ministers, particularly the chancellor. Chancellor Bismarck, who had engineered and supervised Prussia's takeover of Germany, established an authoritarian regime. Many reforms were started in the areas of legal, financial, transportation, social, and military affairs. The tightened regulations facilitated industrial, commercial, educational, and technological expansions. All of these made Germany the foremost manufacturing country in Europe. The socialist-minded workers organized trade unions, demanded concessions and reforms, and in reaction, the government established an extensive social welfare system. Bismarck's foreign policy was an intentional stance carefully designed to avoid war so that Germany could develop. In 1876, civil registration of vital records (births, marriages, deaths) was started throughout Germany.

The emperor who came to the throne in 1888 dismissed Bismarck, adopted an aggressive foreign policy, took the attitude that Germany was surrounded and repressed by hostile powers, began building Germany into a military nation, and firmed up an alliance with Austria-Hungary and Italy. To counter this, an alliance of Britain, France, and Russia took shape during 1894-1904. In 1914, a Serb assassinated the heir to the throne of Austria-Hungary, and Austria-Hungary declared war on Serbia, an ally of Russia. Germany then declared war on Russia, and within a few days all of Europe was at war. On one side were Germany, Austria-Hungary, and Italy; on the other side were Serbia, Russia, France, and Britain. Italy would change sides in 1915. German armies invaded Belgium, France, and Russia. The US entered the war in 1917; in that same year, a revolution in Russia caused its withdrawal from the war.

The German forces in the west were driven back in 1918, and Germany surrendered late in 1918. In the peace treaty of 1919, Germany lost the Alsace-Lorraine to France; the northern part of Schleswig to Denmark; Upper Silesia, most of Posen, and West Prussia to the recreated Poland; three small border districts to Belgium; Memel to Lithuania; and a small area to the newly-formed Czechoslovakia. Please note that the loss of West Prussia separated East Prussia from the rest of Germany. See Figure 11.

12. The Time from 1918–1945	12. Die Zeit von 1918–1945
12. Die Zeit von 1918-1945	12. Die Zeit vom 1918-1945

In 1919, the German people elected a national assembly which drew up a constitution at Weimar for a democratic republic, known as the Weimar Republic. From the very beginning, the new government was beset with numerous problems: unemployment, hunger, war debts, demands of the victors for reparations, over 6 competing political parties, riots, strikes, inflation, radical political movements, and the efforts of the royalty and the military to regain power. A complete economic collapse was narrowly averted in 1923 when a new currency was introduced and arrangements were made with Western countries for foreign loans and an extended schedule of reparation payments. There was a slow fitful improvement thereafter, but just when recovery was imminent, the stock market in New York crashed in 1929, and a world-wide depression set in.

A small ultra-right-wing nationalistic party, the Nazis, had been active for several years, and they took advantage of the depression to push their program of saving the nation. Many were attracted by their radical ideas, and by 1930 the party had become the second largest in

30

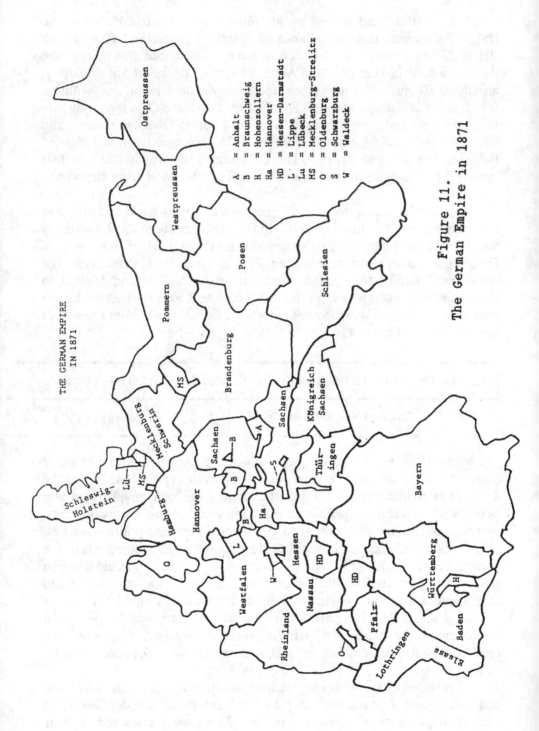

Figure 11.

The German Empire in 1871

Germany. In 1933, their leader Hitler was appointed chancellor, the Nazis won a majority in the assembly, and in 1934 Hitler assumed the dictatorship of Germany, taking the title of Leader of the Empire (Reichsführer), and he set up a totalitarian police state. An anti-Jewish campaign was launched, trade unions were abolished, the treaty of World War I was repudiated, army recruitment was accelerated, and German soldiers occupied the Rhineland. In 1936, Germany entered into alliances with Fascist Italy and Japan. By this time, Hitler had the most powerful motorized army and the largest air force in the world. In 1938 German troops took Austria without resistance and in 1939, most of Czechoslovakia was occupied. The former German territory of Memel was also annexed.

When Hitler's forces invaded Poland, Britain and France declared war, and World War II was underway. Acting rapidly, the soldiers of Germany moved during 1939-40 to take Western Poland, Belgium, the Netherlands, Denmark, Norway, most of France, most of Eastern Europe, most of the Balkans, and sizable parts of Northern Africa. Then in 1941, Germany invaded the Soviet Union. Late in that year the US declared war on Germany, and during 1942-43, the Soviet forces defeated the Germans at Stalingrad. The Nazi invaders were thereafter gradually driven back toward their homeland, while they were forced to surrender in North Africa. In Germany and occupied areas, the Nazis carried out a Jewish genocidal program, over 6 million being sent to concentration camps and killed. In the middle of 1944, US and British armies invaded France, and strategic and saturation bombing continued. By the spring of 1945, US, British, French, and Soviet armies were rapidly converging on Berlin. In May, Germany surrendered unconditionally.

13. Germany after 1945	13. Deutschland nach 1945
13. Deutschland nach 1945	13. Deutschland nach 1945

Shortly after the German surrender of 1945, the peace agreement caused Germany to lose all territories east of the Oder and Neisse Rivers. Silesia, Eastern Pomeria, the eastern part of Brandenburg, and most of East Prussia went to Poland. The Soviet Union took over the remaining portion (northeastern) of East Prussia. In the west, the Saarland was occupied by France (but only until 1957). What remained of Germany was divided into four military occupation zones, those of Great Britain (in the northwest), France (in the southwest), the US (in the central and south central), and the Soviet Union (in the east). Berlin, though within the Russian area, was similarly divided into four zones. During 1944-47, about 10 million Germans moved from the Soviet zone of Germany, Czechoslovakia, Hungary, and the above named Polish and Soviet areas to the other three zones of Germany (British, US, French).

Tensions mounted between the Soviet Union and the other three powers (Britain, US, France) during 1946-49, and in 1949, Germany was divided into two countries: the Federal Republic of Germany (Die Bundesrepublik Deutschland) in the west, and the German Democratic Republic (Die Deutsche Demokratische Republik) in the east. This division can be readily seen in Figure 2 if you will recognize that the following states were constituted in the German Democratic Republic: Mecklenburg-Vorpommern, Sachsen-Anhalt, Brandenburg, Ost-Berlin, Thüringen, and Sachsen. These states were soon reorganized by the new government into 15 districts (Bezirke). Mecklenburg-Vorpommern became the districts of Neubrandenburg, Rostock, and Schwerin; Sachsen-Anhalt became Frankfurt, Potsdam, and Cottbus; Thüringen became Erfurt, Suhl, Gera, and a small part of Leipzig; Sachsen became Leipzig, Karl-Marx Stadt, Dresden, and a small part of Cottbus; and Ost-Berlin remained Ost-Berlin.

Recovery in the Federal Republic of Germany (West Germany) was quite rapid, but such was not the case in the Deutsche Demokratische Republik (erroneously called East Germany), which came under a repressive Communist regime. By 1955, the Federal Republic of Germany was completely independent and its economy was in such good shape that it could absorb the 10 million German refugees from Eastern Europe. In 1955, the German Democratic Republic became officially free from the Soviet Union, but Soviet control continued. So bad were the conditions that between 1953-1961 almost 3 million left for the Federal Republic of Germany (West Germany). To stem these departures, the German Democratic Republic in 1961 built a wall between East and West Berlin and further strengthened their border blockades elsewhere. Slowly, conditions improved in the German Democratic Republic (east), but the Federal Republic of Germany (west) surged further ahead economically. In 1973, the two Germanies signed a treaty supporting closer relations between them, both joined the United Nations, and cooperation increased during the 1970s and 1980s. In the late 1980s when Communist systems grew weak and began to fail in Eastern Europe, the German Democratic Republic (east) also experienced these changes. In 1990, they led to the reunification of the two Germanies to give a new Bundesrepublik

Deutschland, which is pictured in Figure 2. Notice that the 15 districts (Bezirke) of the Deutsche Demokratische Republik have been redissolved into six states (Länder), almost identical to those of 1945-52.

14. States and provinces – names	14. Länder und Provinzen – Namen
14. Länder und Provinzen - Namen	*14. Länder und Provinzen*

In this section, we return briefly to the maps of 1871-1914 Germany (Figures 3, 4, and 11) and the many states (Länder) making it up. Please look back at these Figures, especially Figure 11. Then, take another careful look at Figure 2 which shows you Germany and its states (Länder) at the present time. These sixteen modern states are as follows (with abbreviations for them given in parentheses): Baden-Württemberg(BW), Bayern(B), Berlin(Be), Brandenburg(BR), Bremen(Br), Hamburg(Ha), Hessen(H), Mecklenburg-Vorpommern(MV), Niedersachsen(NS), Nordrhein-Westfalen(NW), Rheinland-Pfalz(RP), Saarland(Sa), Sachsen(S), Sachsen-Anhalt(SA), Schleswig-Holstein(SH), and Thüringen(T).

The states and sections of Germany as of 1871-1914 are very important because you will find their names cropping up very often in the records of ancestors who came to this country during the 1800s and the 1900s. Your forebears will often refer to these places as their places of origin, and it is of utmost importance that you know where they are now. The list below will help you find the present location of them. They are given in alphabetical order and then in parentheses you will find the abbreviations of the present location of them. The abbreviations given in the previous paragraph are the ones used. When the present location is not in today's Germany, the parentheses will tell you the present country and the state or states in that country.

Anhalt(SA), Baden(BW), Bayern/Pfalz(RP and Sa), Bayern(B), Birkenfeld[Oldenburg](RP), Brandenburg[Preussen](BR and Poland: Szczecin, Zielona, Poznan), Braunschweig(NS and SA), Bremen(Br),
Darmstadt[Hessen](H), Eisenach[Thüringen/Sachsen-Weimar-Eisenach](T), Elsass(Bas-Rhin and Haut-Rhin, France), Elsass-Lothringen(Moselle, Bas-Rhin, and Haut-Rhin, France), Frankenhausen[Thüringen/Schwarzburg-Rudolstadt](SA),
Hamburg(Ha), Hannover[Preussen](NS), Hessen/Wimpfen(BW), Hessen(H, RP, and BW), Hessen-Darmstadt(H), Hessen-Nassau/

Schmalkalden[Preussen](T),Hessen-Nassau/Schaumburg[Preussen](NS), Hessen-Nassau[Preussen](RP, H, T, and NS), Hohenzollern [Preussen] (BW), Holstein[Preussen/Schleswig-Holstein](SH and Southern Däne-mark),

Ilmenau[Thüringen/Sachsen-Weimar-Eisenach](T), Kamburg[Thür-ingen/Sachsen Meiningen](T and SA), Langewiesen[Thüringen/Schwarz-burg-Sonderhausen](T), Lippe(NW), Lothringen(Moselle and Bas-Rhin, France), Lübeck(SH), Lübeck[Oldenburg](SH), Mecklenburg-Schwerin (MV and BR), Mecklenburg-Strelitz(MV and BR),

Neustadt[Thüringen/Sachsen-Weimar-Eisenach](T), Oberhessen(H),Oldenburg/Lübeck(SH),Oldenburg/Birkenfeld(RP),Old-enburg(NS)Ostheim[Thüringen/Sachsen-Weimar-Eisenach/Eisenach](T), Ostpreussen[Preussen](Poland: Olsztyn, Biaystok, and Russia: Kalinin-grad),

Pfalz[Bayern](RP and Sa), Pommern[Preussen](MV, BR, and Poland: Szczecin, Koszalin, Gdansk), Posen[Preussen](Poland: Koszalin, Zielona Gora, Poznan), Preussen/Westpreussen(Poland: Koszalin, Byd-goszcz, Gdansk, and Olsztyn), Preussen/Brandenburg(BR, and Poland: Szczecin, Zielona, Poznan), Preussen/Hessen-Nassau/Schmalkalden(T), Preussen/Hohenzollern(BW), Preussen/Westfalen(NW), Preussen/Hessen-Nassau/Schaumburg(NS), Preussen/Pommern(MV, BR, and Poland: Szczecin, Koszalin, Gdansk), Preussen/Hessen-Nassau(RP, H, T, and NS), Preussen/Schleswig-Holstein(SH and Süd-Dänemark), Preussen/Ost-preussen(Poland: Olsztyn, Biaystok, and Russia: Kaliningrad), Preus-sen/Hannover(NS), Preussen/Provinz Sachsen(SA, BR, S, and T), Preus-sen/Rheinland/Wetzlar(H),Preussen/Rheinland(NW,RP,Sa,H,Belgium: Liege), Preussen/Schlesien(BR, Poland: Zielona G, Wrocaw, Opole, Katowice, Czech: Severomoravsky), Preussen/Posen(Poland: Koszalin, Zielona Gora, Poznan), Provinz Sachsen[Preussen](SA, BR, S, and T),

Rhein-Hessen(RP), Rheinland[Preussen](NW, RP, Sa, H, Belgium: Liege), Sachsen Provinz[Preussen](SA, BR, S, and T), Sachsen-Meiningen[Thüringen](T), Sachsen-Weimar-Eisenach[Thüringen](T), Schaumburg-Lippe(NS), Schaumburg[Preussen/Hessen-Nassau](NS), Schlesien[Preussen](BR, Poland: Zielona G, Wrocaw, Opole, Katowice, Czech: Severomoravsky), Schleswig-Holstein[Preussen](SH and Southern Dänemark), Schmalkalden[Preussen/Hessen-Nassau](T), Schwarzburg-Rudolstadt[Thüringen](T and SA), Schwarzburg-Sonderhausen[Thür-ingen](T),

Thüringen/Schwarzburg-Sonderhausen(T), Thüringen/Sachsen-Meiningen(T), Thüringen/Schwarzburg-Rudolstadt(T and SA), Thüringen/Sachsen-Meiningen/Kamburg(T and SA), Thüringen/Sachsen-Weimar-Eisenach(T), Waldeck(NS and H), Weimar[Thüringen/Sachsen-Weimar-

Eisenach](T), Westfalen[Preussen](NW), Westpreussen[Preussen](Poland: Koszalin, Bydgoszcz, Gdansk, and Olsztyn), Wetzlar [Preussen/Rheinland](H), Wimpfen[Hessen](BW), Württemberg(BW).

    You may find that records relating to your German progenitor refer to regions or territories different than those listed above. It is possible that these regions or territories are ones which were in the Germanic-speaking portion of Europe at earlier times, that is, before 1800. Lists of such territories for 1521-1806 and as of 1648 are given in the following:

___C. N. and A. P. Smith, ENCYCLOPEDIA OF GERMAN-AMERICAN GENEALOGICAL RESEARCH, Bowker, New York, NY, 1976, pp. 104-145. For territories 1521-1806.

___GERMAN BOUNDARY AND LOCALITY NAME CHANGES, Research Papers, Series C, Number 4, Family History Library, Salt Lake City, UT, 1978, pp. 38-39. For territories as of 1648, with notes describing changes up to 1978.

15. Recommended reading	15. Empfehlenswerte Literatur
15. Empfehlenswerte Literatur	15. Empfehlenswerte Literatur

    It is exceedingly important that you have a good understanding of German history and geography if you are to do good ancestor research in the country. This is particularly pertinent for the period from the Protestant Reformation (1517-) forward. You have been given an overview of this history in the previous pages. However, you can fix this information in your mind, and expand it, especially for your forebear's areas in Germany, by doing some further reading. It is first recommended that you read a couple of the extensive German history sections in encyclopedias:

___THE WORLD BOOK, World Book, Inc., Chicago, IL, Vol. 8, latest edition.

___ENCYCLOPEDIA AMERICANA, Grolier, Danbury, CT, Vol. 12, latest edition.

___COLLIER'S ENCYCLOPEDIA, Macmillan, New York, NY, Vol. 11, latest edition.

___ENCYCLOPEDIA BRITANNICA, Encyclopedia Britannica, Inc., Chicago, IL, Macropedia, Vol. 20, latest edition.

Once you have completed this, then it would be well if you will turn to a good brief history of Germany, and go through it in detail, paying particular attention to any areas from which you know you have ancestors:

___D. D. Detwiler, GERMANY, A SHORT HISTORY, Southern IL Univ. Press, Carbondale, IL, latest edition.

___F. Russell, editor, HORIZON CONCISE HISTORY OF GERMANY, American Heritage, New York, NY, latest edition.

___A. Maurois, AN ILLUSTRATED HISTORY OF GERMANY, Viking, New York, NY, latest edition.

Then, you should select one of the following larger histories and give it a thorough reading:

___J. E. Rodes, GERMANY, A HISTORY, Holt-Rinehart, and Winston, New York, NY, latest edition.

___V. Valentin, THE GERMAN PEOPLE, Knopf, New York, NY, latest edition.

___M. Dill, GERMANY, A MODERN HISTORY, Univ. of MI Press, Ann Arbor, MI, latest edition.

___W. H. Maehl, GERMANY IN WESTERN CIVILIZATION, Univ. of AL Press, University, AL, latest edition.

Finally, we will recommend to you a multi-volumed work which may be used for details on specific time periods or on specific areas of Germany:

___H. Holborn, A HISTORY OF MODERN GERMANY, Knopf, New York, NY, 3 volumes, latest edition.

CHAPTER 2
(KAPITEL 2)
GERMANS TO AMERICA
(DEUTSCHE NACH AMERIKA)

1. Introduction	1. Einleitung
1. Einleitung	*1. Einleitung*

During the past three centuries, over 7 million Germans (Deutsche) left the area defined as the 1871 German Empire and made their way for the area defined now as the US. These Germans, the largest non-English-speaking group to come, have had a profound influence on the cultural, social, scientific, and technological aspects of American life. They left the Germanic area for many reasons: religious oppression, governmental tyranny, military devastation, crop failures and famine, overtaxation, unemployment produced by industrialization, and overpopulation. They came to the colonies and to the US with hopes that their situation could be changed for the better. These hopes were generated by recruiting agents, recruiting literature, information from Germans who had been over, and letters from Germans who were living in the colonies or later the US.

In order for the factors pushing people out of Germany and those pulling them to America to be fulfilled, transportation out of Germany and across the Atlantic Ocean had to be possible, and it had to be available cheaply. During colonial times (1607-1775), no German state was engaged in maritime (sea-going) activity to any extent or was pursuing a colonization policy. Such was not the case with England, Holland, France, Spain, and Portugal. Many Germanic states were tied in economically with England and Holland, and England and Holland had strong Protestant sympathies. The earliest Germans coming to the colonies were individuals who came along with the English or the Dutch, there being a small number as early as 1607. Groups of Germans who established German settlements did not come until 1683.

When groups of German settlers began to migrate, they used the transportation facilities of England and/or Holland. The English or certain colonies financed some of the early trips, but a system known as the redemptioner system grew up in Rotterdam. Under it, an emigrant sold his/ her labor for 4 to 7 years to a person in the colonies in exchange for the transportation cost. The system was developed in Rotterdam because the earliest emigrants were largely from areas around the Rhine River. They came down the river or its valley to Rotterdam which sits at its mouth. This port of Rotterdam became the major departure point during the colonial period. Some departures were also from Amsterdam. Only English ships could carry passengers to the colonies, so enterprising Englishmen ran the trade out of Rotterdam. After a required stop at an English port, the ships sailed across the Atlantic. The main ports in the colonies to which most of the ships travelled were Philadelphia, New York, Baltimore, and Charleston. Philadelphia received far more than all of the others because of Pennsylvania's policy of religious freedom for all Protestants.

2. Early German immigrants, 1607–1710	2. Frühe deutsche Einwanderer 1607–1710
2. Frühe deutsche Einwanderer 1607-1710	*2. Frühe Deutsche Ein- wanderer 1607-1710*

In 1607, Jamestown was founded in VA. Among the early settlers were several Germans as the names Unger, Keffer, and Volday suggest. There were also Germans among the Dutch who set up New Amsterdam (NY) in NY in 1624, and some Germans were in and out of this trade center during the years following. As of 1638, Swedish settlers established New Sweden, a colony on the DE River, and Germans were among them.

The first group of Germans that came to the colonies in 1683 and established a German settlement were 13 families from Krefeld (15 miles WNW of Düsseldorf) in what is now Nordrhein-Westfalen. They were Mennonites and Pietists who had converted to Quakerism and were responding to Penn's invitation to Pennsylvania for their religious freedom. They travelled from Krefeld to Rotterdam to England (Gravesend) to Philadelphia, and just outside of Philadelphia set up Germantown (Deutschstadt). This little beginning became a magnet for other German immigrants who came soon, moved into neighboring areas, and later beyond. Another contingent from Krefeld came in the next year. The year 1684 also saw about 100 Labadists from Friesland settle in MD on the Bohemian River. These people were followers of the French revivalist De la Badie, and there were Germans among them. Their port of entry was New York. The sect had dwindled away by about

1705-10. In 1685, a Quaker congregation from Kriegsheim (near Worms in Rheinland-Pfalz) came to Germantown. Forty Rosicrucians (religious mystics) arrived in Philadelphia in 1694. They had left Germany, gone to Rotterdam, then to London, to Deal, to Plymouth, and finally across the Atlantic to Philadelphia. After a brief time in Germantown, they took up residence nearby on Wissahickon Creek. Records of about 1700 indicate the presence of Germans in Tidewater VA. By this time, the redemptioner system was beginning to take shape and to be used.

Now, let us turn our attention to the area from which most German settlers came to the colonies. This area is southwest Germany, particularly the sections along the Rhine River: Palatinate (Pfalz), Baden, and Wuerttemberg (Württemberg). The majority were from the Palatinate, and therefore the term Palatines was often used to refer to all Germans who came during these times. The Thirty Years War had devastated this area 1618-1648, it was invaded violently by the French in 1668, again in 1674, in 1680 many cities were completely destroyed, and in 1707 French despoliation came again. The rulers of the many petty principalities of the region overtaxed their miserable subjects to support their opulence. Further, the area was beset by religious intolerance and persecution. The official religion of each principality was either Lutheran or Reformed or Catholic. Those who did not hold to the official faith were at the least simply tolerated or at the most were actively persecuted. These persecutions were often vented with vigor on the people who belonged to unofficial religions such as the Quakers, Mennonites (Anabaptists), Amish, and Schwenkfelders. Spreading among the populace was information that the English were sympathetic to persecuted Protestants, that there was freedom and cheap fertile land in English America, that the American colonies wanted settlers, and that there were transportation connections in Rotterdam (at the mouth of the Rhine). This was all topped off with a devastatingly cruel winter in 1708-1709, which killed the orchards and vineyards.

Starting in the late fall of 1708, people along the Rhine River and its tributaries began moving toward Rotterdam, hoping to get to England, and then to be sent to America. By summer, thousands had gathered in London, and the British government began sending them to various places. About 600 were sent to NC in 1709 where they established Newbern, NC. Other Germans came later, and settled there or nearby. In that same year of 1709, 41 Germans from Landau (in Rheinland-Pfalz, 21 miles NW of Karlsruhe) were sent to NY and established the town of Newburgh, about 55 miles north of New York City on the Hudson River.

In 1710, England dispatched about 3000 of the Germans who had gathered in London to NY. After leaving about 400 in New York City, the rest went to an area on the east bank of the Hudson River, 100 miles north of New York City, near the present city of Rhinebeck. Later quite a number of them moved into the Mohawk and Schoharie Valleys of NY. And many eventually moved to PA. These initial settlements served as centers to which other German immigrants tended to come, as was the case with the first German town established in PA. This would also come to be the case in other colonies when Germans settled them.

3. Other colonies	3. Andere Kolonien
3. Andere Kolonien	3. Andere Kolonien

While an increasing number of Germans were entering PA, Germans also came to other colonies. The PA stream was headed by Anabaptists who settled in Lancaster Co in 1710. The number coming to NY did not increase as greatly as in PA because of numerous adverse experiences the early arrivals had, this making PA even more attractive. By 1713, Germans were known to be in German Valley (Morris County) of NJ. It is not known exactly when they entered the colony, but more followed them, so that by 1760, over 300 families were in the region. In 1714, twelve German families belonging to the Reformed Church, were brought to VA to operate the iron works at Germanna (10 miles NW of Fredericksburg). They had come from Muesen and Siegen (60 miles east of Cologne) now in Nordrhein-Westfalen. They were soon joined by numerous others from Germany. From Germanna, settlers spread to establish Germantown (now in Fauquier County) and to occupy land in Madison County.

The French set out to colonize LA with German settlers from the Palatinate beginning about 1718-1719. By 1721, there were more than 250 living in three small villages on the MS River north of New Orleans. A colony was also started at Biloxi but did not succeed. In 1734, 42 Lutheran families exiled from Catholic Salzburg went to England, then to GA, where they established Ebenezer. The settlement was located on the bank of the Savannah River 25 miles northwest of Savannah. They were joined shortly by others, and in 1736 by more, including some Moravians. The Moravians went to Bethlehem, PA in 1740 after they were persecuted for refusing to fight Spanish incursions. By 1741, there were over 1200 Germans in GA. In that same year of 1734, Germans settled at the falls where the Potomac and Shenandoah Rivers joined. They founded Harper's Ferry, VA (now WV), and in the years afterward, many settled nearby. Sizable numbers of Germans began to arrive in western MD in 1735, and soon established Monocacy (Frederick) and Hagerstown. Many also went to Baltimore to engage in commerce, trade, and manufacturing. Germans came into western MD and Baltimore from both PA and Germany, those from Germany landing at Annapolis, Alexandria, and Philadelphia.

Following upon the heels of the Swiss, Germans settled the Orangeburg and Lexington (Saxe-Gotha) Districts of SC beginning about 1735, probably earlier. More came and spread northward and westward, their port of arrival generally being Charleston. As of 1740, 40 German families from Brunswick and Saxony set up the town of Waldoborough (Waldoburg) on the Medomak River in the Broad Bay District of ME. Their port of entry was Marblehead, near Boston. The colony of MA set aside some areas for foreign Protestants in 1749, and starting shortly after that, Germans came and took up land in the northwestern corner. Notice that by 1740 there were German settlements from ME (which was then MA) down to GA. The major concentrations were in southeastern PA, in the Hudson and Mohawk River areas of NY, in coastal and western MD, in coastal NC, and in GA and SC along the Savannah River. Movements of the Germans were now in process down the back country of MD and VA (the Shenandoah Valley) southward toward NC and TN. Figure 12 depicts the sites of the most important early settlements. In practically every instance, these early sites functioned as dispersal centers for many immigrants who came later.

4. Migrations of the Germans	4. Wanderungen der Deutschen
4. Wanderungen der Deutschen	*4. Wanderungen der D.*

Now, let us return to PA, into which most of the immigrants were coming, with Philadelphia being their port of arrival. Of course, some continued to arrive at New York City, Baltimore, and Charleston, but not in the numbers coming to Philadelphia. To illustrate the accelerating pace of immigration, 3 ships came to Philadelphia in 1717, 80 ships during 1727-1740, and 159 ships during 1740-1755. In the time span 1717-1732 over 3000 Anabaptists (Mennonites and Amish) came from the Palatinate and the Rhineland. In 1719, Dunkers came, settled near Germantown, and were followed by more about 10 years later. In 1723 NY Palatines

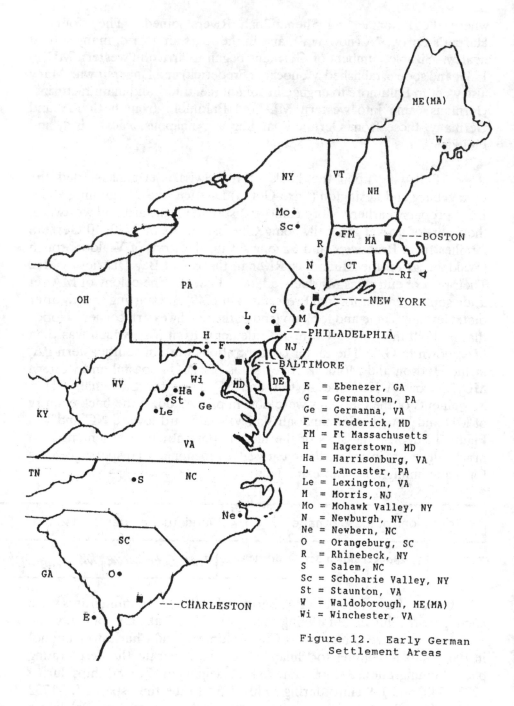

E = Ebenezer, GA
G = Germantown, PA
Ge = Germanna, VA
F = Frederick, MD
FM = Ft Massachusetts
H = Hagerstown, MD
Ha = Harrisonburg, VA
L = Lancaster, PA
Le = Lexington, VA
M = Morris, NJ
Mo = Mohawk Valley, NY
N = Newburgh, NY
Ne = Newbern, NC
O = Orangeburg, SC
R = Rhinebeck, NY
S = Salem, NC
Sc = Schoharie Valley, NY
St = Staunton, VA
W = Waldoborough, ME(MA)
Wi = Winchester, VA

Figure 12.   Early German
        Settlement Areas

came to Bucks County, PA, and in 1728-9 to Berks County, PA. The redemption system and pre-paid passengers fed the colony of PA extremely well: about 15,000 in the 1720s, almost 50,000 in the 1730s, and a peak was reached in the five years 1749-53, when about 30,000 entered. In 1732 Sabbatarian (7th Day) Anabaptists founded Ephrata Cloister on the Cocalico River. Two years later Schwenkfelders came to PA from Silesia and settled in Montgomery County.

By 1735, Lutherans and members of the German Reformed Church, the major Protestant denominations of Germany, were greatly outnumbering the sects. They came from the Palatinate and the Rheinland areas, but as time went on people from other regions came: Württemberg, Baden, Elsass, Hessen, Nassau, Hanau, Anhalt, Lippe, and Bremen. Beginning in 1726-1728, Germans started moving out of overpopulated south-central PA and central MD into western MD and the northern portion of the Shenandoah Valley of VA. This valley is a fertile region running between two mountain ranges from northeast to southwest. These mountains and the valley and its extension rest along the western border of the present state of VA, and run down into east TN, northwestern GA, and northeastern AL. Off to its east are the rest of VA, NC, and SC; to its west are WV, KY, and the rest of TN. The Germans moving out of PA and MD were previous settlers of these two colonies, their descendants, and new immigrants. By about 1740, they had moved south as far as the present site of Lexington, and were spilling eastward through mountain passes into VA's Piedmont.

In 1751, a group of Moravians in PA bought 100,000 acres near the Yadkin River in north-central NC, and soon after moved down the VA Valley, then eastward out of the valley, and south to NC. Many more Moravians, and then many other Germans, followed. Meanwhile, SC continued to be settled by Germans moving northwest in the colony. Practically all of these or their ancestors had come to SC through Charleston, although some came through NC. Immigration came almost to a halt during the French and Indian War, 1756-1763, but resumed afterwards. About 88 ships came to Philadelphia in 1763-1775.

By 1775, the estimated numbers of Germans in the various colonies are: PA(110,000), NY (25,000), VA (25,000), MD-DE (21,000), NJ (15,000), SC (15,000), NC (8,000), GA (5,000), New England (2000); or a total of about 226,000. The map shown in Figure 13 shows the major areas of settlement. The counties (present-day) which showed the heaviest German populations were: PA (Adams, Berks, Chester,

44

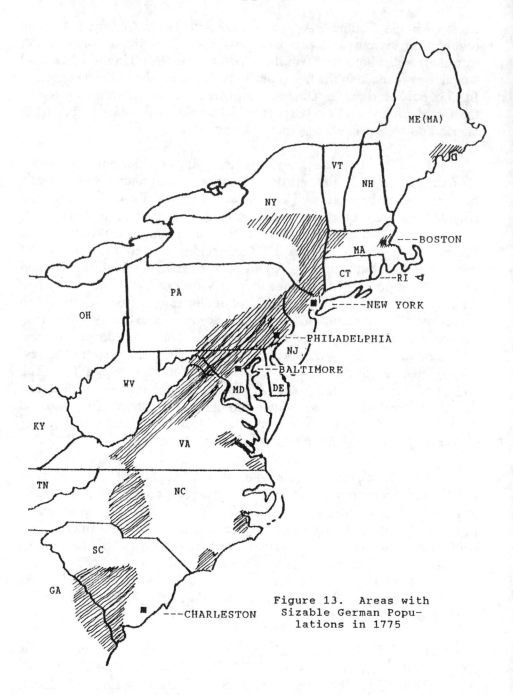

Figure 13. Areas with
Sizable German Popu-
lations in 1775

Cumberland, Dauphin, Lancaster, Lebanon, Lehigh, Monroe, Montgomery, Northumberland, Philadelphia, York), NY (Columbia, Dutchess, Fulton, Greene, Herkimer, Montgomery, Oneida, Saratoga, Schenectady, Schoharie, Ulster), VA (Albemarle, Augusta, Bath, Botetourt, Clarke, Fauquier, Frederick, Greene, London, Louisa, Madison, Montgomery, Orange, Page, Prince William, Rappahannock, Rockbridge, Rockingham, Warren, Wythe), WV (Berkeley, Hampshire, Hardy, Grant, Jefferson, Mineral, Morgan, Pendleton), MD (Baltimore, Carroll, Frederick, Washington), NJ (Essex, Hunterdon, Morris, Passaic, Salem, Somerset, Sussex), SC (Abbeville, Barnwell, Beaufort, Charleston, Edgefield, Fairfield, Lexington, Newberry, Orange), NC (Brunswick, Cabarrus, Catawba, Craven, Davidson, Forsyth, Iredell, Lincoln, Rowan, Stanly, Stokes), GA (Burke, Chatham, Effingham, Screven), ME (Knox, Lincoln, Waldo), and MA (Franklin). The German settlers occupied the best farming lands in the colonies, and they were present all along the ME to GA frontier.

5. The American Revolution and after, 1775–1815	5. Die amerikanische Revolution und die Zeit danach, 1775–1815

5. Die amerikanische Revolution und die Zeit danach, 1775-1815

Germans played several roles in the Revolutionary War. Those living in the colonies overwhelmingly supported the cause of freedom from England largely because of their anti-monarchial sentiments. It is estimated that fewer than 14% had Loyalist inclinations. In every colony, Germans answered the call to arms, and pacifist sects (Mennonites, Amish, Quakers, Dunkers, and Schwenkfelders) gave material help, even though their convictions forbad them to fight. Because of their settlement on the frontier, German families often suffered attacks by Indian allies of the British. Both frontier people and those farther back toward the coast were often subject to aggression by Loyalists. Many experienced German officers came over to serve with the Continental forces, the majority of them having fought in the Seven Years War for Frederick the Great.

Germans also fought for the colonies as soldiers in the troops which the French sent over. There were several German regiments and some of the French regiments contained Germans. They were chiefly from Zweibrücken, the Saar, the Elsass, and Lothringen. These troops were particularly active during the last years of the war, 1780-1783.

Approximately 30,000 German mercenaries were hired by the British to participate in the war. Since the majority, about 17,000, were from Hessen-Kassel, they are generally referred to as Hessians. However, there were about 5700 from Braunschweig, 2400 from Hessen-Nassau, 2400 from Ansbach, 1200 from Waldeck, and 1200 from Anhalt-Zerbst. Of the total, about 17,000 returned to Germany, about 7000 were killed, and about 6000 remained in the US. Many of these had been taken prisoner or had deserted. They were sent to prisoner centers in places such as Winchester, VA, Frederick MD, and Lancaster, PA. Here and in other such places they were absorbed into the German settlements, most in PA, NJ, and MD, but some in places all the way from NY to GA.

During the period following the war (1783-1815), very few immigrants entered the US (an average of fewer than 1000 per year 1783-1806, and even fewer afterwards). The major reason was that Europe was locked into warfare most of this time. In 1789, the French Revolution began, and resulted in the declaration of a French Republic in 1792. Prior to this declaration or shortly thereafter, Austria, Prussia, Britain, The Netherlands, and Sweden declared war on France to restore the monarchy to power. A series of wars between France and European powers was thereby started, these hostilities lasting for 23 years. In 1796 Napoleon defeated Austria, in 1799 Italy and Egypt, in 1805 the British-Austrian-Prussian-Russian-Swedish at Ulm and Austerlitz, in 1806 Prussia and Poland at Jena, in 1807 Russia at Eylau and Friedland, in 1809 Austria at Eckmühl and Wagram. In 1812, Napoleon was repelled by the Russians, and in 1813, the allies forced him to retreat from Leipzig, then captured Paris in 1814. He was finally defeated at Waterloo in 1815. During his periods of conquest, Napoleon ruled Germany by occupation, and as protector of the Confederation of the Rhine (1806-1813). Tremendous devastation occurred as many areas of Germany were turned into battlefields. And all this warfare essentially cut Europe off from the rest of the world. In addition, during much of this period, the US was alternately at odds with France and England, and the War of 1812 (1812-1815) was fought.

The movement of Germans from Germany was very little 1775-1815, but their movement within the US was another matter. After the Revolutionary War, a tremendous surge of westward migration took place along four routes: (a) south in the VA Valley into TN and west through Cumberland Gap into KY and north to OH, (b) west to Pittsburgh then down the OH River to OH and KY, or directly into OH by roads through MD and WV, (c) west from NC into TN and KY, and (d) west along the

Mohawk Valley then along the shores of Lake Erie to northern OH. Germans had come in colonial times and their descendants followed all these routes. As you can see from Figure 13, they were poised on the frontier in proper position to do so. The Germans not only took up farm lands, but they were instrumental in founding many towns. Areas of special concentrations of German settlers were the Blue Grass Region of central KY, just south of the Western Reserve in OH, the Scioto Valley of southern OH (Cincinnati), and somewhat fewer in eastern TN.

During these years (1775-1815), many Germans were being absorbed into the English-speaking culture, especially in cities and on the frontier. They were anglicizing their names, abandoning the German language for English, and marrying into other ethnic groups. Of course, there were numerous German communities which carefully guarded their German characteristics and customs, but when a member left such a community, assimilation was often rapid.

6. The pre–Civil War era, 1815–1860	6. Die Zeit vor dem Bürgerkrieg 1815–1860
6. Die Zeit vor dem Bürgerkrieg 1815-1860	6. Die Zeit vor dem Bürgerkrieg 1815-1860

After the defeat of Napoleon and the end of the War of 1812, both in 1815, Germans from the southwest of Germany began to reopen the Rhine route to Rotterdam and Amsterdam, and to land in Philadelphia and New York as redemptioners. The ever-increasing emigration which was to follow had many causes: the devastations of the wars of 1792-1815, continuing political unrest, economic deprivation, high taxes, crop failures, overpopulation, unemployment produced by industrialization, religious persecution, letters and prepaid tickets from America, and the activities of recruiters. Fairly sizable numbers of Germans came to the US 1816-1818, but a severe US depression which began in 1819 caused German emigrants to go elsewhere. With the passing of the depression, US immigration began to increase slowly in the early 1820s. The collapse of the redemptioner system out of Rotterdam in 1819 caused many German emigrants to seek other routes. Such became available about this time through LeHavre, which was bringing cotton from New Orleans to supply the cloth-making industry in the Alsace. Since the cotton ships returned to New Orleans practically empty, transportation could be offered at low rates. Hence, Germans from southwest Germany began crossing the Alsace to Paris, then going down the Seine River to LeHavre. Here they boarded ships for passage to the US. Some of the ships stopped at New York or other ports, but most went directly to New Orleans. From there, the Germans took steam boats up the MS River to settle the midwestern US. In the pre-Civil War period (1815-1860), New Orleans was second only to New York City in the number of German immigrants. Recognizing the growing emigration, other European ports also began to compete for the German passenger trade to the US: Antwerp, Bremen, and Hamburg.

In the late 1820s the port of Bremen arranged for the tobacco trade from Baltimore (serving MD and VA) and built extensive new harbor facilities in 1830. Troubles in the Netherlands relating to the revolt and subsequent independence of Belgium, plus the loss of the redemptioner systems diverted a sizable portion of the emigrant traffic from Rotterdam and Amsterdam to Bremen. In about 10 years Bremen slightly surpassed LeHavre as a departure port for Germans. Ships headed for Baltimore in many cases made an intermediate stop to discharge passengers at Philadelphia or New York. The location of Bremen was moderately convenient for Rhine connections, and also facilitated emigration from central Germany since the Weser River flows to Bremen from Hannover, Westphalia, and Thuringia. When Hamburg saw the success of Bremen, they too moved to provide for the transport of emigrants. Since few ships from the US came to Hamburg, they worked out a way to use the numerous ships that came to Liverpool in England. Emigrants were shipped to Hull on the east coast of England, were transported to Liverpool on the west coast by canal or train, then took ship for the US. Hamburg sits at the mouth of the Elbe River, which connects to Mecklenburg, Saxony-Anhalt, and Saxony. This fit the emigration pattern very well, because as the 1815-60 period went on, emigration spread eastward and northward from southwestern Germany. In 1842, the Belgians completed a railroad from Antwerp to Cologne, permitting Germans coming down the Rhine Valley to go to Antwerp for transport to the US. This further partially syphoned off emigrants from the Dutch ports. Thus, by 1842, there were five major ports of departure (Bremen, Hamburg, LeHavre, Rotterdam, Amsterdam), and Antwerp was beginning to develop further.

During 1815-1860, the peak year for German immigration was 1854. In that year, about 215,000 Germans came to the US: about 76,000 from Bremen, 50,000 from LeHavre, 50,000 from Hamburg, 21,000 from Antwerp, and 18,000 from Liverpool. These figures are approximations only, meant to give you an idea of major emigration ports. These 215,000 Germans of 1854 arrived in the US approximately as follows: 163,000 to New York, 27,000 to New Orleans, 14,000 to Boston, 8,000 to Philadelphia, and about 3000 to Baltimore. This pattern of immigration to the US began to be established at the outset of this period (1815-1860). You will recall that during the colonial years (1607-1775) the main port of immigration was Philadelphia because of PA's liberal religious policy. When immigration picked up once again in the 1820s, remarkable changes had occurred. LeHavre had established the cotton connection with New Orleans, Bremen had set up the tobacco connection with Baltimore, and in the 1820s NY was in the process of building a quick, direct, and inexpensive route to the west: New York City north up the Hudson River to the Mohawk, up the Mohawk River west to the Erie Canal, on the canal to Buffalo, then into the midwest by land or by ships on the Great Lakes.

The NY route to the west (later enhanced by railroad), a spacious NY City harbor, New York City's growth as a trade center, and good business practices caused New York City to quickly become the major port of entry to the US. By the 1840s over 75% of immigrants to the US were coming through New York City. So important did New York City become that ships headed elsewhere increasingly had to stop there first to let immigrants off. As traffic across the Atlantic increased, all the major ports on both sides of the Atlantic began to offer connections with most or all others. For example, it was not long before one could leave Bremen for Boston, Baltimore, New York, New Orleans, and Philadelphia. People arriving at the Atlantic ports would usually head for OH and the states directly west and northwest of OH. They would use the Hudson-Mohawk-Erie Canal route, or they would head for Pittsburgh and go into OH and beyond from there. By about 1850 the entire trip could be made by railroads which extended through the midwest to the MS River. Two other settlement patterns were used: (a) from overseas to New Orleans, then up the MS River and its tributaries into the midwest, and (b) overseas to Galveston or Indianola, then to inland TX. The approximate numbers of German immigrants to the US during half-decades in 1820-60 are: 1820-1824 (1900), 1825-1829 (3800), 1830-1834 (39,300), 1835-1839 (85,500), 1840-1844 (100,500), 1845-1849 (184,900), 1850-1854 (654,300), 1855-1859 (321,800). The emigration from Germany spread from the southwest (Palatinate, Baden, Wuerttemberg) in the 1830s, to Hesse-Darmstadt, Hesse-Cassel, Franconia, Westphalia, Hannover, and Oldenburg by the 1840s, then by about 1855 to Brandenburg, Mecklenburg, Pomerania, and Silesia, and in the years

1855-1859 to West Prussia, Posen, and East Prussia. Unlike the colonial era, more and more of the immigrants were Catholic, although Lutherans remained the predominant religious denomination.

As of the end of this period, that is, 1860, the densest German settlement occupied five areas of the US. The largest was (1) the mid-Atlantic states (NY, PA, MD) and the territory directly west of them, namely, the midwestern or the north central states (OH, IN, IL, MI, IA, WI, MN). The other four areas were (2) the region of MO from St. Louis west along the MO River and from St. Louis north along the MS River, (3) the rural TX area around San Antonio and Austin, (4) New Orleans and its immediate vicinity, and (5) San Francisco and its vicinity. Some very small colonies developed elsewhere (Norfolk, Wilmington, Charleston, Savannah, Jacksonville, Pensacola, Mobile, northwestern SC, Knoxville, Chattanooga, Nashville, Memphis). Now we will describe the history of the settlement of each of these five areas by the over 1,200,000 Germans who came 1815-1860.

The first area consists of a broad band about 200 miles wide (from NY to MD) sweeping westward. It is obvious that Germans and German descendants in their migrations largely avoided the South and New England. This was a direct reflection of where opportunities for economic betterment were, and the German aversion to southern climate. All the major cities that attracted Germans were in the north (Cincinnati, Cleveland, Toledo, Detroit, Chicago, Milwaukee, St. Louis, Louisville), and the major ports of entry were in the middle Atlantic states (New York City, Philadelphia, Baltimore). The best developed transportation routes connected NY, PA, and MD with the midwest: canals, the OH River, and the Great Lakes (steamboats in the 1830s); roads; and then railroads (1850s). Many immigrants remained in the eastern cities (New York, Baltimore), but many joined descendants of previous German settlers in the westward movement. Most of the immigrants came in the hope of improving their economic situation, although some came for religious reasons and some for political reasons. They followed native-born German-Americans and other settlers into the newly opened agricultural lands and newly developing cities of the midwest. It is also noteworthy to recognize the series of German communities running from east to west in this broad settlement area: Albany-Rochester-Buffalo-Great Lakes-Cleveland-Toledo-Detroit-Chicago-Milwaukee. In 1850, the states with the largest German-born populations were as follows, with the approximate numbers in thousands in parentheses:

				MA(4)
				CT(2)
MN(18)	WI(38)	MI(10)		NY(119)
IA(7)	IL(38)	IN(29)	OH(111)	PA(79)
CA(3)--- MO(45)				NJ(11)
			KY(14)	MD(27)
TX(8)	LA(18)			

Notice that the states are shown in the same general relation they have to each other geographically. Both the German settlement band and the westward movement can be seen clearly. The corresponding data for 1860 are:

				MA(10)
				CT(9)
MN(41)	WI(124)	MI(39)		NY(256)
IA(39)	IL(130)	IN(66)	OH(168)	PA(138)
CA(22)---MO(88)				NJ(34)
			KY(27)	MD(44)
TX(21)	LA(25)			

The cities in these states with sizable German populations were: NY (New York City, Albany, Rochester, Buffalo), MD (Baltimore), OH (Cleveland, Toledo, Columbus, Cincinnati), KY (Louisville), MI (Detroit), IN (Fort Wayne), IL (Chicago), WI (Milwaukee), MO (St. Louis).

The migration of Germans to the St. Louis area in the 1830s was initiated by the favorable report of an earlier settler. Thousands from Westphalia and Hannover responded and settled about 35 miles west of St. Louis just north of the MO River. A society hoping to establish a German state in the US sent Hessen colonists in 1834 from Bremen to New Orleans to the MO area where the MO and MS Rivers came together (St. Louis). Many more Germans came to the region in the characteristic pattern of chain immigration, in which previous settlers encouraged and supported the coming of others. This soon led to the settlement of Germans west of St. Louis on both sides of the MO River and north and south of St. Louis on both sides of the MS River. Large numbers also came into St. Louis, and it became a German Lutheran stronghold.

In the 1820s, a few Germans went into TX, which was a part of Mexico at the time. Sizable immigration began in 1834 when Germans from Oldenburg, Westphalia, and Holstein came to the area of Austin

County. Another small group came to TX in 1839. Later immigration was sponsored by a society which brought over 7000 settlers to TX through the ports of Galveston and Indianola during 1844-1846. They were followed by numerous others, most coming through Galveston or New Orleans. The densest area of German settlement was along a band running westward from Galveston to Yorktown-Austin-Fredericksburg-New Braunfels-San Antonio. By 1860, approximately 30,000 Germans were in TX, 21,000 of them being German-born. Many of them had come from Hannover, Braunschweig, Hesse-Darmstadt, Wuerttemberg, and Thuringia.

As mentioned in a previous section, the French brought German colonists to LA in the early 1720s. They settled on the MS River north of New Orleans. More came in the late 1740s, but not until about 1830 did sizable numbers enter at New Orleans. Many remained in the city, but most went to lands bordering the upper MS River and its tributaries. Several small German settlements were established in other places in LA, and a few in what is now AR. By 1860, the number of Germans in New Orleans had declined significantly, and many of those north of New Orleans had been absorbed in the surrounding culture.

The fifth area to be considered is that in CA around San Francisco. In 1847, gold was found on the land of Sutter, a German who was born in Baden. Not too many Germans came seeking gold, but many came to San Francisco as merchants and workers and to the fertile lands in the Sacramento Valley as farmers. From 1850 to 1860, the number of German-born in CA increased from about 3000 to about 22,000.

In areas where the Germans were dispersed, they quickly were assimilated into the culture, losing their German distinctiveness: language, customs, religion, and social connections. In places where Germans settled in large groups, they retained their distinctiveness for long periods of time, some of this still remaining in a few places even today.

7. The Civil War and after, 1861–1900	7. Der Bürgerkrieg und dïe Zeit danach, 1861–1900
7. Der Bürgerkrieg und die Zeit danach, 1861-1900	*7. Der Bürgerkrieg und danach 1860-1900*

The German-born and their descendants in the US as of 1860 were largely opposed to slavery, except for some who had settled in the south. About 177 thousand German-born enlisted in the Union forces, a number of them serving in units made up chiefly or entirely of Germans. Of these, the following states furnished the largest numbers (in thousands): NY (37K), MO (31K), OH (20K), IL (18K), PA (17K), WI (16K). If men of German ancestry are included, the number of Germans fighting for the north exceeded 700 thousand. During the war, immigration dropped somewhat, but German immigrants coming during the time were often successfully recruited at the port of entry. Once the war was over, the flood of immigrants from Germany resumed. From 1860-1899, Germans coming to the US in half-decades in thousands were: 1860-1864 (204K), 1865-1869 (520K), 1870-1874 (451K), 1875-1879 (120K), 1880-1884 (798K), 1885-1889 (453K), 1890-1894 (429K), 1895-1899 (120K). The sharp drop in 1875-1879 reflects the effects of the 1873 panic in the US and the ensuing economic stagnation and rise in unemployment. The drop in 1895-1899 is a result of world-wide financial panic and economic depression which began in the spring of 1893. The US had about 2.5 million out of work in 1893-1894, and it was 1897 before things got better.

The settlement of the German immigrants may be followed in the following charts. They reflect the German-born population in the censuses of 1870, 1880, 1890, and 1900, but you must remember that they entered earlier, sometimes much earlier. For 1870, the data are (in thousands):

```
                                                      MA(13)
                                                      CT(12)
                MN(18)  WI(162)  MI(64)               NY(317)
        NE(11)  IA(66)  IL(203)  IN(78)   OH(183)     PA(79)
CA(30)---KS(13)  MO(45)                               NJ(54)
               ¦                          KY(30)      MD(47)
        TX(24) LA(19)
```

For 1880, the corresponding information is:

```
                                                              MA(17)
                                                              CT(16)
                    MN(67)  WI(184)   MI(89)                  NY(356)
           NE(31)   IA(88)  IL(236)   IN(81)  OH(193)  PA(168)
CA(42)---  KS(28)   MO(107)                                   NJ(65)
              ¦                                   KY(30)   MD(45)
           TX(36)  LA(17)
```

The data for 1890 are as follows:

```
                                                              MA(28)
                                                              CT(28)
           ND(10)                                             NY(498)
           SD(17)  MN(117)  WI(251)  MI(136)  OH(236)  PA(231)
           NE(73)  IA(127)  IL(338)  IN(85)                   NJ(106)
CA(61)---  KS(46)  MO(125)                        KY(29)   MD(52)
              ¦
           TX(49)  LA(15)
```

And for 1900, the pattern is:

```
                                                              MA(31)
                                                              CT(32)
              ND(12)                                          NY(480)
WA(17)        SD(18)  MN(117)  WI(243)  MI(125)  OH(204)  PA(212)
OR(13)        NE(66)  IA(123)  IL(332)  IN(74)                NJ(120)
CA(72)  CO(15)  KS(40)  MO(109)                     KY(28)   MD(45)
                 ¦
              TX(48)  LA(12)
```

The period after the Civil War was one in which the US was expanding: agriculturally, industrially, geographically, technologically, and commercially. The German immigrants and people of German stock participated thoroughly in all of these movements. Ninety percent of the emigrants leaving Germany during 1860-1900 were bound for the US. Never less than 25% of the total immigrants to the US during this period were Germans, and in the 1850s and 1860s, it was over 33%. The major ports of departure were Bremen and Hamburg, and the major port of arrival was New York, with some also coming into Boston, Baltimore, and Philadelphia. One of the losses of the Civil War was the importance of New Orleans as a port of immigration. Many factors served to produce the large volume of immigration: (1) the industrial revolution in Germany, (2) agricultural reform in Germany, (3) rural overpopulation in Germany,

(4) the unification of Germany in 1871, (5) transportation improvements in Germany [steamboats, railroads], (6) transportation improvements across the Atlantic Ocean [steamboats, regular schedules, better facilities, lower fares], (7) transportation improvements in the US [steamboats, railroads], and (8) religious oppression of Catholics by Bismarck in the 1870s.

However, probably the chief cause of German immigration 1860-1900 was recruitment; in other words, they were actively invited, and even given various inducements such as reduced fares and housing until they could get settled. The Germans were recruited by states, railroads, industries, transatlantic shipping companies, and by their friends and relatives in the US. This recruitment was to support the great expansions that were in process in the US. The midwestern US states (MI, WI, MN, IA, NE, KS, MO, OR, MT, Dakota Territory) set up commissions to attract German settlers to come to advance the states economically. The railroads (WI Central, Burlington, Northern Pacific, St. Paul and Pacific) recruited Germans to settle on lands along the rail lines which they had been granted. The settlers were encouraged to farm the lands and then ship the produce on the railroad. Industries, mostly in the larger cities, were seeking ordinary and semi-skilled workers for their expanding production. Shipping companies, particularly those in Bremen and Hamburg, were recruiting passengers, as they attempted to take trade away from ports in Holland (Amsterdam, Rotterdam), Belgium (Antwerp), France (LeHavre), and England. A very important factor was letters from Germans in the US to Germans in Germany encouraging them to come, arranging for employment before they set out, and often sending them prepaid tickets.

In 1873, Germans began coming to the US from German colonies in southwestern Russia. Something around 120,000 would arrive before 1920. Between 1763 and 1859, the Russian government invited Germans to settle on its southwestern frontiers in order to develop the land and secure the territory. They were given land, the right to establish German colonies and keep their culture, freedom of religion, tax exemptions for a period of time, and exemption from military service. They first settled in the valley of the Volga River (1763-1768), then in the Chernigov and Voronezh regions (1764-1768), the area along the Dnieper River (Mennonites, 1789-1820), the Volhynian area (1790-1850), the Black Sea region (1804-1840), the Bessarabian area (1814-1830), the Tiflis section of Transcaucasia (1818-1820), the Don River, North Caucasia, and some areas east of the Urals (1850-1900). These areas were settled by Lutherans, Reformed, Mennonites (Hutterites), and Catholics. In 1804, the invitation to Russia did not afford all these benefits, in 1859 Russia terminated its colonization program, in 1871 almost all privileges were withdrawn and integration into Russian society was demanded, and in 1874 military conscription was instituted. The Russian-Germans began emigrating to the US, such that by 1920, they and their descendants numbered about 301,000. ND had about 70,000, KS about 32,000, SD about 31,000, NE about 22,000, and the remainder were in states with smaller numbers. Prior to the immigration of Russian-Germans, it was believed that the Great Plains could not be cultivated, but their experience with similar land and their bringing of Turkey red hard wheat turned the area into a fruitful wheat-growing region.

Among the Germans who came after 1873 were others who had previously settled in various regions of the Austro-Hungarian Empire: Galicia (now in Poland), Bohemia (now in Czechoslovakia), Moravia (now in Czechoslovakia), Slovenia (now in Yugoslavia), Batschka (now in Yugoslavia), Banat (now in the Danube region where Hungary, Yugoslavia, and Romania intersect), Transylvania (now in Romania), Bukowina (now where Romania and the Ukraine intersect), and Dobrudscha (now in Bulgaria-Romania).

8. German immigration, 1900–	8. Die Einwanderung der Deutschen nach 1900
8. Die Einwanderung der Deutschen nach 1900	8. Die Einwanderung der Deutschen nach 1900

The numbers of German immigrants in thousands following the year 1900 were as follows: 1900-1904 (129K), 1905-1909 (124K), 1910-1914 (84K), 1915-1919 (1K), 1920-1924 (150K), 1925-1929 (230K), 1930-1934 (62K), 1931-1940 (114K), 1941-1950 (226K), 1951-1960 (478K), 1961-1965 (119K), 1966-1870 (72K), 1971-1975 (37K). The total Germans coming during 1820-1975 was about 6,954,000. In 1910, there were approximately 2,260,000 German-born persons in the US. The comparable figure for 1930 was 1,609,000, for 1950 was 984,000, for 1960 was 990,000, and for 1970 was 833,000. During 1899-1952, about 1,892,000 Germans came to the US, but about 344,000 departed. This amounts to approximately an 18% departure rate, which suggests that many returned.

In the 1890s there was depression in the US along with the end of the US frontier, both of which discouraged immigration. In Germany, the people in overpopulated areas moved within Germany rather than out of Germany. When recovery from the depression occurred, immigration to the US picked up a bit, then decreased markedly when the US went to war with Germany in World War I, 1917-1918. Post-war economic and governmental chaos in the 1920s caused much immigration, but depression, American immigration quotas (about 26K per year for Germans), and hope generated in the early Hitler years dropped the numbers. As this hope faded with Hitler's racist and political violence, immigration of refugees increased the numbers. The onset of warfare between the US and Germany again in World War II (1941-1945) dropped the immigration, but it resumed very soon after the war. German prosperity dropped the number of emigrants leaving the country from the 1960s up to now.

German emigrants to the US during the 1900-1940 period were chiefly industrial workers, although many farmers were still coming (the Russian Germans, for example). The industrial workers settled mainly in the cities where the industries were located. In 1920, about 67% of the Germans in the US lived in large or small cities. The largest concentration of urban Germans was in New York City, with Chicago, Milwaukee, Detroit, Cleveland, and Toledo also having sizable German communities. The German communities in Cincinnati, Louisville, and St. Louis were decreasing in size by this time. The decreases were due to fewer later immigrants and losses to absorption by the larger society.

9. Recommended reading	9. Empfehlenswerte Literatur
9. Empfehlenswerte Literatur	9. Empfehlenswerte Literatur

It is strongly recommended that every German researcher do some additional reading with reference to German emigration, ocean transportation, and German immigration. The first item that should be carefully gone through is a brief and excellent review article:

___K. N. Conzen, essay on GERMANS, in S. Thernstrom, editor, HARVARD ENCYCLOPEDIA OF ETHNIC GROUPS, Harvard Univ. Press. Cambridge, MA, 1980, pages 405-425. Also see related essays beginning on pages 29, 122, 164, 401, 425, 476, 486, 496, 734, and 770.

Then, a more-detailed book will broaden your knowledge and give you greater facility for understanding the circumstances of your ancestors' coming to the US:

58

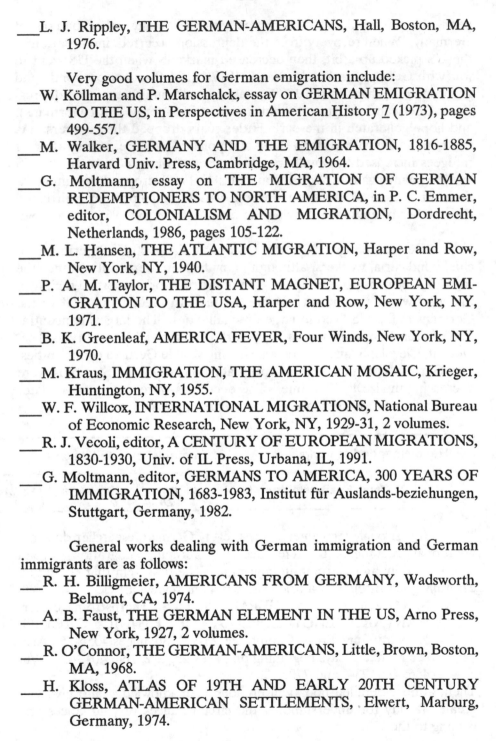

___L. J. Rippley, THE GERMAN-AMERICANS, Hall, Boston, MA, 1976.

Very good volumes for German emigration include:
___W. Köllman and P. Marschalck, essay on GERMAN EMIGRATION TO THE US, in Perspectives in American History 7 (1973), pages 499-557.
___M. Walker, GERMANY AND THE EMIGRATION, 1816-1885, Harvard Univ. Press, Cambridge, MA, 1964.
___G. Moltmann, essay on THE MIGRATION OF GERMAN REDEMPTIONERS TO NORTH AMERICA, in P. C. Emmer, editor, COLONIALISM AND MIGRATION, Dordrecht, Netherlands, 1986, pages 105-122.
___M. L. Hansen, THE ATLANTIC MIGRATION, Harper and Row, New York, NY, 1940.
___P. A. M. Taylor, THE DISTANT MAGNET, EUROPEAN EMIGRATION TO THE USA, Harper and Row, New York, NY, 1971.
___B. K. Greenleaf, AMERICA FEVER, Four Winds, New York, NY, 1970.
___M. Kraus, IMMIGRATION, THE AMERICAN MOSAIC, Krieger, Huntington, NY, 1955.
___W. F. Willcox, INTERNATIONAL MIGRATIONS, National Bureau of Economic Research, New York, NY, 1929-31, 2 volumes.
___R. J. Vecoli, editor, A CENTURY OF EUROPEAN MIGRATIONS, 1830-1930, Univ. of IL Press, Urbana, IL, 1991.
___G. Moltmann, editor, GERMANS TO AMERICA, 300 YEARS OF IMMIGRATION, 1683-1983, Institut für Auslands-beziehungen, Stuttgart, Germany, 1982.

General works dealing with German immigration and German immigrants are as follows:
___R. H. Billigmeier, AMERICANS FROM GERMANY, Wadsworth, Belmont, CA, 1974.
___A. B. Faust, THE GERMAN ELEMENT IN THE US, Arno Press, New York, 1927, 2 volumes.
___R. O'Connor, THE GERMAN-AMERICANS, Little, Brown, Boston, MA, 1968.
___H. Kloss, ATLAS OF 19TH AND EARLY 20TH CENTURY GERMAN-AMERICAN SETTLEMENTS, Elwert, Marburg, Germany, 1974.

59

___L. F. Bittinger, THE GERMANS IN COLONIAL TIMES, Russell
and Russell, New York, NY, 1901.

___J. S. Olson, THE ETHNIC DIMENSION IN AMERICAN HIS-
TORY, St. Martin's Press, New York, NY, 1979.

___R. J. Vecoli, editor, A CENTURY OF EUROPEAN MIGRATIONS,
1830-1930, Univ. of IL Press, Urbana, IL, 1991.

___G. Moltmann, essay on THE MIGRATION OF GERMAN
REDEMPTIONERS TO NORTH AMERICA, in P. C. Emmer,
editor, COLONIALISM AND MIGRATION, Dordrecht,
Netherlands, 1986, pages 105-122.

___K. Wust and H. Moos, THREE HUNDRED YEARS OF GERMAN
IMMIGRANTS IN NORTH AMERICA, Moos Publishing Co.,
New York, NY, 1983.

Special books dealing with particular regions in the US or with
particular groups of Germans are listed below. Some of these should be
of assistance to you depending on exactly when your ancestors came and
where they settled.

___D. Cunz, THE MD GERMANS, Princeton Univ. Press, Princeton,
NJ, 1948.

___K. Wust, THE VA GERMANS, Univ. of VA Press, Charlottesville,
VA, 1969.

___T. G. Jordan, GERMAN SEED IN TX SOIL, Univ. of TX Press,
Austin, TX, 1966.

___R. L. Gerlach, IMMIGRANTS IN THE OZARKS, Univ. of MO
Press, Columbia, MO, 1976.

___K. N. Conzen, IMMIGRANT MILWAUKEE, 1836-1860, Harvard
Univ. Press, Cambridge, MA, 1976.

___R. Ernst, IMMIGRANT LIFE IN NY CITY, 1825-1863, New York,
NY, 1965.

___J. W. Wayland, THE GERMAN ELEMENT OF THE
SHENANDOAH VALLEY, Carrier, Bridgewater, VA, 1964.

___G. G. Benjamin, THE GERMANS IN TX, Philadelphia, PA, 1909.

___F. C. Luebke, IMMIGRANTS AND POLITICS, THE GERMANS
OF NE, 1880-1900, Univ. of NE Press, Lincoln, NE, 1969.

___J. H. Deiler, THE SETTLEMENT OF THE GERMAN COAST OF
LA, R and E Associates, San Francisco, CA, 1968.

___R. von Biesele, THE HISTORY OF GERMAN SETTLEMENTS IN
TX, 1831-1861, Von Boeckmann-Jones, Austin, TX, 1930.

___E. G. Gudde, GERMAN PIONEERS IN EARLY CA, R and E
Associates, San Francisco, CA, 1970.

___K. Stump, THE GERMAN-RUSSIANS, TWO CENTURIES OF PIONEERING, Atlantic Forum, Bonn, Germany, 1971.

___R. Sallet, THE RUSSIAN-GERMAN SETTLEMENTS IN THE US, Fargo Institute for Regional Studies, Fargo, ND, 1974.

___R. Wood, editor, THE PA GERMANS, Princeton Univ. Press, Princeton, NJ, 1942.

___C. Wittke, REFUGEES OF REVOLUTION, THE GERMAN FORTY-EIGHTERS IN AMERICA, Univ. of PA Press, Philadelphia, PA, 1952.

___E. Rothan, THE GERMAN CATHOLIC IMMIGRANT IN THE US, 1830-1860, Washington, DC, 1946.

___W. O. Forster, ZION ON THE MS: THE SETTLEMENT OF THE SAXON LUTHERANS IN MO, 1839-1841, Concordia, St. Louis,MO, 1953.

___R. A. Hofmeister, THE GERMANS OF CHICAGO, Stipes, Chicago, IL, 1976.

___J. F. Nau, THE GERMAN PEOPLE OF NEW ORLEANS, 1850-1900, Brill, Leiden, Holland, 1958.

___A. L. Olson, ST. LOUIS GERMANS, 1850-1920, Arno Press, New York, NY, 1980.

___W. T. Parsons, THE PA DUTCH, Twayne, Boston, MA, 1976.

___A. J. Towsend, THE GERMANS IN CHICAGO, Deutsch-Amerikanische Historische Gesellschaft, Chicago, IL, 1932.

Two bibliographies are of considerable value in locating further information on Germans in America.

___D. H. Tolzmann, GERMAN-AMERICANA, A BIBLIOGRAPHY, Scarecrow Press, Metuchen, NJ, 1975.

___P. Meynen, BIBLIOGRAPHY ON GERMAN SETTLEMENTS IN COLONIAL NORTH AMERICA, Harrassowitz, Leipzig, Germany, 1937.

CHAPTER 3
(KAPITEL 3)
BRIDGING THE ATLANTIC
(DIE ÜBERQUERUNG DES ATLANTIK)

1. Introduction	1. Einleitung
1. **Einleitung**	*1. Einleitung*

Now that you have had a look at German history, German emigration, US immigration of Germans, and German settlement in the US, we will now address ourselves to tracing your German ancestor back across the Atlantic Ocean. It is assumed that you have used the standard genealogical research procedures and have identified the immigrant ancestor. Your next task is to find the exact place in Germany from which your ancestor came, at which your ancestor was married, where your ancestor's children were born, or best of all, where your ancestor was born. In other words, a precise location in Germany where there are records on your forebear must be found. By an exact place or a precise location is meant the city, town (Stadt), village (Dorf), community (Gemeinde), hamlet (Flecken), group of houses (Häusergruppe), rural settlement (Landgemeinde), or small village (Weiler). It is not enough to know your progenitor was from Germany; neither is it enough to know he/she was from a certain state (Land) such as Baden or Thuringia (Thüringen); or even to know the province such as Brandenburg or Pomerania (Pommern). The reason is that there is no single, overall, central German archive, neither are all the records in a given state or province necessarily in one central repository. As a result, in order to find records on your forebear, you need to know the exact place, because only if you know that can you discover where the records for that place are stored.

In the majority of cases, it is possible to find the precise location of your ancestor's origin in Germany from records or copies of records available here in the US. In some instances, it will be necessary to make contacts in Germany, but not most. Following is a treatment of the better types of records available in the US for finding the precise location of your ancestor's place or places of origin (departure, marriage, births of children, birth) and the dates of these events. One of the better ways of approaching this search is to seek the answers to five questions relating to the precise location from which your progenitor originated:

1. Does some family member know? One or more of the many descendants of the immigrant ancestor may know his\her place of origin. This information may be in the form of family oral tradition, of family records, of items handed down through the family, or of originals or copies of organizational or governmental records. Details for searching out the answer to this first question are given in the next section of this chapter. If this search does not turn up the exact location, then you should proceed to the next question.

2. Has someone else here in the US reported the exact place? This search involves investigations into numerous large published indexes which may either give the exact place or lead you to it. Descriptions of these indexes, and how to use them will be given in later sections of this chapter. If these searches do not yield the exact location, then you should proceed to the third question.

3. Do US records give the exact place? An answer to this third question entails the use of numerous genealogical records available here in the US. These records include town, city, county, colony, state, federal, and private US records, as well as copies of numerous German records which are in US repositories. Considerable space in the later sections of this chapter will be devoted to the best of the records, and details on finding them and using them will be presented. Should they still not lead you to the place of origin of your ancestor (birth, marriage, births of children, departure), you can try the approaches invoked by the fourth question.

4. Might some contacts in Germany know the exact place? The question brings up the possibility of contacting agencies, organizations, and individuals in Germany. The hope is that they will have available some special indexes, lists, finding aids, or locating procedures which will tell you what you want to know. This approach will be discussed toward the end of the present chapter. Now, supposing and hoping that these procedures will have revealed your German progenitor's birth place, or marriage place, or birth places of his/her children, or the place from which he/she departed for America, the fifth questions needs to be asked.

5. Precisely where on the German map is the place? Once you have found the name of the exact place, it is necessary for you to identify its precise geographical location. This is done by consulting American and German atlases, gazetteers, and maps. Instructions for carrying out this will be detailed at the end of this chapter.

Now, let us summarize what is to be done. <u>First</u>, you should explore family sources very thoroughly. <u>Second</u>, you need to look at numerous American and German indexes. <u>Third</u>, your quest will involve exploration of American genealogical records and copies of German genealogical records which are available here in the US. <u>Fourth</u>, contacts in Germany are to be made. <u>Fifth</u>, once you locate the name of the precise place, it is necessary to identify it on a map of Germany. A successful locating of this exact place is essential to continuing your research, because you must have this information in order to locate the records back in Germany. We will now provide you with some detail which will assist you to do a thorough job of searching.

2. Family sources	2. Familienquellen
2. Familienquellen	2. Familienquellen

The first step in your quest for the exact place of origin of your German immigrant forebear is to contact as many as possible of the living descendants of that ancestor. The reason for this is that one or more of them may know the place of origin or may have materials passed down the family line which tell the place of origin or provide clues to it. Unfortunately, this is not as easy as it might sound. If it is assumed that your immigrant German male was born in 1739 in Germany, came to the American colonies in 1760 at an age of 21, that the average time between generations is 25 years, that each generation had 4 children (2 girls and 2 boys), and that you were born in 1940, then you have 65,536 cousins to find and contact. And only 256 of them will have the same surname as the immigrant. If the immigrant arrived in 1810, using the same assumptions, you will have 4096 cousins to contact, with only 64 carrying the immigrant's surname. And if your German immigrant arrived in 1860, there will be 256 cousins, with only 16 bearing the immigrant's surname. Of course, if your immigrant was female, the surname was wiped out at her marriage, and none of the cousins will have it.

As many of your cousins, and their parents and children, should be contacted as you can find. Ask each of them that you locate if he or she knows of others. What you are looking for is verbal information (family tradition, remembrances), or better, for written or printed indications of the place. It is very important to ask about Bibles, certificates, diaries, family history notes, funeral cards, legal papers, letters, newspaper clippings, passports, permits, photographs, pictures, receipts, and other such items. Even such things as engraved jewelry, imprints on china, and manufacturer's names on tools must not be overlooked. It is also well to remember that certificates may be of many sorts: baptism, birth, confirmation, communion, christening, naturalization, military service, insurance, membership, marriage, death, voter, school. Do not overlook the possibility that pertinent state and local libraries may have family Bible record collections and/or indexes. Many state libraries do, and some local libraries do.

Caution must be exercised with oral information, since data tend to become distorted with the passage of time and with the covert aspirations of the teller. Thus, you must treat such data as only clues which might lead you to reliable records. Even so, fairly often verbal remembrance is uncannily accurate. One of the major problems you may experience is with spelling. Some of our German ancestors were not literate, and as descendants came along, facility with the German language was often lost. Hence, spellings of place names are sometimes badly mangled and even anglicized almost to the point of non-recognition.

One sometimes-fruitful method of contacting distant relatives is to place a query or an ad in local and state genealogical society journals, and/or in newspapers in the pertinent places in the US. These journals are listed in:
___E. P. Bentley, GENEALOGIST'S ADDRESS BOOK, Genealogical Publishing Co., Baltimore, MD, latest edition.
___V. N. Chambers, editor, THE GENEALOGICAL HELPER, Everton Publishers, Logan, UT, latest May-June issue.
___J. Konrad, DIRECTORY OF GENEALOGICAL PERIODICALS, Summit Publications, Munroe Falls, OH, latest edition.
And newspapers are listed in:
___GALE DIRECTORY OF PUBLICATIONS, AN ANNUAL GUIDE TO NEWSPAPERS, MAGAZINES, JOURNALS, AND RELATED PUBLICATIONS, Gale Research Co., Detroit, MI, latest annual edition.
Another way of contacting distant relatives and/or finding data they have reported is to look into single-name journals devoted to the surnames of your immigrant ancestors. Such publications are listed in:
___V. N. Chambers, editor, THE GENEALOGICAL HELPER, Everton Publishers, Logan, UT, latest Mar-Apr issue.
___J. Konrad, FAMILY ASSOCIATIONS, Munroe Falls, OH, latest edition.

___J. Konrad, DIRECTORY OF FAMILY ONE-NAME PERIODI-
CALS, Summit Publications, Munroe Falls, OH, latest edition.
___K. Cavanaugh, DIRECTORY OF FAMILY NEWSLETTERS, The
Author, Fort Wayne, IN, latest edition.
___SURNAME PERIODICALS, L and H Enterprises, Sacramento, CA,
latest edition.

You should also contact pertinent family organizations listed in the references above, even if they do not publish a journal or newsletter.

3. Indexes at the FHL and FHC	3. Verzeichnisse in der FHL und dem FHC
3. Verzeichnisse in der FHL und dem FHC	3. Verzeichnisse in den FHL und dem FHC

It is quite possible that some remote relative or in-law of yours or
that some institution or agency has discovered the exact place of origin of
your German ancestor, and has entered it into a large index. A sizable
number of these exist, and they can save you an immense amount of
research time and expense if the pertinent information has been entered.
In short, the likelihood of your finding either the place or data which will
lead you to it in these indexes is high enough that this should be done
next.

The largest indexes of this sort are located at the Family History
Library (FHL), 35 North West Temple, Salt Lake City, UT 84150.
Copies of most of them are to be found in every Family History Center
(FHC), these being located in practically every metropolitan area of the
US. They give you references to vital record data (mostly births and
marriages), to published genealogies, and to compiled family data on over
200 million individuals, including millions who lived in Germany and came
from Germany. These indexes are:

___INTERNATIONAL GENEALOGICAL INDEX (IGI), Family
History Library, Salt Lake City, UT, latest edition. Available at
FHL and every FHC on microfiche and computer. Over 200
million entries of vital record data, more than 21 million entries
from Germany. Check under Germany and all the colonies or
states of the US in which your forebear lived.
___FAMILY HISTORY LIBRARY CATALOG, SURNAME SECTION
(FHLC-SS), Family History Library, Salt Lake City, UT, latest
edition. Available at FHL and every FHC on microfiche and

computer. Search for your immigrant's surname to identify published family histories, genealogies in manuscript form, research collections, and other previous work that has been done on the family.

___FAMILY GROUP RECORDS COLLECTION (FGRC), Family History Library, Salt Lake City, UT. Indexes available at FHC and FHL in Subject Section of the FHL Catalog. Records available at FHL. Over 8 million family genealogy sheets.

___ANCESTRAL FILE (AF), Family History Library, Salt Lake City, UT, latest edition. Available on computer at FHL and every FHC. Millions of indexed records from numerous contributors. Much of it undocumented.

A careful search of all these indexes for your ancestor must be made. When you come across references that you think are to her/him, copy down the code numbers and ask for the materials at FHL, or ask the attendant at the FHC to order them for you. You must not fail to remember that probably some of the friends (neighbors) and certainly the siblings (sisters and brothers) of your immigrant progenitor also came from the same place. Thus, it is well to look for them, if you fail to find your immigrant's place of origin.

4. Indexes to histories	4. Verzeichnisse der Geschichts-bücher
4. Verzeichniſſe der Geſchichtſ-bücher	4. Verzeichniſſe der Geſchichtſbücher

Another set of highly useful indexes is made up of reference works which list or refer to family histories. You have already made a search for family histories when you used the FHLC-SS. The volumes listed below will give you a much more comprehensive survey of those that are available. Once again, remember that family histories of close friends of your immigrant forebear may give the friend's place of origin, and it could well be the same as your ancestor's.

___M. J. Kaminkow, GENEALOGIES IN THE LIBRARY OF CONGRESS, with SUPPLEMENTS, Magna Carta Book Co., Baltimore, MD, 1976-86.

___M. J. Kaminkow, COMPLEMENT TO GENEALOGIES IN THE LIBRARY OF CONGRESS, Magna Carta Book Co., Baltimore, MD, 1981. Lists family histories in 45 other large genealogical libraries.

___New York Public Library, DICTIONARY CATALOG OF THE LOCAL HISTORY AND GENEALOGY DIVISION, Hall, Boston, MA, 1974.

___J. Munsell, INDEX TO AMERICAN GENEALOGIES, Genealogical Publishing Co., Baltimore, MD, 1967 (originally published in 1900/8). Refers to family histories published before 1908.·

___F. Rider, AMERICAN GENEALOGICAL INDEX, Godfrey Memorial Library, Middletown, CT, 1942-51. And F. Rider, AMERICAN-GENEALOGICAL-BIOGRAPHICAL INDEX, Godfrey Memorial Library, Middletown, CT, 1952-.

These volumes are available at most large genealogical libraries.

Your next approach is to look into some reference works which list county, city, and town histories. Many of these books, especially the earlier ones, contained biographical sketches and family histories of the residents. Use these reference volumes to locate the local histories for all counties, cities, and towns in which your immigrant ancestor, his/her children, his/her grandchildren, and even his/her great-grandchildren lived. A personal or family sketch on any of these descendants could reveal the place of origin of the immigrant. Such is also true for brothers and sisters of your immigrant. It is also well to look for genealogical sketches of German friends living near your immigrant, since they may have come from the same place. This means, of course, that there may be sketches on the friend's descendants which will tell the place. The reference books which refer you to local histories will be found in most medium- and large-sized genealogical libraries. They are:

___M. J. Kaminkow, US LOCAL HISTORIES IN THE LIBRARY OF CONGRESS, Magna Carta Book Co., Baltimore, MD, 1975, 5 volumes, index in the 5th volume.

___P. W. Filby, A BIBLIOGRAPHY OF AMERICAN COUNTY HISTORIES, Genealogical Publishing Co., Baltimore, MD, 1985.

In addition, you should check for local histories in the pertinent state, county, city, and town libraries where your immigrant, his siblings, and his friends lived (and their descendants). Once you identify one or more local histories which might contain data on your German's origin, you can usually borrow them on interlibrary loan from state or university or city libraries in the region.

5. Indexes to immigrations	5. Verzeichnisse der Einwander- ungen
5. Verzeichniſſe der Einwander- ungen	*[handwritten German script]*

There are numerous large immigration indexes which lead to immigration records of Germans coming to the American colonies and the US. These immigration records do not always give the exact place. In many cases they do, but in other instances, they name only the German state or province, and in still other cases, all they say is Germany. However, the probability of finding the precise location is high enough that you must seek your ancestor, his siblings, and his friends (Germans living near him) in them. For the period from 1607 to about 1820, you can look in a very sizable compilation of early passenger and immigrant lists:

___P. W. Filby and M. K. Meyer, PASSENGER AND IMMIGRANT LISTS INDEX, Gale Research Co., Detroit, MI, 1981, with annual SUPPLEMENTS, 1982ff.

If your ancestor arrived during or after 1820, or during 1800-19 at Philadelphia, you can use the following indexes:

___National Archives, BALTIMORE PASSENGER ARRIVAL LIST INDEXES, 1820-1952, Microfilms M326, M327, M334, T520, Washington, DC. Lead to microfilm lists M255, M596, T844, and original records.

___National Archives, BOSTON PASSENGER ARRIVAL LIST INDEXES, 1820-1940, Microfilms M265, M334, T521, T617, T790, Washington DC. Lead to microfilm lists M277, T843.

___National Archives, NEW YORK PASSENGER ARRIVAL LIST INDEXES, 1820-46, 1897-1943, Microfilms M261, T519, T612, T621, Washington, DC. Lead to microfilm lists M237, T715.

___National Archives, PHILADELPHIA PASSENGER ARRIVAL LIST INDEXES, 1800-1948, Microfilms M334, M360, T526, T791, Washington, DC. Lead to microfilm lists M425, T840.

___National Archives, NEW ORLEANS PASSENGER ARRIVAL LIST INDEXES, 1820-1952, microfilms M334, T527, T618, Washington, DC. Lead to microfilm lists M259, M272, T905.

___National Archives, A SUPPLEMENTAL INDEX TO PASSENGER LISTS OF VESSELS ARRIVING AT ATLANTIC AND GULF COAST POSTS, EXCLUDING NEW YORK, 1820-74, Microfilm M334, Washington, DC. Leads to microfilm list M575, which gives passengers to many ports. The records have many years missing for most ports. These indexes apply to the following ports (with dates): Alexandria, VA (1820-65), Annapolis, MD (1849), Bangor, ME (1848), Barnstable, MA (1820-26), Bath, ME (1825-32g, 1867), Belfast, ME (1820-31, 1851), Bridgeport, CT (1870), Bridgetown, NJ (1828), Bristol, RI (1820-28, 1843-71), Beaufort, NC (1865),Cape May, NJ (1828), Charleston, SC (1820-29), Darien, GA (1823, 1825), Dighton, MA (1820-63g), East River, VA (1830), Edenton, NC (1820), Edgartown, MA (1820-70), Fairfield, CT (1804-21g), Fall River, MA (1837-65g), Falmouth, ME (1820-68g), Frenchman's Bay, ME (1821-27g), Georgetown, DC (1820-21), Gloucester, MA (1820-39g, 1867-70g), Hampton, VA (1820-32), Hartford, CT (1832), Havre de Grace, MD (1820), Hingham, MA (1852), Kennebunk, ME (1820-72), Key West, FL (1837-68g), Little Egg Harbor, NJ (1831), Marblehead, MA (1820-36, 1849), Mobile, AL (1820-74g), Nantucket (1820-62g), Newark, NJ (1836), New Bedford, MA (1823-99), New Bern, NC (1820-45, 1865), Newburyport, MA (1821-39g), New Haven, CT (1720-91g), New London, CT (1820-47g), Newport, RI (1820-75g), Oswegatchie, NY (1821-23), Passamaquoddy, ME (1820-59), Penobscot, ME (1851), Perth Amboy, NJ (1801-37g), Plymouth, MA (1821-36, 1843), Plymouth, NC (1820-30, 1840), Portland-Flamouth, ME (1820-68g), Port Royal, SC (1865), Providence, RI (1820-67g), Richmond, VA (1820-44g), Rochester, NY (1866), Sag Harbor, NY (1829-34g), St. Augustine, FL (1821-27, 1870), St. Johns, FL (1822-24, 1865), Salem-Beverly, MA (1798, 1800, 1823, 1865-66), Sandusky, OH (1820), Savannah, GA (1820-31g, 1847-67g), Waldsboro, ME (1820-21, 1833), Washington, NC (1828-37g, 1848), Wilmington, DE (1820, 1830-33g, 1840-49), Wiscasset, ME (1819-1829), Yarmouth, ME (1820). The letter g means there are gaps.

Immigration passenger lists are available for many ports during 1883-1945. Many are indexed. They are listed in:
__ GUIDE TO GENEALOGICAL RESEARCH IN THE NATIONAL ARCHIVES, The National Archives Staff, Washington, DC, 1984, Chapter 2.

These microfilms are available at the National Archives, its Field Branches, the FHL, through FHC, and in pertinent large genealogical libraries, state libraries, and state archives.

There are also numerous published lists and indexes dealing with immigrant and emigrant Germans. Among them are:

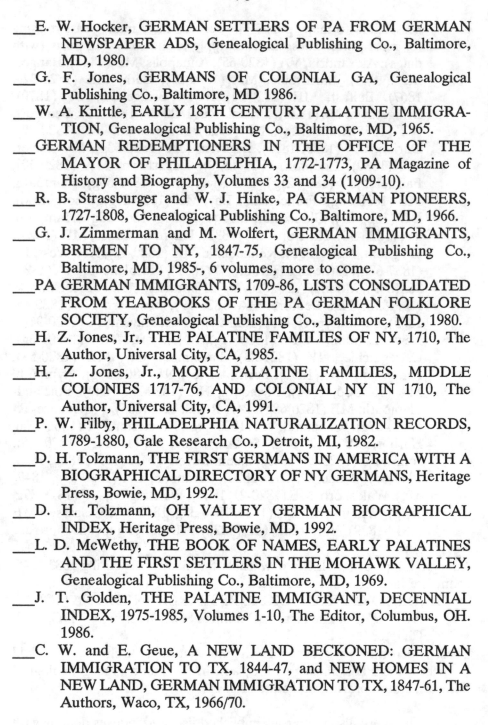

___E. W. Hocker, GERMAN SETTLERS OF PA FROM GERMAN NEWSPAPER ADS, Genealogical Publishing Co., Baltimore, MD, 1980.

___G. F. Jones, GERMANS OF COLONIAL GA, Genealogical Publishing Co., Baltimore, MD 1986.

___W. A. Knittle, EARLY 18TH CENTURY PALATINE IMMIGRATION, Genealogical Publishing Co., Baltimore, MD, 1965.

___GERMAN REDEMPTIONERS IN THE OFFICE OF THE MAYOR OF PHILADELPHIA, 1772-1773, PA Magazine of History and Biography, Volumes 33 and 34 (1909-10).

___R. B. Strassburger and W. J. Hinke, PA GERMAN PIONEERS, 1727-1808, Genealogical Publishing Co., Baltimore, MD, 1966.

___G. J. Zimmerman and M. Wolfert, GERMAN IMMIGRANTS, BREMEN TO NY, 1847-75, Genealogical Publishing Co., Baltimore, MD, 1985-, 6 volumes, more to come.

___PA GERMAN IMMIGRANTS, 1709-86, LISTS CONSOLIDATED FROM YEARBOOKS OF THE PA GERMAN FOLKLORE SOCIETY, Genealogical Publishing Co., Baltimore, MD, 1980.

___H. Z. Jones, Jr., THE PALATINE FAMILIES OF NY, 1710, The Author, Universal City, CA, 1985.

___H. Z. Jones, Jr., MORE PALATINE FAMILIES, MIDDLE COLONIES 1717-76, AND COLONIAL NY IN 1710, The Author, Universal City, CA, 1991.

___P. W. Filby, PHILADELPHIA NATURALIZATION RECORDS, 1789-1880, Gale Research Co., Detroit, MI, 1982.

___D. H. Tolzmann, THE FIRST GERMANS IN AMERICA WITH A BIOGRAPHICAL DIRECTORY OF NY GERMANS, Heritage Press, Bowie, MD, 1992.

___D. H. Tolzmann, OH VALLEY GERMAN BIOGRAPHICAL INDEX, Heritage Press, Bowie, MD, 1992.

___L. D. McWethy, THE BOOK OF NAMES, EARLY PALATINES AND THE FIRST SETTLERS IN THE MOHAWK VALLEY, Genealogical Publishing Co., Baltimore, MD, 1969.

___J. T. Golden, THE PALATINE IMMIGRANT, DECENNIAL INDEX, 1975-1985, Volumes 1-10, The Editor, Columbus, OH. 1986.

___C. W. and E. Geue, A NEW LAND BECKONED: GERMAN IMMIGRATION TO TX, 1844-47, and NEW HOMES IN A NEW LAND, GERMAN IMMIGRATION TO TX, 1847-61, The Authors, Waco, TX, 1966/70.

Take note that indexes for New York arrivals during 1847-96 are not included in the above listings. This is because these very voluminous lists are just now being partially indexed and are appearing in the published form:

___I. A. Glazier and P. W. Filby, GERMANS TO AMERICA, LISTS OF PASSENGERS ARRIVING AT US PORTS, 1850-, Scholarly Resources, Wilmington, DE, 1988- (in progress).

___INDEX OF PASSENGERS ENTERING THE PORT OF NEW YORK, 1847-1897, Precision Indexing, Bountiful, UT, 1993.

Until these indexes are complete, you must go through the unindexed lists page-by-page looking for Germans. Any information you might have on the date of immigration, the port of origin, or the name of the ship could shorten your work considerably.

6. Indexes to periodicals	6. Verzeichnisse der Zeitschriften
6. Verzeichniſſe der Zeitſchriften	6. Vuznichniſſn Dru Zrif.

Further sources of exceptional value are a US genealogical periodical index and a German genealogical periodical index:

___For many US genealogical periodicals 1847-1985, then annually from 1986 to the present, consult Allen County Public Library Foundation, PERIODICAL SOURCE INDEX, The Foundation, Fort Wayne, IN, 1986-present.

___For many German genealogical periodicals from 1872 forward, consult DER SCHLÜSSEL (THE KEY), Heinz Reise Verlag, Göttingen, Deutschland, 1950 forward, in progress. For many German periodicals from 1897 forward, check J. Hohlfeld, F. Wecken, et al., FAMILIENGESCHICHTLICHE QUELLEN UND BIBLIO-GRAPHIE, Verlag Degener, Neustadt/Aisch, Deutschland, 1920-1945, over 17 volumes. Volume 6 has a cumulative index covering all entries for 1897-1927.

In these, you should look up the surname of your immigrant ancestor to see if you can locate periodical articles relating to the family. Don't fail to also look up the names of German friends, neighbors, and associates of your ancestor, especially those whose names are not common. Do not be afraid of the German language in DER SCHLÜSSEL and the BIBLIOGRAPHIE. You will be able to read the surnames you are hunting, and the references to periodicals are fairly evident. Instructions on reading German for those who know very little German will be given in a later chapter. The US index is in most medium and large genealogical libraries, but the German index is usually only in the large ones. Similarly, good collections of US periodicals are available in quite a number of genealogical libraries, but only a few of the largest have good holdings of German periodicals.

7. Indexes to German compilations	7. Verzeichnisse der deutschen Sammlungen
7. Verzeichniſſe der deutſchen Sammlungen	*7. Verzeichniſſe der deutſchen Sammlungen*

The next indexes which may lead you to the exact place of origin of your immigrant German forebear are some large German compendia of alphabetized German genealogical data. These indexes will be found only in the largest US genealogical libraries. The major ones of these are:

___J. Glenzdorf, GLENZDORFS INTERNATIONALES GENEAL-LOGEN-LEXIKON (GLENZDORF'S INTERNATIONAL DIRECTORY OF GENEALOGISTS), Wilhelm Rost Verlag, Bad Münder/Deister, Deutschland, 1977-present, 4 volumes. Alphabetical listing of surnames being researched by genealogists along with index of places where surnames are found.

___O. Spohr, FAMILIENGESCHICHTLICHE QUELLEN (FAMILY HISTORY SOURCES), Verlag Degener, Neustadt/Aisch, Deutschland, 1927-1959, 13 Bände (volumes). Check for your progenitor's surname.

___STAMMFOLGENVERZEICHNIS ZUM DEUTSCHEN GE-SCHLECHTERBUCH, GENEALOGISCHES HANDBUCH BÜRGERLICHER FAMILIEN (INDEX TO LINES OF DE-SCENT IN THE GERMAN FAMILY BOOK, A GENEALOGI-CAL HANDBOOK OF ORDINARY FAMILIES), Stark Verlag, Limburg/Lahn, Deutschland, 1986. Indexes over 186 volumes (Bände) of collected family histories. Look for your forebear's surname.

___DIE DEUTSCHE AHNENLISTEN-KARTEI, Verlag Degener, Neustadt/Aisch, Deutschland, 1975-, 12 Lieferungen (issues). Each issue separately indexed.

___F. Wecken, u.a., FAMILIENGESCHICHTSLICHE BIBLIO-GRAPHIE, Zentrallstelle, Leipzig, und Verlag Degener, Neustadt/Aisch, Deutschland, 1928-, 21 Bände.

___E. Wasmannsdorff, GESAMT NAMENVERZEICHNIS UMFASS-END BAND 1-50 DEUTSCHES GESCHLECHTERBUCH, C.

A. Starke Verlag, Görlitz, Deutschland, 1938. An every name index to the first 50 volumes of the GESCHLECHTERBUCH. Covers only A-Reinisch.

___T. von Fritsch, DIE GOTHAISCHEN TASCHENBÜCHER, HOF-KALENDER, UND ALMANACH, Starke Verlag, Limburg/Lahn, Deutschland, 1987. Indexes over 450 volumes of German noble families. In large genealogical libraries and in FHL (FHC). Be sure and look at both indexes, the one starting on page 187, and the one starting on page 350.

___DEUTSCHES FAMILIENARCHIV (GERMAN FAMILY AR-CHIVE), Verlag Degener, Neustadt/Aisch, Deutschland, 1952-present, over 100 volumes (Bände). Indexes to volumes 1-50, 51-75, 76-100 published in 1980-1989. Check for your ancestor's surname.

___F. Heinemann und C. Lenhartz, BIBLIOGRAPHIE GEDRUCKTER FAMILIENGESCHICHTEN, 1946-60, Heinzmann, Düsseldorf, Deutschland, 1990.

___Deutsche Zentralstelle für Genealogie, DIE AHNENSTAMMKART-EI DES DEUTSCHEN VOLKES, FHL Microfilm of 2.4 million cards, Salt Lake City, UT, 1991-2.

8. Indexes to German emigrations	8. Verzeichnisse der deutschen Auswanderungen
8. Verzeichniffe der deutfchen Aufwanderungen	*[handwritten] 8. Verzeichniffe der deutschen Auswanderungen*

Another step that you can take is to make use of some German emigration record indexes. The most important of these records are the Hamburg passenger lists, which are available on microfilm for 1850 to 1934. There are two distinct indexes, a direct index (for passengers going directly to the US), and an indirect index (for passengers who stopped at some intermediate port).

___DIRECT HAMBURG PASSENGER LISTS, 1850-1854, arranged alphabetically, microfilmed by Family History Library, Salt Lake City, UT; ALPHABETICAL CARD LIST OF DIRECT HAMBURG PASSENGER LISTS, 1856-1871, microfilmed by Family History Library, Salt Lake City, UT; PARTIALLY ALPHABETICAL INDEX OF DIRECT HAMBURG PASSEN-GER LISTS, 1855-1934, microfilmed by Family History Library, Salt Lake City, UT; PARTIALLY ALPHABETICAL INDEX OF

INDIRECT HAMBURG PASSENGER LISTS, 1855-1910, microfilmed by Family History Library, Salt Lake City, UT.
These indexes lead to the passenger lists themselves: direct (1850-1934), and indirect (1854-1910). They give the passenger's name, hometown, age, occupation, and accompanying family members. Both the indexes and the lists can be obtained at the Family History Library (FHL), or they can be ordered through the Library's numerous branch Family History Centers (FHC).

Now we will consider passenger records from other ports which departing Germans used: Bremen, LeHavre, Amsterdam, and Antwerp. The earlier Bremen records were destroyed by the port authorities who did not have room to store them, and the later records were destroyed in World War II. However, the records are being reconstructed from American immigration lists. Those of the records which show the place of origin of the passengers are being published in:

___G. J. Zimmerman and M. Wolfert, GERMAN IMMIGRANTS, LISTS OF PASSENGERS BOUND FROM BREMEN TO NEW YORK, WITH PLACES OF ORIGIN, 1847-forward, Genealogical Publishing Co., Baltimore, MD, 1988-, 5 volumes, more to come.

The LeHavre passenger records are only in France and searches must be carried out there by a hired researcher. The records for 1749-1830 are:

___LeHAVRE EMIGRATION LISTS, 1749-1830, Register Colonies F/5B45-48, located at Archives Nationale de la France, 60 rue des France-Bourgeois, F-75003 Paris, FRANCE.
Those for 1830 up to the present are at:

___LeHAVRE EMIGRATION LISTS, 1830-present, located at Archives de la Seine-Maritime, Cours Clemenceau, F-76036 Rouen, FRANCE.
These lists are difficult and very time consuming to search unless you can give your hired researcher a good idea of the time period and/or the ship. Such information can often be obtained from the New York immigration records. A listing of many of the passengers (including Germans) who went through LeHavre 1803-1869 is on microfilm at the Family History Library (FHL). The microfilms can be borrowed through all of the local branches of the FHL, the Family History Centers (FHC).

___Family History Library, PASSENGERS GOING THROUGH LeHAVRE, 1803-1869, 2 reels of microfilm, Microfilm Nos. 1070234-1070235, FHL, Salt Lake City, UT.

Most Germans heading for the port of LeHavre proceeded through Elsass-Lothringen (Alsace-Lorraine). The French authorities there kept registers of many of them during 1817-1866. These registers, which have numerous gaps in them and are also otherwise incomplete, have been microfilmed by the FHL (available through FHC).

___Family History Library, REGISTERS OF EMIGRANTS [REGISTERS DES ÉMIGRES], 6 reels of microfilm, Microfilm Nos. 1125002-1125007, FHL, Salt Lake City, UT.

Also consult the following index, which lists a large number of Germans:

___Family History Library, ALSACE EMIGRATION INDEX, 8 reels of microfilm, Microfilm Nos. 1069293-1069294, 1070142, 1070232-1070235, FHL, Salt Lake City, UT.

Practically all of Rotterdam's departing passenger lists were destroyed in World War II, and those of Antwerp met the same fate in World War I, except for some passport applications during 1854-1855. They are on microfilm at FHL (available through FHC).

___Family History Library, ANTWERP PASSENGER LISTS [actually PASSPORT APPLICATIONS], 3 reels of microfilm, not indexed, Film Nos. 392910-392912, FHL, Salt Lake City, UT.

There are also numerous published lists of emigrants from the Germanic areas. Some of these were mentioned in the previous section on immigration, but here are others

___W. Hacker, EIGHTEENTH CENTURY REGISTER OF EMIGRANTS FROM SW GERMANY TO AMERICA AND OTHER COUNTRIES, Closson Press, Apollo, Pa, 1994.

___T. Schenk, R. Froekle, J. Bork, WÜRTTEMBURG EMIGRATION INDEX, Ancestry, Salt Lake City, UT, 1986-92, 6 volumes.

___C. Schrader-Muggenthaler, THE ALSACE EMIGRATION BOOK, 1817-1869, Closson Press, Apollo, PA, 1990-1, 2 volumes.

___C. Schrader-Muggenthaler, THE BADEN EMIGRATION BOOK, Closson Press, Apollo, PA, 1992.

___A. K. Burgert, EIGHTEENTH CENTURY EMIGRANTS FROM GERMAN-SPEAKING LANDS TO NORTH AMERICA, (Northern Kraichgau, Western Palatinate, Northern Alsace), PA German Society, Birdsboro, PA, 1983/85/92, 3 volumes.

___A. K. Burgert and H. Z. Jones, Jr., WESTERWALD TO AMERICA, SOME 18TH CENTURY GERMAN IMMIGRANTS, Picton Press, Camden, ME, 1989.

___A. K. Burgert, PA GERMAN MONOGRAPH SERIES, AKB Publications, Myerstown, PA, 1983ff.

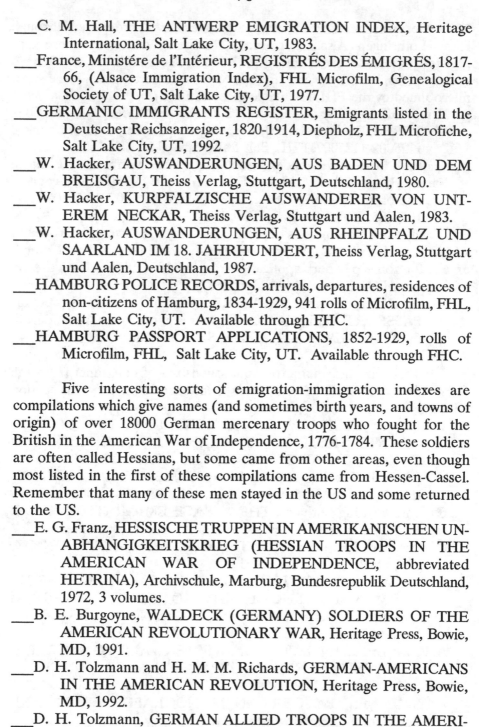

___C. M. Hall, THE ANTWERP EMIGRATION INDEX, Heritage International, Salt Lake City, UT, 1983.

___France, Ministére de l'Intérieur, REGISTRÉS DES ÉMIGRÉS, 1817-66, (Alsace Immigration Index), FHL Microfilm, Genealogical Society of UT, Salt Lake City, UT, 1977.

___GERMANIC IMMIGRANTS REGISTER, Emigrants listed in the Deutscher Reichsanzeiger, 1820-1914, Diepholz, FHL Microfiche, Salt Lake City, UT, 1992.

___W. Hacker, AUSWANDERUNGEN, AUS BADEN UND DEM BREISGAU, Theiss Verlag, Stuttgart, Deutschland, 1980.

___W. Hacker, KURPFALZISCHE AUSWANDERER VON UNT-EREM NECKAR, Theiss Verlag, Stuttgart und Aalen, 1983.

___W. Hacker, AUSWANDERUNGEN, AUS RHEINPFALZ UND SAARLAND IM 18. JAHRHUNDERT, Theiss Verlag, Stuttgart und Aalen, Deutschland, 1987.

___HAMBURG POLICE RECORDS, arrivals, departures, residences of non-citizens of Hamburg, 1834-1929, 941 rolls of Microfilm, FHL, Salt Lake City, UT. Available through FHC.

___HAMBURG PASSPORT APPLICATIONS, 1852-1929, rolls of Microfilm, FHL, Salt Lake City, UT. Available through FHC.

Five interesting sorts of emigration-immigration indexes are compilations which give names (and sometimes birth years, and towns of origin) of over 18000 German mercenary troops who fought for the British in the American War of Independence, 1776-1784. These soldiers are often called Hessians, but some came from other areas, even though most listed in the first of these compilations came from Hessen-Cassel. Remember that many of these men stayed in the US and some returned to the US.

___E. G. Franz, HESSISCHE TRUPPEN IN AMERIKANISCHEN UN-ABHANGIGKEITSKRIEG (HESSIAN TROOPS IN THE AMERICAN WAR OF INDEPENDENCE, abbreviated HETRINA), Archivschule, Marburg, Bundesrepublik Deutschland, 1972, 3 volumes.

___B. E. Burgoyne, WALDECK (GERMANY) SOLDIERS OF THE AMERICAN REVOLUTIONARY WAR, Heritage Press, Bowie, MD, 1991.

___D. H. Tolzmann and H. M. M. Richards, GERMAN-AMERICANS IN THE AMERICAN REVOLUTION, Heritage Press, Bowie, MD, 1992.

___D. H. Tolzmann, GERMAN ALLIED TROOPS IN THE AMERI-CAN REVOLUTION: J. R. ROSENGARTEN'S SURVEY OF

GERMAN ARCHIVES AND SOURCES, Heritage Press, Bowie, MD, 1993.

___M. Von Eelking and J. R. Rosengarten, THE GERMAN ALLIED TROOPS IN THE NORTH AMERICAN WAR OF INDEPENDENCE, 1776-1783, Heritage Books, Bowie, MD, 1987.

Another good source is a card index to numerous emigrants from Germany whose names have been listed in the periodical Deutsches Familienarchiv:

___EMIGRANTS TO AND FROM GERMANY FROM THE 18TH TO THE 20TH CENTURY, FHL Microfilm 1,125,001, Salt Lake City, UT, 1976.

9. Other indexes	9. Andere Verzeichnisse
9. Andere Verzeichnisse	*9. Andere Verzeichnisse*

There are several other types of indexes which may give your progenitor's place of origin or provide you with clues which might lead to its discovery.

Biographical indexes. Numerous biographical collections have been published in the US on all levels: local, regional, state, and national. Perhaps your immigrant or one of his/her descendants appears in one of these. There is a very good overall computer-based index to over 500 of them, in which over 6 million names have been entered. It can be accessed in large libraries:

___BIOBASE, Gale Research, Detroit, MI, latest edition.

In addition, contact with your ancestor's and his/her descendants' state library, state archives, and local (county, city, town) library should be made to inquire about possible biographical publications.

Library and archives indexes. State libraries and state archives often have numerous state-wide indexes which may lead to data on your German immigrant or his/her descendants. Types of state-wide indexes which you should inquire about include alien registrations (particularly 1802-1825), Bible, biography, birth, cemetery, colonial, court, death, directories, family records, genealogical compilations, Germans, immigrants, land grants, marriage, military, naturalization, probate, published genealogies, settlers, state censuses, surnames, taxation, and will. Addresses for these libraries and archives will be found in:

___George K. Schweitzer, HANDBOOK OF GENEALOGICAL
    SOURCES, Genealogical Sources, Unltd., 407 Ascot Court,
    Knoxville, TN, 37923-5807 (1995).
Inquiries about items such as those listed above should also be sent to
local libraries (county, city, town) in the places where your forebear and
his/her descendants lived.

    Census indexes. Most federal census records (1790, 1800, 1810,
1820, 1830, 1840, 1850, 1860, 1870, 1880, 1900, 1910, 1920) have been
indexed, so your progenitor should be relatively easy to find in them.
They will lead you to the actual census records which seldom give the
exact place of origin, but sometimes provide you with clues to finding it.
The 1790-1840 censuses list the names of the heads of the households
only, along with some age brackets (for example, free white females aged
26-45).   All persons are listed by name, sex, age, and place of origin
(state, territory, or country) in the 1850-1920 census, along with some
other data.   The 1870 census added whether the parents were foreign
born. The 1880 census added the parents' places of birth (state, territory,
or country). The 1900 census added the month and year of birth, the
number of years married, the year of immigration, the years in the US,
and the country of citizenship if foreign born. The 1910 census added
whether each foreign-born person had been naturalized. Notice that only
the country is called for in the case of the foreign-born. However, in
some instances, the census-taker has entered more detail. Census indexes
and records are available in medium and large-sized genealogical libraries.

    Alphabetized city directories.   For many major cities, city
directories are available beginning sometime in the 1800s, in a few
instances as early as the late 1700s. They can be useful in indicating
approximately when an ancestor came to a city and when he left it or
died. Thousands of city directories have been microfilmed:
___CITY DIRECTORIES OF THE US, 1752-1901, GUIDE TO THE
    MICROFILM COLLECTION, Research Publications,
    Woodbridge, CT, 1983.
A few of the larger genealogical libraries in the US have complete collections of these.

    Military record indexes. The military conflicts of the US
generated a number of federal records, most notably service, bounty land,
and pension records. In general, they are not useful for identifying an
exact place of origin, but sometimes they do contain the birth date and
place, even though the place may be recorded only as the country or

province. Instructions for locating and searching these records for the Revolutionary War, War of 1812, Mexican War, and Civil War are provided in the book by Schweitzer mentioned in the third paragraph above.

Passport applications. Prior to 1916, passports were not mandatory for US citizens going out of the country. However, many citizens applied for and received them. The National Archives has the applications and some incomplete indexes for 1791-1925. Sometimes the applications give the birth place and date of the applicant, and sometimes data on arrival in the US and naturalization are provided. These records are in
___Record Groups 59 and 84, National Archives, Washington, DC 20408.

Surname indexes. In addition to the surname indexes that have been mentioned before, there are several private companies which have produced them. Usually, it is not fruitful to consult such indexes since they are so small that your chances of success are low. However, there are several very large ones which could be productive:
___Everton Publishers, COMPUTERIZED ROOTS CELLAR, FAMILY FILE, AND PEDIGREE LIBRARY, PO Box 368, Logan, UT 84321.
___K. A. Johnson and M. R. Sainty, GENEALOGICAL RESEARCH DIRECTORY, The Authors, Glendale, CA, one issue each year. Be sure to examine all of them.
___GENESIS, THE INTERNATIONAL FAMILY FILE, PO Box 2607, Salt Lake City, UT 84110.

A number of other indexes and finding aids are available for trying to discover a German immigrant's exact place of origin. These are discussed in detail in:
___A. Eakle and J. Cerny, THE SOURCE, Ancestry Publishing Co., Salt Lake City, UT, 1984.
___George K. Schweitzer, HANDBOOK OF GENEALOGICAL SOURCES, Genealogical Sources, Unltd., 407 Ascot Court, Knoxville, TN 37923-5807 (1995).

10. Records of death	10. Sterbeurkunden
10. Sterbeurkunden	*10. Sterbeurkunden*

Having considered family sources and then numerous large indexes, we now turn to look at the original records and copies of original records available here in the US. Emphasis will be placed upon those which are the most likely sources for permitting you to bridge the Atlantic, that is, to trace your forebear back to German territory. Again, it must be emphasized that searches for friends, neighbors, and associates of your progenitor can often succeed, since it is possible that they came from the same place. Now let us turn to the first category of records, which is the category most likely to lead to your German immigrant's precise place of origin. These are the records associated with his/her death.

When one considers the records surrounding a person's death, these come to mind: hospital, physician, death record or certificate, mortuary, church burial, church funeral, funeral mass, fraternal organization rites, cemetery record, gravestone inscription, obituary, death notice, probate (will), land, and tax. Now a few words will be said about each of these, with some remarks regarding where they may be found and the possibility that they might reveal the place of origin in Germany (birth, marriage, births of children, departure).

Hospital records should be sought in the place where your ancestor died in the hope that they might show the birth place and date. Unfortunately, as one goes back in time, the records get poorer, and finally are non-existent. Further, many have not been preserved. Nonetheless, they should be looked for.

The records of physicians who might have attended your forebear should be sought out. The same difficulties that burden hospital records apply here, but the effort must be made.

In some states, county or town governmental death record keeping goes back to colonial times. However, in most states, centralized state record keeping began in the second half of the 1800s or even early in the 1900s. State, county, or city death records and certificates sometimes reveal the exact place of birth, often give the date of birth, and usually state the age. It is well to remember, however, that the information is only as good as the knowledge and/or memory of the person who gave it. This person was ordinarily a relative, usually a daughter or son. Death records and certificates may be found as microfilm copies in the FHL (FHC), in state libraries or archives, and originals are located in state archives, county court houses, city halls, and town halls.

Following are the sources of governmental (state, county, town) death records presently available in the US. The date in brackets after the name of the state indicates the date on which the state initiated the collection of death records at a central repository, usually at the state capital. The address from which records after this date may be obtained is then given. Then information regarding the sources of governmental death records before this date is given (usually the counties or towns, if at all).

_In AL [1908] AL Department of Public Health, Montgomery, AL 36130. From 1881-1908, very incomplete registration in counties. Before 1881, a few records in county probate courts.

_In AK [1913] AK Bureau of Vital Statistics, PO Box H-02G, Juneau, AK 99811-0675. Before 1913, church records are the best source.

_In AZ [1909] AZ Vital Records Section, PO Box 3887, Phoenix, AZ 85030-3887. They also have abstracts of some county records before 1909.

_In AR [1914] AR Division of Vital Records, 4815 West Markham Street, Little Rock, AR 72201. They also have some Little Rock and Fort Smith deaths from 1881.

_In CA [1905] CA Vital Statistics Branch, 410 N Street, Sacramento, CA 95814. For 1850-1905, records are in counties, in most for only part of this period.

_In CO [1900] CO Vital Records Section, 4210 E. 11th Avenue, Denver, CO 80220. For 1872-1910, some counties have some records, mostly for only part of this time.

_In CT [1897] CT Vital Records Section, 79 Elm Street, Hartford, CT 06115. For 1640-1897, contact town or city clerk, or CT State Library.

_In DE [1861-3, 1881] For records after 1930 DE Bureau of Vital Statistics, State Health Building, PO Box 637, Dover, DE 19901-0637. For records 1861-3 and 1881-1930 DE State Archives, Dover, DE 19901.

_In DC [1855] DC Vital Records Section, Room 3007, 425 I Street, Washington, DC 20001. Earlier records very poor.

_In FL [1917] FL Office of Vital Statistics, PO Box 210, Jacksonville, FL 32231. Also some records 1865-1917. A few counties have records 1875-1917, mostly for only part of this time.

_In GA [1919] GA Vital Records Unit, Room 217-H, 47 Trinity Avenue, SW, Atlanta, GA 30334. Atlanta 1896-1919, Savannah 1803-1919, Macon 1882-1919 from county health departments. A few counties have earlier records.

_In HI [1853] HI State Health Department, 1250 Punchbowl Street, Honolulu, HI 96813. Early records incomplete. Records 1853-1896 also at HI State Archives.

_In ID [1911] ID Vital Statistics Unit, Statehouse Mall, Boise, ID 83720-9990. For 1907-1911 county recorder.

_In IL [1916] IL Division of Vital Records, 535 West Jefferson Street, Springfield, IL 62761. For 1877-1916, contact counties. For Chicago 1871-1916, contact county. A few counties have earlier records.

_In IN [1900] IN Division of Vital Records, PO Box 1964, Indianapolis, IN 46206. For 1882-1907, contact counties. A few counties have earlier records.

_In IA [1880] IA Vital Records Section, Lucas State Office Building, Des Moines, IA 50319.

_In KS [1911] KS Department of Health, 900 South Jackson, Topeka, KS 66612. For 1880-1911, some counties have some records, mostly for a part of this time.

_In KY [1911] KY Office of Vital Statistics, 275 East Main Street, Frankfort, KY 40621. For 1852-1911 KY Department for Libraries and Archives, 300 Coffee Tree Road, Frankfort, KY 40601, or contact counties.

_In LA [1914] LA Division of Vital Records, PO Box 60630, New Orleans, LA 70160. New Orleans 1790-1914 very incomplete, available from city.

_In ME [1892] ME Office of Vital Records, State House, Augusta, ME 04333. For 1892-1955 also at ME State Archives, State House, Augusta, ME 04333. For 1635-1892, records incomplete, contact towns.

_In MD [1898] MD Division of Vital Records, PO Box 13146, Baltimore, MD 21203. For 1898-1982 and Baltimore 1875-1982 also at MD State Archives, 350 Rowe Boulevard, Annapolis, MD 21401. For earlier records, contact MD State Archives.

_In MA [1841] For 1896 and later, MA Registry of Vital Records and Statistics, 150 Tremont Street, Boston, MA 02111. For 1841-1896

MA State Archives, 220 Morrissey Boulevard, Boston, MA 02125. For 1620-1896, consult town or city. Most records published.

_In MI [1867] MI Office of the State Registrar, PO Box 30035, Lansing, MI 48909.

_In MN [1908] MN Section of Vital Statistics, 717 Delaware Street, SE, Minneapolis, MN 55440. For 1870-1908, contact county or health departments in St. Paul and Minneapolis.

_In MS [1912] MS Bureau of Vital Statistics, PO Box 1700, Jackson, MS 39205.

_In MO [1909] MO Bureau of Vital Records, Jefferson City, MO 65101. For 1863-1909, contact counties. For St. Louis 1870-1910 or Kansas City before 1909, write city vital records departments.

_In MT [1907] MT Bureau of Records and Statistics, Helena, MT 59601. For 1878-1907, some counties have some records, usually only for a part of this time.

_In NE [1904] NE Bureau of Vital Statistics, PO Box 95007, Lincoln, NE 68509.

_In NV [1911] NV Section of Vital Statistics, 505 East King Street, Carson City, NV 89710. For 1887-1911, contact counties.

_In NH [1901] NH Bureau of Vital Records, 6 Hazel Drive, Concord, NH 03301. Also has some records since 1640. For 1640-1901, contact towns. Also NH State Library, 20 Park Street, Concord, NH 03301.

_In NJ [1848] For 1848-1923 NJ State Archives, 185 West State Street, Trenton, NJ 08625-0307. For after 1923, NJ State Registrar, Trenton, NJ 08625-0360.

_In NM [1920] NM Vital Statistics Office, PO Box 968, Santa Fe, NM 87504-0968.

_In NY [1880] NY Vital Records Section, Room 244, Corning Tower Building, Albany, NY 12237. For records before 1914 in Albany, Buffalo, and Yonkers, and for records before 1880 for Rochester, Syracuse, and Utica, contact city registrar. For New York City records since 1920, contact Bureau of Vital Records, 125 Worth Street, New York, NY 10013. For Manhattan records 1865-1919, contact Municipal Archives, 31 Chambers Street, New York, NY 10007.

_In NC [1913] For 1913-1929, contact State Records Center, 215 North Blount St., Raleigh, NC 27602. For 1930 and after, contact NC Vital Records Branch, PO Box 2091, Raleigh, NC 27602. A few counties have a few records prior to 1913.

_In ND [1907] ND Division of Vital Records, First Floor, Judicial Wing, Bismarck, ND. Also have some incomplete records 1893-1907. For before 1907, also consult counties.

_In OH [1908] OH Department of Health, 65 South Front Street, Columbus, OH 43215. For 1867-1908, consult probate court offices in counties.

_In OK [1908] OK Vital Records Section, PO Box 53551, Oklahoma City, OK 73152. A few counties have incomplete records before 1908.

_In OR [1903] OR Vital Records Unit, PO Box 116, Portland, OR 97207. For Portland records 1864-1903 contact OR State Archives, 1005 Broadway, NE, Salem, OR 97130.

_In PA [1906] PA Division of Vital Records, PO Box 1528, New Castle, PA 16103. For 1860-1915 Philadelphia records contact Vital Statistics, City Hall Annex, Philadelphia, PA 19107. For 1870-1906 incomplete records of Allegheny City, Easton, Harrisburg, Pottsville, Pittsburgh, and Williamsport, contact cities. Some early records also with county registers of wills.

_In RI [1853] RI Division of Vital Statistics, 75 Davis Street, Providence, RI 02908. For 1636-1853, consult town clerks. Also 1636-1850 mostly in book by J. N. Arnold.

_In SC [1915] SC Office of Vital Records, 2600 Bull Street, Columbia, SC 29201. For 1821-1915 Charleston, 1895-1915 Florence, and 1895-1915 Newberry records, contact county health departments.

_In SD [1905] SD Health Statistics Program, Joe Foss Building, Pierre, SC 57501. Some incomplete earlier records available in counties.

_In TN [1914] TN Division of Vital Records, Cordell Hull Building, Nashville, TN 37219. Also have 1908-1912 records, and 1874-1914 for Nashville, 1887-1914 for Knoxville, and 1872-1914 for Chattanooga. For 1848-1914 Memphis records, contact city health department. For 1881-1914 some counties and larger cities have incomplete records.

_In TX [1903] TX Bureau of Vital Statistics, 1100 West 49th Street, Austin, TX 78756. A few counties have incomplete earlier records.

_In UT (1905) UT Bureau of Health Statistics, PO Box 16700, Salt Lake City, UT 84116. Some counties have incomplete records 1887-1905. For Salt Lake City and Ogden 1890-1904, contact city health departments.

_In VT [effectively 1857] VT Public Records Division, 6 Baldwin Place, Montpelier, VT 05602 for index, abstracts, and microfilm copies for 1760-1954. But original record must be obtained from town clerk.

_In VA [effectively 1853] VA Division of Vital Records, PO Box 1000, Richmond, VA 23208. There is a gap of no records 1896-1912. For the few records before 1853, contact VA State Archives, 11th and Capitol Streets, Richmond, VA 23219. For 1896-1912, inquire at VA State Archives, county, and city about other records.

_In WA [1907] WA Vital Records, PO Box 9709, Olympia, WA 98504. For 1891-1907, contact WA State Archives, 12th and Washington, Olympia, WA 98504, or county auditor.

_In WV [1917] WV Division of Vital Statistics, Charleston, WV 25305. For 1853-1900, contact WV Archives and History Library, Charleston, WV 25305, or clerk of county court.

_In WI [1907] WI Bureau of Health Statistics, PO Box 309, Madison, WI 53701. For 1852-1907, contact county register of deeds and State Historical Society of WI. Earlier records incomplete.

_In WY [1909] WY Vital Records Services, State Office Building West, Cheyenne, WY 82002.

Further details on seeking and using these records are given in the books by Eakle/Cerny and Schweitzer mentioned at the end of section 9 of this chapter.

Mortuary records sometimes contain information regarding the birth place and date of the deceased. They date back to the origin of mortuaries, but earlier records are less likely to have the desired data. The earliest mortuaries in the pertinent community should be identified, and their records examined. Present-day mortuaries may have inherited records from their predecessors. A book which lists almost all present-day mortuaries is:

___AMERICAN BLUE BOOK OF FUNERAL DIRECTORS, National Funeral Directors Association, New York, NY, latest issue.

This volume or a similar one will be found in practically every mortuary in the US.

Church records of deaths, burials, funerals, and funeral masses can contain the sought-after data on German origins. You will recall that early-arriving Germans were those of Pietistic sects (Mennonites, German Baptists, Dunkards, Schwenkfelders, Moravians), but soon Lutherans and Reformed came to predominate, then in the latter half of the 1800s Catholics in large numbers came. Every possible attempt must be made to locate US church records on your ancestor, but you need to be reminded that many Germans, particularly after 1848, were anti-church or neutral toward religious organizations because of adverse experiences in Germany with church-state cooperative oppression. Many of the records will be in German, but you should not worry, because we will give you instructions on reading them in a later chapter.

Church records are to be found in many places in many forms. Original records are located in the local churches, in churches that have superseded previous ones, in churches that have inherited records of defunct congregations, in state denominational archives, in national denominational archives, in denominational colleges, in large universities in the state, and in the state archives and/or libraries. Transcribed records, both hand-written and typescript, are most likely to be found in local libraries, in state libraries, in state and national denominational archives, and in the DAR Library in Washington, DC. The DAR chapters in many states have copied very large numbers of church records. Published transcribed records, both books and genealogical periodical articles, are chiefly to be found in local libraries and state libraries. Microfilmed copies of church records are stored in state and national denominational archives, and in the Family History Library in Salt Lake City, UT. Those in the Family History Library may be borrowed through its numerous branch Family History Centers. Microfilmed abstracts from church records are available in every Family History Center in the International Genealogical Index.

Some of the major German-related church archives in the US are:
__(Brethren) Archives of the Brethren in Christ Church, Messiah College, Grantham, PA 17027.
__(Church of the Brethren) Brethren Historical Library and Archives, 1451 Dundee Avenue, Elgin, IL 60120.
__(Evangelical United Brethren) Historical Society, Evangelical United Brethren Church, 1810 Harvard Building, Dayton, OH 45406. Now part of the United Methodist Church. The Evangelical United Brethren had resulted from a merger of the Evangelical Church and the United Brethren in Christ.
__(Lutheran) Archives of the American Lutheran Church, 333 Wartburg Place, Dubuque, IA 52001; Lutheran Archives Center, 7301 Germantown Avenue, Philadelphia, PA 19119; Wentz Library, Lutheran Theological Seminary, Gettysburg, PA 17325; Lutheran Southern Seminary Library, 4201 Main Street, Columbia, SC 29203; Archives of the Lutheran Church in America, 1100 East 55th Street, Chicago, IL 60615; Archives of the Evangelical

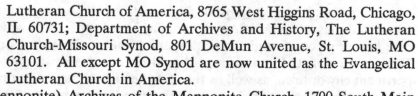

Lutheran Church of America, 8765 West Higgins Road, Chicago, IL 60731; Department of Archives and History, The Lutheran Church-Missouri Synod, 801 DeMun Avenue, St. Louis, MO 63101. All except MO Synod are now united as the Evangelical Lutheran Church in America.

___(Mennonite) Archives of the Mennonite Church, 1700 South Main Street, Goshen, IN 46526.

___(Moravian) The Archives of the Moravian Church, 1228 Main Street, Bethlehem, PA 18018; Moravian Archives, Southern Provinces, Drawer M, Salem Station, Winston-Salem, NC 27108.

___(Roman Catholic Church) Catholic Archives of America, Notre Dame University, South Bend, IN 46624; Department of Archives and Manuscripts, Catholic University of America, Washington, DC 20019.

___(Schwenkfelders) Schwenkfelder Library, Seminary Avenue, Pennsburg, PA 18073.

___(United Church of Christ, a merger of Evangelical and Reformed with some Congregational Churches) Congregational Library, 14 Beacon Street, Boston, MA 02108; Eden Archives, Evangelical and Reformed Churches, 475 East Lockwood Avenue, Webster Groves, MO 63119; Evangelical and Reformed Historical Society, 555 West James Street, Lancaster, PA 17603. The Evangelical and Reformed Church had resulted from a merger of the Evangelical Synod of North America and the Reformed Church in the US.

If the denomination you are concerned with does not appear above, take a look in the following volumes, from which many of the above listings were taken, and which contain much more church archival and headquarters information:

___National Council of Churches, YEARBOOK OF AMERICAN AND CANADIAN CHURCHES, Abingdon Press, Nashville, TN, latest annual issue.

___F. S. Mead, HANDBOOK OF AMERICAN DENOMINATIONS, Abingdon Press, Nashville, TN, latest edition.

___J. G. Melton, ENCYCLOPEDIA OF AMERICAN RELIGIONS, Gale Research Co., Detroit, MI, latest edition.

In addition to national church archives such as those listed in the previous paragraph, there are often state church archives, especially for denominations which have large memberships in the state being considered. National church archives can and will often refer you to these.

Fraternal organizations to which your ancestor belonged may have conducted rites at the burial, or better, may have kept records which indicate his/her place of origin. Such organizations as the Masons and the Turners are meant. Inquiries regarding their records may be made in the pertinent city or town, as well as the state headquarters and the national headquarters. The national headquarters of a large number of these are listed in:

___ENCYCLOPEDIA OF ASSOCIATIONS, Gale Research Co., Detroit, MI, latest edition.

___A. J. Schmidt., FRATERNAL ORGANIZATIONS, Greenwood Press, Westport, CT, 1980.

Cemetery records in the cemetery office and gravestone inscriptions in the cemetery sometimes yield the place of origin of an immigrant ancestor. Many cemeteries have been read, that is, their gravestone inscriptions have been recorded. Some of these are still in manuscript form, some are available as card files, and quite a larger number have been published as books and in journals, and others have been microfilmed. Your search for cemetery records will therefore involve contacts with your nearest FHC, libraries in the place of your progenitor's death, the state library, and the local genealogical society in an effort to find published or manuscript transcriptions. Or, it may be necessary, or even more convenient to search the suspected cemeteries yourself.

Obituaries and death notices published in US newspapers and church journals, especially ones in the German language, are a particularly good source of places of origin of forebears who have come from Germany. Numerous older newspapers have been collected and many are available on microfilm. These will be found at state libraries, state archives, state university libraries, city libraries, and other repositories. Many newspaper offices also have collections of older issues. To discover what newspapers are available for your ancestor's location at the time of her/his death, consult these listings:

___C. S. Brigham, HISTORY AND BIBLIOGRAPHY OF AMERICAN NEWSPAPERS, 1690-1820, American Antiquarian Society, Worcester, MA, 1947, 2 volumes.

___W. Gregory, AMERICAN NEWSPAPERS, 1821-1936, H. W. Wilson Co., New York, NY, 1937.

___NEWSPAPERS IN MICROFORM, US, Library of Congress, Washington, DC, latest edition. Many of these can be borrowed.

___US NEWSPAPER PROGRAM, NATIONAL UNION LIST, Online Computer Library Center, Dublin, OH, latest edition.

It is, of course, of immense importance that you look for German newspapers. An excellent resource for locating them is:

    K. J. R. Arndt and M. E. Olson, THE GERMAN LANGUAGE PRESS OF THE AMERICAS, Verlag Dokumentation, Pullach/München, Deutschland, 1973, and K. G. Saur Verlag, München, 1980, 3 Bände (3 volumes). Use the 1st volume carefully, and don't overlook the supplemental material in volume 2.

All sorts of special periodicals are included in these volumes such as those for religious groups, fraternal organizations, and social clubs.

The towns and cities of the US in which German newspapers and periodicals were published, according to Arndt and Olson, are:

AL: Birmingham, Cullman, Mobile, Warrior, AZ: St. Michaels, AR: Fort Smith, Little Rock, St. Joe, CA: Anaheim, Fresno, Glendale, Lodi, Los Angeles, Mokelumne Hill, Mountain View, Oakland, Petaluma, Sacramento, San Diego, San Francisco, San Jose, Santa Barbara, Santa Rosa, Stockton, CO: Denver, Greeley, Leadville, Pueblo, CT: Bridgeport, Hartford, Meriden, New Haven, Norwich, Rockville, Southbury, Waterbury, DC: Washington, DE: Wilmington, FL: Jacksonville, Miami, Pensacola, San Antonio, GA: Atlanta, Savannah, ID: Cottonwood,

IL: Addison, Alton, Apple River, Arlington Heights, Aurora, Beardstown, Beecher, Belleville, Bloomington, Brookfield, Cairo, Carlinville, Carlyle, Carmi, Centralia, Champaign, Chester, Chicago, Danville, Decatur, Dundee, East St. Louis, Edwardsville, Effingham, Elgin, Evanston, Forest Park, Freeport, Galena, German Valley, Hawthorne, Highland, Hoyleton, Joliet, Kankakee, Kewanee, La Salle, Lensburg, Leonore, Lincoln, Litchfield, McHenry, Mascoutah, Mattoon, Mendota, Mundelein, Mt. Olive, Naperville, Nashville, Nauvoo, Nokomis, Okawville, Ottawa, Pekin, Peoria, Peru, Quincy, Ravenswood, Red Bud, Rock Island, Rockford, Springfield, Staunton, Sterling, Streator, Techny, Urbana, Vandalia, Warsaw, Waterloo, Wheaton, Woodstock,

IN: Anderson, Batesville, Berne, Bowling Green, Brazil, Brookville, Collegeville, Crown Point, Elkhart, Evansville, Fort Wayne, Goshen, Hamburg, Hammond, Huntingburg, Indianapolis, Jeffersonville, Lafayette, La Port, Logansport, Michigan City, Mount Vernon, New Albany, Richmond, Rockport, St. Meinrad, Seymour, South Bend, Tell City, Terre Haute, Vincennes, IA: Ackley, Alton, Andrew, Boone, Breda, Burlington, Carroll, Cascade, Cedar Bluffs, Cedar Rapids, Charles City, Clinton, Council Bluffs, Davenport, Decatur, Denison, Des Moines, Dubuque, Dumont, Dysart, Earling, Elkader, Essex, Fort Dodge, Grundy Center, Guttenberg, Holstein, Ida Grove, Independence, Iowa City,

Keokuk, Lansing, Le Mars, Lyons, Manning, Maquoketa, Marshalltown, Monticello, Muscatine, New Hampton, Newton, Osage, Ottumwa, Postville, Reinbeck, Remson, Rock Rapids, Rockford, Schleswig, Sigourney, Sioux City, Spirit Lake, Sumner, Tama City, Toledo, Vinton, Walcott, Waterloo, Waverly, Wellsburg, Wheatland,

KS: Alma, Atchison, Atwood, Burrton, Canada, Ellinwood, Emporia, Fort Scott, Great Bend, Halstead, Hays, Hillsboro, Hutchinson, Inman, Kansas City, Kingman, Kinsley, Lacrosse, Lawrence, Leavenworth, Lehigh, Lindsborg, Marion, Marysville, McPherson, Newton, Paola, Pittsburg, Russell, Topeka, Wichita, Winfield, Wyandotte, KY: Berea, Covington, Louisville, Newport, Stanford,

LA: Lafayette, New Orleans, MD: Baltimore, Cumberland, Fredericktown, Hagerstown, New Windsor, MA: Boston, Clinton, Fitchburg, Greenfield, Holyoke, Lawrence, Lowell, Springfield, West Roxbury, MI: Adrian, Ann Arbor, Au Gres, Battle Creek, Bay City, Coldwater, Detroit, Grand Rapids, Jackson, Lansing, Manistee, Marquette, Menominee, Monroe, Muskegon, Pigeon, Port Huron, Saginaw, Sebewaing, Sturgis, W. Bay City,

MN: Carver, Chaska, Duluth, Fairmont, Freeport, Glencoe, Jordan, Lake City, Little Falls, Mankato, Melrose, Minneapolis, Mountain Lake, New Ulm, Owatonna, Perham, Red Wing, Rochester, St. Cloud, St. Paul, Shakopee, Springfield, Stillwater, Wabasha, Waconia, Winona, Wykoff, MO: Boonville, California, Cape Girardeau, Centreton, Chamois, Clayton, Clyde, Concordia, Festus, Franklin, Fulton, Hannibal, Hermann, Higginsville, Jackson, Jefferson City, Joplin, Kansas City, Lexington, Marthasville, Moberly, O'Fallon, St. Charles, St. Joseph, St. Louis, Ste. Genevieve, Sedalia, Springfield, Starkenburg, Stewartsville, Warrenton, Washington, Westphalia,

MT: Butte, Great Falls, Helena, Plevna, NE: Arago, Auburn, Beatrice, Bellevue, Bloomfield, College View, Columbus, Crete, Deshler, Fairbury, Falls City, Fremont, Grand Island, Hartington, Hastings, Jansen, Leigh, Lincoln, Meadow Grove, Nebraska City, Norfolk, Omaha, Schuyler, Seward, Steinauer, Sterling, Sutton, West Point, York, NV: Virginia City, NH: Manchester, NJ: Atlantic City, Bayonne, Bound Brook, Camden, Carlstadt, Egg Harbor, Elizabeth, Fairview, Hoboken, Irvington, Jersey City, Newark, New Brunswick, Orange, Passaic, Paterson, Riverside, Sea-Isle City, Town of Union, Trenton, Union, Union City,

NY: Albany, Amsterdam, Auburn, Bardonia, Brooklyn, Buffalo, Camden, College Point, East New York, Elmhurst, Elmira, Erie, Forest Hills, Long Island, Haverstraw, Hicksville, Huntington, Ithaca, Jamaica, Kingston (Rondout), Lockport, Long Island City, Morrisania, Mount Vernon, Newburgh, Newtown, New York, Oswego, Poughkeepsie,

Rochester, Schenectady, Sea Cliff, Staten Island, Syracuse, Tonawanda, Troy, Utica, Williamsburgh, Yonkers, <u>NC</u>: Goldsboro,

<u>ND</u>:Arthur, Ashley, Berwick, Beulah, Bismarck, Dickinson, Fargo, Fessenden, Golden Valley, Harvey, Havelock, Hebron, Jamestown, Linton, McClusky, Mannhaven, Medina, Minot, New Salem, Richardton, Rugby, Stanton, Strassburg, Wahpeton, Wishek, Zap,

<u>OH</u>: Akron, Baltic, Bellaire, Berea, Bluffton, Bowling Green, Bridgeport, Bucyrus, Canton, Carthagena, Celina, Chillicothe, Cincinnati, Cleveland, Columbiana, Columbus, Coshocton, Dayton, Defiance, Delphos, East Liverpool, Elyria, Findlay, Fremont, Germantown, Greenville, Hamilton, Ironton, Kenton, Kingsville, Lancaster, Lima, Lorain, Mansfield, Marietta, Marion, Massillon, Millersburg, Minster, Morrow, Napoleon, New Bremen, New Philadelphia, Newark, Norwalk, Oak Harbor, Osnaburgh, Ottawa, Pauling, Perrysburg, Piqua, Pomeroy, Port Clinton, Portsmouth, Sandusky, Sidney, Springfield, Steubenville, Teutonia, Tiffin, Toledo, Upper Sandusky, Wapakoneta, Waterloo, Weinsberg, Woodsfield, Woodville, Wooster, Worthington, Xenia, Youngstown, Zanesville, Zoar,

<u>OK</u>: Bessie, El Reno, Enid, Guthrie, Kingfisher, Medford, Okeene, Oklahoma City, Perry, <u>OR</u>: Astoria, Bend, Portland, St. Benedict, Salem, <u>PA</u>: Aaronsburg, Abbottstown, Adamsburg, Allegheny (see Pittsburgh), Allentown, Altoona, Berlin, Bath, Berwick, Bethlehem, Boyertown, Carlisle, Cattawissa, Chambersburg, Chartiers, Chestnut-Hill, Columbia, Danville, Doylestown, Easton, Economy, Ephrata, Erie, Gap, Germantown, Gettysburg, Greensburg, Hamburg, Hanover, Harrisburg, Hazleton, Hellertown, Herman, Honesdale, Huntingdon, Jefferson, Jim Thorpe, Johnstown, Kutztown, Lancaster, Lansdale, Lebanon, Lewisburg, Mansfield, Marietta, Marklesburg, Mauchchunk, McKeesport, Meadville, Mercersburg, Meyerstown, Middleburg, Mifflintown, Milford Square, Millheim, Nanticoke, Nazareth, New Berlin, Norristown, Orwigsburg, Pennsburg, Perkasie, Philadelphia, Philipsburg, Pittsburgh, Pottstown, Pottsville, Quakertown, Reading, Schellsburg, Scottdale, Scranton, Selinsgrove, Sharpsburg, Shrewsbury, Skippack, Somerset, Souderton, South Bethlehem, Strassburg, Stroudsburg, Sumneytown, Sunbury, Telford, Thurlow, Vincent, Weissport, West Chester, Wilkes-Barre, Williamsport, Womelsdorf, York, Zieglerville,

<u>RI</u>: Providence, <u>SC</u>: Charleston, <u>SD</u>: Aberdeen, Eureka, Herreid, Java, Mitchell, Olivet, Orient, Parkston, Pierre, Redfield, Sioux Falls, Watertown, Yankton, <u>TN</u>: Chattanooga, Columbia, Hohenwald, Memphis, Nashville, Robbins, <u>TX</u>: Austin, Bastrop, Bellville, Bocrnc, Brenham, Castroville, Comfort, Cuero, Dallas, Denison, Fort Worth, Franklin, Fredericksburg, Gainesville, Galveston, Giddings, Gonzales, Hallettsville, Hous-

ton, Independence, La Grange, Lockart, Marlin, Meyersville, New Braunfels, Rosebud, San Antonio, Schulenberg, Seguin, Shiner, Taylor, Temple, Victoria, Waco, Windthorst, <u>UT</u>: Logan, Salt Lake City,

<u>VA</u>: Alexandria, Bridgewater, New Market, Norfolk, Richmond, Staunton, Winchester, <u>WA</u>: Bellingham, Everett, Ritzville, Seattle, South Bend, Spokane, Tacoma, Walla Walla, <u>WV</u>: Wheeling, <u>WI</u>: Antigo, Appleton, Arcadia, Ashland, Athens, Beaver Dam, Beloit, Burlington, Cedarburg, Chilton, Chippewa Falls, Clintonville, Cochrane, Columbus, Cumberland, Dorchester, Durand, Eagle, Eau Claire, Fond Du Lac, Fort Atkinson, Fountain City, Glidden, Grand Rapids, Green Bay, Hamburg, Horicon, Janesville, Jefferson, Juneau, Kaukauna, Kenosha, Kewaunee, Kiel, La Crosse, Lomira, Madison, Manitowoc, Marathon, Marinette, Marshfield, Mauston, Mayville, Medford, Menasha, Menomonie, Merrill, Merrimack, Milwaukee, Monroe, Neillsville, New Glarus, Oshkosh, Phillips, Platteville, Plymouth, Port Washington, Portage, Princeton, Racine, Reedsburg, Ripon, St. Francis, St. Nazianz, Sauk City, Schlessingerville (now Slinger), Shawano, Sheboygan, Spokane, Stevens Point, Stockbridge, Superior, Theresa, Watertown, Wasau, Wauwatosa, West Bend, Weyauwega, Wittenberg, <u>WY</u>: Laramie.

<u>Other</u> <u>records</u> associated with the death of a progenitor which have a small possibility of identifying the exact place of origin back in Germany are wills, probate records (executor, administrator, inventory, sales, appraisal, list of heirs, accounts, receipts, distributions, probate packets, case files), land records, and tax records. Court actions in which a will or the probate was challenged are sometimes productive sources because relatives back in Germany may be involved, and their addresses may be given. In concluding this section, let us remind you once again that the friends, neighbors, and associates of your German ancestor could very well have come from the same place in the old country. Thus, if the above sources do not lead you to your ancestor's place of origin, it is quite possible that investigations into the records of these people will work.

11. Post-entry records	11. Urkunden kurz nach der Ein- wanderung
11. Urkunden kurz nach der Ein- wanderung	*11. [handwritten German text]*

In the few years following your German immigrant ancestor's arrival in the colonies or the US, there might be records generated on him/her which may reveal the place of origin. Included in these are redemptioner or indentured servant records, land grant records, marriage records, alien registration lists, naturalization records, records of children (births, deaths, and/or confirmations), voter lists, homestead records, state census records, lists of immigrants brought over under sponsorship by states and railroads, and manuscripts of various sorts. Exactly which ones of these will be the most important depends on the age at which your immigrant came and his/her marital-family status at the time. Many single German men came, and many with a wife and young children came.

Redemptioners made up a sizable proportion of the Germans who came over before 1819. As you will recall, redemptioners were arrivals who sold their services to the highest bidders in America in exchange for their passages. Records on them should be sought in the appropriate state archives and libraries, and in libraries and archives in the port of immigration. The probability that the documents will show the exact place of origin is low, but the chance should be taken if nothing has been successful up to now.

Land grant records also have a low probability of yielding the desired place of origin. Even so, they should be investigated. The records are usually found in the appropriate state archives in microfilm form, in the appropriate state library in published form, in large genealogical libraries in published form, and in the FHL (FHC) in one or both forms.

Marriage records in America show a somewhat higher probability of naming the birth place and date or giving some other origin data, but not much. Nonetheless, it is possible, the chances rising with the later records. In most places, the county or city or town office was the place for the recording of marriage information. Some time later, many (but not all) states required that copies or originals of marriage records be sent to a central state registry. You may obtain records by addressing inquiries to these county, town, city, and/or state offices. In some cases, the State Archives or State Historical Society has been made the repository for earlier records. Because of their value, numerous marriage records have also been microfilmed, and many have been published, especially the earlier ones. The microfilmed records should be sought in the appropriate State Archives, State Library, State Historical Society, and the Family History Library (with its branch Family History Centers). Published marriage records can be sought in the relevant state, county, and/or town libraries, and in large genealogical libraries.

In many instances official (state, county, city) marriage records cease to be available when you go back far enough. You will also often find that early records are incomplete, especially in frontier areas and times, and that they contain nothing on your forebears. In such situations, you will need to seek marriage information or indications from other sorts of records. The most likely sources include records of the following types: Bible, biography, cemetery, census, church, city directory, county and city history, directories, family records, fraternal organizations, gravestones, hereditary societies, military, mortuary, newspaper, pension, probate, published genealogy, tax, will.

Alien registrations in a local court were required by US law during 1802-1828, This meant that all men who were not citizens had to register. These registration records still exist in some counties, and they, therefore, should be sought out. Inquiries to the counties and to the relevant state archives and libraries might turn them up.

Naturalization records can often supply the exact place of origin, their usefulness increasing the later they are. In the colonial period, many of the immigrants to the territory that later became the US were from the British Isles, and since the colonies were British, they were citizens. When immigrants of other nationalities began to arrive, they found that British traditions, customs, governmental structures, and language generally prevailed. During the period 1607-1740, English law set forth that only the Crown and the Parliament could issue naturalization. However, because of the long distance to London, the critical need for settlers to work the new land, the general spirit of independence, and the British reluctance to alter the law, colonies often took it upon themselves to naturalize alien immigrants. The naturalizations, given by the colonial governor, proprietor, council, or legislature, were for the individual colony, not for total British citizenship. Some alien groups came through London to secure naturalization before coming to the colonies. The major tests for naturalization were an oath of allegiance, and a Protestant religious test, one which the Crown sometimes did not invoke. For three years, 1709-12, a law allowed for naturalization by (a) an oath of allegiance to the Crown, (b) the recent taking of the sacrament, and (c) the disavowal of transubstantiation. The law was repealed in 1712 and aliens once again had to petition the Crown or Parliament, or obtain naturalization by a colony.

In 1740, a law providing for naturalization of foreigners in the colonies was enacted by Parliament. It required (a) residence in a colony for seven years, (b) an oath of allegiance to the Crown and the profession of Christian belief in a colonial court, and (c) evidence of the taking of the sacrament in a Protestant and Reformed Congregation. Exemptions were allowed for Quakers and Jews, but not for Catholics. Just after the beginning of the Revolution, each newly formed American state declared all patriotic inhabitants citizens, and passed naturalization laws. Most states required an oath of allegiance, a demonstration of good character, a specified period of residency, and a disavowal of allegiance to any foreign power. The Articles of Confederation (1778/81) required that all states honor citizenship in all other states. The Constitution (1789) provided for federal naturalization which replaced the individual states' control. The new national naturalization act required one year's state residence, two years' US residence, and a loyalty oath taken in court. In 1795, a five years' residence came to be required along with a declaration of intent three years before the oath. Then in 1798, these times became 14 and 5 years respectively. Revised statutes of 1802 reverted to the 5 and 3 years of 1795. The declaration and oath could be carried out in any court which kept records (US, state, county, city). Wives and children of naturalized males became citizens automatically. And persons who gave military service to the US and received an honorable discharge also received citizenship.

In 1906, the Bureau of Immigration and Naturalization was set up, and this agency has kept records on all naturalizations since then. Thus, if you suspect your ancestor was naturalized after September 1906, write to the following address for a Form 6641 which you can use to request records:

___Immigration and Naturalization Service, 425 I Street, Washington, DC, 20536.

For naturalization records before October 1906, you need to realize that the process could have taken place in any of several courts, in fact, any court which kept records could have been used.

For the period before 1906, your first move should be to seek out colony-wide and state-wide naturalization indexes in state libraries, state archives, and in the FHL (FHC). Such indexes can save you much time, and a sizable number are in existence. If you do not discover them, then a court-by-court search needs to be inaugurated, starting with county courts in counties where you ancestor lived, then going to state and federal courts. Don't forget to look for oaths of allegiance and sacramental certificates in colonial times, and for declarations of intentions (first papers), petitions (second or final papers), and certificates of naturalization after that. Oaths of allegiance generally carried the name of the foreign government. Declarations could carry the birthplace (sometimes only the country), the US port of entry, date of entry, and the ship. Petitions might give the date of emigration, the birth date and place (sometimes only the country), the time in the US, the name and age of the spouse, the names and ages of children, the last foreign address, the port of entry, the date of entry, and the name of the ship. Certificates might carry the same sort of data as the petitions.

Children's records can be useful, particularly if one or more were born in Germany. For those children, if they came before they were teen-aged, their confirmation records here in the US may indicate where in Germany they were christened or baptized. Their death records (church, county, state, obituary, gravestone, cemetery, mortuary) might also yield up the desired data. And biographical and county history sketches on all the children (both those born in Germany and US) may reveal the parents' places of birth. Birth and marriage records of the children are less likely to be of help, but they should all be examined.

Voter lists may contain information on places of origin of naturalized immigrants. In the pre-Revolutionary War period, it was necessary to be a citizen in order to own land or vote or serve in public office. Sometimes these regulations were not enforced, especially on the frontier. The requirement of citizenship was carried over to the US, except that the declaration of intention was generally accepted as sufficient to permit the immigrant to purchase land.

Homestead records may function as an indirect lead to data on your progenitor's place of origin. In 1862 the US Congress passed a law that a settler could gain title to 160 acres or more of public land for a small filing fee and/or a 5-year residency on the land cultivating and improving it. There were also requirements that the age of the settler be 21 and that the settler be a US citizen or have declared in court an intention to become one. Homestead records are filed in the National Archives in Washington, DC, and in the Washington National Records Center in Suitland, MD. A file of homestead records may contain an application, a publication of the claim, proofs of the homestead, naturalization papers, and military discharge records. The application gives much data on the land and the applicant: description, location, and improvements of the land, description of the house, nature of crops, number of acres under cultivation; name, address, and age of the applicant, number and relationship of members of the family. About 1,970,000 entries for homestead land were made, but only about 780,000 were completed and had patents (the first deeds) issued. However, the most valuable genealogical materials, the applications, are available for all entries.

In order to obtain copies of homestead records for before 1908, it is necessary to send a legal description of the land to:
___General Branch, Civil Archives Division, National Archives, Washington, DC 20408.
The easiest way to obtain the legal description is to obtain it from the county deed records, plat maps, or tax records. If this search is unsuccessful, you can then search the tract books which were kept by the land offices. You need to know the general location. Microfilm copies of the tract books are available at the Family History Library and may be borrowed through Family History Centers. A third possibility is to use a county atlas which shows your ancestor's land. And a fourth way is to use township plats (maps) which are in the National Archives, Regional Branches of the National Archives, the Bureau of Land Management in Alexandria, VA, and Bureau of Land Management Offices in the western states. The value of the homestead records to the immigrant forebear searcher is that they contain naturalization papers and/or military records, either or both of which may lead to the place of origin.

State census records were taken by some of the states of the US. The information which they recorded and the dates for which they are available vary from state to state. To discover this, and you should do so, write the state archives and state library in the state where your ancestor lived. If you find that pertinent censuses are available, obtain them from the state archives or library, get them from FHL (FHC), or have them read for you by a hired searcher.

State and railroad records for the recruitment and bringing over of Germans as laborers and to establish farms might list the places from which the Germans came. Searches for records of this sort should be begun with the appropriate state libraries and archives.

Manuscripts are a further source of pertinent material which might reveal your immigrant's place of origin. There are thousands of collections of manuscripts (unpublished hand-written materials) in hundreds of repositories (archives, libraries, societies, churches, businesses, organizations, museums, private) all over the US. Manuscript collections consist of all sorts of records of religious, educational, patriotic, business, social, civil, professional, governmental, and political organizations; documents, letters, memoirs, notes and papers of early settlers, ministers, politicians, business men, educators, physicians, dentists, lawyers, judges, land speculators, storekeepers, and farmers; records of churches, cemeteries, mortuaries, schools, corporations, and industries; works of artists, musicians, writers, sculptors, photographers, architects, and historians; and records, papers, letters, and reminiscences of participants in various wars, as well as records of military organizations and campaigns. It is quite possible that some of these materials may relate to your progenitor.

The major finding aid for locating manuscripts is a series of indexed annual volumes which have been published since 1959.

__US Library of Congress, THE NATIONAL UNION CATALOG OF MANUSCRIPT COLLECTIONS, The Library, Washington, DC, issued annually 1959-. Cumulative indexes 1959-62, 1963-6, 1967-9, 1970-4, 1975-9, 1980-4, volumes indexed separately thereafter.

There is also an overall name index and an overall subject index:

__E. Altham and others, INDEX TO PERSONAL NAMES IN THE NATIONAL UNION CATALOG OF MANUSCRIPT COLLECTIONS, 1959-84, Chadwyck-Healey, Arlington, VA, 1988, 2 volumes.

__INDEX TO SUBJECTS IN THE NATIONAL UNION CATALOG OF MANUSCRIPT COLLECTIONS, 1959-84, Chadwyck-Healey, Alexandria, VA, 1994, 4 volumes.

Examine all the above indexes for your family surname, then look under pertinent states, counties, cities, and towns to see what records are available. Don't overlook the many listings in the NATIONAL UNION CATALOG indexes under the heading genealogy. You will find all the above volumes in large libraries, including large genealogical libraries. If you discover materials which you suspect relate to your forebear, write the appropriate repository asking for details. Be sure to send a long SASE and to request names of searchers if you cannot go in person.

Church letters of transfer are a further possible source of place of origin data. When church members left Germany, they sometimes brought with them a letter which was presented in the US to a new local church. These letters of transfer should be sought in the church to which your ancestor first belonged when he/she came to America.

Again, you are reminded that if the above sources do not reveal the sought-after place of origin for your ancestor, the same sorts of records should be investigated for his/her friends, neighbors, and associates. Such work will often unearth the place of origin of the friend, neighbor, or associate. And in many cases, this will be the place of origin of your ancestor.

12. German genealogical societ- ies in the US	12. Deutsche genealogische Vereine in den US
12. Deutsche genealogische Vereine in den US	*[handwritten] 12. Deutsche genealogische Vereine in den US*

There are numerous genealogical societies and centers in the U.S. which are specially dedicated to German research in general or to a specific German region, group of German immigrants, or time period. Some of these societies publish very useful journals and/or newsletters, and they can often assist you if you experience difficulty in locating your progenitor's place of origin back in Germany. You may want to write one or more for membership information. Then, after ascertaining whether they can assist you, you can join one or two, and then request their help. Among the most active of these societies and some very valuable centers are:

___ALLIANCE OF TRANSYLVANIA SAXONS, 5393 Pearl Road, Cleveland, OH 44129. Saxons who went to area now in central Rumania.

___AMERICAN HISTORICAL SOCIETY OF GERMANS FROM RUSSIA, 631 D Street, Lincoln, NE 68502-1199. Many local chapters.

___GERMAN-ACADIAN COAST HISTORICAL AND GENEALOGI-CAL SOCIETY, PO Box 517, Destrehan, LA 70047. For LA Germans.

___GERMAN-AMERICAN HERITAGE INSTITUTE, Altenheim, 7824 W. Madison St., Forest Park, IL 60130.

___GERMAN AMERICAN RESEARCH CENTER, UNIVERSITY OF WI, 702 Langdon St., Madison, WI 53706.

___GERMAN GENEALOGICAL SOCIETY OF AMERICA, PO Box 291818, Los Angeles, CA 90029. Very large, very active.

___GERMAN INTEREST GROUP, CHICAGO GENEALOGICAL SOCIETY, PO Box 1160, Chicago, IL 60690.

___GERMAN INTEREST GROUP, IOWA GENEALOGICAL SOCIETY, PO Box 3815, Des Moines, IA 50322.

___GERMAN INTEREST GROUP, WESTERN PA GENEALOGICAL SOCIETY, 4338 Bigelow Blvd., Pittsburgh, PA 15213.

___GERMAN INTEREST GROUP, WESTERN RESERVE HISTORI-CAL SOCIETY, 10825 East Blvd., Cleveland, OH 44106.

___GERMAN RESEARCH ASSOCIATION, INC., PO Box 711600, San Diego, CA 92171.

___GERMAN RESEARCH GROUP [OF ID]. Ed Sarbach, PO Box 7683, Boise, ID 83707.

___GERMAN SOCIETY OF NY, 150 Fifth Ave., New York, NY 10011.

___GERMAN-TEXAS HERITAGE SOCIETY, PO Box 684171, Austin, TX 78768-4171.

___GERMANIC GENEALOGY SOCIETY, PO Box 16312, St. Paul, MN 55116-0312.

___GERMANS FROM RUSSIA HERITAGE SOCIETY, 219 7th St., North, Bismarck, ND 58502.

___IMMIGRANT GENEALOGICAL SOCIETY, PO BOX 7369, Burbank, CA 91510-7369.

___IN GERMAN HERITAGE SOCIETY, 401 E. Michigan St., Indianapolis, IN 46204. For IN.

___JOHANNES SCHWALM HISTORICAL ASSOCIATION, PO BOX 99, Pennsauken, NJ 08110. For German mercenaries in the Revolutionary War.

___MAX KADE INSTITUTE FOR GERMAN-AMERICAN STUDIES, UNIVERSITY OF WI, 901 University Bay Shore Drive, Madison, WI 53705.

___MAX KADE GERMAN-AMERICAN STUDIES RESEARCH CENTER, UNIVERSITY OF KS, 2080 Wescoe Hall, Lawrence, KS 66045.

___MAX KADE GERMAN-AMERICAN CENTER, IU-PU at Indianapolis, Athenaeum, 401 E. Michigan St., Indianapolis, IN 46204.

___MAX KADE INSTITUTE FOR AUSTRIAN-GERMAN-SWISS STUDIES, 2714, S. Hoover St., Los Angeles, CA 90000.

___MID-ATLANTIC GERMANIC SOCIETY, 347 Scott Drive, Silver Spring, MD 20904. For DC, MD, and VA.

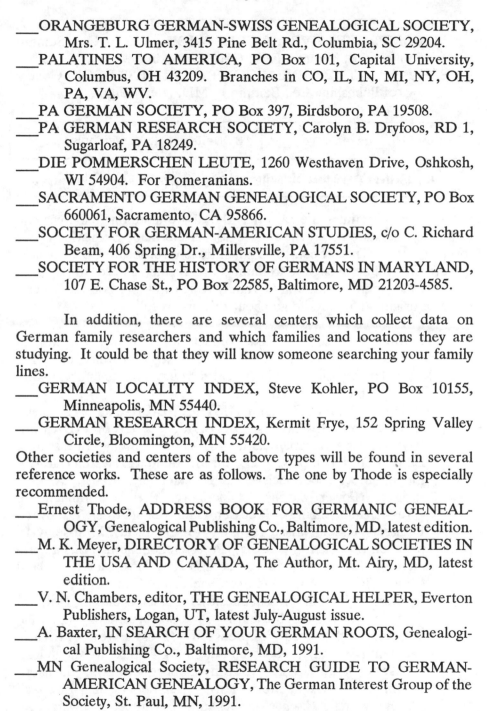

___ORANGEBURG GERMAN-SWISS GENEALOGICAL SOCIETY, Mrs. T. L. Ulmer, 3415 Pine Belt Rd., Columbia, SC 29204.

___PALATINES TO AMERICA, PO Box 101, Capital University, Columbus, OH 43209. Branches in CO, IL, IN, MI, NY, OH, PA, VA, WV.

___PA GERMAN SOCIETY, PO Box 397, Birdsboro, PA 19508.

___PA GERMAN RESEARCH SOCIETY, Carolyn B. Dryfoos, RD 1, Sugarloaf, PA 18249.

___DIE POMMERSCHEN LEUTE, 1260 Westhaven Drive, Oshkosh, WI 54904. For Pomeranians.

___SACRAMENTO GERMAN GENEALOGICAL SOCIETY, PO Box 660061, Sacramento, CA 95866.

___SOCIETY FOR GERMAN-AMERICAN STUDIES, c/o C. Richard Beam, 406 Spring Dr., Millersville, PA 17551.

___SOCIETY FOR THE HISTORY OF GERMANS IN MARYLAND, 107 E. Chase St., PO Box 22585, Baltimore, MD 21203-4585.

In addition, there are several centers which collect data on German family researchers and which families and locations they are studying. It could be that they will know someone searching your family lines.

___GERMAN LOCALITY INDEX, Steve Kohler, PO Box 10155, Minneapolis, MN 55440.

___GERMAN RESEARCH INDEX, Kermit Frye, 152 Spring Valley Circle, Bloomington, MN 55420.

Other societies and centers of the above types will be found in several reference works. These are as follows. The one by Thode is especially recommended.

___Ernest Thode, ADDRESS BOOK FOR GERMANIC GENEAL-OGY, Genealogical Publishing Co., Baltimore, MD, latest edition.

___M. K. Meyer, DIRECTORY OF GENEALOGICAL SOCIETIES IN THE USA AND CANADA, The Author, Mt. Airy, MD, latest edition.

___V. N. Chambers, editor, THE GENEALOGICAL HELPER, Everton Publishers, Logan, UT, latest July-August issue.

___A. Baxter, IN SEARCH OF YOUR GERMAN ROOTS, Genealogical Publishing Co., Baltimore, MD, 1991.

___MN Genealogical Society, RESEARCH GUIDE TO GERMAN-AMERICAN GENEALOGY, The German Interest Group of the Society, St. Paul, MN, 1991.

___J. Konrad, GENEALOGICAL AND HISTORICAL SOCIETIES, A
COMPREHENSIVE WORLD-WIDE LISTING, Summit
Publications, Munroe, Falls, OH, latest edition.
___E. P. Bentley, THE GENEALOGIST'S ADDRESS BOOK, Genea-
logical Publishing Co., Baltimore, MD, latest edition.

13. Further FHL Indexes	13. Weitere FHL Verzeichnisse
13. Weitere FHL Verzeichnisse	*13. ᴍ ᴏ ᴜ ᴜ ᴜ .*

It is sometimes the case that the above-mentioned sources will
yield only the state or province or region of Germany from which your
forebear came. This, of course, is not sufficient for locating the records,
but often it will be enough to examine some further indexes in the FHL
and to make some contacts in Germany which will give you the precise
place of origin. The ways to go about this are as follows.

Before proceeding to make contacts in Germany, it is well to
examine indexes to the records of the pertinent state, province, or region
in the Family History Library (FHL). Go to your nearest Family History
Center (FHC), and ask for
___Family History Library, FAMILY HISTORY LIBRARY CATALOG,
LOCALITY SECTION, for Baden, Bayern (Bavaria),
Bayern/Pfalz (Bavaria/Palatinate), Braunschweig (Brunswick),
Elsass-Lothringen (Alsace-Lorraine), Hamburg, Hessen (Hesse),
Lippe, Mecklenburg-Schwerin, Mecklenburg-Strelitz, Nieder-
sachsen (Lower Saxony), Oldenburg, Preussen/Brandenburg
(Prussia/Brandenburg), Preussen/Hannover (Prussia/Hanover),
Preussen/Hessen-Nassau (Prussia/Hesse-Nassau), Preussen/Ost-
preussen (Prussia/East Prussia), Preussen/Pommern (Prussia/Pom-
erania), Preussen/Posen (Prussia/Posen), Preussen/Rheinland
(Prussia/Rhineland), Preussen/Sachsen (Prussia/ Saxony),
Preussen/ Schlesien (Prussia/Silesia), Preussen/Schleswig-Holstein
(Prussia/ Schleswig-Holstein), Preussen/Westfalen (Prussia/
Westfalia), Preussen/Westpreussen (Prussia/West Prussia),
Sachsen (Saxony), Sachsen-Altenburg (Saxony-Altenburg),
Sachsen-Coburg-Gotha (Saxony-Coburg-Gotha), Sachsen-
Meiningen (Saxony-Meiningen), Sachsen-Weimar-Eisenach
(Saxony-Weimar-Eisenach), Schaumburg-Lippe, Schwarzburg-
Rudolstadt, Schwarzburg-Sonderhausen, Sudetenland, Thüringen

(Thuringia), Waldeck, Württemberg (Wuerttemberg), The Library, Salt Lake City, UT.

Examine the appropriate sections of the catalog looking for large state, province, or regional indexes which might list your progenitor. Pay particular attention to the entries headed EMIGRATION AND IMMIGRATION and GENEALOGY, but do not overlook others. If you locate indexes which you think may be useful, request that the FHC borrow them for you from the FHL. They will, of course, be in German, but we will give you sufficient instruction in a succeeding chapter to be able to make your way through them.

Among the emigration lists from states, provinces, and regions of Germany which you will find in the Family History Library Catalog are the following very important ones.

___For Baden, BADEN EMIGRATIONS LISTS, 17th to 20 centuries, Microfilm Nos. 1180095-118012, 1180209-1180213; and EMIGRANTS FROM BADEN AND ELSASS WITH PLACES OF ORIGIN, Microfilm Nos. 0934610, 1125248-1125254. Also books and articles by A. K. Burgert, K. Ehmann, W. Hacker, G. Kuhn, C. S. Smith, C. Schrader-Muggenthaler.

___For Bayern (Bavaria), books by F. Blendinger and H. Huber.

___For Braunschweig (Brunswick), EMIGRATION NOTICES OF BRAUNSCHWEIG EXCLUDING CITY OF BRAUNSCHWEIG AND HOLZMINDEN, 1846-1871, Microfilm No. 1045468; also in book by F. Gruhne.

___For Bremen, books by W. Dehlwes and G. Zimmerman.

___For Elsass-Lothringen (Alsace-Lorraine), EMIGRATION FROM AACHEN, RHINELAND, 1816-1925, Microfilm Nos. 1347248, 1347158-1347212; EMIGRATION TO AMERICA AND OTHER PLACES FROM THE BAS-RHIN, 1803-1869, Microfilm Nos. 1070233-1070236. Also books by H. Neu, C. Schrader-Muggenthaler, A. K. Burgert.

___For Hamburg, PASSPORT RECORDS, 1852-1929, Microfilm Nos. 0561267-0561304, 0563176-0563208, 0565557-0565575, 0566787-0566817, 0567092-0567113, 0566818-0566826, etc.; HAMBURG PASSENGER LISTS, 1850-1934, Microfilm Nox. 0884668-0884677, 0473070-0473174, 0470833-0470842, etc.

___For Hessen (Hesse), EMIGRATIONS FROM DARMSTADT, 1819-1880, Microfilm Nos. 1457684, 1442143-1442144; EMIGRATION CARD INDEXES FOR HESSEN, 1800-1900, Microfilm Nos. 1124278-1124280, 1124319-1124320; TX IMMIGRANTS FROM RHINEHESSE, Microfilm 1183866; ALPHABETICAL COL-

LECTION OF MATERIALS ON GERMAN FAMILIES, Microfilm Nos. 1204024-1204066, 1204253-1204329, etc.

___For Lippe, books by F. Verdenhalven and F. Engel.

___For Mecklenburg, publication by K. Schomaker.

___For Nordrhein-Westfalen (North Rhine-Westphalia), books by J. Walterscheid and C. N. Smith.

___For Oldenburg, books by J. Ostendorf and C. N. Smith.

___For Pfalz (Palatinate), books by H. Jones, W. Knittle, J. Golden, L. McWethy, A. K. Burgert, W. Hacker, H. Guth, H. F. Macco.

___For Preussen/Hessen-Nassau (Prussia/Hesse-Nassau), EMIGRATION RECORDS OF THE 18TH CENTURY, Microfilm No. 0071553. Also books by A. Gerber and W. Struck.

___For Preussen/Ostpreussen (Prussia/East Prussia), book by M. J. Anuta.

___For Preussen/Pommern (Prussia/Pomerania), books by C. N. Smith and M. A. Wellauer.

___For Preussen/Rheinland (Prussia/Rhineland), EMIGRATIONS FROM AACHEN, 1816-1925, Microfilm Nos. 1347248, 1347158-1347212; EMIGRATIONS FROM DÜSSELDORF, 1822-1920, Microfilm Nos. 1347213-1347248; TEXAS IMMIGRANTS FROM RHEINHESSEN, Microfilm No. 1183866. Also books by W. Hacker, J. Mergen, H. Richter, and C. N. Smith.

___For Preussen/Schlesien (Prussia/Silesia), book by C. N. Smith.

___For Preussen/Westfalen (Prussia/Westphalia), books by A. Dorider, B. C. Holtzclaw, F. Mueller, and W. D. Camphöfner, also book entitled LET'S GO TO AMERICA.

___For Saarland (Saar), books by W. Hacker and J. Mergen.

___For Sachsen (Saxony), MIGRATION REGISTRATIONS OF CHEMNITZ, 1765-1868, Microfilm Nos. 1346513-134562; DEPARTURE PERMITS OF ZWICKAU, 1769-1873, Microfilm Nos. 1340804, 145614-1456430.

___For Sachsen-Weimar-Eisenach (Saxony-Weimar-Eisenach), books by C. N. Smith, H. Koch, H. Rosenthal, and R. Schwemmer.

___For Schleswig-Holstein, book by C. N. Smith.

___For Waldeck, EMIGRANTS LEAVING WALDECK, 1829-1872, Microfilm No. 1183583, item 7.

___For Westfalen (Westphalia): books by F. Miller.

___For Württemberg (Wuerttemberg), EMIGRATION FROM ASPERG, 18TH AND 19TH Centuries, Microfilm No. 1183567, item 40; EMIGRATION FROM CRAILSHEIM, 1811-1891, Microfilm Nos. 0563975-0563981; EMIGRANTS TO AMERICA, 18TH CENTURY, Microfilm Nos. 0962292, items 4-5; EMIGRATION

FROM SCHWABISCH GMUND, 1811-1872, Microfilm Nos. 0582009-0582014, 0598678; EMIGRATION FROM SCHWABISCH HALL, 1803-1876, Microfilm Nos. 0589685, 0598114; EMIGRATION FROM HEIDENHEIM, 1666-1786, Microfilm No. 0550809; EMIGRATION FROM HOHENBERG, Microfilm Nos. 0550833-0550844; EMIGRANTS TO THE US FROM BADEN AND WUERTTEMBERG, Microfilm Nos. 1045409; EMIGRATION FROM LEUTKIRCH, 1807-1889, Microfilm Nos. 0837969-0837977; EMIGRATION FROM LUDWIGSBURG, 1808-1924, Microfilm Nos. 0530090-0530098, 0530809-0530818, etc; EMIGRANTS FROM MARBACH (NECKAR), 1811-1869, Microfilm Nos. 0838261-0838278; EMIGRATION FROM MAULBRONN, 1832-1925, Microfilm Nos. 0531782, 0838279-0838302; EMIGRANTS FROM (BAD) MERGENTHEIM, 1835-1902, Microfilm Nos. 0838303-0838305; EMIGRANTS FROM MÜNSINGEN, 1804-1880, Microfilm Nos. 0838306-0838309, 0838473-0838478; EMIGRANTS FROM LUDWIGSBURG, 1833-1895, Microfilm Nos. 0838488-0838497; EMIGRANTS FROM NECKARSULM, 1853-1921, Microfilm Nos. 0531782-0531786, 0838479-0838487; EMIGRANTS FROM NELLENBURG, 1587-1806, Microfilm Nos. 0550845-0550850, 0530059-0530061; EMIGRANTS FROM NERESHEIM, 1871-1880, Microfilm No. 0838498, ITEMS 1-2; EMIGRANTS FROM NEUENBURG, 1817-1879, Microfilm Nos. 0838498-0838513; EMIGRANTS FROM NÜRTINGEN, 1526-1899, Microfilm Nos. 0550806, 0838514-0838520, 0838618-0838628; EMIGRANTS FROM OBERNDORF, 1808-1881, Microfilm Nos. 0838629-0838638, 0841015-0841016; EMIGRANTS FROM OHRINGEN, 1851-1890, Microfilm Nos. 0841017-0841030; EMIGRANTS FROM RAVENSBURG, 1807-1930, Microfilm Nos. 0841031-0841050; EMIGRANTS FROM RIEDLINGEN, 1807-1927, Microfilm Nos. 0841059-0841080; EMIGRANTS FROM ROTTENBURG, 1811-1923, Microfilm Nos. 0841081-0841110; EMIGRANTS FROM ROTTWEIL, 1830-1896, Microfilm Nos. 084111-084117, 0841167; EMIGRANTS FROM SAULGAU, 1806-1919, Microfilm Nos. 0841169-0841189, 0801457-0801459; EMIGRANTS FROM SCHORNDORF, 1808-1909, Microfilm Nos. 0801460-0801472; EMIGRANTS FROM SCHWABEN, 1587-1806, Microfilm Nos. 0530062-0530088, 0527051-0527053; EMIGRANTS FROM SPAICHINGEN, 1706-1870, Microfilm Nos. 0527054-0527056, 0801475-0801481, 0849646-0849650; EMIGRANTS FROM STUTTGART, 1806-1917, Microfilm Nos.

0535536-0535543, 0849651-0849688, 0849605-0849624; EMI-GRANTS FROM WUERTTEMBERG, 1799-1898, Microfilm Nos. 0527057-0527062, 0461414-0461415, 0529417-0529428, etc.; PASSPORTS AND VISAS FOR WUERTTEMBERG, 1845-1920, Microfilm Nos. 0849689-0849697, 0849597-0849604; EMIGRANTS FROM SULZ, 1754-1900, Microfilm Nos. 0550807, 0849625-0849644; EMIGRATION FROM TETTNANG, 1835-1871, Microfilm Nos. 0849645, 0855322-0855331; EMI-GRANTS FROM TÜBINGEN, 1806-1900, Microfilm Nos. 0855332-0855346, 0849984-0849986; EMIGRANTS FROM TUTTLINGEN, 1806-1891, Microfilm Nos. 0849987-0850006, 0856361-0856363; EMIGRANTS FROM ULM, 1843-1972, Microfilm Nos. 0856364-0856377; EMIGRANTS FROM LEINE VALLEY, Microfilm No. 1183567, Item 34; EMIGRANTS FROM URACH, 1726-1873, Microfilm Nos. 0550808, 0856378-0856392; EMIGRANTS FROM VAIHINGEN, 1811-1918, Microfilm Nos. 0856383-0856402; EMIGRANTS FROM WAIBLINGEN, 1815-1922, Microfilm Nos. 0535547, 0534575-0534577, 0856402-0856405, 0856453-0856475; EMIGRATION FROM WALDSEE, 1833-1890, Microfilm Nos. 0548404, 0856476; EMIGRANTS FROM WANGEN, 1827-1932, Microfilm Nos. 0856477-0856491; EMIGRANTS FROM WEINBERG, 1871-1922, Microfilm Nos. 0534578-0534582, 0856492-0856498; EMI-GRANTS FROM WELTZHEIM, 1818-1892, Microfilm Nos. 0856499-0856500, 0859113-0859116; EMIGRANTS FROM WÜRTTEMBERG, 1500-1819, Microfilm Nos. 0550794-0550801, 0550810-0550815. Also books by T. Schenk, K. Ehmann, W. Hacker, H. Roemer, and C. N. Smith.

Fortunately, indexes to this extensive Württemberg collection are now available:

___T.Schenk, R. Froelke, and I. Bork, WÜRTTEMBERG IMMIGRA-TION INDEX, Ancestry, Salt Lake City, UT, 1986-, several volumes.

The following professional researcher also has a large indexed collection of Württemberg emigrants during 1800-1858.

___Herr Alfred Laun, Aspenwaldstrasse 2, D-70173 Stuttgart, Bundes-republik Deutschland, GERMANY.

Now, let us mention a source which must not by any means be overlooked. Among the extremely useful indexed volumes are an extensive and detailed collection of family genealogical information (192 volumes). Most of the volumes apply to specific regions, but a few cover all of Germany. You should look into the indexes in the backs of the volumes which pertain to the state/province/region of your ancestor. You can then look into the indexes of the books which have an overall coverage.

___DEUTSCHES GESCHLECHTERBUCH, GENEALOGISCHES HANDBUCH BÜRGERLICHER FAMILIEN, Starke, Limburg/Lahn, Deutschland, 1889-, 192 volumes. FHL Book No. 943 D2dg.

The following volumes apply to various states/provinces/regions: Baden (81, 101, 120, 161, 189) Baltisches Staaten (79), Berg (24, 35, 83, 168, 183), Brandenburg (111, 150, 160), Darmstadt (69, 96), Hamburg (18, 19, 21, 23, 27, 44, 51, 63, 127, 128, 142, 171), Harz (106), Hessen (32, 47, 52, 54, 64, 66, 69, 84, 94, 96, 98, 107, 119, 121, 124, 139, 144, 157, 159, 175, 176), Lippe (72), Magdeburg (39), Mecklenburg (57, 74, 88, 105), Nassau (49), Neumark (93), Niedersachsen (46, 76, 89, 102, 113, 122, 129, 131, 141, 143, 151, 158, 166, 167, 180, 187), Obersachsen (33), Ostfriesland (26, 31, 59, 103, 134, 190), Ostpreussen (61, 68, 117), Pfalz (58, 86, 149), Pommern (40, 67, 90, 115, 136, 137, 145, 155, 174, 191), Posen (62, 78, 116, 140), Ravensberg (82, 194), Rentlingen (34, 41), Sauerland (38, 53, 97), Schlesien (73, 112, 153, 178), Schleswig-Holstein (91, 162, 186), Schwaben (34, 41, 43, 55, 71, 75, 110, 146, 170), Siegerland (95, 139, 163, 164), Thüringen (87, 114), Westfalen (108, 152, 156, 172, 182, 184, 187), Westpreussen (126, 132, 133), Coverage over all Germany (1-17, 20, 22, 25, 28-30, 36, 37, 45, 50, 60, 70, 80, 85, 92, 100, 104, 109, 118, 125, 130, 135, 147, 148, 154, 165, 169, 172, 177, 185, 188, 192). These volumes are available in FHL and other large genealogical libraries. Some of them have been microfilmed by FHL and can be borrowed through FHC. Overall indexes to the GESCHLECHTERBUCH were listed in Section 7 of this chapter.

14. Contacts in Germany	14. Kontakte mit Deutschland
14. Kontakte mit Deutschland	14. Kontakte mit Deutschland

We will now look at a number of contacts that you can make with organizations and individuals in Germany. There is a good chance that one or more of them may be able to supply you with the exact place of origin of your immigrant progenitor.

Contacting genealogical societies in the areas of interest is the first of the contacts that should be made in Germany. This can best be done by writing to the appropriate society, enclosing a small fee, and asking that they consult any large indexes they might have for your ancestor.

Here is a sample letter which will serve your purposes:

ARBEITSGEMEINSCHAFT GENEALOGIE THÜRINGEN e.V.
Dr. Harold Bergner
Hainrich-Heine-Strasse 16
D-07749 Jena
Bundesrepublik Deutschland, GERMANY

Dear Director:
    My ancestor, Georg Emil Schweitzer came to America in 1848 from Saxe-Weimar-Eisenach. His age was approximately 18 years. Please examine any appropriate indexes which you have, and provide me with his exact place of origin, if possible. Enclosed you will find $15 for return air mail postage and your search fee.
                With best greetings,
                George K. Schweitzer
                407 Ascot Court
                Knoxville, TN 37923-5807
                U.S.A.

You should make the appropriate substitutions for the society, its address, your ancestor's name, the state, province, or region from which he/she came, his/her age at the time of coming, and your name and address. The letter should then be typed in the following German form and sent by air mail, enclosing $15 in cash.

ARBEITSGEMEINSCHAFT GENEALOGIE THÜRINGEN e.V.
Dr. Harold Bergner
Heinrich-Heine-Strasse 16
D-07749 Jena
Bundesrepublik Deutschland, GERMANY

Werter Direktor!
    Mein Vorfahr, Georg Emil Schweitzer, ist 1848 von Sachsen-Weimar-Eisenach nach Amerika gekommen. Zu der Zeit war er ungefähr 18 Jahre alt. Bitte seien Sie so freundlich und untersuchen alle Ihnen zugänglichen Register und informieren mich, wenn möglich, über seine genaue Herkunft. Anbei finden Sie $15 für Porto (Luftpost) und als Honorar für Ihre Nachforschungen.

Mit freundlichen Grüssen,
George K. Schweitzer
407 Ascot Court
Knoxville, TN 37923-5807
U.S.A.

Among the major state, province, and genealogical societies of Germany are the following, along with their addresses:
__For all of Germany: DEUTSCHE ARBEITSGEMEINSCHAFT GENEALOGISCHER VERBANDE e.V., Schlossstrasse 12, D-50321, Brühl, Bundesrepublik Deutschland, GERMANY. This association of German genealogical societies coordinates the activities of these groups and acts as a clearing house to direct inquiries to the proper society. If in doubt where to write, ask them.
__For all of Germany, BUND DER FAMILIENVERBANDE e.V., Lorenz-von-Stein-Ring 20, D-24340, Eckernförde, Bundesrepublik Deutschland, GERMANY. This organization is an alliance of surname societies. They can tell you if there is such a society for your ancestor's surname.
__For all of Germany, but mostly what was once the Deutsche Demokratische Republik (the DDR, commonly called East Germany): ZENTRALSTELLE FÜR GENEALOGIE, Käthe-Kollwitz-Strasse 82, Postfach 100947, D-04009, Leipzig, Bundesrepublik Deutschland, GERMANY. Not really a society, but a valuable research center which has many indexes and will arrange for further research for you.
__For all of Germany: AHNENLISTENUMLAUF, Rainer und Jutta Bien, Hauptstrasse 70, D-31669 Beckedorf bei Stadthagen, Bundesrepublik Deutschland, GERMANY. Has an extensive file of family pedigrees submitted by genealogical researchers.
__For Baden: VEREIN FÜR FAMILIEN- UND WAPPENKUNDE IN WÜRTTEMBERG UND BADEN e.V., Konrad-Adenauer-Strasse 8, Postfach 105441, D-70047, Stuttgart 1, Bundesrepublik Deutschland, GERMANY.
__For the Baltic States (Estonia, Latvia, Lithuania): FORSCHUNGS-STELLE BALTIKUM DER AGoFF, Winno von Löwenstern, Parkstrasse 45, Frankenforst, D-51427, Bergisch Gladbach, Bundesrepublik Deutschland, GERMANY; and DEUTSCH-BALTISCHE GENEALOGISCHE GESELLSCHAFT, Herdweg 79, D-64285, Darmstadt, Bundesrepublik Deutschland, GERMANY.

__For Bayern (Bavaria): BAYERISCHER LANDESVEREIN FÜR FAMILIENKUNDE, Hauptstaatsarchiv, Ludwigstrasse 14,I, D-80539, München 22, Bundesrepublik Deutschland, GERMANY.

__For Bessarabien (Bessarabia): LANDMANNSCHAFT DER BESSARABIENDEUTSCHEN, Florianstrasse 17, D-70188, Stuttgart, Bundesrepublik Deutschland, GERMANY.

__For Böhmen (Bohemia in Czechoslovakia): FORSCHUNGSSTELLE FÜR DIE BÖHMISCHEN LANDER, Thierschstrasse 11/III, D-80538, München, Bundesrepublik Deutschland, GERMANY.

__For Brandenburg (eastern part): FORSCHUNGSSTELLE OST-BRANDENBURG-NEUMARK DER AGoFF, Director Dipl-Ing. Alfred Bley, Im Langewann 65, D-69469 Weinheim-Lützelsachsen, Bundesrepublik Deutschland, GERMANY, and ARBEITS-GEMEINSCHAFT FÜR MITTELDEUTSCHE FAMILIEN-FORSCHUNG e.V, Prof. Dr. Hans-Joachim Anderson, Cappel, Goldbergstrasse 23, D-35043, Marburg/Lahn, Bundesrepublik Deutschland, GERMANY.

__For Bremen: "DIE MAUS" GESELLSCHAFT FÜR FAMILIEN-FORSCHUNG, Am Staatsarchiv 1, Fedelhören (Staatsarchiv), D-28203 Bremen, Bundesrepublik Deutschland, GERMANY.

__For Bukovina (in Rumania): FORSCHUNGSSTELLE GALIZIEN DER AGoFF, Ernst Hexel, Buchenaustrasse 28, D-82256 Fürstenfeldbrück, Bundesrepublik Deutschland, GERMANY; and RAIMUND-FRIEDRICH-KAINDL-GESELLSCHAFT, Prof. Dr. Herbert Mayer, Raingarten 19, D-73650 Winterbach, Bundesrepublik Deutschland, GERMANY.

__For Burgenland (in Hungary): FORSCHUNGSSTELLE BURGEN-LAND DER AGoFF, Heinz Somogyvár, Bei der Rolandsmühle 9, D-22763 Hamburg 50, Bundesrepublik Deutschland, GERMANY.

__For Donauschwaben (Danube Swabian colonies in Hungary, Rumania, and Yugoslavia): FORSCHUNGSSTELLE DONAUSCHWABEN DER AGoFF, Dr. Helmut Flacker, Fichtenweg 5, D-79189 Bad Krozingen, Bundesrepublik Deutschland, GERMANY.

__For Easternmost Germany (all territory east of the former East Germany): ARBEITSGEMEINSCHAFT OSTDEUTSCHER FAMILIENFORSCHER e.V., Detlef Kühn, Fuhrweg 29, D-53229, Bonn 3, Bundesrepublik Deutschland, GERMANY.

__For Elsass (Alsace): CERCLE GÉNÉALOGIQUE D'ALSACE, Archives departmentales, 5 rue Fischart, F-67000 Strasbourg, FRANCE. Correspond in French, not German.

__For Franken (Franconia in northern Bavaria): GESELLSCHAFT FÜR FAMILIENFORSCHUNG IN FRANKEN, Archivstrasse 17

(Staatsarchiv), D-90408, Nürnberg 10, Bundesrepublik Deutschland, GERMANY.

___For Galizien (Galicia in Poland and Russia): FORCHUNGSSTELLE GALIZIEN DER AGoFF, Ernst Herxel, Buchenaustrasse 28, D-82556 Fürstenfeldbrück, Bundesrepublik Deutschland, GERMANY.

___For Hamburg: GENEALOGISCHE GESELLSCHAFT, SITZ HAMBURG e.V., Alsterchaussee 11, Postfach 302047, D-20307 Hamburg , Bundesrepublik Deutschland, GERMANY.

___For Hessen (Hesse): ARBEITSGEMEINSCHAFT DER FAMILIEN-KUNDLICHEN GESELLSCHAFT IN HESSEN, Loreleystrasse 28, D-65929 Frankfurt, Bundesrepublik Deutschland, GERMANY.

___For Hessen-Darmstadt (Hesse-Darmstadt): HESSISCHE FAMILIEN-GESCHICHTLICHE VEREINIGUNG e.V., Sitz Darmstadt, Karolinenplatz 3, D-64289 Darmstadt, Bundesrepublik Deutschland, GERMANY.

___For Hessen-Kassel and Waldeck (Hesse-Cassel and Waldeck): GE-SELLSCHAFT FÜR FAMILIENKUNDE IN KURHESSEN UND WALDECK e.V., Grafestrasse 35, Postfach 410328, D-34065 Kassel-Wilhelmshöhe, Bundesrepublik Deutschland, GERMANY.

___For Hessen-Nassau und Frankfurt (Hesse-Nassau and Frankfurt): FAMILIENKUNDLICHE GESELLSCHAFT FÜR NASSAU UND FRANKFURT e.V., Mosbacher Strasse 55, D-65187 Wiesbaden, Bundesrepublik Deutschland, GERMANY.

___For Hugenotten (Huguenots): DEUTSCHER HUGENOTTEN-VEREIN e.V., Deutsches Hugenotten-Zentrum, Hafenplatz 9a, D-34385 Bad Karlshafen, Bundesrepublik Deutschland, GERMANY.

___For Lippe: ARBEITSGEMEINSCHAFT FÜR SCHAUMBURG-ISCHE FAMILIENKUNDE, Gut Nienfeld, D-31867 Pohle über Hameln, Bundesrepublik Deutschland, GERMANY.

___For Lothringen (Lorraine): CERCLE GÉNÉALOGIQUE DE LORRAINE, Archives départementales de Meurthe et Moselle, 1 rue de la Monnaie, F-54000, Nancy, France. Correspond in French, not German.

___For Mecklenburg: P. Götze, Eggerstrasse 4, 0-2500 Rostock, Bundesrepublik Deutschland, GERMANY. Write Herr Götze to get in touch with the genealogical society. Also contact the society listed under Hamburg, and ARBEITSGEMEINSCHAFT FÜR MITTELDEUTSCHE FAMILIENFORSCHUNG e.V., Prof. Dr.

Hans-Joachim Anderson, Cappel, Goldbergstrasse 23, D-35043 Marburg/Lahn, Bundesrepublik Deutschland, GERMANY.

___For Mitteldeutschland (Central or Middle Germany, including Brandenburg, Mecklenburg, Sachsen, and Thüringen): ARBEITSGEMEINSCHAFT FÜR MITTELDEUTSCHE FAMILIENFORSCHUNG e.V., Prof. Dr. Hans-Joachim Anderson, Cappel, Goldbergstrasse 23, D-35043 Marburg/Lahn, Bundesrepublik Deutschland, GERMANY.

___For Niedersachsen (Lower Saxony): NIEDERSACHSISCHER LANDESVEREIN FÜR FAMILIENKUNDE e.V., Am Bokemohle 14-16 (Stadtarchiv), D-30171 Hannover, Bundesepublik Deutschland, GERMANY.

___For Nordrhein (North Rhine): WESTDEUTSCHE GESELLSCHAFT FÜR FAMILIENKUNDE, Wallstrasse 96, D-51063 Köln, Bundesrepublik Deutschland, GERMANY.

___For Oldenburg: OLDENBURGISCHE GESELLSCHAFT FÜR FAMILIENKUNDE, Lerigauweg 14, D-26131 Oldenburg, Bundesrepublik Deutschland, GERMANY.

___For Ostpreussen (East Prussia): VEREIN FÜR FAMILIEN-FORSCHUNG IN OST- UND WESTPRESUSSEN e.V., Dr. E. Heling, In der Krümm 10, D-21147 Hamburg, Bundesrepublik Deutschland, GERMANY; and FORSCHUNGSSTELLE OSTPREUSSEN DER AGoFF, Dr. Wolf Konietzko, Eichstrasse 6, D-25336 Elmshorn, Bundesrepublik Deutschland, GERMANY.

___For the Pfalz (Bayerische Pfalz, Bavarian Palatinate, Palatinate): AR-BEITSGEMEINSCHAFT FÜR PFALZISCH-RHEINISCHE FAMILIENKUNDE e.V., Rottstrasse 17, D-67061 Ludwig-shafen/Rhein, Bundesrepublik Deutschland, GERMANY. Also write INSTITUT FÜR PFALZISCHE GESCHICHTE UND VOLKSKUNDE, Benzinoring 6, Postfach 2860. D-67616 Kaiserslautern, Bundesrepublik Deutschland, GERMANY. They have a very sizable card file of emigrants.

___For Pommern (Pomerania): POMMERSCHE VEREINIGUNG FÜR SAMM- UND WAPPENKUNDE, Ladenbergstrasse 1, D-14195 Berlin, Bundesrepublik Deutschland, GERMANY; and FORSCHUNGSSTELLE POMMERN DER AGoFF, Elmar Bruhn, Lohkamp 13, D-22117 Hamburg, Bundesrepublik Deutschland, GERMANY.

___For Posen (in Poland): FORSCHUNGSSTELLE POSEN DER AGoFF, Otto Firchau, Nachtigallenweg 6, D-32105 Bad Salzuflen, Bundesrepublik Deutschland, GERMANY.

___For Rheinland (Rhineland): WESTDEUTSCHE GESELLSCHAFT FÜR FAMILIENKUNDE, Wallstrasse 96, D-51063 Köln, Bundesrepublik Deutschland, GERMANY.

___For Russland (Russia): FORSCHUNGSSTELLE RUSSLAND-DEUTSCHE DER ARBEITSGEMEINSCHAFT OST-DEUTSCHER FAMILIENFORSCHER e.V., Sitz Herne, Dr. Paul Edel, Ziegelstrasse 11, D-73431 Aalen, Bundesrepublik Deutschland, GERMANY.

___For Saarland (Saar): ARBEITSGEMEINSCHAFT FÜR SAAR-LANDISCHE FAMILIENKUNDE IM HISTORISCHEN VEREIN FÜR DIE SAARGEGEND E.v., Norbert Emanuel, Hebbelstrasse 3, D-66356 Püttlingen, Bundesrepublik Deutschland, GERMANY.

___For Salzburger (Protestants from Salzburg in 1730-1739): SALZ-BURGER VEREIN e.V., Memeler Strasse 35, D-33605 Bielefeld, Bundesrepublik Deutschland, GERMANY.

___For Sachsen (Saxony): Write Prof. Dr. W. Lorenz, Burgauenstrasse 3, D-04177 Leipzig, Bundesrepublik Deutschland, GERMANY; write Bernd Hofestädt, Block 109/1, D-06124 Halle-Neustadt, Bundesrepublik Deutschland, GERMANY; ARBEITSGEMEIN-SCHAFT FÜR MITTELDEUTSCHE FAMILIENFORSCHUNG e.V., Prof. Dr. Hans-Joachim Anderson, Cappel, Goldbergstrasse 23, D-35043 Marburg/Lahn 7, Bundesrepublik Deutschland, GERMANY.

___For Schaumburg-Lippe: ARBEITSGEMEINSCHAFT FÜR SCHAUMBURGISCHE FAMILIENKUNDE, Gut Nienfeld, D-31867 Pohle über Hameln, Bundesrepublik Deutschland, GERMANY.

___For Schlesien (Silesia, now in Poland): FORSCHUNGSSTELLE SCHLESIEN DER AGoFF, Kraft Niethard von Stein, Talstrasse 3, D-31707 Bad Eilsen, Bundesrepublik Deutschland, GER-MANY; ARBEITSGEMEINSCHAFT OSTDEUTSCHER FAM-ILIENFORSCHER e.V., Sitz Herne, Detlef Kühn, Holzlar, Fuhrweg 29, D-53229 Bonn, Bundesrepublik Deutschland, GERMANY.

___For Schleswig-Holstein: SCHLESWIG-HOLSTEINISCHE GESELL-SCHAFT FÜR FAMILIENFORSCHUNG UND WAPPEN-KUNDE e.V., Postfach 3809, D-24037 Kiel, Bundesrepublik Deutschland, GERMANY; AUSWANDERER ARCHIV SCHLESWIG-HOLSTEIN DER AMERIKA-GESELL-SCHAFT, Oldesloer Strasse 20, D-23795 Bad Segeberg, Bundesrepublik Deutschland, GERMANY.

__For Südosteuropa (Southeast Europe including Hungary, Rumania, Slovakia, Slovenia, and the Ukraine): FORSCHUNGSSTELLE SÜDOSTEUROPA DER AGoFF, Dr. Martin Armgart, Graitengraben 41, D-45326 Essen/Ruhr, Bundesrepublik Deutschland, GERMANY.

__For Sudetenland (Bohemia, now in Czech Republic): FORSCHUNGSSTELLE SUDENTENLAND DER AGoFF, Adolph Fischer, Juttastrasse 20, D-90480 Nürnberg, Bundesrepublik Deutschland, GERMANY.

__VEREINIGUNG SUDENTENDEUTSCHER FAMILIENFORSCHER, Wittelsbacher Strasse 33, D-93155 Hemau, Bundesrepublik Deutschland, GERMANY.

__For Tschechoslowakei (Czech Republic): COLLEGIUM CAROLINUM, FORSCHUNGSSTELLE FÜR DIE BÖHMISCHEN LANDER, Thierschstrasse 11/III, D-80538 München, Bundesrepublik Deutschland, GERMANY; VEREINIGUNG SUDETENDEUTSCHER FAMILIENFORSCHER, Juttastrasse 20, D-90480 Nürnberg, Bundesrepublik Deutschland, GERMANY.

__For Thüringen (Thuringia): ARBEITSGEMEINSCHAFT GENEALOGIE THÜRINGEN e.V., Sitz Weimar, Helmut Wlokka, Martin-Andersen-Nexoe-Strasse 62, D-99096 Erfurt, Bundesrepublik Deutschland, GERMANY.

__For Volhynia (now in Poland): FORSCHUNGSSTELLE MITTELPOLENVOLHYNIA DER AGoFF, Heinz Ulbrich, Sperberweg 6, Postfach 1039, D-92661 Altenstadt an der Waldnaab, Bundesrepublik Deutschland, GERMANY.

__For Westfalen (Westphalia): WESTFALISCHE GESELLSCHAFT FÜR GENEALOGIE UND FAMILIENFORSCHUNG, Warendorferstrasse 25, D-48145 Münster, Bundesrepublik Deutschland, GERMANY.

__For Westpreussen (West Prussia, now in Poland): FORSCHUNGSSTELLE WESTPREUSSEN-DANZIG DER AGoFF, Dr. Wolf Konietzko, Eichstrasse 6, D-25336 Elmshorn, Bundesrepublik Deutschland, GERMANY.

__For Württemberg: VEREIN FÜR FAMILIEN- UND WAPPENKUNDE IN WÜRTTEMBERG UND BADEN e.V., Konrad-Adenauer Strasse 8, Württembergische Landesbibliothek, Zimmer 103, Postfach 105441, D-70047 Stuttgart, Bundesrepublik Deutschland, GERMANY.

Many more societies, including numerous local ones, are listed in the following compilations:

___Ernest Thode, ADDRESS BOOK FOR GERMANIC GENEAL-
OGY, Genealogical Publishing Co., Baltimore, MD, latest edition.

___W. Ribbe and E. Henning, TASCHENBUCH FÜR FAMILIENGE-
SCHICHTSFORSCHUNG, Neustadt/Aisch, Bundesrepublic
Deutschland, letzte Ausgabe (latest edition).

___P. Bahn, FAMILIENFORSCHUNG, AHNENTAFEL, WAPPEN-
KUNDE, WEGE ZUR EIGENEN FAMILIENCHRONIK,
Falken, Niederhausen, 1989.

___V. N. Chambers, editor, THE GENEALOGICAL HELPER, Everton
Publishers, Logan, UT, latest July-August issue.

___A. Baxter, IN SEARCH OF YOUR GERMAN ROOTS, Genealogi-
cal Publishing Co., Baltimore, MD, 1991.

___R. Hövel, MITGLIEDERVERZEICHNIS DER DEUTSCHEN
ARBEITSGEMEINSCHAFT GENEALOGISCHER VER-
BANDE, Verlag Degener und Co., Neustadt/Aisch, Bundes-
republik Deutschland, letzte Ausgabe (latest edition).

___MN Genealogical Society, RESEARCH GUIDE TO GERMAN-
AMERICAN GENEALOGY, The German Interest Group of the
Society, St. Paul, MN, 1991.

___J. Konrad, GENEALOGICAL AND HISTORICAL SOCIETIES, A
COMPREHENSIVE WORLD-WIDE LISTING, Summit Publications, Munroe Falls, OH, latest edition.

Genealogical advertisements placed in two appropriate genealogical journals can often be of value in discovering the exact place of your
ancestor's origin, if you know the state, province, or regions, and if his/her
surname is not too common. These publications are:

___FAMILIENKUNDLICHE NACHRICHTEN, Verlag Degener,
Postfach 1340, D-91403 Neustadt/Aisch, Bundesrepublik Deutschland, GERMANY.

___ARCHIV FÜR SIPPENFORSCHUNG, PRAKTISCHE FOR-
SCHUNG-HILFE, C. A. Starke Verlag, Frankfurter Strasse 51,
D-65549 Limburg/Lahn, Bundesrepublik Deutschland, GERMA-
NY.

You may write to these publications in English. Send one or each of
them $25 and a brief ad asking for information on your ancestor. They
will translate your ad into German, publish it in their magazine, and it will
be circulated to thousands of German genealogists. A sample ad in
English, and its translation in German are shown here:

HEINOLD, Andreas Johann, born where? (Baden) 14-Apr-1808, came 1835-8 to Boston, USA, his brother Jacob Friedrich HEINOLD, born where? (Baden) 6-Mar-1814, came 1840 to Boston, USA. Who knows anything about these brothers? 407 Ascot Court, Knoxville, TN 37923-5807, USA. Dr. George K. Schweitzer.

HEINOLD, Andreas Johann, *wo? (Baden) 14.4.1808, kam 1835-8 nach Boston, USA, sein Bruder Jakob Friederich HEINOLD, *wo? (Baden) 6.3.1814, kam 1840 nach Boston, USA. Wer weiss etwas über diese Brüder? 407 Ascot Court, Knoxville, TN 37923-5807, USA. Prof. Dr. George K. Schweitzer.

German telephone directories can sometimes be of use to you if all you know is the state or region and if the surname you are seeking is not too common. The procedure is to look the name up in the German telephone directories for the state or region (now on CD-ROM), then to write to six people who have the surname. Give them information about the immigrant ancestor, and ask them if they are related or know who might know. You should write in German. A sample letter follows. Make the needed substitutions in it.

Addressee
Address
Zip code City/town
Bundesrepublik Deutschland, GERMANY

Dear Sir: [Dear Madam:]
My ancestor Andreas Johann HEINOLD came to the US from Baden about 1835. If you are related to him [her], or if you can tell me who might be, please respond. I am especially interested in his [her] place of birth. Enclosed you will find $2 for air mail postage.

With friendly greetings,
George K. Schweitzer
407 Ascot Court
Knoxville, TN 37923-5087
U.S.A.

Addressee
Address
Zip code City/town
Bundesrepublik Deutschland, GERMANY

Sehr geerhter Herr! [Sehr geehrte Frau!]

    Mein Ahn Andreas Johann HEINOLD ist etwa 1835 von Baden in die Vereinigten Staaten gekommen. Falls Sie mit ihm verwandt sind oder jemanden wissen, der mir Auskunft über ihn geben könnte, antworten Sie bitte. Ich bin speziell am Geburtsort von Andreas Johann HEINOLD interessiert. Anbei finden Sie $2 für das Rückporto (Luftpost).

        Mit freundlichen Grüssen,
        George K. Schweitzer
        407 Ascot Court
        Knoxville, TN 37923-5087
        U.S.A.

If no reply is received after a reasonable amount of time, you may wish to try another six of the listings. Telephone directories of Germany may be found in very large municipal and university libraries in the US.

    State archives in Germany are another resource for attempting to find your progenitor's place of origin if all you know is the state (Land) or region. A letter in German directed to one of them and an enclosure of $15 for air mail postage may be of help. You should ask them to examine any pertinent emigration and genealogical indexes for him. The following letter, with appropriate substitutions, may be employed.

Archive
Address
Zip code City/state
Federal Republic of Germany

Dear Director:

    My ancestor Andreas Johann HEINOLD came to the US from Baden about 1835. Please look for him in any pertinent emigration and genealogical indexes. I am especially interested in his place of origin. Enclosed you will find $15 for return air mail postage and your research fee.

        Sincerely,
        Your name
        Address
        City/town, state, zip code
        U.S.A.

Archive
Address
Zip code City/state
Bundesrepublik Deutschland, GERMANY

Werter Herr Direktor!
    Mein Ahn Andreas Johann HEINOLD ist etwa 1835 von Baden in die Vereinigten Staaten gekommen. Bitte seien Sie so freundlich und forschen in den entsprechenden Auswanderungs- und Stammbaumverzeichnissen nach ihm. Ich bin besonders am Ort seiner Herkunft bzw. Abstammung interessiert. Anbei finden Sie $15 für Ruckporto (Luftpost) und als Entgeld für ihre Nachforschungen.

Mit freundlichen Grüssen,
George K. Schweitzer
407 Ascot Court
Knoxville, TN 37923-5807
U.S.A.

    The state archives in Germany are:

__FOR BADEN-WÜRTTEMBERG (BW): Generallandesarchiv, Nördliche Hilda-Promenade 2, D-76133 Karlsruhe, Bundesrepublik Deutschland, GERMANY.

___For BW-Baden: Staatsarchiv, Columbistrasse 4, Postfach 323, D-79003 Freiburg, Bundesrepublik Deutschland, GERMANY. Note that BW means that this archive is in Baden-Württemberg.

___For BW-Württemburg: Hauptstaatsarchiv, Konrad-Adenauer-Strasse 4, D-70173 Stuttgart, Bundesrepublik Deutschland, GERMANY; Staatsarchiv, Schloss-Strasse 30, D-71634 Ludwigsburg, Bundesrepublik Deutschland, GERMANY.

___For BW-Hohenzollern: Staatsarchiv, Karlstrasse 3, Postfach 526, D-72488, Sigmaringen, Bundesrepublik Deutschland, GERMANY.

___For BW-Wertheim: Staatsarchiv Wertheim, Muehlenstrasse 26, D-97877 Wertheim, Bundesrepublik Deutschland, GERMANY.

___FOR BAYERN (B): Haupstaatsarchiv I, Arcisstrasse 12, Postfach 200507, D-80005 München, Bundesrepublik Deutschland, GERMANY.

___For B-Coburg: Staatsarchiv, Schloss Ehrenburg, D-96450 Coburg, Bundesrepublik Deutschland, GERMANY.

___For-B-Mittelfranken: Staatsarchiv, Archivstrasse 17, Postfach 120346, D-90110 Nürnberg, Bundesrepublik Deutschland, GERMANY.

___For B-Niederbayern: Staatsarchiv, Burg Trausnitz, D-84036 Landshut, Bundesrepublik Deutschland, GERMANY.

___For B-Oberbayern: Staatsarchiv, Schönfeldstrasse 3, D-80539 München 22, Bundesrepublik Deutschland, GERMANY.

___For B-Oberfranken: Staatsarchiv, Hainstrasse 39, Postfach 2668, D-96017 Bamberg, Bundesrepublik Deutschland, GERMANY.

___For B-Oberpfalz: Staatsarchiv, Archivstrasse 3, D-92224 Amberg, Bundesrepublik Deutschland, GERMANY.

___For B-Schwaben: Staatsarchiv Augsburg, Salomon-Idler-Strasse 2, D-86159 Augsburg, Bundesrepublik Deutschland, GERMANY.

___For B-Unterfranken: Staatsarchiv, Residenzplatz 2, D-97070 Würzburg, Bundesrepublik Deutschland, GERMANY.

___FOR BERLIN (EAST): Magistrat von Berlin, Breite Strasse 30/31, D-10178 Berlin, Bundesrepublik Deutschland, GERMANY.

___FOR BERLIN (WEST): Staatsarchiv, Archivstrasse 12-14, D-14195 Berlin 33, Bundesrepublik Deutschland, GERMANY.

___FOR BRANDENBURG:Staatsarchiv, Sanssouci-Orangerie, D-14469 Potsdam, Bundesrepublik Deutschland, GERMANY.

___FOR BREMEN: Staatsarchiv, Am Staatsarchiv 1, D-28203 Bremen, Bundesrepublik Deutschland, GERMANY.

___FOR ELSASS-LOTHRINGEN (EL)-Bas-Rhin: Archives départementales du Bas-Rhin, 5-9 rue Fischart, F-67000 Strasbourg, FRANCE.

___For EL-Haut-Rhin: Archives départmentales du Haut-Rhin, Cité administrative, Rue Fleischauer, F-68000 Colmar, FRANCE.

___For EL-Moselle: Archives départmentales de la Moselle, Préfecture de la Moselle, Hôtel du Département, 9 Place de la Prêfecture, F-57036 Metz, FRANCE.

___For EL-Meurthe-et-Moselle: Archives départementales de Meurthe-et-Moselle, 1 rue de la Monnaie, F-54000 Nancy, FRANCE.

___FOR HAMBURG: Staatsarchiv, ABC-Strasse 19, D-20354 Hamburg, Bundesrepublik Deutschland, GERMANY.

___FOR HESSEN (H)-Nassau: Hauptstaatsarchiv, Mosbacher Str. 55, D-65187 Wiesbaden, Bundesrepublik Deutschland, GERMANY.

___For H-Darmstadt: Staatsarchiv Darmstadt, Karolinenplatz 3, D-64289 Darmstadt, Deutschland, GERMANY.

___For H-Kassel: Staatsarchiv, Friedrichsplatz 15, Postfach 540, D-35017 Marburg a.d. Lahn, Bundesrepublik Deutschland, GERMANY.

___For H-Nassau-Siegen: Staatsarchiv Münster, Bohlweg 2, Postfach 7629, D-48041 Münster, Bundesrepublik Deutschland, GERMANY.

___For LIPPE: Personenstandsarchiv für Westfalen-Lippe, Willi-Hofmann-Strasse 2, D-32765 Detmold, Bundesrepublik Deutschland, GERMANY.

__For LIPPE: Landschaftsverband Westfalen-Lippe, Westfälisches Landesamt für Archivpflege, Warendorfer Strasse 24, D-48145 Münster, Bundesrepublik Deutschland, GERMANY.

__FOR MECKLENBURG-VORPOMMERN (MV)-Mecklenburg: Staatsarchiv, Graf-Schack-Allee 2, D-19053 Schwerin, Bundesrepublik Deutschland, GERMANY.

__For MV-Vorpommern: Staatsarchiv, Alte Kaserne Kreishaus, D-17489 Greifswald, Bundesrepublik Deutschland, GERMANY.

__FOR NIEDERSACHSEN (N): Niedersächsisches Hauptstaatsarchiv, Am Archiv 1, D-30169 Hannover, Bundesrepublik Deutschland, GERMANY.

__For N-Braunschweig: Staatsarchiv, Forstweg 2, D-32302 Wolfenbüttel, Bundesrepublik Deutschland, GERMANY.

__For N-Bückeburg: Staatsarchiv, Schloss, D-31675 Bückeburg, Bundesrepublik Deutschland, GERMANY.

__For N-Oldenburg: Staatsarchiv, Damm 43, D-26135 Oldenburg, Bundesrepublik Deutschland, GERMANY.

__For N-Osnabrück: Staatsarchiv, Schloss-Strasse 29, D-49074 Osnabrück, Bundesrepublik Deutschland, GERMANY.

__For N-Ostfriesland: Niedersächsisches Hauptstaatsarchiv Aurich, Oldersumer Strasse 50, D-26603 Aurich, Bundesrepublik Deutschland, GERMANY.

__For N-Stade: Staatsarchiv, Am Sande 4c, D-21682 Stade, Bundesrepublik Deutschland, GERMANY.

__For N-Wolfenbüttel: Niedersächsisches Staatsarchiv, Wolfenbüttel, Forstweg 2, D-32302 Wolfenbüttel, Bundesrepublik Deutschland, GERMANY.

__FOR NORDRHEIN-WESTFALEN (NW): Haupstaatsarchiv, Mauerstrasse 55, D-4-476 Duesseldorf 30, Bundesrepublik Deutschland, GERMANY.

__For NW-Lippe: Staatsarchiv, Willi-Hofmann-Strasse 2, D-32756 Detmold, Bundesrepublik Deutschland, GERMANY.

__For NW-Westfalen: Staatsarchiv, Bohlweg 2, Postfach 7629, W-48041 Münster, Bundesrepublik Deutschland, GERMANY.

__FOR RHEINLAND-PFALZ (RP)-Rheinland: Personenstandsarchiv für Kirchenbücher und Zivilstandregister, Schloss-Strasse 12, D-50321 Brühl, Bundesrepublik Deutschland, GERMANY.

__For RP-Pfalz: Landesarchiv Speyer, Otto-Mayer-Strasse 9, Postfach 1608, D-67326 Speyer/Rhein, Bundesrepublik Deutschland, GERMANY.

__For RP-Rheinland: Staatsarchiv, Karmeliterstrasse 1-3, W-5400 Koblenz, Bundesrepublik Deutschland, GERMANY.

___FOR SAARLAND: Landesarchiv, Scheidter Strasse 114, Postfach 101010, D-66010 Saarbrücken, Bundesrepublik Deutschland, GERMANY.

___FOR SACHSEN (S)-Dresden: Staatsarchiv, Archivstrasse 14, D-01097 Dresden, Bundesrepublik Deutschland, GERMANY.

___For S-Coburg-Gotha, Staatsarchiv Coburg, Schloss Ehrenburg, D-96450 Coburg, Bundesrepublik Deutschland, GERMANY.

___For S-Leipzig: Staatsarchiv Leipzig, Postfach 100947, D-04009 Leipzig, Bundesrepublik Deutschland, GERMANY.

___For S-Bautzen: Staatsarchiv, Ortenburg, D-02625 Bautzen, Bundesrepublik Deutschland, GERMANY.

___For S-Altenburg: Staatsarchiv, Schloss 2a, D-06429 Altenburg, Bundesrepublik Deutschland, GERMANY.

___For S-Schwarzburg-Rudolstadt/Sonderhausen: Staatsarchiv Rudolstadt, Schloss Heidecksburg, D-07407 Rudolstadt, Bundesrepublik Deutschland, GERMANY.

___For S-Weimar-Eisenach: Thüringisches Hauptstaatsarchiv, Postschliessfach 726, D-99408 Weimar, Bundesrepublik Deutschland, GERMANY.

___FOR SACHSEN-ANHALT (SA)-Magdeburg: Staatsarchiv, Hegelstrasse 25, D-39104 Magdeburg, Bundesrepublik Deutschland, GERMANY.

___For SA-Wernigerode: Staatsarchiv, Schloss, D-38855 Wernigerode (Harz), Bundesrepublik Deutschland, GERMANY.

___For SA-Oranienbaum: Staatsarchiv, Schloss, D-06785 Oranienbaum, Bundesrepublik Deutschland, GERMANY.

___FOR SCHLESWIG-HOLSTEIN: Landesarchiv, Schloss Gottorf, D-24837 Schleswig, Bundesrepublik Deutschland, GERMANY.

___FOR THÜRINGEN (T)-Gotha: Staatsarchiv, Schloss Friedenstein, D-99867 Gotha, Bundesrepublik Deutschland, GERMANY.

___For T-Greiz: Staatsarchiv, Oberes Schloss 7, D-O7973 Greiz, Bundesrepublik Deutschland, GERMANY.

___For T-Meiningen: Staatsarchiv, Schloss Bibrabau, D-98617 Meiningen, Bundesrepublik Deutschland, GERMANY.

___For T-Rudolstadt: Staatsarchiv, Schloss Heidecksburg, D-07407 Rudolstadt, Bundesrepublik Deutschland, GERMANY.

___For T-Weimar: Thüringisches Hauptstaatsarchiv, Postschliessfach 726, D-99408 Weimar, Bundesrepublik Deutschland, GERMANY.

Precisely which archive or archives you should contact depends completely on exactly what information you already have on your forebear.

For German areas which were once in Germany but are in other countries now, the institutions listed under genealogical societies should be consulted. These areas are Brandenburg (East), Elsass (Alsace), Lothringen (Lorraine), Ostpreussen (East Prussia), Pommern (Pomerania), Posen, Schlesien (Silesia), and Westpreussen (West Prussia). Also see and use the listing there under Easternmost Germany. If called for, you may also write the institutions listed previously under genealogical societies for German ancestors who settled outside of Germany: Baltikum (Baltic States), Bassarabien (Bessarabia), Bukovina, Burgerland, Donauschwaben (Danube Swabians), Galizien (Galicia), Russland (Russia), Südosteuropa (Southeastern Europe), Sudetenland, Tschechoslowakei (Czechoslovakia), and Volhynia. For other archival sources in these areas, consult

___J. O. R. Nuthack and A. Goertz, translators, GENEALOGICAL GUIDE TO GERMAN ANCESTORS FROM EASTERN (actually EASTERNMOST) GERMANY AND EASTERN EUROPE, Verlag Degener, Neustadt/Aisch, Deutschland, 1984.

More archives for all the areas of Germany will be found in a very valuable listing:

___E. Thode, ADDRESS BOOK FOR GERMANIC GENEALOGY, Genealogical Publishing Co., Baltimore, MD, latest edition.

Central archives serving very large regions may be of some help to you if all the previous measures have failed. The one of these with the highest likelihood of finding your ancestor's precise place of origin is the following. This archive serves all of what was once the Deutsche Demokratische Republik (the DDR, East Germany), and it has an incredibly large number of records and indexes.

___Deutsche Zentralstelle für Genealogie, Postfach 100947, D-04009 Leipzig, Bundesrepublik Deutschland, GERMANY.

15. Finding the place on the map	15. Auffinden des Ortes auf einer Karte
15. Auffinden des Ortes auf einer Karte	15. Auffinden des Ortes auf einer Karte

Once you find the exact place of origin in Germany, your next step is to locate it precisely on a detailed map. This will clarify for you exactly which state/province/region the place was in when your ancestor left and which state the place now is in. Such information is necessary to facilitate finding the greatest number of records pertaining to your forebear. Most of the time you will know both the name of the city/town/village and the state/ province/region in which it is located. This is particularly valuable in the case of city/town/village names which are common and occur in several or many areas (states/provinces/regions). However, sometimes you will know only the name of the city/town/village, and if that name is commonly used, it will be necessary for you to investigate all places by that name. For example, suppose you have only one bit of evidence, namely, an old Bible entry that says your ancestor was from Neustadt. When you look this town name up, you will discover there are at least 28. You will need to locate all of them, then invoke migration and immigration patterns, and even places of origin of friends, neighbors, and associates, to arrange these in the order of likelihood of success. That is, you will need to speculate on the most likely ones to search first.

To locate a German city/town/village on a map, it is necessary to look into indexed atlases and gazetteers. These are volumes which list places in alphabetical order and tell you where to find them on maps. With regard to Germany, it is well for you to remember that there was no unified Germany before 1871. Also you need to recall that during 1871-1918, a unified Germany reached its largest size. It then contained much territory that is now in France, Poland, Czechoslovakia, Russia, Lithuania, Denmark, and Belgium. In these areas, especially in Poland, the cities/towns/villages often had German names which were changed when the areas ceased to be German. For example, in Poland Stettin became Sczecin, Stolp became Stupsk, Belgard became Bialogord, Liegnitz became Legnica, and Breslau became Wroclaw. A German ancestor from this region who came when it was still in Prussia (Preussen), would use the German name of the city/town/village. Thus, you must bear in mind that each city/town/village has a German and a Polish name. Similarly, in Czechoslovakia, what is now Skalna was Wildstein, now Luby was Schönbach, and now Mariánské Lazne was Marienbad.

The first effort to identify the exact map location is to look the city/ town/village up in gazetteers and atlases of modern Germany. Please bear in mind that the former German territories are not included in these, so if you know your ancestor was from one of them, skip on down to the next paragraph. The four items which are recommended are:
___NATIONAL GEOGRAPHIC ATLAS OF THE WORLD, National Geographic Society, Washington, DC, 1981. A very useful indexed atlas which will locate most places in modern Germany.

In English.
___POSTLEITZAHLEN VERZEICHNIS [ZIP-CODE DIRECTORY],
Bundesministerium für das Post- und Fernmeldewesen, Bonn,
Deutschland, a recent issue. This is a directory which gives zip
codes for cities/towns/ villages/suburbs in Germany. Once the zip
code is discovered, the place can be readily found on the zip-code
map of Germany, which is listed next. In German, but no
knowledge of German necessary.
___POSTLEITEINHEITEN [ZIP-CODE MAP], Bundesministerium für
das Post- und Fernmeldewesen, Bonn, Deutschland, a recent
issue.
___DER GROSSE SHELL ATLAS [THE LARGE SHELL ATLAS],
Mairs Geographischer Verlag, Ostfildern, Deutschland, a recent
issue. Very detailed listings extending to small villages, suburbs,
and settlements. In German, but easily used by non-German
speakers.
These items may be found in large genealogical libraries, including FHL,
large university libraries, and large municipal libraries. The German zip-
code index and map, and the Shell atlas may be purchased from Ernest
Thode, RR7, Box 306 AB, Marietta, OH 45750-9437.

Good gazetteers and atlases of the world which list in many cases
(but not all) both the modern and the old German Empire names for
cities/ towns/villages are:
___THE TIMES ATLAS OF THE WORLD, Times Books, Ltd., London,
England, 1985, one-volume edition.
___THE TIMES INDEX-GAZETTEER OF THE WORLD, Time
Publishing Co., London, England, 1965.
___J. Bartholomew, THE TIMES ATLAS OF THE WORLD, Times
Publishing Co., London, England, 1955, multi-volumed edition,
Volume 3.
___THE NEW INTERNATIONAL ATLAS, Rand McNally, Chicago, IL,
1987.
___COLUMBIA LIPPINCOTT GAZETTEER OF THE WORLD,
Columbia University Press, New York, NY, 1962.
These volumes will be found in FHL, other large genealogical libraries,
and large universities and city libraries.

A highly-detailed gazetteer listing over 107,000 places in modern
Germany can be consulted if the above reference words do not lead you
to the geographical location of your ancestor's city/town/village. The book
is in German, but a little use of a German-English dictionary will allow

you to employ it successfully. This detailed work even covers communities with less than 200 inhabitants.

___J. Müller, MÜLLERS GROSSES DEUTSCHES ORTSBUCH [MÜLLER'S LARGE GERMAN GAZETTEER], Post- and Ortsbuch Verlag, Wuppertal, Deutschland, 1974.

The most valuable overall gazetteer is a large volume which was published in 1912. At this time the German Empire had its largest extension. Therefore, this book lists the names of the cities/towns/villages in this large area (see Figures 3 and 4). This gazetteer is in the old German Gothic print, but you will be able to handle it with the aid of the material on the German language to be presented in a later chapter.

___E. Ütrecht, MEYERS ORTS- UND VERKEHRS-LEXIKON DES DEUTSCHEN REICHS [MEYER'S GAZETTEER AND TRANSPORTATION LEXICON], Bibliographisches Institut, Berlin, Deutschland, 1912.

This work not only locates places, but it also indicates whether the city/town/village has a civil registration office (Standesamt), and whether there are church parishes (Pfarrkirchen) there. The abbreviation StdA stands for Standesamt, Pfk for Pfarrkirche, ev. for evangelische (Lutheran or later united Lutheran-Reformed), kath. for katholische (Catholic), and reform. for reformierte (Reformed). If there is no Standesamt, then the civil registration office which serves the village will be given. If the village has no church parish, however, only the fact is stated. The MÜLLER'S and MEYER'S GAZETTEERS can be found in very large genealogical libraries, the libraries of universities with German research centers, a few very large municipal libraries, and the FHL.

In order to locate the parish in which a village having no parish was included, the appropriate one of the following references may be consulted. It will either give you the parish or will name the place nearest the town/ village which has a parish. Most of the volumes also indicate the places having civil registration offices (Standesämter), and for those places which do not, they give the nearest one.

___For Anhalt, M. Starke, STADTISCHES HANDBUCH DER LANDWIRTSCHAFT UND GEOGRAPHISCHES ORTSLEXIKON VOM HERZOGTUM ANHALT, Verlag Starke, Leipzig, Deutschland, 1879. FHL Film No. 496846. Look for the nearest city/town/village that has a listing reading Pfarrdorf (parish seat).

___For Baden, F. Hermann, DIE KIRCHENBÜCHER IN BADEN, Verlag G. Braun, Karlsruhe, Deutschland, 1957. FHL Film No.

492899. Look for Lutheran parishes (ePf), Catholic parishes (kPf), and note that the symbol zPf means that the pertinent parish is located in the place following this symbol.

___For Bayern (Bavaria), ORTSCHAFTEN-VERZEICHNIS FÜR DEN FREISTAAT BAYERN, Lindauersche Universitats Buchhandlung, München, Deutschland, 1928. FHL Film No. 924721. Look for these abbreviations: Pfd. (place has a parish), k.Pf. (Catholic parish), e.Pf. (Lutheran parish), z.k.Pf. (word following this is location of the Catholic parish), and z.e.Pf. (word following this is location of the Lutheran parish). Remember that Bavaria owned the Palatinate (Pfalz) for a long time. This area is included in the above volume.

___For Elsass-Lothringen (Alsace-Lorraine), H. Koch, articles in MIT-TEILUNGEN DER ZENTRALSTELLE FÜR DEUTSCHE PERSONEN- UND FAMILIENGESCHICHTE, Degener, Leipzig, Deutschland, Band 9 (1911) 14-61, Band 10 (1912) 8-52. FHL Film Nos. 492890 and 492892. Look for the nearest city/town/village that has a parish.

___For Hessen (Hesse), O. Praetorius, KIRCHENBÜCHER UND STANDESREGISTER FÜR ALLE WOHNPLATZE IM LAND HESSEN, Selbstverlag der Historischen Kommission für das Land Hessen, Darmstadt, Deutschland, 1939, FHL Film No. 496714. Look for k bei (word following this is location of the Catholic parish) and e bei (word following this is location of Lutheran parish).

___For Lippe, DIE BESTANDE DES STAATSARCHIVS UND PERSONENSTANDSARCHIVS DETMOLD, Selbstverlag des Staatarchivs Detmold, Deutschland, 1970. Use listings in the book to locate nearest place with a parish. FHL Book 943.55 B4nw Ser. B, No. 3.

___For Mecklenburg, MECKLENBURGS FAMILIENGESCHICHT-LICHE QUELLEN, Hermes Verlag, Hamburg, Deutschland, 1936. FHL Film No. 496473. In the index, places without a parish are followed by a dash and the location of the parish which serves them.

___For Oldenburg, ORTSCHAFTVERZEICHNIS DES GROSS-HERZOGTUMS OLDENBURG, Druck und Verlag von A. Littmann, Oldenburg, Deutschland, 1911. FHL Film No. 806633. Look up the name of the place, then in the next column, you will find the parish in which it is located.

___For Preussen (Prussia), GEMEINDE LEXIKON FÜR DAS KÖNIGREICH PREUSSEN, Verlag des Landesamts, Berlin,

1908, Volumes 1-14. FHL Film Nos. 491042, 806633, 806634, 806635, 1186701, and 1186702. Includes volumes for Brandenburg (806635), Hannover (806634), Hessen-Nassau (1186702), Hohenzollern (806635), Ostpreussen (East Prussia-1186701), Pommern (Pomerania-806634), Posen (806634), Rheinland (1186702), Sachsen (Saxony-806634), Schlesien (Silesia-806633), Schleswig-Holstein (806635), Westfalen (491042), and Westpreussen (West Prussia-1186701). Index in each volume. Indexes give city/town/village and Kreis (district). Look under Kreis (district) for the city/town/village. Column 2 gives the city/town/ village, column 25 names the Lutheran parish, column 26 names the Catholic parish.

___For Preussen (Prussia), there is another multi-volumed gazetteer, GEMEINDELEXIKON FÜR DEN FREISTAAT PREUSSEN, Verlag des Landesamts, Berlin, Deutschland, 1931-1932, Volumes 1-14. FHL Film Nos. 475862, 806636, and 806637. Includes volumes for Berlin and Brandenburg (806636), Grenzmark, Posen, and Westpreussen (Grenzmark, Posen, and West Prussia-80636), Hannover (806637), Hessen-Nassau (806637), Hohenzollern (475862), Niederschlesien (Lower Silesia-806636), Oberschlesien (Upper Silesia-806637), Ostpreussen (East Prussia-806636), Pommern (Pomerania-806636), Rheinland (475862), Sachsen (Saxony-806637), Schleswig-Holstein (806637), Westfalen (806637). Index in each volume. Indexes give city/town/ village and Kreis (district). Look under Kreis (district) for the city/town/ village. Column 2 gives the city/town/village, column 14 names the Lutheran parish, column 15 names the Catholic parish.

___For Königreich Sachsen (Kingdom of Saxony), A. Schumann, VOLL-STANDIGES STAATS-, POST-, UND ZEITUNGS LEXIKON VON SACHSEN, Verlag der Gebrüder Schumann, Zwickau, Deutschland, 1825, 13 Bande. FHL Film Nos. 824319, 824320, 824321, 824322, 824323, 824324, and 824325. Also includes Reuss-Greiz, Reuss-Schleiz, Sachsen-Altenburg (Saxony-Altenburg), Sachsen-Coburg-Gotha (Saxony-Coburg-Gotha), Sachsen-Meiningen (Saxony Meiningen), Sachsen-Weimar-Eisenach (Saxony-Weimar-Eisenach), Schwarzburg-Rudolstadt, Schwarzburg-Sonderhansen, and Thüringen (Thuringia). City/town/village entries name the parish to which it belongs.

___For Schaumburg-Lippe, DAS LAND SCHAUMBURG-LIPPE, in O. Spohr, FAMILIENGESCHICHTLICHER WEGWEISER DURCH STADT UND LAND, Verlag Degener, Neustadt/Aisch,

No. 12 (1939) 4-5. FHL Book 943 B4fw. Find town/village, use reference work to locate the nearest parish.

___For Württemberg, ORTSCHAFTSVERZEICHNIS DES KÖNIGREICHS WÜRTTEMBERG, Druck von W. Kohlhammer, Stuttgart, Deutschland, 1912. FHL Film No. 806333. Look up place in index. Refer to the page number given to find place listing. Column 1 gives the name of the place, column 7 names the Lutheran parish, column 8 names the Catholic parish.

All the above parish-locating materials will be found in FHL, and all but the books can be borrowed through FHC. Some of them are available in large genealogical libraries and large municipal libraries in the US.

In some difficult cases, you will not have found the modern name of the place in areas that were previously German, but are now in other countries. The works listed in the second paragraph of this section are usually fruitful, but if they fail you, some more detailed works can be consulted.

___AMTLICHES GEMEINDE- UND ORTSNAMEN VERZEICHNIS DER DEUTSCHEN OSTGEBIETE UNTER FREMDEN VERWALTUNG, Bundesanstalt für Landeskunde, Reuragen, Deutschland, 1955, 3 Bände. Place name changes in the area taken from Germany after World War II. Volume 2 gives German place names and new foreign names. Volume 3 gives new foreign names and previous German names. FHL Film No. 6053256.

___O. Kredel und F. Thierfelder, DEUTSCH-FREMDSPRACHTIGES ORTSNAMENVERZEICHNIS, Deutsche Verlagsgesellschaft, Berlin, 1931, 3 Bände. German place name changes after World War I in France, Belgium, Denmark, Poland, Lithuania, Russia, Czechoslovakia, Hungary, Yugoslavia, Italy, Switzerland, Latvia, Estonia, Luxembourg, and Romania. FHL Film No. 583457.

___F. Vanderhalven, NAMENSANDERUNGEN EHEMALS PREUSSISCHER GEMEINDEN VON 1850 NACH 1942, Verlag Degener, Neustadt/Aisch, Deutschland, 1971. Name changes of places which were formerly in Prussia. FHL Book No. 943.8 B4sw no. 43.

___GEMEINDEVERZEICHNIS FÜR DIE HAUPTWOHNGEBIETE DER DEUTSCHEN AUSSERHALB DER BUNDES-REPUBLIK DEUTSCHLAND, Verlag für Standesamtwesen, Frankfurt am Main, Deutschland, 1982. Over 60,000 cities, towns, and villages outside of present-day Germany where Germans settled with their present locations. These are available at FHL (FHC) and also at a few other large libraries.

Occasionally in attempting to locate the exact place of origin of your progenitor, family materials or other records will tell you he/she came from one of the old principalities/duchies/districts/regions which was in the Germanic area long before there was any united Germany. You will need to identify where that old principality/duchy/district/region is today. To assist you, here is an alphabetical list of many of these old places and where they are today. Today's locations are presented in parentheses and refer to the following states (Länder) which are in Germany now: Baden-Württemberg (BW), Bayern (B), Brandenburg (BR), Hessen (H), Mecklenburg-Vorpommern (MV), Niedersachsen (N), Nordrhein-Westfalen (NW), Rheinland-Pfalz (RP), Saarland (SL), Sachsen (S), Sachsen-Anhalt (SA), Schleswig-Holstein (SH), Thüringen (T). The old territories are: Aachen(NW), Aalen (BW), Aix-la-Chapelle(NW), Altenkirchen(B), Anhalt(SA), Anholt(NW), Ansbach(B), Aremberg(N), Augsburg(B), Aulendorf(BW), Baden(BW), Baindt (BW), Bamberg(B), Barby(SA), Bayreuth(B), Beilstein(RP), Berchtesgaden (B), Berg(NW), Bernburg(SA), Biberach(BW), Birstein(H), Bitsch(Lorraine, France), Blankenburg(Lorraine, France), Böhmen(Czechoslovakia), Bonndorf(BW), Bopfingen(BW), Brakel(NW), Braunschweig(N), Buchau(BW), Buchhorn(BW), Bückeburg(N), Büdingen(H), Burscheid(NW), Castell(B), Chiemsee(B), Colmar(Haut-Rhin), Comburg(NW), Corvey(NW), Danzig (Poland), Degenberg(B), Diepholz(N), Diessen(B), Dinkelsbühl(B), Dortmund(NW), Duisburg((NW), Düren(NW), Durlach(BW), Dyck(NW), Eberstein(BW), Eglingen(BW), Eglof(BW), Ehrenfels(H), Eichstädt(B), Elbing (Poland), Elchingen(B), Ellwangen(BW), Elsass(Alsace, France), Emden(N), Eppstein(H), Erbach(H), Essen(NW), Esslingen/Neckar(BW), Falkenstein (BW), Finstingen(Lorraine, France), Frankfurt/Main(H), Freising(B), Friedberg(H), Friedrichshafen(BW), Fulda(H), Fürstenberg(BW), Gandersheim (NS), Geldern(NW), Gelnhausen(H), Gemen(NW), Gengenbach(BW), Genrode(SA), Gera(T), Geroldstein(RP), Giech(B), Giengen/Brenz(BW), Gimborn-Neustadt(NW), Gleichen(T), Goslar(N), Göttingen(N), Gundelfingen (BW), Guntersblum(RP), Gutenzell(BW), Haag in Oberbayern(B), Hachenburg(RP), Hagenau(Bas-Rhin, France), Halberstadt(SA), Hanau-Lichtenberg(H), Hanau-Münzenberg(H), Hannover(N), Havelberg(SA), Heben(BW), Heggbach(BW), Heideck(B), Heilbronn(BW), Heiligenberg(BW), Helfenstein(BW), Henneberg(T), Herford(NW), Herrenalb(BW), Hersfeld(H), Hessen-Darmstadt(H), Hessen-Kassel(H),

Hessen-Nassau(H), Hildesheim(N), Hohenfels(BW), Hohengeroldseck(BW), Hohenlohe(BW/B), Hohenstein(B), Hohenzollern(BW), Holstein(SH), Holzappel(RP), Hoya(N), Isenburg(H), Isny(BW), Jülich und Berg(NW), Kammin(b), Kaufbeuren(B), Kaufungen(H), Kempten(B), Kerpen-Lommersum(NW), Kitzinger(B), Klettgau(BW), Koblenz(RP), Köln(NW), Königsbronn(BW), Königstein und Eppstein(H), Konstanz(BW), Kornelmünster(NW), Kriechingen(Moselle, France), Kronberg (H), Lahr(BW), Landau/Pfalz(RP), Laubach(H), Lauenburg(SH), Lebus(BR), Lemgo(NW), Leuchtenberg(B), Leutkirch(BW), Lich(H), Lichtenberg(H), Limpurg(BW), Lindau(B), Lippe(NW), Lommersum(NW), Lothringen (Lorraine, France), Löwenstein(BW), Lübeck(SH), Lüneburg(N), Magdeburg (SA), Mainz(RP), Manderscheid(RP), Mansfeld(SA), Maulbronn(BW), Mecklenburg(MV), Meerholz(H), Meissen(S), Memmingen(B), Merseburg(SA), Metz(Moselle, France), Minden(NW), Moers(NW), Mühlhausen(Alsace, France), Mühlhausen(T), Mühlingen(SA), Münster(NW), Münzenberg(H), Murbach(Alsace, France), Nassau(H), Naumburg/Saale(SA), Neresheim (BW), Neuburg(B), Neuenahr(RP), Niederwesel(NW), Nomeny(Lorraine, France), Nordhausen(T), Nördlingen(B), Nürnberg(B), Oberehnheim(Bas-Rhin, France), Oberstein(RP), Ochsenhausen(BW), Oettingen(BW/B), Offenburg(BW), Oldenburg(N), Ortenburg(BW), Osnabrück(N), Ostfriesland(N), Paderborn(NW), Passau(N), Petershausen(BW), Pfalz(RP), Pfullendorf(BW), Plauen(S), Plesse(N), Pommern(MV, Poland), Prüm(RP), Pyrmont(N), Quedlinburg(SA), Ratzeburg(SH), Ravensburg(BW), Recklinghau sen(NW), Regensburg(B), Regenstein(SA), Reichenau(BW), Reichenstein (NW), Reifferscheid(RP), Reipoltskirchen(RP), Reuss-Gera(T), Reuss-Greiz(T), Reutlingen(BW), Rheineck(RP), Riddagshausen(N), Rieneck(B), Rietberg(NW), Roggenburg(B), Rosheim(Bas-Rhin, France), Rothenburg/ Tauber(B), Rottweil(BW), Runkel(H), Ruppin(B), Saalfeld(T), Saarbrücken (SL), Saarburg(Moselle, France), Saffenburg(RP), Salmannsweiler(BW), Savoyen(France), Schaumburg und Gemen(N), Schenken(S), Schleiden (NW), Schleswig(SH), Schlettstadt(Bas-Rhin, France), Schussenried(BW), Schwäbisch Hall(BW), Schwäbisch Wörth(B), Schwäbish Gmünd(BW), Schwarzburg-Rudolstadt(T), Schwarzburg-Sonderhausen(T), Schweinfurth(B), Schwerin(MV), Seinsheim(B), Simmern(RP), Soest(NW), Solms(H), Sonnenberg(H), Speyer(RP), St. Georgenschild(BW), St. Blasien(BW), St. Agidien zu Nürnberg(B), Stauffen(BW), Steinfurt(NW), Strassburg(Bas-Rhin, France), Sulz(BW), Tecklenburg(NW), Tengen(BW), Toul(Meurthe-et-Moselle, France), Trier(RP), Tübingen(BW), Türkheim(Haut-Rhin, France), Überlingen(BW), Ulm-

(BW), Urspring(BW), Usingen(H), Verden(N), Virneburg(RP), Wachters-bach(H), Waldburg(B/BW), Waldeck(H), Waldsassen/ Oberpfalz(B), Wal-kenried(N), Wangen/Allgau(BW), Warburg(NW), Weil der Stadt(BW), Weilburg(H), Weingarten(BW), Weinsberg(BW), Weissenburg/ Nordgau(B), Weissenburg(Bas-Rhin, France), Wernigerode(SA), Wert-heim(BW), Westerburg(RP), Wetzlar(H), Wied und Runkel(H), Wimpfen(BW), Windsheim(B), Winneburg und Beilstein(RP), Wittgenstein(NW), Wolfenbüttel(N), Wolgast(MV), Worms(RP), Wunstorf(N), Württemberg(BW), Würzburg(B), Zell am Harmersbach(BW), Zwiefalten(BW).

Greyffenstein

Waldenburg.

CHAPTER 4
(KAPITEL 4)
TYPES OF GERMAN RECORDS
(VERSCHIEDENE ARTEN VON AUFZEICHNUNGEN)

1. Introduction	1. Einleitung
1. Einleitung	*1. Einleitung*

The most important question in all of genealogy is: "Who were the parents?" This is because the child-parent identification is what connects the generations, and therefore what permits the family lines to be extended farther and farther back. Hence, the original records which make these child-parent connections are the most important records in genealogy. The German records that fit this category best are vital records (birth, marriage, death) and records that surround these events (christening, baptism, confirmation, banns, divorce, will, probate, funeral, burial, cemetery). The two major agencies that kept such records were the church and the government. The main church groups were the Catholic, Lutheran, and Reformed, with the Lutheran and the Reformed uniting in 1817 to make up the Evangelical (or Protestant) Church. The governmental agencies were the many independent states/principalities/duchies/bishoprics/fiefdoms/free cities which from time to time made up the area which became in 1871 the German Empire. These independent governments also often had subdivisions which kept records of a more local sort: districts, regions, counties, cities, towns, villages, communities.

In addition to the above vital records and the records which surround them, numerous other records which refer to individuals were kept. In some instances these records give the names of parents and/or children. In other instances, these records lead to data on the parents and/or children. In still other cases, the records simply locate the individual in time and place, and relate him/her to some particular activity. Typical auxiliary records of these types include records of the following sorts: alien registration, arrival registration, censuses, citizenship lists, court records, departure registration, dwelling house histories, emigration documents, inhabitant lists, land records, local histories, military records, newspaper reports, occupational records, organization memberships, parish histories, personal recordings (account books, autobiographies, biographies, diaries, letters, memoirs, family history materials), tax records, university enrollment data, and welfare records.

Since Germans have been keeping records for so long, and since genealogical research has been active in Germany for many years, numerous collections of genealogical material have been made. Some are published, and some are still in manuscript form. For the most part, the compilations have been gathered from the records mentioned above. These compilations include large multi-volumed series of genealogical data, massive indexes to numerous records, many detailed family histories, a large number of genealogical periodicals, indexes to this periodical literature, and sizable collections of microfilmed documents and indexes.

When you begin to look into the genealogical records of Germany, you will encounter many of the following:

Abendmahlgästelisten - Communion attendance lists
Adressbücher - Address books
Almosenliste - Welfare lists
Aufgebote - Marriage banns
Armenregister - Poor registers
Auswanderungsakten - Emigration records
Auswanderungslisten - Emigration lists
Bestattungsbücher - Burial books
Bevölkerungslisten - Population lists
Bruderschaftsurkunde - Brotherhood records
Bürgerbücher - Citizen books
Bürgerlisten - Citizen lists
Dorfsippenbücher - Village lineage books
Eheregister - Marriage registers
Einnahmeregister-Receipt register
Einwohnerlisten - Inhabitant lists
Einwohnermelderegister - Inhabitant registration register
Familiengeschichten - Family histories
Familienregister - Family register
Geburtsbrief - Birth letter
Geburtsregister - Birth register
Geburtsschein - Birth certificate
Geburtsurkunden - Birth documents
Geburtszeugnis - Birth certificate
Gerichtsbücher - Court books
Gerichtsprotokolle - Court minutes
Geschlechterbücher - Family lineage books
Gildenbücher - Guild books
Glockenbücher - Bell tolling books
Grabregister - Grave register

Grundbücher - Land books
Hausbücher - House books (all owners of a house)
Hochschulmatrikeln - Institute enrollments
Innungsbücher - Guild books
Kirchen Zweitschriften - Church transcripts
Kirchenbücher - Church books
Konfirmationsregister - Confirmation register
Kopfzahlregister - Census registers
Lagerbücher - Military levy books
Lehrlingsbücher - Apprentice books
Leichenpredigten - Funeral sermons
Mannzahlregister - Census registers
Mitgliederlisten - Membership lists
Musterungslisten - Military lists
Nachlässe - Estates
Ortslexika - Gazetteers
Ortssippenbücher - Locality lineage books
Polizeiregister - Police register
Proklamationsbücher - Banns register
Ranglisten - Military lists
Seelenregister - Person register
Stadtchroniken - City chronicles
Stammrollen - Military rosters
Standesamtregister - Vital record office register
Sterberegister - Death registers
Steuerbücher - Tax books
Taufregister - Christening registers
Testamentsakten - Probate records
Todesregister - Death register
Totengeläutbücher - Death bell tolling books
Trauregister - Marriage register
Universitätsmatrikeln - University enrollments
Volkszahlungslisten - Census lists
Vormünderbücher - Guardian books
Zehntregister - Tithe register
Zeitungen - Newspapers
Zivilstandsregister - Vital records registers
Zunftbücher - Guild books

Here is a list of the same records with the English language titles given first:

Address books - Adressbücher
Apprentice books - Lehrlingsbücher
Banns register - Proklamationsbücher
Bell tolling books - Glockenbücher
Birth certificate - Geburtsschein
Birth certificate - Geburtszeugnis
Birth documents - Geburtsurkunde
Birth letter - Geburtsbrief
Birth register - Geburtsregister
Brotherhood records - Bruderschafturkunde
Burial books - Bestattungsbücher
Census lists - Volkszahlungslistlen
Census registers - Mannzahlregister
Census registers - Kopfzahlregister
Christening registers - Taufregister
Church books - Kirchenbücher
Church transcripts - Kirchen Zweitschriften
Citizen books - Bürgerbücher
Citizen lists - Bürgerlisten
City chronicles - Stadtchroniken
Communion attendance lists - Abendmahlgästelisten
Confirmation register - Konfirmationsregister
Court minutes - Gerichtsprotokolle
Court books - Gerichtsbücher
Death bell tolling books - Totengeläutbücher
Death registers - Sterberegister
Death register - Todesregister
Emigration lists - Auswanderungslisten
Emigration records - Auswanderungsakten
Estates - Nachlässe
Family histories - Familiengeschichten
Family lineage books - Geschlechterbücher
Family register - Familienregister
Funeral sermons - Leichenpredigten
Gazetteers - Ortslexika
Grave register - Grabregister
Guardian books - Vormünderbücher
Guild books - Gildenbücher
Guild books - Zunftbücher
Guild books - Innungsbücher

House books (all owners of a house) - Hausbücher
Inhabitant lists - Einwohnerlisten
Inhabitant registration register - Einwohnermelderegister
Institute enrollments - Hochschulmatrikeln
Land books - Grundbücher
Locality lineage books - Ortssippenbücher
Marriage banns - Aufgebote
Marriage register - Trauregister
Marriage registers - Eheregister
Membership lists - Mitgliederlisten
Military levy books - Lagerbücher
Military lists - Musterungslisten
Military lists - Ranglisten
Military rosters - Stammrollen
Newspapers - Zeitungen
Person register - Seelenregister
Police register - Polizeiregister
Poor registers - Armenregister
Population lists - Bevölkerungslisten
Probate records - Testamentsakten
Receipt register - Einnahmeregister
Tax books - Steuerbücher
Tithe register - Zehntregister
University enrollments - Universitätsmatrikeln
Village lineage books - Dorfsippenbücher
Vital record office register - Standesamtregister
Vital records registers - Zivilstandsregister
Welfare lists - Almosenlisten

Commonly used words which you will find describing German genealogical record sources are: books (Bücher), collections (Sammlungen), documents (Urkunden), histories (Geschichten), indexes and inventories (Verzeichnisse), lists (Listen), and registers (Register).

German genealogical research resembles American genealogical research in many ways, but the main difference is in the church records. Church records in Germany are relatively good, and as a result have the potential to take you back into the 1500s. This is because all religious groups in the Germanic territories were good record keepers. This makes the churches by far the best source of genealogical data, even though there have been considerable losses, especially for the 1500s and 1600s. Many of the major religious groups in America were not good record-keepers (Baptists, Methodists), and the frontier situation did not lend itself to the preservation of records. As a result, American church records are not nearly as pertinent as German, even though Germans who came to America often persisted in keeping good records. An interesting parallel between American and German records will help you understand the German situation. Before the American Declaration of Independence, there was no central government in America, only 13 colonies. Hence, there was no central place where records were kept. They were kept only in the governmental seats in the 13 colonies. Not until after 1775, when there was a unified government did overall federal centralized records begin to be kept. It was similar in Germany, with the unification not occurring there until 1871. Prior to that, the Germanic territory was occupied by numerous independent countries. Each kept its own records, and regulated that record-keeping differently. This tendency persisted long after 1871, even though some centralized records were gradually brought into being.

The oldest Germanic records which can be of some genealogical assistance are deed, land, guild, and apprentice records (from about 1250). Will and probate records, and citizen lists are the next oldest (from about 1350). House books, which chronicle the histories of houses, including information on owners and inhabitants, developed next (from about 1450). Then came local and regional censuses (about 1500), university registers (about 1530), and funeral sermons (about 1530). Church record books then developed into good sources (about 1550), and much later, duplicates of them began to be sent to central repositories (about 1800). Police registers recorded arrivals and departures, emigration records began to be kept, and city directories were starting to be compiled (all about 1830). Passenger lists then came to be kept (about 1850), and finally (about 1875) civil registers of vital data appeared throughout Germany, even though many states/provinces had started to keep them earlier (1798).

We will now turn to treatments of the various sorts of genealogical records available for doing ancestral research in Germany and former Germanic territories. The governmental and church vital records will be described first, then we will turn our attention to the auxiliary records, and finally to published and unpublished compilations.

2. Civil vital records	2. Standesamtsregister
2. Standesamtsregister	*2. Standesamtsregister*

Governmental registration of vital records (birth, marriage, death) began for all of Germany in 1876. Registration districts (Standesamtsbezirke) were set up, each of them covering a small area with several towns/villages in it. Parts of the Germanic territories had started civil (governmental) registration prior to this. In 1792, the Alsace-Lorraine (Elsass-Lothringen) began the practice, since it was a portion of France then. In 1798 government vital record keeping was initiated in Baden, Pfalz, and Rheinland. Then in 1803, it was inaugurated in Hessen and Hessen-Nassau, in 1808-9 in Westfalen, Hamburg, and Hannover, and in 1811 in Oldenburg. In some areas, including Westfalen and Hannover, civil registration lasted only a few years, and was resumed later. Anhalt began in 1850, Bremen in 1866, and in 1874 Brandenburg, Pommern, Ostpreussen, Westpreussen, Posen, Schlesien, and Schleswig-Holstein. They were joined in 1876 by Bayern, Braunschweig, Lippe, Mecklenburg, Sachsen, Thüringen, and Württenberg.

The events which were recorded in the civil vital record offices were births (Geburten), marriages (Heiraten), and deaths (Sterbefälle). The contents of the birth records are: the name of the new born, sex of the child, religion, the place of birth, the names of the parents, their residence, and their occupations. The contents of the marriage records are: information on the couple (names, religions, ages, occupations, birth places, and residences), information on the parents of the couple (names, ages, occupations, and residence), and information on witnesses (names, ages, occupations, and residences). The contents of the death records are: information on the deceased (name, place of death, date of death, religion, age, occupation, place of birth, last residence, cause of death), name of the surviving spouse, information on the parents of the deceased (names, occupations, and residence), and data on the person giving the information (name, occupation, residence). Before 1876, there are some variations in the contents of records from different states/provinces. The records are often indexed, and often on printed forms with filled-in blanks, which makes them easy to find and easy to read. Duplicates were usually sent to the state capital, so if the originals are missing, the duplicates may be sought.

The civil vital records were originally taken and kept in the registration offices (Standesämter), each of which covered a small area, but an area that could include several towns, villages, and/or communities. Larger cities/towns usually had their own Standesämter, but many smaller towns/villages/communities had the Standesamt in a nearby place. In order to locate the Standesamt for a given city/town/village, you can look into the following volume:

___E. Ütrecht, MEYERS ORTS- UND VERKEHRS-LEXIKON DES DEUTSCHEN REICHS, Bibliographisches Institut, Berlin, 1912. Available in large genealogical libraries and FHL (FHC).

Under the names of the places you will find the abbreviation StdA (Standesamt). If a comma or semicolon follows the abbreviation, there was a Standesamt in the place. If not, then the town following the abbreviation is the location of the pertinent Standesamt. There are three major places where the civil vital records can be found: (1) as original records in the Standesamt, (2) as original records or as duplicate records in archives, and (3) as microfilm copies in the FHL (available through FHC).

The first place to look for these civil registration records is in the locality section of the FHL (Family History Library) catalog. This will be found on computer and on microfiche at every FHC (Family History Center), one or more of which is probably close to you.

___Family History Library, FAMILY HISTORY LIBRARY CATALOG, LOCALITY SECTION, FHL, Salt Lake City, UT, latest edition.

In this catalog, the microfilmed civil registration records which the FHL holds (and lends through its FHC) will be found under listings such as the following:

___Germany, Bayern, Brücken - Civil Registration
___Germany, Preussen, Rheinland, Hochemmerich - Civil Registration

Note that you look under Germany, then under the state, (then under the principality if any), then under the city or town. When you discover records that you believe to apply to your ancestor, then have the FHC borrow them for you from the FHL.

If microfilms of the civil registrations for places now in Germany are not discovered in the FHL, then it is appropriate to write the pertinent civil registration office for the place you are interested in. The proper zip code for the city or town will be found in

___POSTLEITZAHLEN VERZEICHNIS, [ZIP CODE DIRECTORY], Bundesministerium für das Post- und Fernmeldewesen, Bonn, Deutschland, a recent issue.

This is a directory which gives zip codes for cities/towns/ villages/suburbs in Germany. A sample letter follows:

Standesamt
D-71111 Waldenbuch
Bundesrepublik Deutschland, GERMANY

Dear ladies and gentlemen:
My research indicates that my ancestor, Ludwig Adam SCHISSLER, came from your city/town about 1886 at an age of about 23. Please check your records for his birth and his marriage. I am also interested in the names, birth places and dates, marriage places and dates, death places and dates of his parents, and of his wife's parents.
If your records go back to include the next generation, I would also like to have data on them. Enclosed is $10 for return air mail postage and your fee.

> With friendly greetings,
> George K. Schweitzer
> 407 Ascot Court
> Knoxville, TN 37923-5807
> U.S.A.

The German translation is given below. You can make the proper substitutions to adapt the letter for your inquiries to civil registration offices.

Standesamt
D-71111 Waldenbuch
Bundesrepublik Deutschland, GERMANY

Sehr geehrte Damen und Herren!
Meine Nachforschungen weisen darauf hin, dass mein Vorfahr Ludwig Adam SCHISSLER Waldenbuch um 1886, d.h. im Alter von ungefähr 23 Jahren, verlassen hat. Falls Sie über Zivilstandsregister Ihrer Stadt oder Duplikate davon verfügen sollten, überprüfen Sie diese bitte hinsichtlich der Geburt und Heirat meines Vorfahrens. Ich bin ebenso an den Namen, Geburtsorten und -daten, dem Datum und Ort der Heirat, sowie den Sterbedaten und -orten seiner Eltern und der Eltern seiner Frau interessiert.
Falls Ihre Akten bis zur nächsten Generation zurückreichen sollten, würde ich auch gern Daten über diese erhalten.
Beigefügt sind 10 Dollar für Rückporto (Luftpost) und für Ihr Honorar.

Mit freundlichen Grüssen
George K. Schweitzer
407 Ascot Court
Knoxville, TN 37923-5807
U.S.A.

If inquiries at the local Standesamt do not prove successful, then you should contact the nearest large state archives. These archives will be listed later in Chapter 5. The following letter can be dispatched to them.

Hauptstaatsarchiv Stuttgart
Konrad-Adenauer-Strasse 4
D-70173 Stuttgart
Bundesrepublik Deutschland, GERMANY

Dear ladies and gentlemen:
My research indicates that my ancestor, Ludwig Adam SCHISSLER, came from Waldenbuch about 1886 at an age of about 23. If you have civil registration records or duplicates of them for this city/town, please check them for his birth and his marriage. I am also interested in the birth places and dates, marriage places and dates, death places and dates of his parents, and of his wife's parents.
If your records go on back to include the next generation, I would also like to have data on them. Enclosed is $10 for return air mail postage and your fee.

With friendly greetings,
George K. Schweitzer
407 Ascot Court
Knoxville, TN 37923-5807
U.S.A.

The German translation is given below. You can make the proper substitutions to adapt the letter for your purposes.

Hauptstaatsarchiv Stuttgart
Konrad-Adenauer-Strasse 4
D-70173 Stuttgart
Bundesrepublik Deutschland, GERMANY

Sehr geehrte Damen und Herren!
Meine Nachforschungen weisen darauf hin, dass mein Vorfahr Ludwig Adam SCHISSLER Ihre Stadt um 1886, d.h. im Alter von

ungefähr 23 Jahren, verlassen hat. Bitte überprüfen Sie Ihre Unterlagen hinsichtlich seines Geburtsdatums und seiner Heirat. Ich bin ebenso an den Namen, Geburtsorten und -daten, dem Datum und Ort der Heirat, sowie den Sterbedaten und -orten seiner Eltern und der Eltern seiner Frau interessiert.

Falls Ihre Akten bis zur nächsten Generation zurückreichen sollten, würde ich auch gern Daten über diese erhalten.

Beigefügt sind 10 Dollar für Rückporto (Luftpost) und für Ihr Honorar.

> Mit freundlichen Grüssen
> George K. Schweitzer
> 407 Ascot Court
> Knoxville, TN 37923-5807
> U.S.A.

If microfilms of the civil registrations for places now outside of Germany are not discovered in the FHL, then you need to locate them in Europe. The major territories which were once in Germany but are now outside Germany include Elsass Lothringen, Ostpreussen, Westpreussen, Pommern, Brandenburg-Ost, Schlesien, and Posen. The first effort that should be made is to contact several archives in Germany which hold a number of these records (or know where they are):

___GEHEIMES STAATSARCHIV PREUSSISCHER KULTURBESITZ, Archivstrasse 12, D-14195 Berlin, Bundesrepublik Deutschland, GERMANY.

___STANDESAMT I IN BERLIN (WEST), Rheinstrasse 54, D-12161 Berlin, Bundesrepublik Deutschland, GERMANY.

___STANDESAMT I IN BERLIN (EAST), Rückerstrasse 9, D-12163 Berlin, Bundesrepublik Deutschland, GERMANY.

___BUNDESARCHIV, ABT. OSTARCHIV, Am Wöllerhof 12, D-56068 Koblenz, Bundesrepublik Deutschland, GERMANY.

___JOHANN-GOTTFRIED-HERDER-INSTITUT, Gisonenweg 5, D-35037 Marburg/Lahn, Bundesrepublik Deutschland, GERMANY.

___ZENTRALSTELLE FÜR GENEALOGIE, Postfach 100947, D-04009 Leipzig, Bundesrepublik Deutschland, GERMANY.

The following letter of inquiry may be dispatched to them:

Geheimes Staatsarchiv Preussischer Kulturbesitz
Archivstrasse 12
D-14195 Berlin
Bundesrepublik Deutschland, GERMANY.

Dear Direktor:

My ancestor Heinrich Richard Kaiser came from Pyritz, Pomerania (now Pyrzyce in Poland), about 1891 at an age of about 14. I am seeking his birth record in civil registers and church books of Pyritz. If you have either or both, please look for him in them, and send me a copy of the data.

If the records also show his parents, grandparents, and other ancestors, I would like data on them as far back as your records go. Enclosed is $10 for return air mail postage and your fee.

With hearty greetings,
George K. Schweitzer
407 Ascot Court
Knoxville, TN 37923-5807
U.S.A.

The German translation is given below. You can make the proper substitutions to adapt the letter for your purposes.

Geheimes Staatsarchiv Preussischer Kulturbesitz
Archivstrasse 12
D-14195 Berlin
Bundesrepublik Deutschland, GERMANY.

Sehr geehrter Direktor!

Mein Vorfahr Heinrich Richard KAISER had Pyritz, Pommern (heute Pyrzyce in Polen) um 1891, d.h. im Alter von ungefähr 14 Jahren, verlassen. Ich suche nach seiner Geburtsurkunde in den Zivilstandsregistern und Kirchenbüchern von Pyritz. Falls Sie über eines dieser Dokumente oder sogar beide verfügen sollten, forschen Sie bitte darin nach ihm und senden mir eine Kopie seiner Daten.

Falls die Dokumente auch seine Eltern, Grosseltern und weitere Vorfahren aufführen, wäre ich auch an deren Daten, die soweit als möglich zurückreichen sollten, interessiert.

Beigefügt sind 10 Dollar für Rückporto (Luftpost) und für Ihr Honorar.

Mit herzlichen Grüssen
George K. Schweitzer
407 Ascot Court
Knoxville, TN 37923-5807
U.S.A.

Should the above contacts not locate the records for you, then an inquiry can be addressed to the relevant society among the German genealogical societies which specialize in the records of these areas:

___VEREIN FÜR FAMILIENFORSCHUNG IN OST- UND WEST-PREUSSEN, Dr. E. Heling, In de Krümm 10, D-21147 Hamburg, Bundesrepublik Deutschland, GERMANY.

___FORSCHUNGSSTELLE POMMERN DER AGoFF, Elmar Bruhn, Lohkamp 13, D-22117 Hamburg, Bundesrepublik Deutschland, GERMANY.

___FORSCHUNGSSTELLE OSTBRANDENBURG-NEUMARK DER AGoFF, Dipl.-Ing. Alfred Bley, Lützelsachsen, Im Langewann 65, D-69469 Weinheim, Bundesrepublik Deutschland, GERMANY.

___FORSCHUNGSSTELLE POSEN DER AGoFF, Otto Firchau, Nachtigallenweg 6, D-32105 Bad Salzuflen, Bundesrepublik Deutschland, GERMANY.

___FORSCHUNGSSTELLE OSTPREUSSEN DER AGoFF, Dr. Wolf Konietzko, Eichstrasse 6, D-25336 Elmshorn, Bundesrepublik Deutschland, GERMANY.

___FORSCHUNGSSTELLE WESTPREUSSEN-DANZIG DER AGoFF, Dr. Wolf Konietzko, Eichstrasse 6, D-25336 Elmshorn, Bundesrepublik Deutschland, GERMANY.

___FORSCHUNGSSTELLE SCHLESIEN DER AGoFF, Kraft Neithard von Stein, Talstrasse 3, D-31707 Bad Eilsen, Bundesrepublik Deutschland, GERMANY.

___BUND DER VERTRIEBENEN, Kreisverband Braunschweig, Arbeitskreis Genealogie, Auskunftstelle, Gutenbergstrasse 12b, W-3300 Braunschweig, Bundesrepublik Deutschland, GERMANY.

The following letter may be sent to the appropriate one of the above societies:

Forschungsstelle Pommern der AGoFF
Herr Elmar Bruhn
Lohkamp 12
D-22117 Hamburg
Bundesrepublik Deutschland, GERMANY

Dear Dr. Bruhn:

My ancestor Heinrich Richard Kaiser came from Pyritz, Pomerania (now Pyrzyce in Poland), about 1891 at an age of about 14. I am seeking the civil registers and church books of Pyritz in an effort to find his birth record and the birth, marriage, and death records of his ancestors.

If you know where the records are, or if you know of substitute records, please inform me. Enclosed is $3 for return air mail postage.
With friendly greetings,
George K. Schweitzer
407 Ascot Court
Knoxville, TN 37923-5807
U.S.A.

The German translation is given below. You can make the proper substitutions to adapt the letter for your purposes.

Forschungsstelle Pommern der AGoFF
Herr Elmar Bruhn
Lohkamp 12
D-22117 Hamburg
Bundesrepublik Deutschland, GERMANY

Sehr geehrter Dr. Bruhn!
Mein Vorfahr Heinrich Richard KAISER hat Pyritz, Pommern (heute Pyrzyce in Polen), um 1891, d.h. im Alter von ungefähr 14 Jahren, verlassen. Ich suche die Zivilstandsregister und Kirchenbücher von Pyritz, um seine Geburtsurkunde sowie die Geburts-, Heirats-, und Sterbeurkunden seiner Vorfahren zu finden.
Falls Sie wissen, wo sich diese Akten befinden, oder wenn Sie von anderen Dokumenten wissen, die ich an deren Stelle nutzen könnte, informieren Sie mich bitte.
Beigefügt sind 3 Dollar für Rückporto (Luftpost).
Mit herzlichen Grüssen
George K. Schweitzer
407 Ascot Court
Knoxville, TN 37923-5807
U.S.A.

If you have still not located the civil registers for the city/town/village of your progenitor, then you can try contacting state archives in the countries in which your ancestor's place now is. These archives for the territories we have been discussing are:
___(East Prussia, Ostpreussen) for Allenstein/Olsztyn, Wojewódzkie Archiwum Pánstwowe w Olsztynie Zamek, Zamkowa 2, PL-10074 Olsztyn, Polska, POLAND.
___(West Prussia, Westpreussen) Bromberg/Bydgoszcz, Wojewódzkie Archiwum Pánstwowe w Bydgoszczy, ul. Dworcowa 65, PL-83009

Bydgoszcz, Polska, POLAND. For Danzig/Gdansk, Wojewódzkie Archiwum Pánstwowe w Gdansku, ul. Waly Piastowski 5, PL-80855 Gdansk, Poland, POLAND. For Thorn/Torun, Wojewódzkie Archiwum Pánstwowe w Toruniu, pl. Rapackiego 4, PL-87100 Torun, Polska, POLAND.

__(Pomerania, Pommern) For Köslin/Koszalin, Wojewódzkie Archiwum Pánstwowe w Koszalinie, ul. Zwyciestwa 117, skrytka pocztowa, PL-75950 Koszalin, Polska, POLAND. For Stettin/ Szczecin, Wojewódzkie Archiwum Pánstwowe w Szczecinie, ul. sw. Wojciecha 13, PL-70410 Szczecin, Polska, POLAND.

__(East Brandenburg, Brandenburg-Ost) For Frankfurt/Oder, Landsberg/ Warthe, Lebus, Meseritz, Schwerin/Warthe and Weststernberg, Wojewódzkie Archiwum Pánstwowe, Gorzow Wielkopolski, Polska, POLAND. For Königsberg, Wojewódzkie Archiwum Pánstwowe, Szczecin, Polska, POLAND. For Forst/Lausatia, Crossen/Oder, Guben, Oststernberg, Sorau/Lansatia, Zuellichau-Schwiebus, Wojewódzkie Archiwum Pánstwowe, Stary Kiselin 31, PL-66002 Zielona Gora, Polska, POLAND.

__(Silesia, Schlesien) For Breslau/Wroclaw, Archiwum Pánstwowe Miasto Wroclawia i Wojewodztwo Wroclawskiego, ul. Pomorska 2, PL-50215 Wroclaw, Polska, POLAND. For Gruenberg/Zielona Gora, Wojewódzkie Archiwum Pánstwowe w Zielonej Gorze, Stary Kiselin 31, PL-66002 Zielona Gora, Polska, POLAND. For Oppeln/Opole, Wojewódzkie Archiwum Pánstwowe w Opolu, ul. Zamkowa 2, PL-45016 Opole, Polska, POLAND. For Kattowitz/Katowice, Wojewódzkie Archiwum Pánstwowe w Katowicach, ul. Jagiellonska 25, PL-40032 Katowice, Polska, POLAND.

__(Posen, Poznan) Archiwum Panstwowe, ul Dluga 7, PL-00950 Warszawa, Polska, POLAND. Wojewódzkie Archiwum Pánstwowe, Bydgoszcz, Polska, POLAND. Archiwum Panstwowe Torun, pl. Rapackiego, PL-87100 Torun, Polska, POLAND. Archiwum Pánstwowe Miasta Poznanina i Wojewodztwa Poznanskiego, ul. 23 Lutego 41/43, PL-60967 Poznan, Polska, POLAND.

__(Alsace, Elsass) Archives departmentales du Bas-Rhin, 5-9, rue Fischart, F-67000 Strasbourg, FRANCE. Archives departmentales du Haut-Rhin, Cité administrative, Rue Fleischauer, F-68000 Colmar, FRANCE.

__(Lorraine, Lothringen) Archives departmentales de la Moselle, Prefecture de la Moselle, Hotel du Departement, 9 Place de la Prefecture, F-57036 Metz, FRANCE. Archives departementales de Meurthe-et-Moselle, 3 rue de la Monnaie, F-54000 Nancy, FRANCE.

There is a very useful guide to the contents of the Polish archives cited above.

__KATALOG INVENTARZY ARCHIWALNYCH (CATALOG OF INVENTORIES OF ARCHIVES), Pestkowska and Stebelska, Warsaw, Poland, 1971.

Appropriate letters for inquiries follow. They can be modified for your own use by substitutions. Please note that the letters have been translated into Polish and French, the latter for Alsace (Elsass) and Lorraine (Lothringen).

Wojewodzkie Archiwum Pánstwowe
w Szczecinie
ul. sw. Wojciecha 13
PL-71410 Szezecin
Polska, POLAND

Dear Sirs:
My ancestor Heinrich Richard KAISER came from Pyritz, Pomerania (now Pyrzyce in Poland), about 1891 at an age of about 14. I am seeking the civil registers and church books of Pyritz in an effort to find his birth record and the birth, marriage, and death records of his ancestors.
If you can supply the information, or if you know where the records are, or if you know of substitute records, please inform me. Enclosed is $3 for return air mail postage.

> With regards,
> George K. Schweitzer
> 407 Ascot Court
> Knoxville, TN 37923-5807
> U.S.A.

Wojewódzkie Archiwum Pastwowe
w Szczecinie
ul. Św. Wojciecha 13
PL-71410 Szezecin
SZCZECIN, POLAND

Szanowni Pastwo,
Mój przodek Heinrich Richard Kaiser przybyl do U.S.A. z Pyrzyc na Pomorzu okoo roku 1891 mając ok 14 lat. Poszukuje rejestrów cywilnych i ksiag koscielnych, w których móglbym znalezc jego akt urodzenia oraz akty urodzenia, slubów i zgonów jego przodków.

Jezeli wiedza Panstwo, gdzie takie zapisy sa, lub jak moge uzyskac ich odpisy, uprzejmie prosze o informacje. Zalaczam $3 na pokrycie kosztów poczty lotniczej.

Z powazaniem
George K. Schweitzer
407 Ascot Court
Knoxville, TN 37923-5807
U.S.A.

Archives départmentales du Haut-Rhin
Cité administrative
Rue Fleischauer
F-68000 Colmar, FRANCE

Dear Sirs:

My ancestor Emile Jacques FALTER came from Wintzenheim, Alsace (now in Haut-Rhine, France), about 1891 at an age of about 14. I am seeking the civil registers and church books of Wintzenheim in an effort to find his birth record and the birth, marriage, and death records of his ancestors.

If you can supply the information, or if you know where the records are, or if you know of substitute records, please inform me. Enclosed is $3 for return air mail postage.

With my best wishes,
George K. Schweitzer
407 Ascot Court
Knoxville, TN 37923-5807
U. S. A.

Archives départmentales du Haut-Rhin
Cité adminstrative
Rue Fleischauer
F-68000 Colmar, FRANCE

Messieurs:

Mon ancêtre Emile Jacques Falter est venu de Wintzenheim, Alsace (dan le Haut-Rhin), aux alentours de 1891 ayant environ 14 ans. Je cherche les actes publics et documents ecclésiastiques de Wintzenheim afin de trouver des documents officiels liés a sa naissance et aux naissances, marriages, et décès des ses ancêtres.

Si vous pouvez fournir cette information, ou si vous savez où je pourrai trouver de tels documents, ou si vous connaissez d'autres documents qui pourraient me servir, je vous serais reconnaissant de m'en infromer. Vous trouverez $3 ci-inclus pour défrayer le coût de l'affranchissement (par avion) de retour.

Veuillez agreer, messieurs, l'expression de mes sentiments distingués,
George K. Schweitzer
407 Ascot Court
Knoxville, TN 37923-5807
Les États-Unis, U. S. A.

If by now, the civil vital records of your forebear's place have not been found, a further step needs to be taken. This is to make direct contact with the city/town/village. One way of doing this in Poland is to write in English to the Directorate of State Archives. You should enclose $3 for return air mail postage. They will forward your request to the pertinent civil registration office. The address is:
___Naczelna Dyrekcja Archiwów Pánstwowych, Miodowa 10, skr. poczt. 1005, 00950 Warszawa, Polska, POLAND.
Or you may write to the civil registration office directly, but this communication should be in Polish. A sample English letter and a Polish translation appear below. There is also a sample French letter. You can use them after making appropriate data substitutions.

Urzad Stanu Cywilnego
Pyrzyce, Pyrzyce
Polska, POLAND

Dear Sir:
My ancestor Heinrich Richard KAISER came from Pyritz, Pomerania (now Pyrzyce in Poland), about 1891 at an age of about 14. I am seeking the civil registers and church books of Pyritz in an effort to find his birth record and the birth, marriage, and death records of his ancestors.

If you can supply the information, or if you know where the records are, or if you know of substitute records, please inform me. Enclosed is $3 for return air mail postage.

With regards,
George K. Schweitzer
407 Ascot Court
Knoxville, TN 37923-5807
U.S.A.

Urzad Stanu Cywilnego
Pyrzyce, Pyrzyce
Polska, POLAND

Szanowny Panie:
   Mój przodek Heinrich Richard Kaiser przybyl do U.S.A. z Pyrzyc na
Pomorzu okoo roku 1891 mając ok 14 lat. Poszukuje rejestrów cywilnych i
ksiag koscielnych, w których móglbym znalezc jego akt urodzenia oraz akty
urodzenia, slubów i zgonów jego przodków.
   Jeżeli wiedza Panstwo, gdzie takie zapisy sa, lub jak moge uzyskac
ich odpisy, uprzejmie prosze o informacje.   Zalaczam $3 na pokrycie
kosztów poczty lotniczej.

                              Z powazaniem
                              George K. Schweitzer
                              407 Ascot Court
                              Knoxville, TN 37923-5807
                              U.S.A.

État civil
F-68000 Colmar-Wintzenheim
FRANCE

Dear Sirs:
   My ancestor Emile Jacques Falter came from Wintzenheim, Alsace
(now in Haut-Rhine, France), about 1891 at an age of about 14.   I am
seeking the civil registers and church books of Wintzenheim in an effort to
find his birth record and the birth, marriage, and death records of his ancestors.
   If you can supply the information, or if you know where the records
are, or if you know of substitute records, please inform me.   Enclosed is $3
for return air mail postage.

                              With my best wishes,
                              George K. Schweitzer
                              407 Ascot Court
                              Knoxville, TN 37923-5807
                              U.S.A.

État civil
F-68000 Colmar-Wintzenheim
FRANCE

Messieurs:

Mon ancêtre Emile Jacques Falter est venu de Wintzenheim, Alsace (dan le Haut-Rhin), aux alentours de 1891 ayant environ 14 ans. Je cherche les actes publics et documents ecclésiastiques de Wintzenheim afin de trouver des documents officiels liés a sa naissance et aux naissances, marriages, et décès des ses ancêtres.

Si vous pouvez fournir cette information, ou si vous savez où je pourrai trouver de tels documents, ou si vous connaissez d'autres documents qui pourraient me servir, je vous serais reconnaissant de m'en infromer.   Vour trouverez $3 ci-inclus pour défrayer le coût de l'affranchissement (par avion) de retour.

Veuillez agreer, messieurs, l'expression de mes sentiments distingués,

George K. Schweitzer

407 Ascot Court

Knoxville, TN 37923-5807

Les États-Unis, U. S. A.

In addition to the lost territories, there were many German settlements in other eastern and southeastern European areas. These areas were never a part of the 1871 Germany, but were under other governments.   In general, the Germans in these settlements maintained their culture, language, churches, and contacts with Germany. In other words, they kept their distinctiveness from the peoples around them. The major areas of this sort were Central Poland, Volhynia(Poland), Galicia(Poland), Lithuania, Latvia, Estonia, eastern and southeastern Russia, Bohemia(Czechoslovakia), Moravia(Czechoslovakia), Austrian Silesia, Bukovina(Russia-Romania), Dobrudscha(Bulgaria-Romania), Slovakia(Czechoslovakia), western Hungary, Slovenia(Yugoslavia), Transylvania(Romania), Bessarabia(Russia). southwest Hungary, and the Danube-Swabian colonies(Romania, Yugoslavia, and Hungary along the Danube River). For instructions regarding location of the civil register and church records of these areas, see:

___J. O. R. Nuthack and A. Goertz, GENEALOGICAL GUIDE TO GERMAN ANCESTORS FROM EASTERN(MOST) GERMANY AND EASTERN EUROPE, Verlag Degener, Neustadt/Aisch, Deutschland, 1984.

3. Church vital records	3. Kirchliche Lebensdokumente

3. Kirchliche Lebensdokumente

The most valuable genealogical records for the Germanic areas of Europe are church records of baptisms (and/or births), marriages, and burials (and/or deaths). They present the genealogical researcher with the high probability that he/she can trace ancestors back to 1650 and with the possibility of going on back to 1550. The major denominations were the Catholic (katholische), Lutheran (lutherische), and the Reform (reform-ierte), with the latter two merging in 1817 to form the Evangelical (evangelische). As you will recall, Catholics predominate in southern and southwestern Germany, and Evangelicals (Lutheran-Evangelical) are in a majority elsewhere. In large cities, there will be numerous churches, each serving only a portion of the city. In towns and large villages, one church usually served the entire area, often including some small places. In rural areas, one church often served many villages and smaller settlements. Since the boundaries of these church districts sometimes changed, and since even the denomination could change, you need to be alert to such events.

The Protestant Reformation started in 1517, resulted in the split up of the Catholic Church in the Germanic area, and was a major factor in the origins of church record keeping. Lutheran records of baptisms, marriages, and burials began about 1540, and in 1563 Catholic parishes were ordered to keep baptism and marriage records, in 1614 Catholic priests were instructed to keep death records, and Reformed records of the three types began about 1650. The earliest records occurred in the west, with records starting later the farther one goes east. Early Catholic records were in Latin, Lutheran records in mixed German-Latin or German, and Reformed records in mixed German-Latin or German. The German language was written in Gothic script, this persisting until about 1920. Sometimes, especially early on, all three types of records were kept in one book, but later on, the usual pattern is for them to be kept in separate books. Many losses of records occurred during the Thirty Years War (1618-1648). Duplicates of the records began to be filed in regional church offices at various times (1750-1820) in different areas. And in the early 1800s, governments in various Germanic states made increased use of church records to keep track of citizens and to tax them, and entered actively into the processes of collection of the data. The church records may be found in numerous places: (1) as originals in the individual churches (parishes), (2) as originals or duplicates or copies in regional church archives, (3) as microfilm copies in the FHL, and (4) as published extracts in books and genealogical periodicals.

The baptism records (Taufbücher, Taufregister, Taufprotokolle) at their best contain the following information: name of child, baptismal date, birth date, indication of legitimacy, name of father, occupation of father, name of mother, place, sponsors or godparents. Some of these items may not be given in the early records. Careful attention must be given to the date or dates to be sure and identify them as baptismal or birth dates. Children were usually baptized within a few days of birth if nothing hindered their being brought to the church. The marriage records (Eheregister, Trauregister) at their best give these data: date of marriage, date of the banns, name of groom, name of his father, his father's occupation, his father's residence, whether his father is living or not, name of bride, name of father of bride or of her late husband if she is a widow, occupation of her father or late husband, residence of her father or late husband, whether her father is living or not. Again, early records may not contain all of these data. The burial or death records (Todesregister, Sterberegister, Begräbnisregister, Beerdigungregister, Bestattungsbücher, Totenbücher) at their best consist of: name of deceased, date of burial, date of death, place of burial, place of death, age, date of birth, name of surviving spouse, occupation of deceased. Ages may be given in years, in years/months, in years/weeks, or in years/months/days. Care must be exercised with regard to the ages since they were often based on oral information and approximations. Attention must be paid to the dates so that you are clear as to whether they are burial dates or death dates. Sometimes a burial or death note is attached to the birth record if the events occurred in the same parish.

Once you know the exact place of your forebear's origin, then it is necessary to find out if there is a parish church located there, or if not, to find which parish church had jurisdiction over the place. This topic was treated in Chapter 3, section 15, but we will review the procedure here. Your initial step is to look for the place in:

E. Utrecht, MEYERS ORTS- UND VERKEHRS-LEXIKON DES DEUTSCHEN REICHS [MEYERS GAZETTEER AND TRANSPORTATION LEXICON], Bibliographisches Institut, Leipzig, Deutschland, 1912.

If the place had a parish church or churches, this will be indicated by the abbreviations ev. Pfk. (for a Lutheran parish), kath. Pfk (for a Catholic parish), reform. Pfk. (for a Reformed parish), Syn. (for a Jewish synagogue). Other religious faiths are generally spelled out: Baptisten (Baptist), Hugenotten (Huguenots), Mennoniten (Mennonites), Brüdergemeine (Moravians), Methoden (Methodists). If it turns out that your progenitor's place was so small that it had no parish church, you will need to consult one of the reference works which lists places in a state or duchy or province and indicates the parishes which serve them. These works were listed in Chapter 3, section 15. They and the MEYERS GAZETTEER are available as microfilms from the FHL through its many FHC.

The first place to seek the parish registers (baptism, marriage, burial) is in the locality section of the FHL catalog. This will be found on computer and on microfiche at every FHC, one or more of which is probably close to you.

___Family History Library, FAMILY HISTORY LIBRARY CATALOG, LOCALITY SECTION, FHL, Salt Lake City, UT, latest edition.

In this catalog, the microfilmed church registers which the FHL holds (and lends through its FHC) will be found under listings such as the following:

___Germany, Baden, Gremmelsbach - Church Records

___Germany, Preussen, Posen, Gross Kotten - Church Records

Note that you look under Germany, then under the state, (then under the province, if any), then under the city or town. When you discover microfilmed records that you believe apply to your ancestor, then have the FHC borrow them for you from the FHL. Help for you with reference to reading the Old German script will be given in a later chapter.

If microfilms of the church records for places now in Germany are not discovered in the FHL, then it is appropriate to write the pertinent church for the place you are interested in. The proper zip code for the city or town will be found in

___POSTLEITZAHLENVERZEICHNIS [ZIP CODE DIRECTORY], Bundesministerium für das Post- und Fernmeldewesen, Bonn, Deutschland, a recent issue.

This is a directory which gives zip codes for cities/towns/ villages/suburbs in Germany. A sample letter follows:

The Catholic Church Office
D-76275 Ettlingen
Bundesrepublik Deutschland
GERMANY

The Protestant Church Office
Grünwettersbach
D-76228 Karlsruhe
Bundesrepublik Deutschland
GERMANY

Very honored Mr. Pastor:

My ancestor Andreas Jacob HEINOLD came from your city/town to the US about 1835 at the age of about 25. Please check your records for his birth and his marriage. I am also interested in the names, birth places and dates, marriage places and dates, death places and dates of his parents, and of his wife's parents.

If your records go on back to include further generations, I would also like to have data on them. Enclosed is $10 for return air mail postage and a donation. If a larger donation would be appropriate, please inform me.

> With friendly greetings,
> George K. Schweitzer
> 407 Ascot Court
> Knoxville, TN 37923-5807
> U.S.A.

Das Katholische Pfarramt
D-76275 Ettlingen
Bundesrepublik Deutschland
GERMANY

Das evangelische Pfarramt
Grünwettersbach
D-76228 Karlsruhe
Bundesrepublik Deutschland
GERMANY

Sehr geehrter Herr Pfarrer!

Mein Vorfahr Andreas Jacob HEINOLD hat Ihre Stadt um 1835, d. h. im Alter von ungefähr 25 Jahren, verlassen. Bitte überprüfen Sie Ihre Unterlagen hinsichlich seines Geburtsdatum und seiner Heirat. Ich bin ebenso an den Namen, Geburtsorten und -daten, dem Daten und Ort der Heirat, sowie den Sterbedaten und -orten seiner Eltern und der Eltern seiner Frau interessiert.

Falls Ihre Akten bis zu weiteren Generationen zurückreichen sollten, würde ich auch gern Daten über diese erhalten. Beigefügt sind $10 für Rückporto (Luftpost) und eine Spende. Falls eine grössere Spende angemessener ist, informieren Sie mich bitte.

> Mit freundlichen Grüssen
> George K. Schweitzer
> 407 Ascot Court
> Knoxville, TN 37923-5807
> U.S.A.

If inquiries at the local parish do not prove successful, then you should contact the nearest regional church archives. Those for Protestant churches are as follows:

___(For Mecklenburg-Vorpommern, Berlin, Brandenburg, Sachsen-Anhalt, Thüringen, and Sachsen) Zentralstelle für Genealogie, Postfach 100947, D-04009 Leipzig, Bundesrepublik Deutschland, GERMANY.

___(For Anhalt) Evangelische Landeskirche Anhalts, OttD-Grotewohl-Strasse 22, D-06842 Dessau, Bundesrepublik Deutschland, GERMANY.

___(For Baden) Evangelischer Oberkirchenrat, Landeskirchliches Archiv, Blumenstrasse 1, D-76133 Karlsruhe, Bundesrepublik Deutschland, GERMANY; Generallandesarchiv, Nördliche Hilda-Promenade, D-76133 Karlsruhe, Bundesrepublik Deutschland, GERMANY.

___(For Bayern) Evangelisch-Lutherischer Landeskirchenrat, Meiserstrasse 13, D-80333 Muenchen/Munich 2, Bundesrepublik Deutschland, GERMANY; Evangelisch-Lutherische Kirche, Landeskirchliches Archiv, Veilhofstrasse 28, D-90489 Nürnberg/Nuremberg, Bundesrepublik Deutschland, GERMANY; Evangelische-Lutherische Kirche, Landeskirchliches Archiv, Aussenstelle Kirchenbucharchiv, Am Oelberg 2, D-93047 Regensburg, Bundesrepublik Deutschland, GERMANY; Evangelisch-Lutherisches Pfarrarchiv, Pfarrergasse 5, D-93047 Regensburg, Bundesrepublik Deutschland, GERMANY; Evangelisches Kirchenbuchamt, Im Annahof 4, D-86150 Augsburg, Bundesrepublik Deutschland, GERMANY.

___(For Berlin) Archiv des Evangelischen Konsistoriums Berlin-Brandenburg, Bachstrasse 1-2, D-10555 Berlin, Bundesrepublik Deutschland, GERMANY; Evangelisches Zentralarchiv in Berlin, Kirchenbuchstelle, Jebensstrasse 3, D-10623 Berlin (Charlottenburg), Bundesrepublik Deutschland, GERMANY.

___(For Brandenburg) Archiv des Evangelischen Konsistoriums Berlin-Brandenburg, Bachstrasse 1-2, D-10555 Berlin, Bundesrepublik Deutschland, GERMANY; Evangelisches Zentralarchiv in Berlin, Kirchenbuchstelle, Jebensstrasse 3, D-10623 Berlin (Charlottenburg), Bundesrepublik Deutschland, GERMANY; Evangelische Kirche Berlin-Brandenburg, Neue Gruenstrasse 19, D-10179 Berlin, Bundesrepublik Deutschland, GERMANY.

___(For Braunschweig) Braunschweigische Evangelisch-lutherische Landeskirche, Landeskirchliches Archiv, Alter Zeughof 1, D-38100 Wolfenbüttel, Bundesrepublik Deutschland, GERMANY; Stadtkirchenamt, Schützenstrasse 23, D-38100 Braunschweig/Brunswick, Bundesrepublik Deutschland, GERMANY; Evangelisch-Lutherisches Kirchenverband Wolfenbüttel, Kirchenverbandsamt, Neuer Weg 1, D-38100 Wolfenbüttel, Bundesrepublik Deutschland, GERMANY (only for city of Wolfenbüttel).

___(For Bremen) Staatsarchiv, Präsident-Kennedy-Platz 2, D-28203 Bremen, Bundesrepublik Deutschland, GERMANY.

___(For Hamburg) Evangelisch-lutherische Kirche im Hamburgischen Staat, Archiv, Neue Burg 11, D-20354 Hamburg, Bundesrepublik Deutschland, GERMANY; Staatsarchiv Hamburg, ABC-Strasse 19, Eingang A, D-20354 Hamburg, Bundesrepublik Deutschland, GERMANY.

___(For Hannover) Kirchenbuchamt der Evangelisch-lutherischen Landeskirche Hannovers, Landeskirchliches Archiv, Am Steinbruch 14, D-30037 Hannover, Bundesrepublik Deutschland, GERMANY; Evangelisch-lutherische Stadtkirchenverband Hannover, Stadtkirchenkanzlei, Kirchenbuchamt, Arnswaldtstrasse 28, D-30057 Hannover, Bundesrepublik Deutschland, GERMANY (only for city of Hannover).

___(For Hessen) Evangelische Kirche von Kurhessen-Waldeck, Archiv des Lanmdeskirchenamts, D-34131 Kassel-Wilhelmshöher, Bundesrepublik Deutschland, GERMANY; Evangelische Kirche in Hessen und Nassau, Zentralarchiv, Ahastrasse 5a, D-64285 Darmstadt, Bundesrepublik Deutschland, GERMANY; Staatsarchiv für Hessen Darmstadt, Karolinenplatz 3, D-64289 Darmstadt, Bundesrepublik Deutschland, GERMANY; Staatsarchiv für Hessen-Kassel, Friedrichsplatz 15, D-35037 Marburg/Lahn, Bundesrepublik Deutschland, GERMANY; Evangelischer Gemeinde- und Dekanatsverband Darmstadt, Kirchengemeindeamt, Kiesstrasse 14, D-64283 Darmstadt, Bundesrepublik Deutschland, GERMANY.

___(For Lippe) Lippisches Landeskirchenamt, Archiv der Lippischen Landeskirche, Leopoldstrasse 12, D-32756 Detmold, Bundesrepublik Deutschland, GERMANY; Personenstandsarchiv, Staatsarchiv, Willi-Hofmann-Strasse 2, D-32756 Detmold, Bundesrepublik Deutschland, GERMANY.

___(For Mecklenburg) Archiv der Landessuperintendentur der Evangelischen-Lutherischen Landeskirche Mecklenburgs, Strasse des Friedens 50, D-19370 Parchim, Bundesrepublik Deutschland, GERMANY; Domarchiv, Domplatz, Domhof 35, D-23909 Ratzeburg, Bundesrepublik Deutschland, GERMANY; Evangelisches Kirchenarchiv, Münzstrasse 8, D-19010 Schwerin, Bundesrepublik Deutschland, GERMANY.

___(For Niedersachsen, see also Braunschweig, Hannover, Lippe, Oldenburg, Ostfriesland and Westphalia) Staatsarchiv für Osnabrück, Schlossstrasse 29, D-49074 Osnabrück, Bundesrepublik Deutschland, GERMANY; Niedersächisches Staatsarchiv, Am Sande 4 C, D-21682 Stade, Bundesrepublik Deutschland, GERMANY; Evangelische-Lutherischer Gesamtverband Osnabrück, Gemeindeamt, Heger-Tor-Wall 9, D-49008 Osnabrück, Bundesrepublik Deutschland, GERMANY.

___(For Oldenburg) Staatsarchiv für Oldenburg, Damm 43, D-26135 Oldenburg, Bundesrepublik Deutschland, GERMANY.

___(For Pfalz) Evangelischen Kirche der Pfalz, Landeskirchenrat (Protestantische Landeskirche), Domplatz 5, D-67327 Speyer, Bundesrepublik Deutschland, GERMANY; Zentralarchiv der Evangelischen Kirche der Pfalz, Kirchenbuchstelle Koblenz, Karmeliterstrasse 1-3, D-56068 Koblenz, Bundesrepublik Deutschland, GERMANY.

___(For Pommern) Evangelisches Zentralarchiv in Berlin, Kirchenbuchstelle, Jebensstrasse 3, D-10623 Berlin (Charlottenburg), Bundesrepublik Deutschland, GERMANY; Evangelisch-lutherische Kirche im Hamburgischen Staat, Archiv, Neue Burg 1, D-20457 Hamburg, Bundesrepublik Deutschland, GERMANY.

___(For Rheinland) Archiv der Evangelischen Kirche im Rheinland, Evangelische Archivstelle Koblenz, Karmeliterstrasse 1-3, D-56068 Koblenz, Bundesrepublik Deutschland, GERMANY; Archiv der Evangelischen Kirche im Rheinland, Hans-Böckler-Strasse 7, D-40418 Düsseldorf, Bundesrepublik Deutschland, GERMANY; Personenstandsarchiv Brühl, Schlossstrasse 12, D-50321 Brühl, Bundesrepublik Deutschland, GERMANY.

___(For Saarland) Protestantisches Landeskirchenarchiv, Grosse Himmelsgasse 6, D-67346 Speyer, Bundesrepublik Deutschland, GERMANY; Archiv der Evangelischen Kirche im Rheinland, Archivstelle Koblenz, Karmeliterstrasse 1-3, D-56068 Koblenz, Bundesrepublik Deutschland, GERMANY.

___(For Sachsen) Evangelisch-Lutherische Landeskirche Sachsens, Landeskirchenarchiv, Lukasstrasse 6, D-01069 Dresden, Bundesrepublik Deutschland, GERMANY; Evangelisches Konsistorium des Görlitzer Kirchengebietes, Archiv der Evangelischen Kirchen von Schlesien, Berliner Strasse 62, D-02826 Görlitz, Bundesrepublik Deutschland, GERMANY; Archiv der Evangelischen Kirche der Kirchenprovinz Sachsen, Am Dom 2, D-39014 Magdeburg, Bundesrepublik Deutschland, GERMANY; Archiv und Bibliothek des Evangelischen Ministeriums, Comthurgasse 8, D-99084 Erfurt, Bundesrepublik Deutschland, GERMANY; Kirchenbuchamt des Evangelisch-Lutherischen Kirchengemeindeverbands Leipzig, Burgstrasse 1-5-Hof-3. Stock, D04109 Leipzig, Bundesrepublik Deutschland, GERMANY (only for city of Leipzig).

___(For Schleswig-Holstein) Evangelisch-lutherische Landeskirche Schleswig-Holsteins, Dänische Strasse 27-35, D-24033 Kiel, Bundesrepublik Deutschland, GERMANY; The records in Schleswig-Holstein are in 27 small regional archives. See E. Thode, ADDRESS BOOK FOR GERMIC GENEALOGY, Genealogical Publishing Co., Baltimmore, MD, latest edition, for addresses.

___(For Thüringen) Archiv des Landeskirchenrats der Evangelisch-Lutherischen Kirche in Thüringen, Dr.-Moritz-Mitzenheim-Strasse 2, D-99187 Eisenach, Bundesrepublik Deutschland, GERMANY.

___(For Westfalen, also see Lippe and Rheinland) Evangelische Kirche von Westfalen, Landeskirchenarchiv, Alstädter Kirchplatz 4, D-33602 Bielefeld 11, Bundesrepublik Deutschland, GERMANY; Personenstandsarchiv Detmold, Willi-Hofmann-Strasse 2, D-32756 Detmold, Bundesrepublik Deutschland, GERMANY.

___(For Württenberg) Evangelische Landeskirche in Württemberg, Landeskirchliches Archiv, Gänsheidestrasse 4, D-70184 Stuttgart, Bundesrepublik Deutschland, GERMANY; Evangelische Landeskirche in Württemberg, Lauterbadstrasse 31, D-72250 Freudenstadt, Bundesrepublik Deutschland, GERMANY; Evangelisches Kirchenregisteramt Stuttgart, Hospitalhof, Gymnasiumstrasse 36, D-70174 Stuttgart, Bundesrepublik Deutschland, GERMANY.

The regional church archives for Catholic churches are:

___(For inquiring about the location of church records in all of Germany) Katholisches Kirchenbuchamt des Verbandes der Dioezesen Deutschlands München, Theatinerstrasse 31/IX, D-80333 München, Bundesrepublik Deutschland, GERMANY.

___(For Baden) Badisches Generallandesarchiv, Nördliche Hilda-Promenade 2, D-77133 Karlsruhe, Bundesrepublik Deutschland, GERMANY; Erzbistumarchiv, Herrenstrasse 35, Eingang Schoferstrasse, D-79098 Freiburg in Breisgau, Bundesrepublik Deutschland, GERMANY.

___(For Bayern) Archiv des Bistums Augsburg, Hafnerberg 2/II, D-86152 Augsburg 11, Bundesrepublik Deutschland, GERMANY; Erzbistumsarchiv, Domplatz 5, D-96049 Bamberg, Bundesrepublik Deutschland, GERMANY; Bischöfliches Ordinariatsarchiv, Luitpoldstrasse 2, D-85067 Eichstätt, Bundesrepublik Deutschland, GERMANY; Erzbischöfliches Ordinariatsarchiv München und Freising, Karmeliterstrasse 1, D-80333 München/Munich, Bundesrepublik Deutschland, GERMANY; Erzbischöfliches Matrikelamt, Pacellistrasse 7/I, D-80333 München/Munich, Bundesrepublik Deutschland, GERMANY; Bischöfliches Ordinariatsarchiv, Luragogasse 4, D-94032 Passau, Bundesrepublik Deutschland, GERMANY; Bischöfliches Zentralarchiv, St. Petersweg 11-13, D-93047 Regensburg, Bundesrepublik Deutschland, GERMANY; Bischöfliches Ordinariatsarchiv, Am Bruderhof 1, D-97070 Würzburg 1, Bundesrepublik Deutschland, GERMANY.

___(For Berlin) Bistumarchiv, Götzstrasse 65, D-12099 Berlin, Bundesrepublik Deutschland, GERMANY.

___(For Hamburg) see Niedersachsen.

___(For Hessen) Staatsarchiv für Hessen-Darmstadt, Katolinenplatz 3, D-64289 Darmstadt, Bundesrepublik Deutschland, GERMANY; Bischöfliches Generalvikariat, Paulustor 5, D-36001 Fulda, Bundesrepublik Deutschland, GERMANY; Bistumarchiv, Rossmarkt 4, D-65549 Limburg/Lahn, Bundesrepublik Deutschland, GERMANY; Erzbistumsarchiv, Kirchenbuchabteilung, Domplatz 3, D-33098 Paderborn, Bundesrepublik Deutschland, GERMANY; Katholische Kirchenbuchstelle, Bürgistrasse 28, D-34125 Kassel, Bundesrepublik Deutschland, GERMANY (only for city of Kassel).

___(For Niedersachsen, also see Oldenburg and Westphalia) Bistums-archiv, Pfaffenstieg 2, D-31134 Hildesheim, Bundesrepublik Deutschland, GERMANY; Kirchenbucharchiv der Dioezese Hildesheim, Postfach 100263, D-31002 Hildesheim, Bundesrepublik Deutschland, GERMANY; Bistumsarchiv, Hasestrasse 40 a, D-49074 Osnabrück, Bundesrepublik Deutschland, GERMANY.

___(For Nordrhein-Westfalen) see Rheinland and Westphalia.

___(For Oldenburg) Bischöfliches Offizialat, Bahnhofstrasse, D-49377 Vechta, Bundesrepublik Deutschland, GERMANY.

___(For Ostpreussen and Westpreussen) Bischöflisches Zentralarchiv, St. Petersweg 11-13, D-93047 Regensburg, Bundesrepublik Deutschland, GERMANY.

___(For Pfalz) Archiv des Bistums Speyer, Kleine Pfaffengasse 16, D-67321 Speyer/Rhein, Bundesrepublik Deutschland, GERMANY; Bistumsarchiv, Jesuitenstrasse 13 b, D-54290 Trier, Bundesrepublik Deutschland, GERMANY.

___(For Rheinland) Bischöfliches Diözesanarchiv Aachen, Klosterplatz 7, D-52003 Aachen, Bundesrepublik Deutschland, GERMANY; Bistums-archiv, Zwölfling 16, D-45127 Essen, Bundesrepublik Deutschland, GERMANY; Historisches Archiv des Erzbistums Köln, Gereonstrasse 2-4, D-50670 Köln/Cologne, Bundesrepublik Deutschland, GERMANY; Bistumsarchiv, Grebenstrasse 8-12, D-55116 Mainz, Bundesrepublik Deutschland, GERMANY.

___(For Saarland) Archiv des Bistums Speyer, Kleine Pfaffengasse 16, D-67321 Speyer, Bundesrepublik Deutschland, GERMANY; Bistums-archiv, Jesuitenstrasse 13 b, D-54290 Trier, Bundesrepublik Deutsch-land, GERMANY.

___(For Sachsen) Bistumsarchiv, Dresdner Strasse 26, D-01326 Dresden, Bundesrepublik Deutschland, GERMANY; Erzbistumsarchiv, Domplatz 3, D-33098 Paderborn, Bundesrepublik Deutschland, GERMANY; Bischöfliches Amt Erfurt-Meiningen, Hermannsplatz 9, D-99084 Erfurt, Bundesrepublik Deutschland, GERMANY; Bischöfliches Amt Magde-

burg, Max-Josef-Metzger-Strasse, D-39104, Bundesrepublik Deutschland, GERMANY.
___(For Schleswig-Holstein) Bistumsarchiv, Hasestrasse 40 a, D-49074 Osnabrück, Bundesrepublik Deutschland, GERMANY.
___(For Westfalen) Bistumsarchiv, Kardinal-von-Galen-Stift, Georgskommende 19, D-48143 Münster, Bundesrepublik Deutschland, GERMANY; Erzbistumsarchiv, Kirchenbuchabteilung, Domplatz 3, D-33094 Paderborn, Bundesrepublik Deutschland, GERMANY.
___(For Württemberg) Diözesanarchiv, Eugen-Bolz-Platz 5, D-72108 Rottenburg am Neckar, Bundesrepublik Deutschland, GERMANY.

Here is a sample letter for such contacts:

Evangelischer Oberkirchenrat
Landeskirchliches Archiv
Blumenstrasse 1
D-76133 Karlsruhe
Bundesrepublik Deutschland, GERMANY

Very honored Director:
My ancestor Andreas Jacob HEINOLD came from Grünwettersbach to the US about 1835 at the age of about 25. Please check your records for his birth and his marriage. I am also interested in the names, birth places and dates, marriage places and dates, death places and dates of his parents, and of his wife's parents.
If your records go on back to include further generations, I would also like to have data on them. Enclosed is $10 for return air mail postage and for your fee.

With friendly greetings,
George K. Schweitzer
407 Ascot Court
Knoxville, TN 37923-5807
U.S.A.

Evangelischer Oberkirchenrat
Landeskirchliches Archiv
Blumenstrasse 1
D-76133 Karlsruhe
Bundesrepublik Deutschland, GERMANY

Sehr geerhrter Direktor!
Mein Vorfahr Andreas Jacob HEINOLD hat Grünwettersbach um 1835, d. h. im Alter von ungefähr 25 Jahren, verlassen. Bitte überprüfen

Sie Ihre Unterlagen hinsichlich seines Geburtsdatum und seiner Heirat. Ich bin ebenso an den Namen, Geburtsorten und -daten, dem Daten und Ort der Heirat, sowie den Sterbedaten und -orten seiner Eltern und der Eltern seiner Frau interessiert.

Falls Ihre Akten bis zu weiteren Generationen zurückreichen sollten, würde ich auch gern Daten über diese erhalten. Beigefügt sind $10 für Rückporto (Luftpost) und für Ihr Honorar.

Mit freundlichen Grüssen
George K. Schweitzer
407 Ascot Court
Knoxville, TN 37923-5807
U.S.A.

You may also have occasion to correspond with some special archives:

___(For Baptist records) Bund Evangelisch-Freikirchlicher Gemeinden in Deutschland (Baptisten), Friedberger Strasse 101, D-61350 Bad Homburg vor der Hoehe 1, Bundesrepublik Deutschland, GERMANY.

___(For Huguenot records) Deutscher Hugenotten-Verein e.V, Deutsches Hugenotten-Zentrum, Hafenplatz 9a, D-34385 Bad Karlshafen, Bundesrepublik Deutschland, GERMANY.

___(For Jewish records) Gesamtarchiv der deutschen Juden, Joachimstaler Strasse 13, D-10719 Berlin, Bundesrepublik Deutschland, GERMANY; Bundesarchiv Am Wöllershof 12, D-56068 Koblenz, Bundesrepublik Deutschland, GERMANY; Archiv des Institutum Judaicum Delitzschianum, Wilmergasse 1-4, D-48143 Münster, Bundesrepublik Deutschland, GERMANY; Israelitische Religionsgemeinschaft Württembergs, Hospitalstrasse 36, D-70174 Stuttgart, Bundesrepublik Deutschland, GERMANY.

___(For Mennonite records) Archiv des Mennonitischen Geschichtsvereins, D-67297 Weierhof bei Marnheim/Pfalz, Bundesrepublik Deutschland, GERMANY.

___(For Methodist records) Evangelisch-Methodistische Kirche, Wilhelm-Lüschner-Strasse 8, D-60329 Frankfurt/Main, Bundesrepublik Deutschland, GERMANY.

___(For Moravian records) Evangelische Brüder-Unität, Archiv der Brüder-Unität, Zittauer Strasse 24, D-02747 Herrnhut (Oberlausitz), Bundesrepublik Deutschland, GERMANY.

___(For Old Lutheran Church records) Bund freier evangelischer Gemeinden in Deutschland, Goltenkamp 2, D-58452 Witten-Bammern, Bundesrepublik Deutschland, GERMANY.

___(For Quaker records) Religiöse Gesellschaft der Freunde in Deutschland (Quäker), Brombergstrasse 9 a, D-791020 Freiburg im Breisgau, Bundesrepublik Deutschland, GERMANY.

If microfilms of the church records for <u>places</u> <u>now</u> <u>outside</u> <u>of</u> <u>Germany</u> are not discovered in the FHL, then you need to try to locate them in Europe. The major territories which were once in Germany (1871) but are now outside Germany include Elsass-Lothringen, Ostpreussen, Westpreussen, Pommern, Brandenburg-Ost, Schlesien, and Posen. The first move that you should make is to contact several archives in Germany which hold a sizable number of these records (or know where they are):

___(For locations of Catholic and Protestant records in present-day Poland) Arbeitsgemeinschaft ostdeutscher Familienforscher e.V., Sitz Herne, Detlef Kuehn, Holzlar, Fuhrweg 29, D-53229 Bonn, Bundesrepublik Deutschland, GERMANY; Zentralstelle für Genealogie, Käthe-Kollwitz-Strasse 82, D-04009 Leipzig, Bundesrepublik Deutschland, GERMANY.

___(For Catholic records in Ostpreussen, Posen, and Westpreussen) Bischöfliches Zentralarchiv, St. Petersweg 11-13, D-93047 Regensburg, Bundesrepublik Deutschland, GERMANY.

___(For Catholic records in Schlesien) Bistumsarchiv, Biesnitzer Strasse 94, D-02826 Görlitz, Bundesrepublik Deutschland, GERMANY.

___(For Jewish records in Ostpreussen, Pommern, Schlesien, and Westpreussen) Bundesarchiv, Am Wöllershof 12, D-56068 Koblenz, Bundesrepublik Deutschland, GERMANY; Gesamtarchiv der deutschen Juden, Joachimsthaler Strasse 13, D-10719 Berlin, Bundesrepublik Deutschland, GERMANY.

___(For Protestant records in what is now Poland) Evangelisches Zentralarchiv, Jebenstrasse 3, D-10623 Berlin, Bundesrepublik Deutschland, GERMANY; Zentralstelle für Genealogie, Käthe-Kollwitz-Strasse 82, D-04009 Leipzig, Bundesrepublik Deutschland, GERMANY.

___(For Protestant records in Pommern) Evangelisch-lutherische Kirche im Hamburgischen Staat, Archiv, Neue Burg 1, D-20457 Hamburg, Bundesrepublik Deutschland, GERMANY.

___(For Protestant records in Schlesien) Evangelisches Konsistorium des Görlitzer Kirchengebietes, Archiv der Evangelischen Kirchen von Schlesien, Berliner Strasse 62, OD-10623 Görlitz, Bundesrepublik Deutschland, GERMANY.

If you still have not located church records for the city/town/village of your ancestor, then try making the following contacts in the countries in which your ancestor's place now is located. The repositories for the territories we have been discussing are:

___(For both Protestant and Catholic records in Brandenburg-Ost, Ostpreussen, Pommern, Posen, Schlesien, Westpreussen, Elsass, and Lothringen) Write the Polish and French state archives listed toward the end of Section 2 of this chapter.

___(For Catholic records in Brandenburg-Ost, Ostpreussen, Pommern, Posen, Schlesien, and Westpreussen) Sekretariat Prymasa Polski, Polish Central Catholic Office, ul. Miodowa 17, PL-Warszawa, Polska, POLAND; Archiwum Archidiecezalne, PL-62200 GnieznD-Katedra, Polska, POLAND; Archiwum Diecezji (general name for a church archive) in PL-83130 Pelpin (diocese of Chelmno, was Kulm), in PL-Gdansk (diocese of Gdansk, was Danzig), in PL-Gorzów (diocese of Gorzów, was Landsberg), in PL-Olsztyn (diocese of Olsztyn, was Allenstein), in PL-Opole (diocese of Opole, was Oppeln), in PL-Pila (diocese of Pila, was Schneidemühl), in PL-Poznan (diocese of Poznan, was Posen), in PL-Warszawa (diocese of Warszawa, was Warschau), in PL-Wloclawek (diocese of Wloclawek, was Leslau), in PL-Wroclaw (diocese of Wroclaw, was Breslau).

___(For Catholic records in Elsass) Archives départementales du Bas-Rhin, 5 rue Fischart, F-67000 Strasburg, FRANCE; Archives départementales du Haut-Rhin, Rue Fleischauer, F-68000 Colmar, FRANCE.

___(For Catholic records in Lothringen) Archives de l'Évêché de Metz, F-57000 Metz, FRANCE.

Further information and addresses for obtaining church records from places that were previously in Germany will be found in two superb reference works.

___AGoFF, with J. O. R. Nuthack and A. Goertz, GENEALOGICAL GUIDE TO GERMAN ANCESTORS FROM EASTERN(-MOST) GERMANY AND EASTERN EUROPE, Degener, Neustadt/Aisch, Deutschland, 1984.

___E. Thode, ADDRESS BOOK FOR GERMANIC GENEALOGY, Genealogical Publishing Co., Baltimore, MD, latest edition.

Availability of records for the following areas of German settlements are discussed: in Poland (Middle Poland, Volhynia, Galicia), in the Baltic countries (Estonia, Latvia, Lithuania), in Russia (areas of the Volga River, the Black Sea, the Caucausus, and the Crimea), in Slovakia (Spi, Hauerland), in Romania (Transylvania, Banat, Bukovina, Bessarabia,

Dobrudscha, along the Danube), in Yugoslavia (Banat, Bácska, Slavonia, Srem, along the Danube), in Hungary (Banat, Bácska, along the Danube).

There are some very useful descriptions of church records and inventories of church records for various regions. Some are books and some have appeared as journal articles. Many of them are available at the FHL, and therefore can be borrowed through FHC. Several of these works are quite old which means that some listings may be out of date, since records may have been moved or may have been destroyed. Among the better reference works of this sort are:

___(Printed church records) E. Henning and C. Wegelaben, BIBLIOGRAPHY OF PRINTED LISTS FOR BAPTISMS, MARRIAGES, AND DEATHS, Verlag Degener, Neustadt/Aisch, Deutschland, 1996.

___(Protestant) K. Dumrath, u.a., HANDBUCH DES KIRCHLICHES ARCHIVWESENS, DER ZENTRALEN ARCHIVE IN DER EVANGELISCHEN KIRCHE, Degener, Neustadt/Aisch, Deutschland, 1977.

___(Outside present Germany) VERZEICHNIS DER IN BERLIN (WEST) VORHANDENEN ORTSFREMDEN PERSONENSTANDS- UND KIRCHENBÜCHER, Frankfurt/Main, Deutschland, 1955.

___(Catholic, easternmost area) J. Kaps, HANDBUCH ÜBER DIE KATHOLISCHEN KIRCHENBÜCHER IN DER OST-DEUTSCHEN KIRCHEN PROVINZ ÖSTLICH DER ODER UND NEISSE, München, Deutschland, 1962.

___(Ostpreussen and Westpreussen) PERSONENSTANDSUNTER-LAGEN UND KIRCHENBÜCHER AUS OST-DEUTSCH-LAND, in ÜBERSICHT ÜBER DIE BESTANDE DES GEHEIMEN STAATSARCHIVS IN BERLIN-DAHLEM, Köln-Berlin, Deutschland, 1967; R. Rose, DIE KIRCHENBÜCHER DER EVANGELISCHEN KIRCHEN OST- UND WEST-PREUSSEN, VERZEICHNIS DER MILITARKIRCHEN-BÜCHER DER PROVINZ WESTPREUSSEN, UND KIRCH-ENBÜCHER DER DIÖZESE ERMLAND, 1909.

___(Anhalt) R. Specht, DAS LAND ANHALT, Degener, Leipzig, Deutschland, 1937.

___(Baden) H. Franz, DIE KIRCHENBÜCHER VON ELSASS-LOTHRINGEN, Karlsruhe, Deutschland, 1957.

___(Bayerisches Pfalz) A. Müller, DIE KIRCHENBÜCHER DER BAYERISCHEN PFALZ, München, Deutschland, 1925.

___(Bayern) PFARRBÜCHERVERZEICHNISSE FÜR DAS RECHTSRHEINISCHE BAYERN, von der Bayerischen Archivverwaltung, München-Regensburg, Deutschland, 1937-1951, 8 Hefte (volumes).

___(Brandenburg) K. Meyerding de Ahna, DIE KIRCHENBÜCHER DER EVANGELISCHEN KIRCHEN IN DER PROVINZ BRANDENBURG, in Archiv für Sippenforschung 10 (1933) 97; P. Schwartz, DIE KIRCHENBÜCHER DER MARK BRANDENBURG, Landsberg, Deutschland, 1900.

___(Elsass-Lothringen) H. Koch, DIE KIRCHENBÜCHER VON ELSASS-LOTHRINGEN, in Mitteilungen der Zentralstelle 9 (1911) 14, 10 (1912) 8.

___(Hannover) F. Garbe, DIE KIRCHENBÜCHER IN DER EVANGELISCH-LUTHERISCHEN LANDESKIRCHE HANNOVERS, Göttingen, Deutschland, 1960; F. Garbe, INVENTARE KIRCHLICHER ARCHIVE NIEDER-SACHSENS, Göttingen, Deutschland, 1962-1963.

___(Hessen) O. Praetorius, KIRCHENBÜCHER UND STANDES-REGISTER FÜR ALLE WOHNPLATZE IM LAND HESSEN, Darmstadt, Deutschland, 1939.

___(Kurhessen-Waldeck) E. Eisenberg, KIRCHENBUCH-VERZEICHNIS DER EVANGELISCHEN KIRCHE VON KURHESSEN WALDECK, Kassel, Deutschland, 1973.

___(Mecklenburg) C. A. Endler und E. Albrecht, MECKLENBURGS FAMILIENSCHICHTLICHE QUELLEN, Hamburg, Deutschland, 1936.

___(Oldenburg) KIRCHENBUCH-VERZEICHNIS DER EV.-LUTH. KIRCHE IN OLDENBURG, Ev.-Luth. Oberkirchenrat, Oldenburg, Deutschland, 1972.

___(Ostpreussen) E. Grigoleit, NEUES VERZEICHNIS OSTPREUSS-ISCHER KIRCHENBÜCHER SOWIE DER VOR 1874 ABGE-LEGTEN PERSONSTANDSREGISTER, Ailringen, Deutschland, 1958; M. Wermes, u.a., CHURCH RECORDS IN THE GERMAN CENTRAL OFFICE FOR GENEALOGY (POSEN, PRUSSIA, POMERANIA, SILESIA), Verlag Degener, Neustadt/Aisch, Deutschland, 1991.

___(Pfalz) W. Eger, DIE PROTESTANTISCHEN KIRCHENBÜCHER DER PFALZ, Speyer, Deutschland, 1960.

___(Pommern) M. Wehrmann, DIE KIRCHENBÜCHER IN POMMERN, in Baltische Studien 42 (1892) 201-280; M. Wermes, u.a., CHURCH RECORDS IN THE GERMAN CENTRAL OFFICE FOR GENEALOGY (POSEN, PRUSSIA, POM-

168

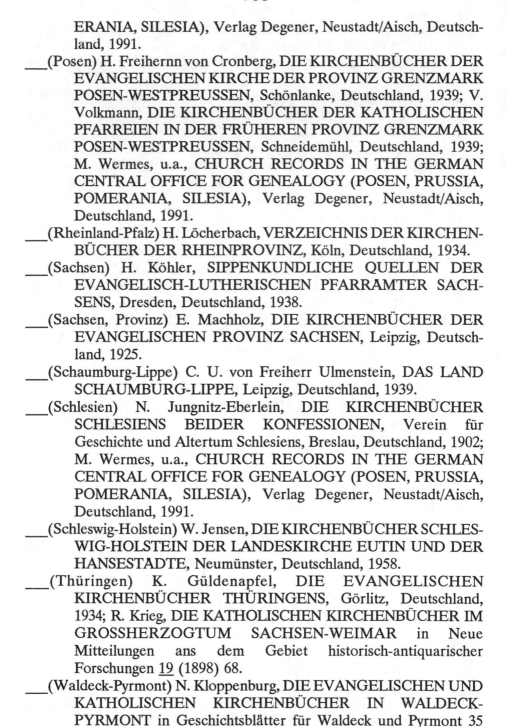

ERANIA, SILESIA), Verlag Degener, Neustadt/Aisch, Deutschland, 1991.

___(Posen) H. Freihernn von Cronberg, DIE KIRCHENBÜCHER DER EVANGELISCHEN KIRCHE DER PROVINZ GRENZMARK POSEN-WESTPREUSSEN, Schönlanke, Deutschland, 1939; V. Volkmann, DIE KIRCHENBÜCHER DER KATHOLISCHEN PFARREIEN IN DER FRÜHEREN PROVINZ GRENZMARK POSEN-WESTPREUSSEN, Schneidemühl, Deutschland, 1939; M. Wermes, u.a., CHURCH RECORDS IN THE GERMAN CENTRAL OFFICE FOR GENEALOGY (POSEN, PRUSSIA, POMERANIA, SILESIA), Verlag Degener, Neustadt/Aisch, Deutschland, 1991.

___(Rheinland-Pfalz) H. Löcherbach, VERZEICHNIS DER KIRCHENBÜCHER DER RHEINPROVINZ, Köln, Deutschland, 1934.

___(Sachsen) H. Köhler, SIPPENKUNDLICHE QUELLEN DER EVANGELISCH-LUTHERISCHEN PFARRAMTER SACHSENS, Dresden, Deutschland, 1938.

___(Sachsen, Provinz) E. Machholz, DIE KIRCHENBÜCHER DER EVANGELISCHEN PROVINZ SACHSEN, Leipzig, Deutschland, 1925.

___(Schaumburg-Lippe) C. U. von Freiherr Ulmenstein, DAS LAND SCHAUMBURG-LIPPE, Leipzig, Deutschland, 1939.

___(Schlesien) N. Jungnitz-Eberlein, DIE KIRCHENBÜCHER SCHLESIENS BEIDER KONFESSIONEN, Verein für Geschichte und Altertum Schlesiens, Breslau, Deutschland, 1902; M. Wermes, u.a., CHURCH RECORDS IN THE GERMAN CENTRAL OFFICE FOR GENEALOGY (POSEN, PRUSSIA, POMERANIA, SILESIA), Verlag Degener, Neustadt/Aisch, Deutschland, 1991.

___(Schleswig-Holstein) W. Jensen, DIE KIRCHENBÜCHER SCHLESWIG-HOLSTEIN DER LANDESKIRCHE EUTIN UND DER HANSESTADTE, Neumünster, Deutschland, 1958.

___(Thüringen) K. Güldenapfel, DIE EVANGELISCHEN KIRCHENBÜCHER THÜRINGENS, Görlitz, Deutschland, 1934; R. Krieg, DIE KATHOLISCHEN KIRCHENBÜCHER IM GROSSHERZOGTUM SACHSEN-WEIMAR in Neue Mitteilungen ans dem Gebiet historisch-antiquarischer Forschungen 19 (1898) 68.

___(Waldeck-Pyrmont) N. Kloppenburg, DIE EVANGELISCHEN UND KATHOLISCHEN KIRCHENBÜCHER IN WALDECK-PYRMONT in Geschichtsblätter für Waldeck und Pyrmont 35 (1935) 141, 39 (1939) 30.

___(Westfalen) H. Kochendörffer, ÜBER KIRCHENBÜCHER IN
WESTFALEN in Mitteilungen der Westdeutschen Gesellschaft
für Familienkunde 5 (1928) 445.
___(Westpreussen) M. Baer, DIE KIRCHENBÜCHER DER PROVINZ
WESTPREUSSEN, Danzig, Deutschland, 1908; M. Wermes, u.a.,
CHURCH RECORDS IN THE GERMAN CENTRAL OFFICE
FOR GENEALOGY (POSEN, PRUSSIA, POMERANIA,
SILESIA), Verlag Degener, Neustadt/Aisch, Deutschland, 1991.
___(Württemberg) M. Duncker, VERZEICHNIS DER WÜRTTEM-
BERGISCHEN KIRCHENBÜCHER, Stuttgart, Deutschland,
1938.

4. Other church records	4. Andere kirchliche Aufzeichnungen
4. Andere kirchliche Aufzeichnungen	*4. Andere kirchliche Aufzeichnungen*

The churches of the Germanic territories kept numerous other records in addition to those of baptisms (births, marriages, and burials
(deaths). These records are usually not as fruitful as the vital records, but
they can be useful because they often supply confirmation of vital records,
substitutes for lost vital records, locations of ancestors in place and time,
and information on your progenitor's life events and activities. You will
not find all of the following supplemental church records for every church,
but you will usually find a few of them for any given church. First, we
will take a look at some records which usually supply birth (baptism),
marriage, and death (burial) data, but of a secondary nature.

Family registers (Familienregister, Familienbücher, Seelenregister,
Einwohmerverzeichnis). Another type of record found in parishes, in regional church archives, and sometimes in regional governmental and state
archives are family registers. These are basically listings of families and/or
households in a parish, along with various amounts of data on the persons
listed. These registers date from the early 1600s, but they did not become
numerous until about 1800, and then chiefly in the southwestern
Germanic area. Both Protestant and Catholic parishes kept them. They
list the names, birth, marriage, and death places and dates of the father,
the mother, and the birth places and dates of the children. Other
information which may appear, especially at later dates, includes names of
the father's and mother's parents, marriage and death places and dates of

the children, emigration data, people who were not immediate family members (uncles, aunts, cousins), non-family members in the household (servants, laborers), grandparents and once in awhile even great-grand-parents. The more information given, the more the likelihood that much of it is secondary, that is, derived from non-current sources. So be careful of such data, and check them out in original sources (birth, marriage, death) if at all possible. Family registers can be found in parishes, regional church archives, and sometimes in governmental archives. Now we will treat several church records or records derived from church records which give indirect witness to births.

Confirmation records (Konfirmationbücher, Konfirmationregister). Sometimes at an age usually between 13-19, children were put into a church class where they received religious instruction in preparation for full church membership which permitted them to take communion. Following satisfactory completion of the instruction, the children in the class were confirmed and took their first communion. Records were kept of these confirmations. They ordinarily contain the date, the names of the confirmands, the names of their fathers, their places of residence and/or birth, and sometimes their ages. These record books are usually not as consistent, nor as continuous, nor as frequently found as baptism, marriage, and burial records, but they are available for many churches during many time periods. They are generally located in the churches and/or in regional church archives.

Other birth records. There are other useful records of births which often appear among church records or which are derived from the church records or inaugurated by the event of birth or baptism. The first of these is the death record which has been treated in the previous section. Death records often contain places and dates of birth or the age at death. The latter permits calculations which estimate the birth date. The second of the auxiliary birth records is known as the Pattenzettel, this being an invitation by the godparents to attend the baptism. A third sort of record is that generated by the payment of a city/town tax assessed on the baptism. Such records are often found in the city/town accounting records, Ratsrechnungen, in the sections listing receipts of taxes. The fourth sort of record is the birth certificate: Geburtsschein, Geburtsbrief, Geburtverzeichnis, Herkunftverzeichnis. This certificate was a document presented for membership in a guild or other occupational organization. The data in it were taken from church records and it was authenticated by governmental authorities. Now we will look at two indirect records of a marriage.

Other marriage records. It was generally required that an engaged couple publicly announce their intention to marry on each of three Sundays prior to the wedding. Such announcements are known as banns (Proklamationen, Aufgebote, Verlobungsanzeige), and the church kept registers of them (Proklamationsbücher, Aufgebotsverzeichnisse). Please recognize that the banns are not conclusive evidence of the marriage, only that a marriage was intended. As in the case of baptisms (christenings), the city/town sometimes collected a marriage tax. The receipts of these tax monies are generally recorded in the municipal records. The banns will be found among the church records in the parish, in church archives, and/or in the microfilms of FHL (available through FHC). There are a number of indirect death records kept by churches or relating to church funerals to which we now turn.

Funeral sermons (Leichenpredigten). Beginning about 1550, well-to-do Protestant families began aranging for sermons (eulogies) to be delivered at the funerals of their members. These were printed up and copies were given to relatives and friends. These printed orations often serve as good secondary genealogical sources because they contain life histories, summaries of military, occupational, and public service, and vital data on the deceased individual. In addition, some of them give extensive family information (chiefly on the surviving spouse and children), and even ancestral data (parents, grandparents). The funeral sermons for young and still-born children are usually filled with family historical material. The practice persisted until about 1750 and then gradually declined. Collections of these sermons have been made and are available in local and regional archives. Some have been microfilmed by the FHL, and may be located in the Locality Section of the FHL Catalog, which is available at every FHC. The heading that you should look under in order to find them is:

___Germany-Obituaries

Inquiries may also be made at local, nearby regional, and state archives.

Other death records. In addition to funeral sermons, there are other church records which have a secondary relation to deaths. The first of these are to be found in books which record the tolling of the church bell during the burial (Totengeläutbücher). The name of the deceased is given and sometimes the fee paid for the service. Well-to-do families would sometimes give money to the church to set up some sort of memorial endowment. These endowments paid for such things as prayers or services on the anniversaries of the death (Anniversarien), or for listings in special books (Nekrologien, Totenannalen). A third type of record is the grave register (Grabregister), which was a listing of the burials in the church cemetery. They often contained burial date information. These records are to be found in parishes and in church archives. Finally, we will turn to some church records which chiefly establish people in place and time.

Communion lists (Kommunikanten, Abendmahlbücher, Abendmahlgäste). As you look more deeply into church records, you will run into lists of persons taking Communion or the Eucharist or the Lord's Supper. These records rarely give any other data than simply to locate persons in time and place. However, it is well to remember that a name on a communion list ordinarily implies that confirmation has occurred, and therefore that the individual is usually older than 11-12.

Personal presence records. Numerous churches kept other records which located persons in a given city/town/district at a particular time. These include lists of those coming for confession (Beichtbücher), those who did penance (Kirchenstrafen), those who remitted penance money (Bussgeldlisten), receipt books kept by churches for payments of many different items (Einnahmeregister) [grave cloths, cemetery plots, bell tolling]. There also may be lists of church members (Mitgleiderlisten), of church admissions (Kircheneintrittsregister), of church dismissals (Kirchenaustrittsregister), of the poor under the care of the church (Armenbücher, Almosenbücher), of those paying pew taxes (Kirchenstuhlbücher), and of the pastors of the church through the years (Pfarrerchroniken). These histories of pastors vary widely in their content, with some of them providing considerable genealogical detail. There were also histories of the parishes (Pfarrchroniken), which sometimes have genealogical information as incidental entries.

Records on pastors. As mentioned above, there were chronicles of the succession of pastors in churches (Pfarrerchroniken), some of them yielding good genealogical data. The making of a pastor was a regulated process, and as a result, records were kept, usually at the regional church headquarters. Heydenreich points out that involved in this process for a Lutheran pastor were the call (Berüfung), the sponsorship of a local church, an examination (Prüfung) before a church council, the education of the candidate, the acceptance (Bestättigung) of the candidate by the ruler of the state, the ordination (Weihe, Ordination), and the installation (Einführung) of the person as a parish pastor. The ordinations were usually listed along with sizable amounts of accompanying information in special books (Ordiniertenbücher).   Records relating to the pastor's education are to be found in the university registration records.

Military church records. During times of war and internal unrest, troops were stationed in certain towns, which were known as garrison towns. Separate records were often kept by churches in the towns for baptisms of soldiers' children, marriages of soldiers, and deaths of soldiers (Garnisonskirchenbücher). However, in many instances, particularly for baptisms, the entries for children and for soldiers, were placed in the regular church records. There were also records kept by the military chaplains who accompanied the military regiments (Militärkirchenbücher). These, too, may contain vital records, especially christenings (baptisms). All of these military church records should be sought in German city, town, state, and church archives.

5. Other civil records	5. Andere Gerichtsakten
5. Andere Gerichtsakten	5. Andern Gerichtsakten

Court records.   Many of the records of German courts are valuable sources of genealogical data. Among those which give vital data (birth, marriage, death, parents, children) and which refer to most of the population are guardian, estate, and land records. As you will recall, before 1871 Germany was not united, but was made up of numerous semi-independent states. Each of these states had its own judicial system, and there were often considerable differences among them. Included in these differences was a great variety in names of courts, however almost all of them carried the word Gericht which means court. There were inheritance, municipal, manorial, baronial, ecclesiastical, monasterial, notarial, military, lay, city, town, civil, criminal, appellate, and other sorts of courts. Since 1871, there have been three levels of German courts: the lower courts acting at the administration, registration and trial levels (Amtsgericht, Schöffengericht, Landgericht, Schwurgericht), those acting at the first appeal level (Landgericht, Oberlandesgericht), and those acting at the final appeal level (Oberlandesgericht, Bundesgerichthof). You will notice that some courts act in two categories, the level of action depending upon the nature of the case. German court records are located in the court offices and in governmental record archives. Some probate and guardian records are available on microfilm at FHL (FHC). They may be found by looking under the locality in the FHLC. Some of the German archives have already been discussed. They will be reviewed, and others will be treated later. The locations of the courts as of 1911 are listed in the following volume:

___E. Ütrecht, MEYERS ORTS- UND VERKEHRS-LEXIKON DES DEUTSCHEN REICHS, Bibliographisches Institut, Leipzig, Deutschland, 1912.

Look up your ancestor's city, town, or community and you will find the court locations listed following the abbreviations AG.(Amtsgericht or local or district court), LG.(Landgerichte or regional or county court), and OLG.(Oberlandesgerichte or provincial higher regional court). This volume will be found in the largest genealogical libraries and on microfilm at FHL (FHC).

Guardian court records. The guardian court (Vormundschaftgericht) is generally a division of the Amtsgericht. It deals with illegitimacy, adultery, underage marriage, annulment of marriage, adoption, minor children, marriage contracts, divorce settlement, incapacitation, foster care, custodial matters, certification of coming of age, release from marriage hindrances, and other such matters. Among the records that can be looked for are the Vormundschaftakten (guardian records), Pflegeschaftakten (foster care records), Sorgerechtakten (custodial rights records), Adoptionakten (adoption records), Volljährigkeitserklärungen (declarations of majority or coming of age), Ehelichtkeitserklärungen (declarations of legitimacy), Vaterschaftanerkenntnissen (paternity findings), Befreiung von Ehehindermissen (release from impediments to marriage), and Fürsorgeerziehungsakten (records of correctional training). Many of these records refer to names of parents, dates of their marriages, dates of their deaths, births of the children, ages of children, and persons who took charge of children in place of their parents.

Probate court records. The probate courts in Germany (Nachlassgerichte) are also usually a division of the Amtsgericht. They concern themselves with wills, administrations of estates, appointments of administrators, partitions of estates, settlements of estates, inherited property distributions, and similar matters. Documents for earlier times, especially wills, are also to be found in collections in regional and state archives. Among the records that should be looked for are the Testamente (wills), Testamentsvollstreckerzeugnisse (administrators' and executors' records), Nachlasspflegerakten (administration records), Nachlasssteuerakten (inheritance tax records), Akten betreffend Vermittlung von Erbauseinandersetzungen (records of settlement of partitions of estates), Todeserklärungen (declaration of death), Erbscheinakten (records of certificates of heirship), Auseinandersetzungen (partitions of inheritances), Nachlassverzeichnisse (estate inventories), and Verwahrungsbücher (books listing and/or indexing records in the probate office). Probate records are of unusual value with reference to death dates and places, and with regard to establishing parent-child connections. Sometimes children had to submit birth information to the probate court to establish their identities, and these data are generally in the records. The best sources of probate data are in the courts themselves and in local and regional archives. The FHL has some probate records on microfilm and they can be borrowed through FHC. They may be located in the FHLC by looking under the locality.

Land records. The Grundbuchämter (land registration offices) in Germany are generally divisions of the local courts (Amtsgerichte). The more recent land transaction records are to be found in these offices and in archives as Grundbücher (land registers) and Grundakten (land records). Land registers contain names of owners, descriptions of the land, mortgages, debts, and transfers of ownership. Extending on back are the Hypothekenbücher (mortgage registers), Höfferollen (farm lists), and Erbhofakten (hereditary farm records). And for earlier times, there arc Güterbücher (chattel books), Flurbücher (registers of parcels of agricultural lands), and Lagerbücher (agricultural warehouse storage records), all of which make direct or indirect reference to lands, landholders, or occupants of lands. In medieval times, and for many years after, there were Lehnbücher (fief registers) and Lehnbriefe (fief certificates). These were related to fiefs, or feudal estates, which were pieces of land held on condition that the landholder give military service and a portion of the produce in return for the protection of the landlord (a nobleman) and for the use of the land. The earlier records are found in castle archives, manorial archives, baronial archives, principality archives, noble family archives, and other such repositories. Later materials are located in governmental archives (town, city, district, regional, state).

Listings of residents. As you will recall, Germany was not a united nation until 1871, so until then, there were no overall listings of residents. All such listings before 1871 were therefore for smaller regions, sometimes provinces, sometimes districts, sometimes counties, at other times towns or cities. The earliest of these were Bürgerbücher (citizen lists) which go back to the 1300s in a few places, and became more prevalent as the years went on. These records list the people in the town who have qualified for citizenship. Their applications generally had to present a birth or baptismal record, had to show gainful occupation, and had to evidence some property ownership. It is important to remember that there were many residents of towns who had not qualified for citizenship. The citizen lists at their best give much detail (name, occupation, wife, dates and places of birth, names of parents, names of children), but sometimes show as little as only the name. There were other broader listings called Einwohnerlisten (resident lists), Kopfzahlregister (head count registers), Bevölkerungslisten (population lists), Hausbesitzerverzeichnisse (house owner lists), Mannzahlregister (population register), and Bauernverzeichnisse (farmer lists). These latter records often applied to areas larger than towns or cities. Records of all the above types may be found in town and city archives and libraries, in regional and state archives, and a few microfilmed copies are in FHL (FHC). The microfilms may be located in FHL by using the Locality Section of the FHLC.

Steuerbücher (tax registers) and Steuerlisten (tax lists) are another source of genealogical data, although they usually do not give any direct information which connects generations. The earlier types of tax records, dating from the 1400s, were Zehntregister (tithe registers). Tax information is also sometimes found in the Ratsrechnungen (town/city account books), but they are ordinarily not indexed. The major thing that tax records do is to locate your ancestor in time and place, but once in awhile there will be additional data. Volkszählungslisten (censuses) of regions larger than towns and cities were also taken in the many districts and principalities of pre-1871 Germany. Usually listed in censuses are name, age, place of origin, occupation, and residence. They are to be found in city and state archives, and some are on microfilm in FHL (FHC). There were also Adresskalender (almanacs) starting in the early 1700s and then later Adressbücher (city directories). They sometimes extended beyond the city/town boundaries to the immediate surroundings, the metropolitan area, the district, or the county. City directories generally contain names, addresses, and occupations, and sometimes more extensive information. They may be found in city and state archives, with some being available on microfilm at FHL (FHC). Detailed listings of many city directories and citizenship lists are provided in:

___W. Ribbe and E. Henning, TASCHENBUCH FÜR FAMILIEN-GESCHICHTSFORSCHUNG, Verlag, Degener, Neustadt/Aisch, Deutschland, 1980, pp. 104-40 (Bürgerbücher), pp. 192-210 (Adressbücher).

Police registration records. Beginning about 1830 many towns and cities began keeping lists of inhabitants and records of all those coming in and moving out. These data were set down in record books called Einwohnermeldelisten and Polizeiregister. The records usually give name, age or date of birth, occupation, sometimes place of birth, and town going to or coming from. Such materials will be found in the Einwohnermeldeamt (inhabitant registration office) in the town or city, and in local and state archives.

Military records. Most families in many times during 1600-1850 had at least one soldier in service. As a result, there are dispersed in numerous archives in Germany sizable amounts of military records. Because of this wide-spread distribution of records, locating the proper ones is often somewhat time-consuming, since several archives must usually be contacted. It is extremely helpful if you happen to know the place or region of enlistment, the approximate dates of service, and the exact regiment. Especially important are the Regimentskirchenbücher (regimental church registers) and the Garnisionskirchenbücher (garrison church registers) in which church records (baptism, marriage, and death) of military personnel and often their families were kept. Among the records that can be sought for officers are the Offiziersstammrollen (officer assignments), Ranglisten (officer lists), and Offiziersnachweise (officer records). Records which deal with enlisted men also are Musterungslisten (muster rolls), Mannschaftsstammrollen (personnel assignments), and Regimentsgeschichte (regimental histories). The German word for a pension is Pension, and records relating to the granting of military pensions are available. Among the major archives which act somewhat as centralized military record repositories are:

___(Brandenburg, Ostpreussen, Westpreussen) Geheimes Staatsarchiv Preussischer Kulturbesitz, Archivstrasse 12-14, D-14195 Berlin (Dahlem), Bundesrepublik Deutschland, GERMANY.

___(Preussen) Deutsches Bundesarchiv, Militärarchiv, Wiesenthalstrasse 10, D-85356 Freiburg, Bundesrepublik Deutschland, GERMANY.

___(Baden) Badisches Generallandesarchiv, Nördliche Hilda-Promenade 2, D-76113 Karlsruhe, Bundesrepublik Deutschland, GERMANY.

___(Bayern) Bayerisches Hauptstaatsarchiv, Kriegsarchiv, Leonradstrasse 57, D-80636 München, Bundesrepublik Deutschland, GER-MANY.

___(Deutschland) Deutsches Bundesarchiv, Zentralnachweisstelle, D-52076 Kornelmünster, Bundesrepublik Deutschland, GERMANY; Militärkirchenbuchamt, Adenauer Allee 115, D-53113 Bonn, Bundesrepublik Deutschland, GERMANY.

___(Darmstadt) Staatsarchiv Darmstadt, Karolinenplatz 3, D-64289 Darmstadt, Bundesrepublik Deutschland, GERMANY.

___(Hessen) Staatsarchiv Darmstadt, Schloss, D-64201 Darmstadt, Bundesrepublik Deutschland, GERMANY; Staatsarchiv Marburg, Friedrichsplatz 15, D-35017 Marburg/Lahn, Bundesrepublik Deutschland, GERMANY; Hessisches Hauptstaatsarchiv, Mosbacher Strasse 55, D-65187 Wiesbaden, Bundesrepublik Deutschland, GERMANY.

___(Lippe-Detmold) Personenstandsarchiv für Westfalen-Lippe, Willi-Hofmann Strasse 2, D-32756 Detmold, Bundesrepublik Deutschland, GERMANY.

___(Mecklenburg) Staatsarchiv Schwerin, Graf-Schack-Allee 2, D-19053 Schwerin, Bundesrepublik Deutschland, GERMANY.

___(Niedersachsen) Niedersächsisches Staatsarchiv, D-31675 Bückeburg, Bundesrepublik Deutschland, GERMANY; Niedersächsisches Staatsarchiv, Damm 43, D-26135 Oldenburg, Bundesrepublik Deutschland, GERMANY; Niedersächsisches Staatsarchiv, Forstweg 2, D-38302 Wolfenbüttel, Bundesrepublik Deutschland, GERMANY; Niedersaechsisches Hauptstaatsarchiv, Am Archiv 1, D-30169 Hannover, Bundesrepublik Deutschland, GERMANY.

___(Sachsen) Staatsarchiv, Archivstrasse 14, D-01097 Dresden, Bundesrepublik Deutschland, GERMANY; Staatsarchiv, Schloss 2a, D-06429 Altenburg, Bundesrepublik Deutschland, GERMANY; Historisches Staatsarchiv, Schloss Friedenstein, D-99867 Gotha, Bundesrepublik Deutschland, GERMANY; Staatsarchiv, Oberes Schloss 7, D-07973 Greiz, Bundesrepublik Deutschland, GERMANY; Staatsarchiv Schloss Bibrabau, D-98617 Meiningen, Bundesrepublik Deutschland, GERMANY; Staatsarchiv, Schloss Heidecksburg, D-07407 Rudolstadt, Bundesrepublik Deutschland, GERMANY; Staatsarchiv Marstallstrasse 2, D-99408 Weimar, Bundesrepublik Deutschland, GERMANY.

___(Schleswig-Holstein) Landesarchiv, Schloss Gottorf, D-24837 Schleswig, Bundesrepublik Deutschland, GERMANY; Rigsarkivet 3. Afdeling, Forsvarets Arkiver, Rigsdagsgarden 5, DK-1218 Kobenhavn/Copenhagen K, Danmark/DENMARK.

___(Württemberg) Hauptstaatsarchiv, Konrad-Adenauer-Strasse 4, D-70173 Stuttgart, Bundesrepublik Deutschland, GERMANY; Heeresarchiv, Gutenbergstrasse 109, D-70197 Stuttgart, Bundesrepublik Deutschland, GERMANY.

Letters of inquiry to the archives nearest your ancestor's area will often locate the military records for you. Not to be overlooked is a valuable publication listing Hessian troops who fought as mercenaries for the British in the American Revolution.

___HESSISCHE TRUPPEN IM AMERIKANISCHEN UNABHANG-
IGKEITSKRIEG, Staatsarchiv Marburg, Marburg, Deutschland,
1972.
This extensive index lists names, birth dates, places from which the
soldiers came, regiments, ranks, enlistment dates, and what happened to
each (deserted, killed, died, returned to Hessen).

House genealogies. A fascinating type of record found in a
number of cities and towns is that which chronicles house genealogies
(Hausbücher). They give histories of dwelling houses along with names
of owners, their occupations, years each owner owned the house, and
sometimes others who occupied the premises. These intriguing materials
are generally found in town and city offices and archives, but sometimes
they will be located in regional and state repositories.

Poor records. One other category of civil records that often
proves genealogical useful is that dealing with records of the poor. These
often are known as Armenregister (poor records) and Almosenregister
(alms records). Look in city, town, and other regional archives.

Emigration records. These were discussed in detail in section 13
of the previous chapter. The major sources of them are state archives
and the FHL (FHC). There are also many published works.

6. Institutional records.	6. Institutionsakten
6. Institutionsakten	6. Institutionsakten

Occupational records. During the middle ages and for some years
afterwards, people with a common interest organized themselves into associations called guilds. These organizations were formed for charitable,
social, religious, and occupational reasons. The most important were the
occupational ones which were set up by merchants and craftworkers. By
about 1250, merchant guilds were very important in towns where they
regulated trade, set prices, enforced quality standards, protected their
members, and strongly influenced the government. The craft guilds included those of apothecaries, architects, artists, bakers, booksellers, butch-
ers, carpenters, goldsmiths, lacemakers, masons, musicians, publishers,
sausage manufacturers, shoemakers, surgeons, tailors, and weavers. The
guilds strongly began to lose influence, by about 1650 were becoming
simply fraternal societies, and about 1860 were abolished in Germany.

Part of the activity of a guild was the training of its members. First, an apprentice served for at least three years learning the craft under the supervision of a master. After an exam, he was promoted to a journeyman, who travelled around working as an assistant to a series of masters in other towns. Then he was made a master and could open his own business or shop. Every stage in the procedure was recorded. Admission to apprenticeship required a birth or origin validation (Geburtsbrief, Herkunftszeugnisse). There were apprentice contracts, apprentice registers (Lehrlingsbücher), journeymen registers (Gesellenbücher), record books kept by journeymen on their work journeys (Wanderzettel), lists of masters (Meisterbücher), membership lists, and financial reports. At their best, these records can supply you with the guild member's name, residence, birth date and place, parent's names, employer's name, and sometimes family information such as names of wife and children, date and place of marriage, and birth dates and places of the children. The guild record books may be found under several names (Gildebücher, Innungsbücher, Zunftbücher). They should be sought in town, city, regional, and state archives, and quite a number are on microfilm in FHL (FHC). The latter may be located by looking under the locality in the locality Section of the FHLC.

Academic records. Higher education, that is, education beyond the level of high school, is given in Germany in universities (Universitäten) and in specialized academies and institutes (Hochschulen). Some of them date back into the 1400s. From these earliest times, Protestant ministers, lawyers, physicians, and teachers were educated in these institutions. As time went on, many other professionals came to be educated in them. The university registers (Universitätsmatrikeln) and the academy and institute registers (Hochschulmatrikeln) are often sources of much information: students' names, entrance date, place of origin, date and place of birth, name of father, years at school, subjects studied, degree granted. Sometimes there is additional family information.

There are also records of secondary schools. These include lists of student acceptances (Inmatrikulation, Inscription), which give students' ages, parentage, and residence. Many secondary schools have printed lists of graduates (Schülerverzeichnisse), which contain varied amounts of family data. School records are to be found in the schools themselves (universities, academies, institutes, secondary schools), in archives in the appropriate towns and cities, and in regional archives. Some are available on microfilm at FHL (FHC), and they may be located by looking in the

FHLC under the appropriate place. A long list of German institutions of higher education with indications of available records is given in

___W. Ribbe and E. Henning, TASCHENBUCH FÜR FAMILIENGE-
 SCHICHTSFORSCHUNG, Verlag Degener, Neustadt/Aisch,
 Deutschland, 1980, pp. 142-157.

7. Secondary sources	7. Sekundäre Quellen
7. Sekundäre Quellen	*7. Vrfründäunt Günllen*

    Germans have been searching out, compiling, and publishing family genealogical information for several centuries. As a result, there are numerous publications of many sorts which contain such compiled data. Among the available materials are genealogical compilations, family histories, local histories, and genealogical periodicals. Several of these were discussed in Sections 6 and 7 of Chapter 3, but more detail will be given here. In addition to these, German newspapers are a very important source for progenitor information. Unlike the various compilations, however, they are seldom indexed.

    <u>Genealogical</u> <u>compilations</u>. An exceedingly valuable series of compiled German genealogies is the Deutsches Geschlechterbuch (German Lineage Book). The first volume in the series was published in 1889 and there are now about 200 volumes, with more in preparation. Each of the volumes contains numerous family histories usually arranged in the form of genealogical tables.

___DAS DEUTSCHE GESCHLECHTERBUCH, C. A. Starke,
 Limburg/Lahn, Deutschland, 1889-, Vol. 1-about 200.

Most of the volumes apply to a specific region of Germany, but some of them cover broader areas. The material which was used to put together these family lineages come mainly from church and civil records. Each volume contains an index to all surnames. Further, there are several more comprehensive indexes to some or all of the books:

___G. Jeske, LOCALITY INDEX TO THE DEUTSCHES
 GESCHLECHTERBUCH, European Reference Desk, Family
 History Library, Salt Lake City, UT. A listing of the many
 volumes with the area covered by each.

___G. Jeske, SURNAME INDEX TO THE DEUTSCHES
 GESCHLECHTERBUCH, European Reference Desk, Family
 History Library, Salt Lake City, UT. List of all surnames for

which detailed family records are available, with the volume and page where the data are given.

___STAMMFOLGENVERZEICHNISSE ZUM DEUTSCHEN GESCH-LECHTERBUCH. Covers over 186 volumes up to 1986.

___E. Wassmannsdorff, GESAMTNAMENSVERZEICHNIS UM-FASSEND BAND 1-50 DEUTSCHES GESCHLECHT-ERBUCH, C. A. Stark, Görlitz, Deutschland, 1938. An index to every name in the first 50 volumes of DAS DEUTSCHE GESCHLECHTERBUCH. Covers only A-Reinisch.

The many volumes of the GESCHLECHTERBUCH are in FHL and very large genealogical libraries. The indexes by Jeske are in FHL, and the other indexes are in FHL and very large genealogical libraries.

Several other indexes to compilations, articles, and researchers should also be used. These include:

___J. Glenzdorf, GLENZDORF'S INTERNATIONALES GEN-EALOGEN-LEXIKON (GLENZDORF'S INTERNATIONAL DIRECTORY OF GENEALOGISTS), Wilhelm Rost Verlag, Bad Münder/Deister, Deutschland, 1977-present, 4 volumes. Alphabetical listing of surnames being researched by genealogists along with index of places where surnames are found.

___O. Spohr, FAMILIENGESCHICHTLICHE QUELLEN (FAMILY HISTORY SOURCES), Verlag Degener, Neustadt/Aisch, Deutschland, 1927-1959, 13 Bände (volumes). Check for your progenitor's surname.

___DIE DEUTSCHE AHNENLISTEN-KARTEI, Verlag Degener, Neustadt/ Aisch, Deutschland, 1975-, 12 Lieferungen (issues). Each issue separately indexed.

___DEUTSCHES FAMILIENARCHIV (GERMAN FAMILY AR-CHIVE), Verlag Degener, Neustadt/Aisch, Deutschland, 1952-present, over 80 volumes (Bände). Indexes to volumes 1-50, 51-75, 75-100 available. Check for your ancestor's surname.

___T. von Fritsch, DIE GOTHAISCHEN TASCHENBÜCHER, HOFKALENDER, UND ALMANACH, Starke Verlag, Limburg/Lahn, Deutschland, 1987. Indexes over 450 volumes of German noble families: families of princes, dukes, counts, barons, noblemen, and knights. Both the indexes and the volumes to which they refer are in large genealogical libraries and in FHL (FHC). Be sure and look at <u>both</u> indexes, the one starting on page 187, and the one starting on page 350. They are in very large genealogical libraries.

Family and local histories. Many German people have compiled and published their family histories in book form. Others have put their family research data in manuscript form. To locate these books and manuscripts, you need to write to the appropriate town, city, and regional libraries. Quite a sizable number of towns and cities have put together local histories. These often contain valuable genealogical information, especially for the earlier years. Letters of inquiry to town, city, and regional libraries will usually locate available volumes. There is a series of about 150 special local family history books which are exceptionally valuable. These books, originally called DORFSIPPENBÜCHER (village genealogy books) began appearing in 1937. They are now called ORTSIPPENBÜCHER (local genealogy books). The books are collections of data from local church books and some other sources arranged under surname. Such volumes are available for the following towns: Ahausen, Alpenrod, Altdorf, Altenheim, Altenroda, Altensteigdorf, Altweilnau, Anhausen, Anraff, Aschach, Aurich-Oldendorf, Backemoor, Baltrum, Bartschdorf, Berich, Binzen, Boitin, Braunsen, Bredenbeck, Breinermoor, Briesen, Britzingen, Bühle, Büren, Büsingen, Dattingen, Dundenheim, Efringen-Kirchen, Egringen, Eimeldingen, Evestorf, Finsternthal, Fischingen, Frebershausen, Frei-Weinheim, Freiamt, Freisen, Freyenstein, Fürstenberg, Fürth, Gabelbach, Gajdobra-Neugajdobra, Gembeck, Gochsheim, Goldhausen, Grafenhausen, Grenzach, Gross-Upahl, Grosswangen, Güttigheim, Hägerfelde, Haltingen, Hambühren, Hangard, Hausen, Helsen, Heppenheim, Herbolzheim, Hesel, Hodschag, Holtensen, Höringhausen, Hüfingen, Huttingen, Ichenheim, Ingelheim, Ingelheim, Istein, Kappel am Rhein, Karcheez, Kassel, Kippenheim, Kippenheimweiler, Kleinkems, Klitten, Königsbruch, Krautsand, Kreuth, Landau, Lauf, Leitersweiler, Lelbach, Lengefeld, Leutewitz, Loga, Logabirum, Lubzin, Lütersheim, Mahlberg-Orschweier, Massenhausen, Mehlbach, Meissenheim, Meineringhausen, Mettlach-Keuchingen, Middels, Mietersheim, Mittelbach-Hemgstbach, Muggardt, Mulsum, Münchweier, Nebringen, Neider-Ingelheim, Nermsdorf, Neuhof, Nieder-Ense, Nonnenweier, Nordenbeck, Oberacker, Oberense, Oberweier, Öschelbronn, Ötlingen, Ottoschwanden, Petersmark, Philippsburg, Pirmasens, Poppenhausen, Reinbek, Remmesweiler, Rheinhausen, Rhena, Ringsheim, Rümmingen, Rust, Sambach, Schlotzau, Schmieheim, Schweigern, Sexau, Sontra, Spiekeroog, Stein-Wingert, Storbeck, Strohte, Tannenkirch, Tottleben, Treisberg, Vasbeck, Vasbeck, Vechelade, Volkhardinghausen, Volkhardinghausen, Wedtlenstedt, Weingarten, Werdum, Wethen,Wetterburg, Wiegleben, Wilhelmsbruch, Winsdorf, Wittenweier, Wittlingen, Wollbach, Woquard, Zaisenhausen. These

ORTSIPPENBÜCHER may be sought at FHL, large US genealogical libraries, and in town, city, and regional libraries in Germany.

German periodicals. A sizable number of German genealogical periodicals have been or are being published by numerous individuals, agencies, and organizations. They carry genealogical data (family histories, church record extracts, land records, poor registers, emigration lists, funeral sermons, guild records, citizen lists), inquiries, articles on genealogical sources and research techniques, archive inventories, book reviews, and information on historical, geographical, and legal matters bearing on ancestor research. Among the better ones currently being published are:

___(Anhalt, Berlin, Brandenburg, Mecklenburg, Thuringia) MITTEL-DEUTSCHE FAMILIENKUNDE, Goldbergstrasse 23, D-35043 Marburg/Lahn, Bundesrepublik Deutschland, GERMANY.

___(All Germany) ARCHIV FÜR SIPPENFORSCHUNG, published by C. A. Starke Verlag, Frankfurter Strasse 51, D-66549 Limburg/Lahn, Bundesrepublik Deutschland, GERMANY.

___(All Germany) BLATTER FÜR FAMILIENKUNDE UND FAMILIENPFLEGE, published by Bund der Familienverbände, Lorenz-von-Stein-Ring 20, D-24340 Eckernförde, Bundesrepublik Deutschland, GERMANY.

___(All Germany) COMPUTERGENEALOGIE, published by Verein zur Förderung EDV-gestützer familienkundlicher Forschungen, Schorlemmers Kamp 20, D-44536 Lünen, Bundesrepublik Deutschland, GERMANY.

___(All Germany) DER HEROLD, published by Verein für Heraldik, Genealogie, und verwandte Wissenschaften, Archivstrasse 12, D-14195 Berlin, Bundesrepublik Deutschland, GERMANY, 1975 ff.

___(All Germany) FAMILIENGESCHICHTLICHE BLATTER DER ZENTRALSTELLE FÜR DEUTSCHE PERSONEN- UND FAMILIENGESCHICHTE, published by Zentralstelle für Personen- und Familiengeschichte, Seulberg, Birkenweg, D-61381 Friedrichsdorf, Bundesrepublik Deutschland, GERMANY, 1962 ff.

___(All Germany) FAMILIENKUNDLICHE NACHRICHTEN, published by Verlag Degener, Nürnberger Strasse 27, D-91413 Neustadt/Aisch, Bundesrepublik Deutschland, GERMANY, 1956 ff.

___(All Germany) GENEALOGIE, published by Verlag Degener, Nürnberger Strasse 27, D-91413 Neustadt/Aisch, Bundesrepublik

Deutschland, GERMANY, 1952 ff.   Called FAMILIE UND VOLK, 1952-1961.

___(Baden) BADISCHE FAMILIENKUNDE, published in Grafen-hausen, Bundesrepublik Deutschland, GERMANY, 1958 ff.

___(Baden and Württemberg) SÜDWESTDEUTSCHE BLATTER FÜR FAMILIEN- UND WAPPENKUNDE, published by Verein für Familien- und Wappenkunde in Württemberg und Baden, Konrad-Adenauer Strasse 8, Zimmer 103, D-70173 Stuttgart, Bundesrepublik Deutschland, GERMANY, 1949 ff.

___(Bavaria) BLATTER DES BAYERISCHEN LANDESVEREINS FÜR FAMILIENKUNDE, published by Bayerischer Landesverein für Familienkunde, Ludwigstrasse 14/I, D-80539 München, Bundesrepublik Deutschland, GERMANY, 1923-1942, 1958 ff.

___(Bremen, East Frisia, Hamburg, Lower Saxony, Oldenburg, Schleswig-Holstein) NORD-DEUTSCHE FAMILIENKUNDE, Verlag Degener, Nürnberger Strasse 17, D-91413 Neustadt/Aisch, Bundes-republik Deutschland, GERMANY, 1952 ff.

___(Central Germany) MITTELDEUTSCHE FAMILIENKUNDE, published by Arbeitsgemeinschaft für mitteldeutsche Familien-forslchung, Goldbergstrasse 23, D-35043 Marburg/Lahn, Bundes-republik Deutschland, GERMANY, 1960 ff.

___(Düsseldorf area) DÜSSELDORFER FAMILIENKUNDE, published by Düsseldorfer Verein für Familienkunde, Monika Degenhard, Krummenweger Strasswe 26, D-40885 Ratingen, Bundesrepublik Deutschland, GERMANY, 1963 ff.

___(Easternmost Germany) OSTDEUTSCHE FAMILIENKUNDE, and ARCHIV OSTDEUTSCHER FAMILIENFORSCHER, pub-lished by Arbeitsgemeinschaft ostdeutscher Familienforscher, Detlef Kühn, Holzlar, Fuhrweg 29, D-53229 Bonn, Bundesrepublik Deutschland, GERMANY, 1953 ff.

___(East Frisian area) QUELLEN UND FORSCHUNGEN ZUR OSTFRIESISCHEN FAMILIEN- UND WAPPENKUNDE, published by Arbeitsgruppe Familienkunden, Genealogie und Heraldik, Landschaftshaus, Bürgermeister-Mueller-Platz 2, D-26603 Aurich, Bundesrepublik Deutschland, GERMANY, 1951 ff.

___(East Prussia, Pomerania, Silesia, West Prussia, eastern settlements) OSTDEUTSCHE FAMILIENKUNDE, Verlag Degener, Nürnberger Strasse 27, D-91413 Neustadt/Aisch, Bundesrepublik Deutschland, GERMANY, 1953 ff.

___(Franconia in northern Bavaria) BLATTER FÜR FRANKISCHE FAMILIENKUNDE, published by Gesellschaft für Familien-forschung in Franken, Staatsarchiv, Archivstrasse 17, D-90408

Nürnberg, Bundesrepublik Deutschland, GERMANY, 1957 ff.

___(Göttingen area) GÖTTINGER MITTEILUNGEN ZUR FÖR-DERUNG GENEALOGISCHER UND HERALDISCHER ARBEIT, published in Göttingen, Bundesrepublik Deutschland, GERMANY, 1937 ff.

___(Hamburg, Lower Saxony, Mecklenburg, Schleswig-Holstein) NIEDER-EUTSCHE FAMILIENKUNDE, published by Genealogische Gesellschaft, Alsterchaussee 11, D-20149 Hamburg, Bundesrepublik Deutschland, GERMANY.

___(Hesse) HESSISCHE FAMILIENFORSCHER, HESSICHE FAMILIENKUNDE and HESSICHE AHNENLISTEN, published by Arbeitsgemeinschaft der Familienkundlichen Gesellschaften in Hessen, Loreleystrasse 28, D-65929 Frankfurt, Bundesrepublik Deutschland, GERMANY, 1948 ff.

___(Hesse) HESSISCHE FAMILIENKUNDE, Verlag Degener, Nürnberger Strasse 27, D-91413 Neustadt/Aisch, Bundesrepublik Deutschland, GERMANY, 1948 ff.

___(Lower Saxony) ZEITSCHRIFT FÜR NIEDERSACHSISCHE FAMILIENKUNDE, published by Genealogische Gesellschaft, Postfach 302042, D-20307 Hamburg, Bundesrepublik Deutschland, GERMANY, 1919 ff.

___(Lübeck area) LÜBECKER BEITRAGE ZUR FAMILIEN- UND WAPPENKUNDE, published by Lübecker Arbeitskreis für Familienforschung, Mühlentorplatz 2, D-23552 Lübeck, Bundesrepublik Deutschland, GERMANY, 1972 ff.

___(North Germany) NORDDEUTSCHE FAMILIENKUNDE, published by Verlag Degener, Nürnberger Strasse 27, D-91413 Neustadt/Aisch, Bundesrepublik Deutschland, GERMANY, 1952 ff.

___(Oldenburg area) OLDENBURGISCHE FAMILIENKUNDE, published by Oldenburgische Gesellschaft für Familienkunde, Lerigauweg 14, D-26131 Oldenburg, Bundesrepublik Deutschland, GERMANY, 1959 ff.

___(Palatinate-Rhine area) PFALZISCH-RHEINISCHE FAMILIEN-KUNDE, published by Arbeitsgemeinschaft für Pfälzisch-Rheinische Familienkunde, Rottstrasse 17, D-67061 Ludwigshafen/Rhein, Bundesrepublik Deutschland, GERMANY, 1952 ff.

___(Pomerania) SEDINA ARCHIV, FAMILIENGESCHICHTLICHE MITTEILUNGEN DER POMMERSCHEN VEREINIGUNG FÜR STAMM- UND WAPPENKUNDE, published in Stettin, 1933-1941, 1955 ff. Under several different titles before 1955.

___(Prussia) ALTPREUSSICHE GESCHLECHTERKUNDE, published by Verein für Familienforschung in Ost- und Westpreussen, Dr. E. Heling, In de Krümm 10, D1147 Hamburg, Bundesrepublik Deutschland, GERMANY.

___(Rhineland) DIE LATERNE, published by Westdeutsche Gesellschaft für Familienkunde, Adolf Paul Quilling, Grossenbuschstrasse 30, D-53229 Bonn, Bundesrepublik Deutschland, GERMANY, 1948 ff.

___(Rhine Valley and surrounding area) MITTEILUNGEN DER WEST-DEUTSCHEN GESELLSCHAFT FÜR FAMILIENKUNDE, published by Westdeutsche Gesellschaft für Familienkunde, Wallstrasse 96, D-51063 Köln, Bundesrepublik Deutschland, GERMANY, 1914 ff.

___(Saarland) SAARLANDISCHE FAMILIENKUNDE, published by Arbeitsgemeinschaft für Saarländische Familienkunde, Hebbelstrasse 3, D-66356 Püttlingen, Bundesrepublik Deutschland, GERMANY.

___(Schleswig-Holstein) MITTEILUNGSBLATT DER GESELL-SCHAFT FÜR SCHLESWIG-HOLSTEINISCHE FAMILIEN-FORSCHUNG UND WAPPENKUNDE, published by Schleswig-Holsteinische Gesellschaft für Familienforschung und Wappenkunde, Postfach 3809, D-24037 Kiel, Bundesrepublik Deutschland, GERMANY, 194 ff.

___(Schleswig-Holstein) FAMILIENKUNDLICHES JAHRBUCH SCHLESWIG-HOLSTEIN, published in Kiel, Bundesrepublik Deutschland, GERMANY, 1962 ff.

___(Thüringen) GENEALOGIE IN DEUTSCHLAND, published by Arbeitsgemeinschaft Genealogie Thüringen e.V., Martin-Andersen-Nexoe-Strasse 62, D-99096 Erfurt, Bundesrepublik Deutschland, GERMANY.

___(Westphalia) BEITRAGE ZUR WESTFALISCHEN FAMILIEN-FORSCHUNG, published by Westfälische Gesellschaft für Genealogie und Familienforschung, Warendorferstrasse 25, D-48145 Münster, Bundesrepublik Deutschland, GERMANY, 1938 ff.

In addition to the above periodicals, there are others which are currently being published, and many others which were published at one time, but are now defunct. A listing of a sizable number of these is in:
___W. Ribbe and E. Henning, TASCHENBUCH FÜR FAMILIENGE-SCHICHTSFORSCHUNG, Verlag Degener, Neustadt/Aisch, Deutschland, 1980, pp. 224-227.

Fortunately, there are some very good indexes which lead you to pertinent articles in the periodicals.

___DER SCHLÜSSEL, Heinz Reise-Verlag, Göttingen, Deutschland, 9 volumes, 1950 ff., more in preparation.

This remarkable research aid lists surnames, place names, and the subject matter of the titles of articles appearing in over 90 German genealogical publications. Two other useful indexes which include periodical references are:

___J. Hohlfeld, F. Wecken, and others, FAMILIENGESCHICHTLICHE BIBLIOGRAPHIE, Degener Verlag, Neustadt/Aisch, Deutschland, 1920-forward, 19 volumes, more to come. Covers articles and books published from 1897 forward. In volume 6, section 3, there is a cumulative index covering all volumes up to that time (1937).

___O. Spohr and F. Heinzmann, FAMILIENGESCHICHTLICHE QUELLEN, Degener Verlag, Neustadt/Aisch, Deutschland, 1926 ff., 13 volumes. Has over 2 million entries taken from about 1600 sources. Each volume separately indexed.

Many German periodicals will be found in the FHL and in very large genealogical libraries. These same repositories also have one or more of the above-mentioned indexes.

German newspapers (Deutsche Zeitungen). The local newspapers of Germany, which were coming to be published in many places by about 1800, are exceedingly rich genealogical sources. They can contain both direct and indirect data relating to births, marriages, emigrations, children, and deaths. The most valuable are usually the death notices which carry the date and place of death, the place of burial, the date of birth, the occupation, survivor's names (spouse, children), and sometimes the place of birth. An excellent bibliography of newspapers held by libraries and archives in Germany is available. It lists over 2000 newspapers located in over 200 places.

___G. Hagelweide, GERMAN NEWSPAPERS IN LIBRARIES AND ARCHIVES, Droste Verlag, Düsseldorf, Deutschland, 1974.

Listings of newspapers in many archives are also given in:

___ARCHIVE IM DEUTSCHSPRACHIGEN RAUM, Minerva Handbücher, Walter de Gruyter und Co., Berlin, Deutschland, 1974, 2 Bände (volumes).

These volumes indicate that your search for newspapers of your forebear's village, town, or city should be made in town and city libraries and archives, and in nearby regional and state libraries and archives. The

FHL also holds a number of German newspapers on microfilm. Among the large German libraries which have sizable newspaper collections are:

___In Berlin: Deutsche Staatsbibliothek, Unter den Linden 8, D-10117; Staatsbibliothek Preussischer Kulturbesitz, D-14195; Institut für Publizistik, D-14195; Deutsches Institut für Zeitgeschichte, D-10916.

___In Bonn: Presse- und Informationsamtes der Bundesregierung, D-53001.

___In Bremen: Universität Bremen Bibliothek, Deutsche Presseforschung, Breitenweg 27, D-28195.

___In Halle: Universitäts- und Landesbibliothek Sachsen Anhalt, D-06001.

___In Munich: Bayerische Staatsbibliothek, Ludwigstrasse 16, D-80539.

It is important that you know the approximate dates of events in your ancestor's life, because very few newspapers are indexed.

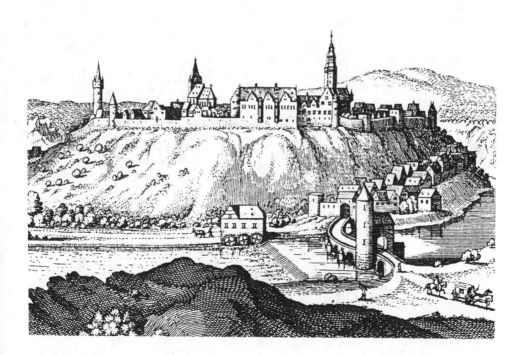

Weilburg.

Schwartzenberg

CHAPTER 5
(KAPITEL 5)
GERMAN RECORD REPOSITORIES
(DEUTSCHE URKUNDENVERWAHRUNGSORTE)

1. Introduction	1. Einleitung
1. **Einleitung**	*1. Einleitung*

The genealogical records of Germany are spread among many repositories because of the political fragmentation of the Germanic area before 1871. The major repositories include governmental offices (Standesämter or civil registry offices, Amter or district offices, Amtsgerichte or district county courts, Domäneämter or estate offices, Bezirksgerichte or local courts, Landesgerichte or county courts, Oberämter or county offices, Oberlandesgerichte or provincial courts, Ritterämter or estate offices, Finanzämter or revenue offices, Arbeitsgerichte or labor courts, Versorgungsämter or pension offices), individual church offices (Pfarrämter), church archives (Kirchliche Archive), national archives (Bundesarchive), state archives (Staatliche Archive), county archives (Kreisarchive), town and city archives (Stadtarchive), manorial archives (Herrschaftsarchive), family archives (Familienarchive), trade and industry archives (Wirtschaftsarchive), business company archives (Firmenarchive), factory archives (Werksarchive), press archives (Pressearchive), university archives (Universitätsarchive), institute and academy archives (Hochschularchive), and archives dealing with specialized subjects (such as art, music, archaeology, theater, the Brothers Grimm, mining). There are also numerous libraries which are good sources of published genealogical materials, newspapers, maps, local histories, and family histories. These libraries are the national libraries (Nationalbibliotheken), the state libraries (Staatsbibliotheken and Landesbibliotheken), and the university libraries (Universitätsbibliotheken).

The governmental offices mentioned above are located in the appropriate towns or cities, with some of the offices being located in a nearby larger place in the case of small towns and villages. The gazetteers by MEYER and MÜLLER can often be of assistance because they list the exact locations of some of the governmental offices for a given village, town, or city. Many of the important archives are listed in the following reference works:

___ARCHIVE IM DEUTSCHSPRACHIGEN RAUM, Walter de
   Gruyter, Berlin, Deutschland, 1974.
___ARCHIVE UND ARCHIVARE, Selbst Verlag des Vereins deutscher
   Archivare, München, Deutschland, 1986.
___E. Thode, ADDRESS BOOK FOR GERMANIC GENEALOGY,
   Genealogical Publishing Co., Baltimore, MD, 1994, pages 60-128,
___E. Henning in W. Ribbe und E. Henning, TASCHENBUCH FÜR
   FAMILIENGESCHICHTSFORSCHUNG, Verlag Degener,
   Neustadt/Aisch, Deutschland, 1990, Seiten (pages) 359-400.
___THE WORLD OF LEARNING, Europa Publications, London, latest
   issue.
The first listing is especially useful because it gives the name of each ar-
chive, its exact address, its telephone number, a brief history of the ar-
chive, a brief summary of its record holdings, and references to literature
(both books and articles) which describe its record collection in detail.
For listings of German libraries, you may consult:
___THE WORLD OF LEARNING, Europa Publications, London, latest
   issue.
___W. Ribbe in W. Ribbe und E. Henning, TASCHENBUCH FÜR
   FAMILIENGESCHICHTSFORSCHUNG, Verlag Degener,
   Neustadt/Aisch, Deutschland, 1980, Seiten (pages) 401-405.
___E. Thode, ADDRESS BOOK FOR GERMAN GENEALOGY,
   Genealogical Publishing Co., Baltimore, MD, 1994, pages 158-161.

2. Family History Library (FHL)	2. Family History Library
2. Family Hiftory Library	2. Family Hiffory Library

   The Family History Library is located at 35 North West Temple,
Salt Lake City, UT 84150. They hold the largest German genealogical
collection in the US. This large collection is open free of charge to all
persons. The hours are 7:30-6:00 Monday, 7:30-10:00 Tuesday through
Friday, and 7:30-5:00 Saturday, except holidays. The German collection
consists of many books, many periodicals, and many microfilm copies of
German records and publications. Included are biographical volumes,
censuses, church records, city directories, city records, civil registers, court
records, emigration records, family histories, funeral sermons, gazetteers,
genealogical compilations, genealogical indexes, guardianship records,
guild records, land records, local histories, maps, military records,
periodicals, probate records, reference works, tax lists, town records,
university records, and wills.

The key which permits you to locate records in the Family History Library (FHL) is the Family History Library Catalog (FHLC) and several very important indexes and locators. The Family History Library Catalog is divided into four sections:

___*(FHLC-SurS) FAMILY HISTORY LIBRARY CATALOG, SURNAME SECTION, latest computer or microfiche edition. To be searched for all surnames you are interested in. Leads you to family histories, genealogies, research collections, and previous work which other people have done on the family. Available at FHL and all FHC branches of FHL which are called Family History Centers).

___*(FHLC-SubS) FAMILY HISTORY LIBRARY CATALOG, SUBJECT SECTION, latest computer or microfiche edition. To be searched for specific types of records, for example, divorce, land, guardian, and postal code guides. Available at FHL and all FHC.

___*(FHLC-A/TS) FAMILY HISTORY LIBRARY CATALOG, AUTHOR/ TITLE SECTION, latest computer or microfiche edition. To be searched for particular volumes, either by their authors or their titles. Microfilm records can be found in this index under the name of the organization that created them. Available at FHL and all FHC.

___*(FHLC-LS) FAMILY HISTORY LIBRARY CATALOG, LOCALITY SECTION, latest computer or microfiche edition. To be searched for your ancestor's nation of Germany, and for your ancestor's state, province, district, county, city, town, village. Leads you to the national, state, province, district, and local records which the Family History Library has, and which are likely to include your ancestor. Available at FHL and all FHC. Since this section of the FHLC is so very important, it will now be discussed in detail.

THE LOCALITY SECTION of the FAMILY HISTORY LIBRARY CATALOG (FHLC-LS) is an exceptionally valuable resource because it lists all the German materials which the FHL holds in its extensive collection. This catalog is organized according to the states and provinces which existed in the united Germany of 1871-1918. The major headings in the German section of the FHLC-LS are as follows: Germany, Anhalt, Baden, Bayern, Braunschweig, Bremen, Elsass-Lothringen, Hamburg, Hessen, Lippe, Lübeck, Mecklenburg-Schwerin, Mecklenburg-Strelitz, Niedersachsen, Oldenburg, Preussen, Preussen-Brandenburg, Preussen-Hannover, Preussen-Hessen-Nassau, Preussen-

Hohenzollern, Preussen-Ostpreussen, Preussen-Pommern, Preussen-Posen, Preussen-Rheinland, Preussen-Sachsen, Preussen-Schlesien, Preussen-Schleswig-Holstein, Preussen-Westfalen, Preussen-Westpreussen, Sachsen, Sachsen-Altenburg, Sachsen-Coburg-Gotha, Sachsen-Meiningen, Sachsen-Weimar-Eisenach, Schaumburg-Lippe, Schwarzburg-Rudolstadt, Schwarzburg-Sonderhausen, Thüringen, Waldeck, and Württemberg. You will notice that the large state of Preussen has been broken up into its constituent provinces, each of which gets a major heading. Do not forget that the Pfalz area (Palatinate) west of the Rhine River was part of Bavaria (Bayern) 1815-1945.

The first major heading is entitled Germany. The initial entry under that category is a very lengthy list of cities, towns, and villages in 1874-1918. It is important to remember that only places with parishes are listed. Therefore, if a hamlet or village had no parish, it will be treated under the name of the city or town whose parish served its people. This list of cities, towns, and villages is alphabetical, and each citation shows you exactly how to find it in the FHLC-LS. After the list, the Germany heading is subdivided into the following sub-headings: Archives and Libraries, Bible Records, Bibliography, Biography, Business and Commerce, Cemeteries, Census, Centennials, Chronology, Church Directories, Church Histories, Church Records, Civil Registration, Collected Works, Colonization, Correctional Institutions, Court Records, Description and Travel, Dictionaries, Directories, Dwellings, Emigration and Immigration, Encyclopedias, Ethnology, folklore, Gazetteers, Genealogy, Guardian Records, Guide Books, Handbooks and Manuals, Handwriting, Heraldry, Historical Geography, History, Indexes, Inventories and Registers, Jewish History, Jewish Records, Land and Property, Languages, Law and Legislation, Manors, Maps, Medical Records, Migration (Internal), Military History, Military Records, Minorities, Names (Geographic), Names (Personal), Native Races, Naturalization, Newspapers, Nobility, Notarial Records, Obituaries, Occupations, Officials and Employees, Orphans, Pensions, Periodicals, Politics and Government, Poor Records, Religion, Schools, Slavery and Bondage, Social Life and Customs, Societies, Statistics, Taxation, Vital Records, Voting Registers, Yearbooks.

Following the Germany heading, the other major headings (states or provinces) then appear: Anhalt, then Baden, then Bayern, and so on. Under each of these, Baden for example, there first appear listings for the overall state of Baden. The categories listed in the previous paragraph are used. Then the cities and towns in Baden are listed, and under each, the same categories are used. When categories are not represented by record holdings, they will be omitted.

There are also several large FHL indexes which contain names of Germans in Germany and of German immigrants to the colonies and/or the US. Chief among these are:
___*(IGI-GS) INTERNATIONAL GENEALOGICAL INDEX, GERMANY SECTION, latest computer or microfiche edition. To be searched for all names which you are seeking in Germany. Over 21 million entries. Available at FHL and all FHC.
___*(IGI-USS) INTERNATIONAL GENEALOGICAL INDEX, US SECTION, latest computer or microfiche edition. To be searched for all names of immigrant German ancestors and their descendants. Available at FHL and all FHC.
___*(FR) FAMILY REGISTRY, latest edition. To be searched for names of immigrant German ancestors and their descendants. Refers to persons who are doing genealogical research on them. Available at FHL and all FHC.
___(FGRC) FAMILY GROUP RECORDS COLLECTION, available at FHL. Over 8 million family genealogy sheets. Obtain order blank at local FHC to have it searched for your German ancestors and their descendants.
___(TIB) TEMPLE INDEX BUREAU, available at FHL. A 30 million name index to persons for whom records are on file. Obtain order blank at local FHC to have it searched for your German ancestor and his/her descendants.
___*(AF) ANCESTRAL FILE, latest computer or microfiche edition. Millions of indexed records. Search for your German ancestors and their descendants. Available at FHL and all FHC.

All the above indexes will lead you to various holdings of records at the FHL (microfilms, books, manuscripts). A detailed description of the holdings of the FHL is given in:
___J. Cerny and W. Elliott, THE LIBRARY, A GUIDE TO THE LDS FAMILY HISTORY LIBRARY, Ancestry Publishing, Salt Lake City, UT, 1988, Chapter 19.
If you cannot go to FHL, most of the above indexes are available at the numerous Family History Centers (FHC) located in most metropolitan areas of the US and at many places in other countries. The indexes marked with asterisks in the previous paragraph are the ones available at all FHC. In addition, most of the microfilmed records listed in the above indexes can be borrowed from FHL by your local FHC for you to read on

their microfilm readers. Family History centers are located in the
following US cities:

___In AL: Birmingham, Dothan, Huntsville, Mobile, Montgomery, In AK:
Anchorage, Fairbanks, Juneau, Ketchikan, Soldotna, Wasilla, In
AZ: Buckeye, Cottonwood, Flagstaff, Globe, Holbrook, Kingman,
Mesa, Page, Peoria, Phoenix, Prescott, Safford, St. David, St.
Johns, Show Low, Sierra Vista, Snowflake, Tucson, Winslow,
Yuma, In AR: Fort Smith, Jacksonville, Little Rock,

___In CA: Anaheim, Anderson, Auburn, Bakersfield, Barstow, Blythe,
Buena Park, Camarillo, Canyon Country, Carlsbad, Cerritos,
Chatsworth, Chico, Clovis, Corona, Covina, El Centro, Escondido,
Eureka, Fairfield, Fresno, Glendale, Goleta, Gridley, Hacienda
Heights, Hanford, Hemet, Highland, Huntington Beach, La
Crescenta, Lancaster, Los Alamitos, Los Angeles, Menlo Park,
Mission Viejo, Modesto, Monterey Park, Moorpark, Moreno
Valley, Napa, Needles, Newbury Park, Norwalk, Oakland, Orange,
Palmdale, Palm Desert, Pasadena, Quincy, Rancho Palos Verdes,
Redding, Ridgecrest, Riverside, Sacramento, San Bernardino, San
Bruno, San Diego, San Jose, San Luis Obispo, Santa Clara, Santa
Maria, Santa Rosa, Seaside, Simi Valley, Sonora, Ukiah, Upland,
Van Nuys, Ventura, Victorville, Visalia, Watsonville, Westminster,
Whittier, Yuba City, Yucaipa,

___In CO: Arvada, Boulder, Colorado Springs, Cortez, Craig, Denver,
Durango, Fort Collins, Grand Junction, Greeley, La Jara,
Littleton, Montrose, Northglenn, Pueblo, In CT: Bloomfield,
Madison, New Canaan, Trumbull, Waterford, In DE: Wilmington,
In FL: Boca Raton, Fort Meyers, Gainesville, Homestead,
Jacksonville, Lake City, Lake Mary, Orange Park, Orlando,
Panama City, Pensacola, Plantation, Rockledge, St. Petersburg,
Tallahassee, Tampa, Winter Haven,

___In GA: Augusta, Columbus, Dunwoody, Macon, Marietta, Roswell,
Savannah, Tucker, Valdosta, in HI: Hilo, Honolulu, Kaneohe,
Kona, Laie, Lihue, Mililani, in ID: Blackfoot, Boise, Burley,
Caldwell, Coeur d'Arlene, Driggs, Emmett, Firth, Idaho Falls,
Iona, Lewiston, Mald, Meridian, Montpelier, Moore, Nampa,
Pocatello, Rexburg, Salmon, Sandpoint, Shelly, Soda Springs,
Twin Falls, Weber, In IL: Carbondale, Cham-paign, Chicago
Heights, Fairview Heights, Joliet, Naperville, Nauvoo, Peoria,
Rockford, Schaumburg, Wilmette,

___In IN: Bloomington, Evansville, Fort Wayne, Indianapolis, Noblesville,
New Albany, South Bend, Terre Haute, In IA: Ames, Cedar
Rapids, Davenport, Sioux City, West Des Moines, In KS: Dodge

City, Olathe, Topeka, Wichita, In KY: Hopkinsville, Lexington, Louisville, Martin, Paducah, In LA: Alexandria, Baton Rouge, Monroe, Metairie, Shreveport, In ME: Bangor, Cape Elizabeth, Caribou, Farmingdale, In MD: Annapolis, Ellicott City, Frederick, Kensington, Lutherville, In MA: Foxboro, Weston,

__In MI: Ann Arbor, Bloomfield Hills, East Lansing, Grand Blanc, Grand Rapids, Kalamazoo, Marquette, Midland, Westland, In MN: Duluth, Minneapolis, Rochester, St. Cloud, St. Paul, In MS: Clinton, Columbus, Gulfport, Hattiesburg, In MO: Columbia, Frontenac, Independence, Joplin, Kansas City, Liberty, Springfield, In MT: Billings, Bozeman, Butte, Great Falls, Helena, Kalispell, Missoula, Stevensville,

__In NE: Grand Island, Lincoln, Omaha, In NV: Elko, Ely, Fallon, Las Vegas, Logandale, Reno, Sparks, In NH: Concord, Nashua, In NJ: Cherry Hill, East Brunswick, Morristown, In NM: Albuquerque, Carlsbad, Farmington, Gallup, Grants, Las Cruces, Santa Fe, Silver City, In NY: Jamestown, Loudonville, Plainview, Pittsford, Syracuse, Vestal, Williamsville, In NC: Charlotte, Fayetteville, Goldsboro, Greensboro, Hickory, Kingston, Raleigh, Skyland, Wilmington, Winston-Salem, In ND: Bismark, Fargo, Minot,

__In OH: Akron, Cincinnati, Dayton, Dublin, Fairbourn, Kirtland, Reynoldsburg, Toledo, Westlake, In OK: Lawton, Muskogee, Norman, Oklahoma City, Stillwater, Tulsa, In OR: Beaverton, Bend, Central Point, Coos Bay, Corvallis, Eugene, Grants Pass, Gresham, Hermiston, Hillsboro, Klamath Falls, La Grande, Lake Oswego, McMinnville, Medford, Nyssa, Ontario, Oregon City, Portland, Prineville, Roseburg, Salem, Sandy, The Dalles, In PA: Broomall, Clarks Summit, Erie, Knox, Pittsburgh, Reading, State College, York,

__In RI: Providence, In SC: Charleston, Columbia, Florence, Greenville, West Columbia, In SD: Gettysburg, Rapid City, Rosebud, Sioux Falls, In TN: Chattanooga, Franklin, Kingsport, Knoxville, Madison, Memphis, In TX: Abilene, Amarillo, Austin, Bryan, Corpus Christie, Dallas, Denton, Duncanville, El Paso, Fort Worth, Friendswood, Harlingen, Houston, Killeen, Kingwood, Longview, Lubbock, McAllen, Odessa, Orange, Pasadena, Plano, Port Arthur, Richland Hills, San Antonio, Sugarland,

__In UT: Altamont, Beaver, Blanding, Bountiful, Brigham City, Cache, Castledale, Cedar City, Delta, Duchesne, Escalante, Ferron, Fillmore, Grantsville, Green River, Heber City, Hurricane, Kanab, Lehi, Loa, Moroni, Mount Pleasant, Nephi, Ogden, Parowan, Price, Provo, Richfield, Roosevelt, Sandy, Santaquin, South

Jordan, St. George, Springville, Tremonton-Garland, Vernal, In
VT: Berlin,
___In VA: Annandale, Charlottesville, Dale City, Falls Church, Newport
News, Oakton, Richmond, Salem, Virginia Beach, In WA:
Auburn, Bellevue, Bremerton, Centralia, Edmonds, Elma, Everett,
Federal Way, Ferndale, Fennewick, Lake Stevens, Longview,
Moses Lake, Mount Vernon, North Bend, Olympia, Othello,
Pasco, Pullman, Quincy, Richland, Seattle, Silverdale, Spokane,
Sumner, Tacoma, Vancouver, Walla Walla, Wenatchee, Yakima,
___In WV: Fairmont, Huntington, In WI: Eau Claire, Hales Corners,
Madison, Shawano, In WY: Afton, Casper, Cheyenne, Cody,
Evanston, Gillette, Green River, Jackson Hole, Kemmerer,
Laramie, Lovell, Rawlins, Riverton, Rock Springs, Sheridan,
Uriks, Worland.

3. German governmental archives	3. Deutsche Regierungs-archive
3. Deutsche Regierungs-archive	3. Deutsche Regierungsarchiven

German governmental archives are an exceptionally important source of practically all types of original records. The most important of these governmental archives are the national, state, regional, district/county, city/town, and some specialized ones. These will be listed in this section.

Having located your ancestral city, town, village, hamlet, or community, you need to recognize that the governmental archives in his/her state, region, district/county, and in nearby cities are likely to hold records of value to your research. Hence, what you should do is locate the place on a map, then using the state and regional archive listings below, identify the archives in his/her state. Having done this, take a look and see if your forebear's city is in the lists of city/town and district/county archives presented below. If it is, this is the city/town or district/county archive which is pertinent. If not, then you need to use your map to locate the two or three nearest cities/towns or district/county towns which do have archives. It is in these archives where further records on your progenitor can possibly be found. Be sure and examine both the city/town listings and the district/county listings.

The state and regional archives in Germany are:

___FOR BADEN-WÜRTTEMBERG (BW): Generallandesarchiv, Nördliche Hilda-Promenade 2, D-76133 Karlsruhe, Bundesrepublik Deutschland, GERMANY.

___For BW-Baden: Staatsarchiv, Columbistrasse 4, D-79098 Freiburg, Bundesrepublik Deutschland, GERMANY. Note that BW means that this archive is in Baden-Württemberg.

___For BW-Württemburg: Hauptstaatsarchiv, Konrad-Adenauer-Strasse 4, D-70173 Stuttgart, Bundesrepublik Deutschland, GERMANY; Staatsarchiv, Schloss-Strasse 30, D-71634 Ludwigsburg, Bundesrepublik Deutschland, GERMANY.

___For BW-Hohenzollern: Staatsarchiv, Strohdorfer Strasse 11, Postfach 526, D-72488, Sigmaringen, Bundesrepublik Deutschland, GERMANY.

___For BW-Wertheim: Staatsarchiv Wertheim, Muehlenstrasse 26, D-97877 Wertheim, Bundesrepublik Deutschland, GERMANY.

___FOR BAYERN (B): Hauptstaatsarchiv I, Arcisstrasse 12, Postfach 200507, D-80333 München, Bundesrepublik Deutschland, GERMANY.

___For B-Coburg: Staatsarchiv, Schloss Ehrenburg, D-96450 Coburg, Bundesrepublik Deutschland, GERMANY.

___For-B-Mittelfranken: Staatsarchiv, Archivstrasse 17, D-90408 Nürnberg, Bundesrepublik Deutschland, GERMANY.

___For B-Niederbayern: Staatsarchiv, Burg Trausnitz, D-84036 Landshut, Bundesrepublik Deutschland, GERMANY.

___For B-Oberbayern: Staatsarchiv, Schönfeldstrasse 3, D-80539 München, Bundesrepublik Deutschland, GERMANY.

___For B-Oberfranken: Staatsarchiv, Hainstrasse 39, Postfach 2668, D-96017 Bamberg, Bundesrepublik Deutschland, GERMANY.

___For B-Oberpfalz: Staatsarchiv, Archivstrasse 3, D-92224 Amberg, Bundesrepublik Deutschland, GERMANY.

___For B-Schwaben: Staatsarchiv, Schloss, D-86333 Neuburg a.d. Donau, Bundesrepublik Deutschland, GERMANY.

___For B-Unterfranken: Staatsarchiv, Residlenzplatz 2, D-97070 Würzburg, Bundesrepublik Deutschland, GERMANY.

___FOR BERLIN (WEST): Staatsarchiv, Archivstrasse 12-14, D-14195 Berlin, Bundesrepublik Deutschland, GERMANY.

___FOR BRANDENBURG:Staatsarchiv, Sanssouci-Orangerie, O-14469 Potsdam, Bundesrepublik Deutschland, GERMANY.

___FOR BREMEN: Staatsarchiv, Präsident-Kennedy-Platz 2, D-28203 Bremen, Bundesrepublik Deutschland, GERMANY.

___FOR ELSASS-LOTHRINGEN (EL)-Bas-Rhin: Archives départementales du Bas-Rhin, 5-9 rue Fischart, F-67000 Strasbourg, FRANCE.

___For EL-Haut-Rhin: Archives départmentales du Haut-Rhin, Cité administrative, Rue Fleischauer, F-68000 Colmar, FRANCE.

___For EL-Moselle: Archives départmentales de la Moselle, Préfecture de la Moselle, Hôtel du Département, 9 Place de la Prêfecture, F-57036 Metz, FRANCE.

___For EL-Meurthe-et-Moselle: Archives départementales de Meurthe-et-Moselle, 3 rue de la Monnaie, F-54000 Nancy, FRANCE.

___FOR HAMBURG: Staatsarchiv, ABC-Strasse 19a, D-20354 Bremen, Bundesrepublik Deutschland, GERMANY.

___FOR HESSEN (H)-Nassau: Hauptstaatsarchiv, Mainzer Strasse 80, D-65187 Wiesbaden, Bundesrepublik Deutschland, GERMANY.

___For H-Darmstadt: Staatsarchiv Darmstadt, Karolinenplatz 3, D-64289 Darmstadt, Bundesrepublik Deutschland, GERMANY.

___For H-Kassel: Staatsarchiv, Friedrichsplatz 15, Postfach 540, D-35017 Marburg a.d. Lahn, Bundesrepublik Deutschland, GERMANY.

___FOR MECKLENBURG-VORPOMMERN (MV)-Mecklenburg: Staatsarchiv, Graf-Schack-Allee 2, D-19053 Schwerin, Bundesrepublik Deutschland, GERMANY.

___For MV-Vorpommern: Staatsarchiv, Martin-Andersen-Nexoe-Platz 1, D-17489 Greifswald, Bundesrepublik Deutschland, GERMANY.

___FOR NIEDERSACHSEN (N): Hauptstaatsarchiv, Am Archiv 1, D-30169 Hannover, Bundesrepublik Deutschland, GERMANY.

___For N-Braunschweig: Staatsarchiv, Forstweg 2, D-38302 Wolfenbüttel, Bundesrepublik Deutschland, GERMANY.

___For N-Bückeburg: Staatsarchiv, Schloss, D-31675 Bückeburg, Bundesrepublik Deutschland, GERMANY.

___For N-Oldenburg: Staatsarchiv, Damm 43, D-26135 Oldenburg, Bundesrepublik Deutschland, GERMANY.

___For N-Osnabrück: Staatsarchiv, Schloss-Strasse 29, D-49074 Osnabrück, Bundesrepublik Deutschland, GERMANY.

___For N-Ostfriesland: Staatsarchiv, Oldersumer Strasse 50,, D-26603 Aurich, Bundesrepublik Deutschland, GERMANY.

___For N-Stade: Staatsarchiv, Am Sande 4c, D-21682 Stade, Bundesrepublik Deutschland, GERMANY.

___For N-Wolfenbüttel: Niedersächsisches Staatsarchiv, Wolfenbüttel, Forstweg 2, D-38302 Wolfenbuettel, Bundesrepublik Deutschland, GERMANY.

___FOR NORDRHEIN-WESTFALEN (NW): Haupstaatsarchiv, Mauerstr. 55, D-404076Düsseldorf, Bundesrepublik Deutschland, GERMANY.

___For NW-Lippe: Staatsarchiv, Willi-Hofmann-Strasse 2, D-32756 Detmold, Bundesrepublik Deutschland, GERMANY.

___For NW-Westfalen: Staatsarchiv, Bohlweg 2, D-48147 Münster, Bundesrepublik Deutschland, GERMANY.

___FOR RHEINLAND-PFALZ (RP)-Rheinland: Personenstandsarchiv für Kirchenbücher und Zivilstandregister, Schloss-Strasse 12, D-50321 Brühl, Bundesrepublik Deutschland, GERMANY.

___For RP-Pfalz: Staatsarchiv, Domplatz 6, D-67346 Speyer, Bundesrepublik Deutschland, GERMANY.

___For RP-Rheinland: Staatsarchiv, Karmeliterstrasse 1-3, D-56068 Koblenz, Bundesrepublik Deutschland, GERMANY.

___FOR SAARLAND: Landesarchiv, Scheidter Str. 114, D-66130 Saarbrücken, Bundesrepublik Deutschland, GERMANY.

___FOR SACHSEN (S)-Dresden: Staatsarchiv, Archivstrasse 14, D-01097 Dresden, Bundesrepublik Deutschland, GERMANY.

___For S-Leipzig: Staatsarchiv, Georgi-Dimitroff-Platz 1, D-04107, Leipzig, Bundesrepublik Deutschland, GERMANY.

___For S-Bautzen: Staatsarchiv, Ortenburg, D-02625 Bautzen, Bundesrepublik Deutschland, GERMANY.

___For S-Altenburg: Staatsarchiv, Schloss 2a, D-04600 Altenburg, Bundesrepublik Deutschland, GERMANY.

___FOR SACHSEN-ANHALT (SA)-Magdeburg: Staatsarchiv, Hegelstrasse 25, D-39104 Magdeburg, Bundesrepublik Deutschland, GERMANY.

___For SA-Wernigerode: Staatsarchiv, Schlossfreiheit 7, D-38855 Wernigerode (Harz), Bundesrepublik Deutschland, GERMANY.

___For SA-Oranienbaum: Staatsarchiv, Schloss, D-06785 Oranienbaum, Bundesrepublik Deutschland, GERMANY.

___FOR SCHLESWIG-HOLSTEIN: Landesarchiv, Schloss Gottorf, D-24837 Schleswig, Bundesrepublik Deutschland, GERMANY.

___FOR THÜRINGEN (T)-Gotha: Staatsarchiv, Schloss Friedenstein, D-99867 Gotha, Bundesrepublik Deutschland, GERMANY.

___For T-Greiz: Staatsarchiv, Oberes Schloss, D-07873 Greiz, Bundesrepublik Deutschland, GERMANY.

___For T-Meiningen: Staatsarchiv, Schloss Bibrabau, D-98617 Meiningen, Bundesrepublik Deutschland, GERMANY.

___For T-Rudolstadt: Staatsarchiv, Schloss Heidecksburg, D-07407 Rudolstadt, Bundesrepublik Deutschland, GERMANY.

___For T-Weimar: Hauptstaatsarchiv, Beethovenplatz 3, D-99423 Weimar, Bundesrepublik Deutschland, GERMANY.

Next we will consider several archives in Germany which deal with records of the former provinces of Ostpreussen, Westpreussen, Pommern, Brandenburg-Ost, Schlesien, and Posen, which are now largely in Poland. Before contacting any archives in Poland, you should inquire at these. It would also be well for you to contact the genealogical societies which are dedicated to research in these former provinces. They were listed in Section 14 of Chapter 3.

___GEHEIMES STAATSARCHIV PREUSSISCHER KULTUR-BESITZ, Archivstrasse 12, D-14195 Berlin, Bundesrepublik Deutschland, GERMANY.

___STANDESAMT I IN BERLIN (WEST), Rheinstrasse 54, D-12161 Berlin, Bundesrepublik Deutschland, GERMANY.

___STANDESAMT I IN BERLIN (EAST), Rückerstrasse 9, D-12163 Berlin, Bundesrepublik Deutschland, GERMANY.

___BUNDESARCHIV, ABT. OSTARCHIV, Am Wöllerhof 12, D-56001 Koblenz, Bundesrepublik Deutschland, GERMANY.

___JOHANN-GOTTFRIED-HERDER-INSTITUT, Gisonenweg 5, D-35037 Marburg/Lahn, Bundesrepublik Deutschland, GERMANY.

___ZENTRALSTELLE FÜR GENEALOGIE, Käthe-Kollwitz-Strasse 1, D-04109 Leipzig, Bundesrepublik Deutschland, GERMANY.

The archives in Poland for the territories we have been discussing and archives in France relating to the Alsace (Elsass) and Lorraine (Lothringen) are:

___(East Prussia, Ostpreussen) for Allenstein/Olsztyn, Wojewódzkie Archiwum Pánstwowe w Olsztynie Zamek, Zamkowa 2, PL-10074 Olsztyn, Polska, POLAND.

___(West Prussia, Westpreussen) Bromberg/Bydgoszcz, Wojewódzkie Archiwum Pánstwowe w Bydgoszczy, ul. Dworcowa 65, PL-83009 Bydgoszcz, Polska, POLAND. For Danzig/Gdansk, Wojewódzkie Archiwum Pánstwowe w Gdansku, ul. Waly Piastowski 5, PL-80855 Gdansk, Poland, POLAND. For Thorn/Torun, Wojewódzkie Archiwum Pánstwowe w Toruniu, pl. Rapackiego 4, PL-87100 Torun, Polska, POLAND.

___(Pomerania, Pommern) For Köslin/Koszalin, Wojewódzkie Archiwum Pánstwowe w Koszalinie, ul. Zwyciestwa 117, skrytka pocztowa, PL-75950 Koszalin, Polska, POLAND. For Stettin/ Szczecin, Wojewódzkie Archiwum Pánstwowe w Szczecinie, ul. sw. Wojciecha 13, PL-70410 Szczecin, Polska, POLAND.

___(East Brandenburg, Brandenburg-Ost) For Frankfurt/Oder, Landsberg/Warthe, Lebus, Meseritz, Schwerin/Warthe and Weststernberg, Wojewódzkie Archiwum Pánstwowe, Gorzow Wielkopolski, Polska, POLAND. For Königsberg, Wojewódzkie Archiwum Pánstwowe, Szczecin, Polska, POLAND. For Forst/Lausatia, Crossen/Oder, Guben, Oststernberg, Sorau/Lansatia, Zuellichau-Schwiebus, Wojewódzkie Archiwum Pánstwowe, Stary Kiselin 31, PL-66002 Zielona Gora, Polska, POLAND.

___(Silesia, Schlesien) For Breslau/Wroclaw, Archiwum Pánstwowe Miasto Wroclawia i Wojewodztwo Wroclawskiego, ul. Pomorska 2, PL-50215 Wroclaw, Polska, POLAND. For Gruenberg/Zielona Gora, Wojewódzkie Archiwum Pánstwowe w Zielonej Gorze, Stary Kiselin 31, PL-66002 Zielona Gora, Polska, POLAND. For Oppeln/Opole, Wojewódzkie Archiwum Pánstwowe w Opolu, ul. Zamkowa 2, PL-45016 Opole, Polska, POLAND. For Kattowitz-/Katowice, Wojewódzkie Archiwum Pánstwowe w Katowicach, ul. Jagiellonska 25, PL-40032 Katowice, Polska, POLAND.

___(Posen, Poznan) Archiwum Pánstwowe, ul Dluga 6, PL-00850 Warszawa, Polska, POLAND. Wojewódzkie Archiwum Pánstwowe, Bydgoszcz, Polska, POLAND. Archiwum Pánstwowe Torun, pl. Rapackiego, PL-87-Torun, Polska, POLAND. Archiwum Pánstwowe Miasta Poznanina i Wojewodztwa Poznanskiego, ul. 23 Lutego 41/43, PL-60967 Poznan, Polska, POLAND.

___(Alsace, Elsass) Archives departmentales du Bas-Rhin, 5-9, rue Fischart, F-67000 Strasbourg, FRANCE. Archives departmentales du Haut-Rhin, Cité administrative, Rue Fleischauer, F-68000 Colmar, FRANCE.

___(Lorraine, Lothringen) Archives departmentales de la Moselle, Prefecture de la Moselle, Hotel du Departement, 9 Place de la Prefecture, F-57036 Metz, FRANCE. Archives departementales de Meurthe-et-Moselle, 3 rue de la Monnaie, F-54000 Nancy, FRANCE.

City/town archives (Stadtarchive) for Germany are as follows. They should be addressed as Stadtarchiv, D-52062 Aachen, Bundesrepublik Deutschland, GERMANY or Stadtarchiv, D-04600 Altenburg, Bundesrepublik Deutschland, GERMANY. The word Stadtarchiv will not be repeated in the following list, but it should be used in each address.

D-52062 Aachen	D-93326 Abensberg
D-73407 Aalen	D-37139 Adelebsen
D-06449 Aaschersleben	D-48683 Ahaus

D-53474 Ahrweiler
D-31061 Alfeld
D-36295 Alsfeld
D-90514 Altdorf
D-58762 Altena
D-04600 Altenburg
D-55232 Alzey
D-92211 Amberg
D-35287 Amöneburg
D-56626 Andernach
D-17389 Anklam
D-09456 Annaberg-Buchholz
D-76855 Annweiler
D-91522 Ansbach
D-99510 Apolda
D-59713 Arnsberg
D-99310 Arnstadt
D-34454 Arolsen
D-06556 Artern
D-63739 Aschaffenburg
D-06449 Aschersleben
D-86150 Augsburg
D-64824 Babenhausen
D-55422 Bacharach
D-71522 Backnang
D-Bad: See second word.
D-72336 Balingen
D-96047 Bamberg
D-18356 Barth
D-34255 Baunatal
D-02625 Bautzen
D-95444 Bayreuth
D-15848 Beeskow
D-64625 Bensheim
D-48455 Bentheim
D-51465 Bergisch Gladbach
D-76887 Bad Bergzabern
D-57319 Berleburg
D-14195 Berlin
D-16321 Bernau
D-06406 Bernburg
D-74354 Besigheim

D-29549 Bevensen
D-88400 Biberach
D-33602 Bielefeld
D-88400 Biberach an der Riss
D-55411 Bingen am Rhein
D-01877 Bischofswerda
D-06749 Bitterfeld
D-89143 Blaubeuren
D-32825 Blomberg
D-46397 Bocholt
D-44722 Bochum
D-53111 Bonn
D-46325 Borken
D-04552 Borna
D-74336 Brackenheim
D-33034 Brakel
D-14770 Brandenburg
D-35619 Braunfels
D-38023 Braunschweig
D-58333 Breckerfeld
D-27568 Bremerhaven
D-59929 Brilon
D-50321 Brühl
D-88422 Bad Buchau
D-31675 Bückeburg
D-33133 Büren
D-23763 Burg
D-39288 Burg
D-91593 Burgbernheim
D-84480 Burghausen
D-96224 Burgkunstadt
D-48565 Burgsteinfurt
D-79325 Burkheim am Kaiserstuhl
D-35501 Butzbach
D-21614 Buxtehude
D-39240 Calbe
D-75365 Calw
D-44575 Castrop-Rauxel
D-29223 Celle
D-93413 Cham
D-09112 Chemnitz
D-96450 Coburg

D-48637 Cösfeld
D-06869 Coswig/Anhalt
D-03046 Cottbus
D-08451 Crimmitschau
D-27472 Cuxhaven
D-64283 Darmstadt
D-94469 Deggendorf
D-67146Deidesheim
D-04509 Delitzsch
D-17109 Demmin
D-06844 Dessau
D-65582 Diez
D-89402 Dillingen
D-84130 Dingolfing
D-91550 Dinkelsbühl
D-46525 Dinslaken
D-04720 Döbeln 1
D-03253 Doberlug-Kirchhain
D-86604 Donawörth
D-39264 Dornburg/Elbe
D-46282 Dorsten
D-44135 Dortmund
D-63266 Dreieichenhain
D-01907 Dresden
D-37104 Duderstadt
D-47051 Duisburg
D-48235 Dülmen
D-52349 Düren
D-67098 Bad Dürkheim
D-40468 Düsseldorf-Derendorf
D-69412 Eberbach
D-16225 Eberswalde
D-72458 Ebingen
D-6748032 Edenkoben
D-85067 Eichstätt
D-04838 Eilenburg
D-37574 Einbeck
D-99817 Eisenach
D-07607 Eisenberg Bezirk Gera
D-98673 Eisfeld
D-06295 Eisleben
D-24340 Eckernförde

D-67480 Edenkoben
D-84302 Eggenfelden
D-73479 Ellwangen
D-26702 Emden
D-46446 Emmerich
D-56130 Bad Ems
D-79346 Endingen
D-78234 Engen
D-99084 Erfurt
D-41812 Erkelenz
D-91054 Erlangen
D-37269 Eschwege
D-73228 Esslingen
D-53879 Euskirchen
D-23701 Eutin
D-91552 Feuchtwangen
D-24937 Flensburg
D-91301 Forchheim
D-03149 Forst/Lausitz
D-06567 Bad Frankenhausen
D-67227 Frankenthal
D-60311 Frankfurt am Main
D-15230 Frankfurt an der Oder
D-50209 Frechen
D-99599 Freiberg
D-79098 Freiburg im Breisgau
D-85354 Freising
D-61169 Friedberg/Hessen
D-34560 Fritzlar
D-72550 Freudenstadt
D-88045 Friedrichshafen
D-64505 Fross
D-49578 Fürstenau
D-11517 Fürstenwalde
D-90768 Fürth
D-87629 Füssen
D-74401 Gaildorf
D-78184 Geisingen
D-73312 Geislingen
D-63571 Gelnhausen
D-45879 Gelsenkirchen-Bür
D-77723 Gengenbach

D-07545 Gera
D-37339 Gernrode
D-64579 Gernsheim
D-97447 Gerolzhofen
D-59590 Geseke
D-58285 Gevelsberg
D-89537 Giengen
D-35390 Giessen
D-08371 Glauchau
D-25348 Glückstadt
D-47574 Goch
D-64560 Goddelau
D-73033 Göppingen
D-37028 Göttingen
D-02826 Görlitz
D-38615 Goslar
D-99867 Gotha
D-17489 Greifswald
D-07973 Greiz
D-97718 Greussen
D-04668 Grimma
D-04838 Groitzsch
D-71723 Grossbottwar
D-64505 Gross-Gerau
D-35305 Grünberg
D-67269 Grünstadt/Pfalz
D-03172 Guben/Wilhelm-Pieck-
        Stadt Guben
D-34281 Gudensberg
D-51643 Gummersbach
D-91710 Gunzenhausen
D-18273 Güstrow
D-57622 Hachenburg
D-58042 Hagen
D-38820 Halberstadt
D-39340 Haldensleben
D-06108 Halle/Saale
D-31785 Hameln
D-63450 Hanau
D-34346 Hannoversch Münden
D-77716 Haslach im Zinzigtal
D-67454 Hassloch/Pfalz

D-45525 Hattingen
D-25746 Heide/Holstein
D-69117 Heidelberg
D-89522 Heidenheim an der Brenz
D-87308 Heiligenstadt
D-74072 Heilbronn
D-38350 Helmstedt
D-91217 Hersbruck
D-32052 Herford
D-44651 Herne
D-71083 Herrenberg
D-36251 Bad Hersfeld
D-45699 Herten
D-04916 Herzberg/Elster
D-98646 Hildburghausen
D-40724 Hilden
D-31134 Hildesheim
D-69434 Hirschhorn
D-89420 Höchstädt
D-34369 Hofgeismar
D-95028 Hof/Saale
D-35315 Homberg
D-61350 Bad Homburg
D-72160 Horb am Neckar
D-38315 Hornburg
D-37671 Höxter
D-78183 Hüfingen
D-35410 Hungen
D-25813 Husum
D-98693 Ilmenau
D-55218 Ingelheim
D-85049 Ingolstadt
D-75864 Iserlohn
D-88305 Isny
D-25524 Itzehoe
D-07747 Jena
D-26441 Jever
D-52428 Jülich
D-14913 Jüterbog
D-67603 aiserslautern
D-47546 Kalkar
D-01917 Kamenz

D-76870 Kandel
D-09112 Karl-Marx-Stadt/Chem-
nitz
D-34385 Karlshafen
D-97753 Karlstadt
D-87577 Kaufbüren
D-93309 Kelheim
D-47906 Kempen
D-87435 Kempten
D-79341 Kenzingen
D-73230 Kirchheim unter Teck
D-55602 Kirn
D-36320 Kirtorf
D-97318 Kitzingen
D-47517 Kleve
D-56077 Koblenz
D-50676 Köln
D-97631 Königshofen i. Grabfeld
D-78467 Konstanz
D-34498 Korbach-Edersee
D-06366 Köthen/Anhalt
D-47559 Kranenburg
D-47727 Krefeld
D-55543 Bad Kreuznach
D-96317 Kronach
D-61467 Kronberg/Taunus
D-95326 Kulmbach
D-66869 Kusel
D-32791 Lage-Lippe
D-77933 Lahr
D-56112 Lahnstein
D-76829 Landau/Pfalz
D-84028 Landshut
D-99947 Bad Langensalza
D-35321 Laubach
D-21481 Lauenburg/Elbe
D-91207 Lauf/Pegnitz
D-83410 Laufen
D-89415 Lauingen/Donau
D-67742 Lauterecken
D-04109 Leipzig
D-32657 Lemgo

D-88299 Leutkirch
D-51311 Leverkusen
D-35423 Lich
D-96215 Lichtenfels
D-65549 Limburg/Lahn
D-88131 Lindau
D-53542 Linz/Rhein
D-59535 Lippstadt
D-02708 Löbau
D-79523 Lörrach
D-64653 Lorsch
D-15907 Lübben
D-14943 Luckenwalde
D-58507 Lüdenscheid
D-71602 Ludwigsburg
D-67061 Ludwigshafen am Rhein
D-32676 Lugde
D-21315 Lünenburg
D-39104 Magdeburg
D-55116 Mainz
D-68199 Mannheim
D-35001 Marburg an der Lahn
D-09496 Marienberg
D-88670 Markdorf
D-04416 Markkleeberg
D-95606 Marktredwitz
D-45772 Marl
D-75433 Maulbrunn
D-56727 Mayen
D-88701 Meersburg
D-98617 Meiningen
D-55590 Meisenheim
D-01662 Meissen
D-25704 Meldorf
D-49324 Melle
D-97638 Mellrichstadt
D-87700 Memmingen
D-58688 Menden
D-49716 Meppen
D-06217 Merseburg
D-88605 Messkirch
D-48629 Metelen

D-40822 Mettmann
D-04610 Meuselwitz
D-64720 Michelstadt
D-87719 Mindelheim
D-32427 Minden
D-09648 Mittweida
D-47441 Mörs
D-78532 Möhringen
D-41061 Mönchengladbach
D-52156 Monschau
D-56410 Montabaur
D-84453 Mühldorf am Inn
D-99974 Mühlhausen
D-45473 Mülheim an der Ruhr
D-95204 Münchberg
D-80797 München
D-97702 Münnerstadt
D-48143 Münster
D-53896 Bad Münstereifel
D-04610 Meuselwitz
D-56377 Nassau
D-61236 Nauheim
D-06618 Naumburg/Saale
D-69239 Neckarsteinach
D-79395 Neuenburg
D-49828 Neuenhaus
D-24516 Neumünster
D-84524 Neuötting
D-67433 Neustadt/Weinstrasse
D-91406 Neustadt an der Aisch
D-23730 Neustadt in Holstein
D-97616 Bad Neustadt a. d. Saale
D-67433 Neustadt an der Wein-
　　　　strasse
D-56566 Neuwied
D-63659 Nidda
D-52385 Nideggen
D-99734 Nordhausen
D-48531 Nordhorn
D-86720 Nördlingen
D-37154 Northeim
D-90403 Nürnberg

D-72609 Nürtingen
D-46015 Oberhausen
D-63785 Obernburg/Main
D-78720 Oberndorf am Neckar
D-61440 Oberursel
D-92526 Oberviechtach
D-97195 Ochsenfurt
D-63065 Offenbach am Main
D-77652 Offenburg
D-99885 Ohrdruf
D-74613 Öhringen
D-26135 Oldenburg
D-23832 Bad Oldesloe
D-57462 Olpe
D-08606 Ölsnitz
D-51379 Opladen
D-55276 Oppenheim
D-16515 Oranienburg
D-04758 Oschatz
D-39387 Oschersleben
D-49074 Osnabrück
D-39606 Osterburg
D-67697 Otterberg
D-33098 Paderborn
D-19370 Parchim
D-94014 Passau
D-05423 Pegau
D-19348 Perleberg
D-75177 Pforzheim
D-88630 Pfullendorf
D-72793 Pfullingen
D-01796 Pirna
D-08523 Plauen
D-51107 Porz/Rhein
D-14469 Potsdam
D-07381 Pössneck
D-17291 Prenzlau
D-16928 Pritzwalk
D-31812 Bad Pyrmont
D-49610 Quakenbrück
D-06484 Quedlinburg
D-78315 Radolfzell

D-86641 Rain
D-76437 Rastatt
D-40878 Ratingen
D-88212 Ravensburg
D-46459 Rees
D-08468 Reichenbach/Vogtland
D-64354 Reinheim
D-53424 Remagen
D-42853 Remscheid
D-24768 Rendsburg
D-72764 Reutlingen
D-33374 Rheda-Wiedenbrück
D-47495 Rheinberg
D-48431 Rheine
D-47239 Rheinhausen
D-41065 Rheydt
D-34474 Rhoden
D-88499 Riedlingen
D-97794 Rieneck
D-01587 Riesa
D-31737 Rinteln
D-36329 Romrod
D-09306 Rochlitz
D-83022 Rosenheim
D-18057 Rostock
D-27356 Rotenburg/Hannover
D-91154 Roth bei Nürnberg
D-91541 Rothenburg ob der
Tauber
D-72108 Rottenburg
D-78628 Rottweil
D-07407 Rudolstadt
D-99842 Ruhla
D-65401 Rüsselsheim
D-59602 Rüthen
D-99996 Saalfeld
D-66111 Saarbrücken
D-66740 Saarlouis
D-38228 Salzgitter-Lebenstedt
D-32108 Bad Salzuflen
D-36463 Bad Salzungen
D-29410 Salzwedel

D-06526 Sangerhausen
D-66386 Sankt (St.) Ingbert
D-96528 Schalkau
D-07907 Schleiz
D-24837 Schleswig
D-36110 Schlitz
D-98553 Schlüsingen
D-98574 Schmalkalden
D-08289 Schneeberg
D-04626 Schmölln
D-39218 Schönebeck/Elbe
D-86956 Schongau
D-73614 Schorndorf
D-63679 Schotten
D-78713 Schramberg
D-91126 Schwabach
D-73525 Schwäbisch Gmünd
D-74501 Schwäbisch Hall
D-97421 Schweinfurt
D-19053 Schwerin
D-68723 Schwetzingen
D-39615 Seehausen/Altmark
D-63500 Seligenstadt
D-48324 Sendenhorst
D-57072 Siegen
D-71063 Sindelfingen
D-78224 Singen
D-74889 Sinsheim
D-59494 Soest
D-42653 Solingen
D-99706 Sondershausen
D-96515 Sonneberg
D-37242 Bad Sooden-Allendorf
D-59494 Söst
D-67346 Speyer
D-03130 Spremberg
D-55576 Sprendlingen
D-21682 Stade
D-31655 Stadthagen
D-39576 Stendal
D-78333 Stockach
D-52222 Stolberg

D-47638 Straelen
D-18437 Stralsund
D-94315 Straubing
D-70049 Stuttgart
D-98527 Suhl
D-72172 Sulz am Neckar
D-39590 Tangermünde
D-36142 Tann
D-48291 Telgte
D-84529 Tittmoning
D-83646 Bad Tölz
D-04860 Torgau
D-83278 Traunstein
D-99830 Treffurt
D-54290 Trier
D-88662 Überlingen
D-29525 Uelzen
D-89073 Ulm
D-35327 Ulrichstein
D-59423 Unna
D-42551 Velbert
D-27283 Verden
D-41747 Viersen
D-78050 Villingen
D-85088 Vohburg
D-66333 Völkingen
D-67157 Wachenheim/Wein-
    strasse
D-71336 Waiblingen
D-04736 Waldheim bei Döbeln
D-88339 Bad Waldsee
D-79761 Waldshut
D-88239 Wangen
D-44649 Wanne-Eickel
D-48231 Warendorf
D-83512 Wasserburg am Inn
D-44866 Wattenscheid
D-92639 Weiden in der Oberpfalz
D-79576 Weil am Rhein

D-35781 Weilburg
D-73235 Weilheim
D-99423 Weimar
D-76356 Weingarten
D-69469 Weinheim
D-96260 Weismain
D-91781 Weissenburg in Bayern
D-06667 Weissenfels
D-86650 Wemding
D-59445 Werl
D-38855 Wernigerode
D-59368 Werne an der Lippe
D-38855 Wernigerode
D-46483 Wesel
D-65205 Wiesbaden
D-25554 Wilster
D-74206 Bad Wimpfen
D-91438 Bad Windsheim
D-21423 Winsen
D-23966 Wismar
D-58453 Witten
D-06886 Wittenberg/Lutherstadt
D-77709 Wolfach
D-38440 Wolfsburg
D-17438 Wolgast
D-39326 Wolmirstedt
D-42489 Wülfrath
D-95632 Wunsiedel
D-42349 Wuppertal
D-97070 Würzburg
D-25938 Wyk auf Föhr
D-46509 Xanten
D-06712 Zeitz
D-98544 Zella-Mehlis
D-39261 Zerbst
D-07937 Zeulenroda
D-02763 Zittau
D-08056 Zwickau

There are also some important <u>district</u>/<u>county</u> archives which you must look for in the region of your ancestor's town, village, or community. These should be addressed as Kreisarchiv, D-86485 Biberach, Bundesrepublik Deutschland, GERMANY or Kreisarchiv, D-99310 Arnstadt, Bundesrepublik Deutschland, GERMANY. The word Kreisarchiv will not be repeated in the following list, but it should be used in each address.

___D-52010 Aachen
___D-73404 Aalen
___D-58762 Altena
___D-58603 Altenkirchen
___D-99310 Arnstadt
___D-53474 Bad Neuenahr-Ahr-
    weiler
___D-51469 Bergisch Gladbach
___D-88386 Biberach
___D-55760 Birkenfeld
___D-71006 Böblingen
___D-46304 Borken
___D-27423 Bremervörde
___D-33142 Büren
___D-29221 Celle
___D-49346 Diepholz
___D-52349 Düren
___D-99817 Eisenach
___D-73728 Esslingen
___D-53861 Euskirchen
___D-24937 Flensburg
___D-65904 Frankfurt
___D-72236 Freudenstadt
___D-88009 Friedrichshafen
___D-47608 Geldern
___D-38503 Gifhorn
___D-08371 Glauchau
___D-73008 Göppingen
___D-41515 Grevenbroich
___D-51643 Gummersbach
___D-38820 Halberstadt
___D-30169 Hannover
___D-37308 Heilbad Heiligenstadt
___D-74072 Heilbronn
___D-32051 Herford

___D-98646 Hildburghausen
___D-31134 Hildesheim
___D-50354 Hürth
___D-25813 Husum
___D-25524 Itzehoe
___D-47906 Kempen
___D-74643 Künzelsau
___D-26766 Leer
___D-29439 Lüchow
___D-71607 Ludwigsburg
___D-98617 Meiningen
___D-59872 Meschede
___D-32387 Minden
___D-99974 Mühlhausen
___D-34311 Naumburg
___D-77609 Offenburg
___D-57445 Olpe
___D-39387 Oschersleben
___D-39606 Osterburg
___D-27711 Osterholz-Scharm-
    beck
___D-21762 Otterndorf
___D-31203 Peine
___D-75175 Pforzheim
___D-25407 Pinneberg
___D-24306 Plön
___D-78304 Radolfzell
___D-40885 Ratingen
___D-23901 Ratzeburg
___D-45608 Recklinghausen
___D-72764 Reutlingen
___D-33378 Rheda-Wiedenbrück
___D-66130 Saarbrücken
___D-66718 Saarlouis
___D-98574 Schmalkalden

___D-74504 Schwäbisch Hall
___D-53721 Siegburg
___D-72482 Sigmaringen
___D-59494 Soest
___D-96515 Sonneberg
___D-39418 Stassfurt
___D-98527 Suhl
___D-97933 Tauberbischofsheim
___D-78509 Tuttlingen
___D-29525 Uelzen

___D-89018 Ulm/Donau
___D-59406 Unna
___D-27265 Verden
___D-88239 Wangen
___D-48231 Warendorf
___D-46483 Wesel
___D-21423 Winsen
___D-06712 Zeitz
___D-39261 Zerbst

There are a few special archives which might be of use to you in your ancestor searches:

___(Emigration records) Heimatauskunftstelle Übersee, Contrescarpe 73, D-28195 Bremen, Bundesrepublik Deutschland, GERMANY; Historisches Seminar, Prof. Dr. G. Moltmann, Universität Hamburg, Von-Melle-Park 6, D-20146 Hamburg, Bundesrepublik Deutschland, GERMANY; Archives départmentales de la Seine-Maritime, Cours Clemenceau, F-76000 Rouen, FRANCE; Institut für Pfälzische Geschichte und Volkskunde, Benzinoring 6, D-67616 Kaiserslautern, Bundesrepublik Deutschland, GERMANY. Also see state archives in the pertinent states.

___(Military) Deutsches Bundesarchiv, Militärarchiv, Wiesenthalstrasse 10, D-79115 Freiburg in Breisgau, Bundesrepublik Deutschland, GERMANY; Bayerisches Hauptstaatsarchiv, Kriegsarchiv, Leonrodstrasse 57, D-80636 München, Bundesrepublik Deutschland, GERMANY; Service Historique de l'Armee de terre, Pavillon du Roi, Chteau de Vincennes, F-94000 Vincennes, FRANCE (for French soldiers in the American Revolution). Also see state archives in the pertinent states.

___(Newspapers) Gesamtkatalog der deutschen Presse, Universitäts-bibliothek Bremen, Achterstrasse, D-28353 Bremen, Bundes-republik Deutschland, GERMANY; Staatsarchiv Leipzig, Georgi-Dimitroff-Platz 1, D-04107 Leipzig, Bundesrepublik Deutschland, GERMANY. Also see pertinent state archives.

___(Polish civil registration records) Urzad Stanu Cywilnego, Praezydium Dzielnacowej Rady Warodowej, Nony Swiat 18, Warszawa, Polska, POLAND; Standesamt I in Berlin (West), Rheinstrasse 54, D-12161 Berlin, Bundesrepublik Deutschland, GERMANY.

___(World War II displaced Germans) Berlin Document Center, Wasser-käfersteig 1, D-14163 Berlin (Zehlendorf), Bundesrepublik Deutschland, GERMANY.

4. Church archives	4. Kirchliche Archive
4. Kirchliche Archive	4. Kirchliche Archive

In addition to the numerous church records which remain in the individual parishes, there are many in church archives in Germany. Some of the parishes have sent their older records to such repositories, parishes which have become extinct have deposited their records there, and almost all of the records of church organizations at a higher level than the individual parish are in these church archives. The two principal types of archives are those of the Evangelical Churches (Evangelische Kirche, the Protestant church body which represents the combined Lutheran and Reformed churches) and those of the Roman Catholic Churches (Katholische Kirche). The archives of the Evangelical Churches are chiefly the Central Church Archives (Zentralarchive) which serve all the churches, and the State Church Archives (Landesarchive) which serve the churches of a given German state. The archives of the Catholic Churches are chiefly the Archbishopric Archives (Erzbistumsarchive), Bishopric Archives (Bistumsarchive), the Diocesan Archives (Diözesanarchive), and the Cathedral Archives (Domarchive). In addition to the major religious groups, which have just been mentioned, there are a number of minor religious groups which have archives in Germany. These are especially important because many of the early emigrants from Germany to the American colonies came out of these minor or dissenting denominations.

Among the major Evangelical Church archives are the following:
___(For Mecklenburg-Vorpommern, Berlin, Brandenburg, Sachsen-Anhalt, Thüringen, and Sachsen) Zentralstelle für Genealogie, Georgi-Dimitroff-Platz 1, D-04107 Leipzig, Bundesrepublik Deutschland, GERMANY.
___(For Anhalt) Evangelische Landeskirche Anhalts, OttD-Grotewohl-Strasse 22, D-06842 Dessau, Bundesrepublik Deutschland, GERMANY.
___(For Baden) Evangelischer Oberkirchenrat, Landeskirchliches Archiv, Blumenstrasse 1, D-76133 Karlsruhe, Bundesrepublik Deutschland, GERMANY; Generallandesarchiv, Nördliche Hilda-Promenade, D-76133 Karlsruhe, Bundesrepublik Deutschland, GERMANY.
___(For Bayern) Evangelisch-Lutherischer Landeskirchenrat, Meiserstrasse 13, D-80333 München/Munich, Bundesrepublik Deutsch-

land, GERMANY; Evangelisch-Lutherische Kirche, Landeskirchliches Archiv, Veilhofstrasse 28, D-90489 Nürnberg/Nuremberg, Bundesrepublik Deutschland, GERMANY; Evangelisch-Lutherische Kirche, Landeskirchliches Archiv, Auenstelle Kirchenbucharchiv, Am Oelberg 2, D-93047 Regensburg, Bundesrepublik Deutschland, GERMANY; Evangelisch-Lutherisches Pfarrarchiv, Pfarrergasse 5, D-93047 Regensburg, Bundesrepublik Deutschland, GERMANY; Evangelisches Kirchenbuchamt, Im Annahof 4, D-86150 Augsburg, Bundes-republik Deutschland, GERMANY.

___(For Berlin) Archiv des Evangelischen Konsistoriums Berlin-Brandenburg, Bachstrasse 1-2, D-10555 Berlin, Bundesrepublik Deutschland, GERMANY; Evangelisches Zentralarchiv in Berlin, Kirchenbuchstelle, Jebensstrasse 3, D-10623 Berlin, (Charlottenburg), Bundesrepublik Deutschland, GERMANY.

___(For Brandenburg) Archiv des Evangelischen Konsistoriums Berlin-Brandenburg, Bachstrasse 1-2, D-10555 Berlin, Bundesrepublik Deutschland, GERMANY; Evangelisches Zentralarchiv in Berlin, Kirchenbuchstelle, Jebensstrasse 3, D-10623 Berlin (Charlottenburg), Bundesrepublik Deutschland, GERMANY.

___(For Braunschweig) Braunschweigische Evangelisch-Lutherische Landeskirche, Landeskirchliches Archiv, Alter Zeughof 1, D-38100 Wolfenbüttel, Bundesrepublik Deutschland, GERMANY; Stadtkirchenamt, Schützenstrasse 23, D-38100 Braunschweig/Brunswick, Bundesrepublik Deutschland, GERMANY; Evangelisch-Lutherisches Kirchenverband Wolfenbüttel, Kirchenverbandsamt, Neuer Weg 1, D-38302 Wolfenbüttel, Bundesrepublik Deutschland, GERMANY (only for city of Wolfenbüttel).

___(For Bremen) Staatsarchiv, Präsident-Kennedy-Platz 2, D-28203 Bremen, Bundesrepublik Deutschland, GERMANY.

___(For Hamburg) Evangelisch-Lutherische Kirche im Hamburgischen Staat, Archiv, Neue Burg 11, D-20354 Hamburg, Bundesrepublik Deutschland, GERMANY; Staatsarchiv Hamburg, ABC-Strasse 19, Eingang A, D-20354 Hamburg, Bundesrepublik Deutschland, GERMANY.

___(For Hannover) Kirchenbuchamt der Evangelisch-Lutherischen Landeskirche Hannovers, Landeskirchliches Archiv, Am Steinbruch 14, D-30037 Hannover, Bundesrepublik Deutschland, GERMANY; Evangelisch-Lutherische Stadtkirchenverband Hannover, Stadtkirchenkanzlei, Kirchenbuchamt, Arnswaldtstrasse 28, D-30057 Hannover, Bundesrepublik Deutschland, GERMANY (only for city of Hannover).

___(For Hessen) Evangelische Kirche von Kurhessen-Waldeck, Landes-kirchenarchiv, Wilhelmshöher Allee 330, D-34064 Kassel-Wilhelm-shöhe, Bundesrepublik Deutschland, GERMANY, Evangelische Kirche in Hessen und Nassau, Paulusplatz 1, D-64285 Darmstadt, Bundesrepublik Deutschland, GERMANY; Staatsarchiv für Hessen-Darmstadt, Karolinenplatz 3, D64289 Darmstadt, Bundesrepublik Deutschland, GERMANY; Staatsarchiv für Hessen-Kassel, Friedrichsplatz 15, D-35017 Marburg/Lahn, Bundesrepublik Deutschland, GERMANY; Evangelischer Gemeinde- und Dekanatsverband Darmstadt, Kirchenge-meindeamt, Kiesstrasse 14, D-64283 Darmstadt, Bundesrepublik Deutschland, GERMANY.

___(For Lippe) Lippisches Landeskirchenamt, Archiv der Lippischen Lan-deskirche, Leopoldstrasse 12, D-32756 Detmold, Bundesrepublik Deutschland, GERMANY; Personenstandsarchiv, Staatsarchiv, Willi-Hofmann-Strasse 2, D-32756 Detmold, Bundesrepublik Deutschland, GERMANY.

___(For Mecklenburg) Archiv der Landessuperintendentur der Evangel-ischen-Lutherischen Landeskirche Mecklenburgs, Strasse des Friedens 50, D-19370 Parchim, Bundesrepublik Deutschland, GERMANY; Domarchiv, Domplatz, Domhof 35, D-23909 Ratzeburg, Bundesrepublik Deutschland, GERMANY; Evangel-isches Kirchenarchiv, Münzstrasse 8, D-19010 Schwerin, Bundes-republik Deutschland, GERMANY.

___(For Niedersachsen, see also Braunschweig, Hannover, Lippe, Olden-burg, Ostfriesland and Westfalen) Staatsarchiv für Osnabrück, Schlossstrasse 29, D-49074 Osnabrück, Bundesrepublik Deutsch-land, GERMANY; Niedersächsisches Staatsarchiv, Am Sande 4 C, D-21682 Stade, Bundesrepublik Deutschland, GERMANY; Evangelische-Lutherischer Gesamtverband Osnabrück, Gemeindeamt, Heger-Tor-Wall 9, D-49008 Osnabrück, Bundes-republik Deutschland, GERMANY.

___(For Oldenburg) Staatsarchiv für Oldenburg, Damm 43, D-26135 Ol-denburg, Bundesrepublik Deutschland, GERMANY.

___(For Pfalz) Evangelische Kirche der Pfalz, Landeskirchenrat (Prote-stantische Landeskirche), Domplatz 5, D-67327 Speyer, Bundesre-publik Deutschland, GERMANY; Zentralarchiv der Evangelischen Kirche der Pfalz, Kirchenbuchstelle Koblenz, Karmeliterstrasse 1-3, D-56068 Koblenz, Bundesrepublik Deutschland, GERMANY.

___(For Pommern) Evangelisches Zentralarchiv in Berlin, Kirchenbuch-stelle, Jebensstrasse 3, D-10623 Berlin, Bundesrepublik Deutschland, GERMANY; Evangelisch-Lutherische Kirche im Hamburg-ischen Staat, Archiv, Neue Burg 1, D-20457 Hamburg, Bundesrepublik Deutschland, GERMANY.

___(For Rheinland) Archiv der Evangelischen Kirche im Rheinland, Evangelische Archivstelle Koblenz, Karmeliterstrasse 1-3, D-56068 Koblenz, Bundesrepublik Deutschland, GERMANY; Archiv der Evangelischen Kirche im Rheinland, Hans-Böckler-Strasse 7, D-40418 Düsseldorf 10, Bundesrepublik Deutschland, GERMANY; Personenstandsarchiv Brühl, Schlossstrasse 12, D-50321 Brühl, Bundesrepublik Deutschland, GERMANY.

___(For Saarland) Protestantisches Landeskirchenarchiv, Grosse Himmelsgasse 6, D-67346 Speyer, Bundesrepublik Deutschland, GERMANY; Archiv der Evangelischen Kirche im Rheinland, Archivstelle Koblenz, Karmeliterstrasse 1-3, D-56068 Koblenz, Bundesrepublik Deutschland, GERMANY.

___(For Sachsen) Evangelisch-Lutherische Landeskirche Sachsens, Landeskirchenarchiv, Lukasstrasse 6, D-01069 Dresden, Bundesrepublik Deutschland, GERMANY; Evangelisches Konsistorium des Görlitzer Kirchengebietes, Archiv der Evangelischen Kirchen von Schlesien, Berliner Strasse 62, D-02826 Görlitz, Bundesrepublik Deutschland, GERMANY; Archiv der Evangelischen Kirche der Kirchenprovinz Sachsen, Am Dom 2, D-39104 Magdeburg, Bundesrepublik Deutschland, GERMANY; Archiv und Bibliothek des Evangelischen Ministeriums, Comthurgasse 8, D-99084 Erfurt, Bundesrepublik Deutschland, GERMANY; Kirchenbuchamt des Evangelisch-Lutherischen Kirchengemeindeverbands Leipzig, Burgstrasse 1-5-Hof-3. Stock, D-04109 Leipzig, Bundesrepublik Deutschland, GERMANY (only for city of Leipzig).

___(For Schleswig-Holstein) Evangelisch-Lutherische Landeskirche Schleswig-Holsteins, Dänische Strasse 27-35, D-24033 Kiel, Bundesrepublik Deutschland, GERMANY; Write Kirchenbuchamt at D-23795 Bad Segeberg, D-24340 Eckernförde, D-25337 Elmshorn, D-23701 Eutin, D-24937 Flensburg, D-25836 Garding, D-23684 Gleschendorf, D-21073 Hamburg-Harburg, D-22769 Hamburg-Niendorf, D-22359 Hamburg-Stormann, D-25746 Heide, D-25813 Husum, D-25524 Itzehoe, D-24376 Kappeln/Schlei, D-24103 Kiel, D-23564 Lübeck, D-24534 Neumünster, D-23730 Neustadt in Holstein, D-24206 Preetz, D-3909 Ratzeburg, D-24768 Rendsburg, or D-24837 Schleswig.

___(For Thüringen) Archiv des Landeskirchenrats der Evangelisch-Lutherischen Kirche in Thüringen, Dr.-Moritz-Mitzenheim-Strasse 2, D-99817 Eisenach, Bundesrepublik Deutschland, GERMANY.

___(For Westfalen, also see Lippe and Rheinland) Evangelische Kirche von Westfalen, Landeskirchenarchiv, Alstädter Kirchplatz 4, D-33602 Bielefeld, Bundesrepublik Deutschland, GERMANY; Personenstandsarchiv Detmold, Willi-Hofmann-Strasse 2, D-32756 Detmold, Bundesrepublik Deutschland, GERMANY.

___(For Württenberg) Evangelische Landeskirche in Württemberg, Landeskirchliches Archiv, Gänsheidestrasse 4, D-70184 Stuttgart, Bundesrepublik Deutschland, GERMANY; Evangelische Landeskirche in Württemberg, Lauterbadstrasse 31, D-72250 Freudenstadt, Bundesrepublik Deutschland, GERMANY; Evangelisches Kirchenregisteramt Stuttgart, Hospitalhof, Gymnasiumstrasse 36, D-70174 Stuttgart, Bundesrepublik Deutschland, GERMANY.

The most important Catholic Church archives in Germany are as follows:

___(For inquiring about the location of church records in all of Germany) Katholisches Kirchenbuchamt des Verbands der Dioezesen Deutschlands München, Theatinerstrasse 31/IX, D-80333 München, Bundesrepublik Deutschland, GERMANY.

___(For Baden) Badisches Generallandesarchiv, Nördliche Hilda-Promenade 2, D-77133 Karlsruhe, Bundesrepublik Deutschland, GERMANY; Erzbistumarchiv, Herrenstrasse 35, Eingang Schoferstrasse, D-79098 Freiburg in Breisgau, Bundesrepublik Deutschland, GERMANY.

___(For Bayern) Archiv des Bistums Augsburg, Hafnerberg 2/II, D-86152 Augsburg, Bundesrepublik Deutschland, GERMANY; Erzbistumsarchiv, Domplatz 5, D-96049 Bamberg, Bundesrepublik Deutschland, GERMANY; Bischöfliches Ordinariatsarchiv, Luitpoldstrasse 2, D-85067 Eichstätt, Bundesrepublik Deutschland, GERMANY; Erzbischöfliches Ordinariatsarchiv München und Freising, Karmeliterstrasse 1, D-80333 München/Munich, Bundesrepublik Deutschland, GERMANY; Erzbischöfliches Matrikelamt, Pacellistrasse 7/I, D-8333 München/Munich, Bundesrepublik Deutschland, GERMANY; Bischöfliches Ordinariatsarchiv, Luragogasse 4, D-94032 Passau, Bundesrepublik Deutschland, GERMANY; Bischöfliches Zentralarchiv, St. Petersweg 11-13, D-93015 Regensburg, Bundesrepublik Deutschland, GERMANY; Bischöfliches Ordinariatsarchiv, Bruderhof 1, D-97070 Würzburg, Bundesrepublik Deutschland, GERMANY.

___(For Berlin) Bistumarchiv, Götzstrasse 65, D-1209 Berlin, Bundesrepublik Deutschland, GERMANY.

___(For Hamburg) see Niedersachsen.

___(For Hessen) Staatsarchiv für Hessen-Darmstadt, Karolinenplatz 3, D-64289 Darmstadt, Bundesrepublik Deutschland, GERMANY; Bischöfliches Generalvikariat, Paulustor 5, D-36001 Fulda, Bundesrepublik Deutschland, GERMANY; Bistumarchiv, Rossmarkt 4, D-65549 Limburg/Lahn, Bundesrepublik Deutschland, GERMANY; Erzbistumsarchiv, Kirchenbuchabteilung, Domplatz 3, D-33044 Paderborn, Bundesrepublik Deutschland, GERMANY; Katholische Kirchenbuchstelle, Bürgistrasse 28, D-34125 Kassel, Bundesrepublik Deutschland, GERMANY (only for city of Kassel).

___(For Niedersachsen, also see Oldenburg and Westphalia) Bistumsarchiv, Pfaffenstieg 2, D-31134 Hildesheim, Bundesrepublik Deutschland, GERMANY; Bistumsarchiv, Hasestrasse 40 a, D-49074 Osnabrück, Bundesrepublik Deutschland, GERMANY.

___(For Nordrhein-Westfalen) see Rheinland and Westphalia.

___(For Oldenburg) Bischöfliches Offizialat, Bahnhofstrasse, D-49377 Vechta, Bundesrepublik Deutschland, GERMANY.

___(For Ostpreussen and Westpreussen) Bischöfliches Zentralarchiv, St. Petersweg 11-13, D-93015 Regensburg, Bundesrepublik Deutschland, GERMANY.

___(For Pfalz) Archiv des Bistums Speyer, Kleine Pfaffengasse 16, D-67321 Speyer/Rhein, Bundesrepublik Deutschland, GERMANY; Bistumsarchiv, Jesuitenstrasse 13 b, D-54203 Trier, Bundesrepublik Deutschland, GERMANY.

___(For Rheinland) Bischöfliches Diözesanarchiv Aachen, Klosterplatz 7, D-52003 Aachen, Bundesrepublik Deutschland, GERMANY; Bistumsarchiv, Zwölfling 16, D-45127 Essen, Bundesrepublik Deutschland, GERMANY; Historisches Archiv des Erzbistums Köln, Gereonstrasse 2-4, D-50670 Köln/Cologne, Bundesrepublik Deutschland, GERMANY; Bistumsarchiv, Grebenstrasse 8-12, D-67321 Mainz, Bundesrepublik Deutschland, GERMANY.

___(For Saarland) Archiv des Bistums Speyer, Kleine Pfaffengasse 16, D-67346 Speyer, Bundesrepublik Deutschland, GERMANY; Bistumsarchiv, Jesuitenstrasse 13 b, D-54203 Trier, Bundesrepublik Deutschland, GERMANY.

___(For Sachsen) Bistumsarchiv, Dresdener Str. 26, D-01326 Dresden, Bundesrepublik Deutschland, GERMANY; Erzbistumsarchiv, Domplatz 3, D-33044 Paderborn, Bundesrepublik Deutschland, GERMANY.

___(For Schleswig-Holstein) Bistumsarchiv, Hasestrasse 40 a, D-49074 Osnabrück, Bundesrepublik Deutschland, GERMANY.

___(For Westfalen) Bistumsarchiv, Kardinal-von-Galen-Stift, Georgskommende 19, D-48003 Münster, Bundesrepublik Deutschland, GERMANY; Erzbistumsarchiv, Kirchenbuchabteilung, Domplatz 3, D-33044 Paderborn, Bundesrepublik Deutschland, GERMANY.

___(For Württemberg) Diözesanarchiv, Eugen-Bolz-Platz 5, D-72108 Rottenburg am Neckar, Bundesrepublik Deutschland, GERMANY.

Other denominational archives and repositories include:

___(For Baptist records) Bund Evangelisch-Freikirchlicher Gemeinden in Deutschland (Baptisten), Friedberger Strasse 101, D-61350 Bad Homburg vor der Höhe, Bundesrepublik Deutschland, GERMANY.

___(For Huguenot records) Arbeitkreis für die Geschichte der Hugenotten und Waldenser, Brachterstrasse 15, D-35282 Rauschenberg-Schwabendorf, Bundesrepublik Deutschland, GERMANY.

___(For Jewish records) International Tracing Service, D-34454 Arolsen, Bundesrepublik GERMANY; Gesamtarchiv der deutschen Juden, Joachimstaler Strasse 13, D-10719 Berlin, Bundesrepublik Deutschland, GERMANY; Bundesarchiv Am Wöllershof 12, D-56068 Koblenz, Bundesrepublik Deutschland, GERMANY; Archiv des Institutum Judaicum Delitzschianum, Wilmergasse 1-4, D-48143 Münster, Bundesrepublik Deutschland, GERMANY; Israelitische Religionsgemeinschaft Württembergs, Hospitalstrasse 36, D-70174 Stuttgart, Bundesrepublik Deutschland, GERMANY.

___(For Mennonite records) Archiv des Mennonitischen Geschichtsvereins, D-67297 Weierhof bei Marnheim/Pfalz, Bundesrepublik Deutschland, GERMANY.

___(For Methodist records) Evangelisch-Methodistische Kirche, Wilhelm-Lüschner-Strasse 8, D-60329 Frankfurt/Main, Bundesrepublik Deutschland, GERMANY.

___(For Moravian records) Evangelische Brüder-Unität, Archiv der Brüder-Unität, Zittauer Strasse 24, D-02747 Herrnhut (Oberlausitz), Bundesrepublik Deutschland, GERMANY.

___(For Old Lutheran Church records) Bund freier evangelischer Gemeinden in Deutschland, Goltlenkamp 2, D-58452 Witten-Bammern, Bundesrepublik Deutschland, GERMANY.

___(For Quaker records) Religiöse Gesellschaft der Freunde in Deutschland (Quäker), Brombergstrasse 9 a, D-79102 Freiburg im Breisgau, Bundesrepublik Deutschland, GERMANY.

5. German libraries	5. Deutsche Bibliotheken

5. Deutsche Bibliotheken

In addition to the exceptionally useful governmental and church archives of Germany, there are a number of large libraries which are good sources of published genealogical materials (family histories, local histories, gazetteers, genealogical compilations, genealogical periodicals, and so forth). They often have good collections of old newspapers, and some of them have valuable manuscript collections.

Among the better of these libraries in Germany are:
___Aachen, Bibliothek der Technischen Hochschule, D-52056
___Aachen, Öffentliche Bibliothek, D-52058
___Amberg, Staatliche Provinzialbibliothek, D-92224
___Amorbach, Fürstlich-Leiningensche Bibliothek, D-63916
___Ansbach, Regierungsbibliothek, D-91522
___Aschaffenburg, Hof- und Stiftsbibliothek, D-94347
___Augsburg, Staats- und Stadtbibliothek, D-86152
___Bamberg, Staatsbibliothek, D-96049
___Bautzen, Stadt- und Kreisbibliothek, D-02625
___Bayreuth, Universitätsbibliothek, D-95440
___Berlin, Deutsche Staatsbibliothek, D-10001
___Berlin, Berliner Stadtbibliothek, D-10121
___Berlin, Universitätsbibliothek der Humboldt Universität, D-10001
___Berlin, Staatsbibliothek Stiftung Preuischer Kulturbesitz, D-10117
___Berlin, Universitätsbibliothek, D-14195
___Bochum, Stadtbücherei, D-44777
___Bochum, Universitätsbibliothek, D-44879
___Bonn, Universitätsbibliothek,, D-53001
___Braunschweig, Stadtbibliothek, D-38001
___Bremen, Staats- und Universitätsbibliothek, D-28331
___Celle, Bibliothek des Oberlandesgerichtes in Celle, D-09306
___Celle, Kirchen-Ministerial Bibliothek, D-09306
___Chemnitz, Stadtbibliothek, D-17039
___Chemnitz, Universitätsbibliothek, D-09009
___Coburg, Landesbibliothek, D-96450
___Darmstadt, Hessische Landes- und Hochschulbibliothek, D-64283
___Dessau, Universitäts- und Landesbibliothek Sachsen-Anhalt, D-39606
___Detmold, Lippische Landesbibliothek, D-39291
___Dillingen, Studienbibliothek, D-89401

___Donaueschingen, Fürstlich Fürstenbergberische Hofbibliothek, D-78151
___Donauworth, Bibliothek Cassianeum, D-86601
___Dortmund, Stadt- und Landesbibliothek, D-44137
___Dresden, Sächsische Landesbibliothek, D-01099
___Dresden, Stadtbibliothek, D-18573
___Duisburg, Stadtbibliothek, D-47049
___Düsseldorf, Universitätsbibliothek, D-40225
___Düsseldorf, Bücherei Haus des deutschen Ostens, D-40001
___Eichstatt, Universitätsbibliothek, D-85071
___Emden, Bibliothek der Groen Kirche zu Emden, D-39343
___Erfurt, Wissenschaftliche Bibliothek der Stadt Erfurt, D-99084
___Erlangen, Universitätsbibliothek, D-91054
___Frankfurt, Deutsche Bibliothek, D-60235
___Frankfurt, Stadt- und Universitätsbibliothek, D-60325
___Freiburg im Breisgau, Universitätsbibliothek, D-79016
___Freiburg i. S., Bergakademie-Bibliothek, D-09596
___Fulda, Hessische Landesbibliothek, D-36037
___Giessen, Bibliothek der Justus-Liebig-Universität, D-35331
___Göttingen, Niedersächische Staats- & Universitätsbibliothek, D-37070
___Gotha, Forschungsbibliothek Gotha, D-99851
___Greifswald, Universitätsbibliothek, D-16278
___Halle, Universitäts- und Landesbibliothek Sachsen-Anhalt, D-06098
___Hamburg, Staats- und Universitätsbibliothek, D-20146
___Hannover, Niedersächische Landesbibliothek, D-30001
___Hannover, Stadt Bibliothek, D-30169
___Heidelberg, Universitätsbibliothek, D-69047
___Helmstedt, Ehemalige Universitätsbibliothek, D-38350
___Herne, Bücherei des deutschen Ostens, D-99510
___Hildesheim, Stadtbibliothek, D-36115
___Ilmenau, Bibliothek der Technischen Hochschule, D-98693
___Ingolstadt, Wissenschaftliche Stadtbibliothek, D-88456
___Jena, Universitätsbibliothek, D-07740
___Karlsruhe, Badische Landesbibliothek, D-76133
___Kassel, Bibliothek der Stadt Kassel und Landesbibliothek, D-34111
___Kiel, Schleswig-Holsteinische Landesbibliothek, D-19370
___Kiel, Universitätsbibliothek, D-24118
___Koblenz, Stadtbibliothek, D-56068
___Köln, Universitäts- und Stadtbibliothek, D-50931
___Köln, Zentralkatalog Nordrhein-Westfalen, D-50679
___Konstanz, Bibliothek der Universität, D-78461
___Leipzig, Deutsche Bücherei, D-04103

___Leipzig, Stadtbibliothek, D-04001
___Leipzig, Universitätsbibliothek, D-04107
___Lindau, Stadtbibliothek, D-88101
___Lübeck, Bibliothek der Hansestadt Lübeck, D-23501
___Lüneberg, Ratsbücherei, D-54597
___Magdeburg, Kulturhistorisches Museum, Klosterbibliothek, D-39001
___Magdeburg, Stadt- und Bezirksbibliothek, D-39001
___Mainz, Stadtbibliothek, D-55126
___Mainz, Universitätsbibliothek, D-55126
___Mannheim, Universitätsbibliothek, D-68131
___Marburg, Universitätsbibliothek, D-35001
___Marburg, Bibliothek der Herder Instituts, D-35037
___Minden, Bibliothek des Stadtsarchiv, D-54310
___Mönchengladbach, Stadtbibliothek, D-41050
___München, Bayerische Staatsbibliothek, D-80328
___München, Stadtbibliothek München, D-80001
___München, Universitätsbibliothek, D-80539
___Münster, Universitätsbibliothek, D-48043
___Neuburg, Staatliche Bibliothek, D-86616
___Nürnberg, Bibliothek des Germanischen Nationalmuseums, D-90402
___Nürnberg, Stadtbibliothek, D-90317
___Oldenburg, Landesbibliothek, D-26024
___Passau, Staatliche Bibliothek, D-94032
___Potsdam, Brandenburgische Landesbibliothek, D-14467
___Regensburg, Staatliche Bibliothek, D-93047
___Rostock, Universitätsbibliothek, D-18051
___Saarbrücken, Universitätsbibliothek, D-66041
___Schweinfurt, Stadtbibliothek, D-01920
___Schwerin, Mecklenburgische Landesbibliothek, D-19010
___Speyer, Pfälzische Landesbibliothek, D-67343
___Stuttgart, Württembergische Landesbibliothek, D-18146
___Stuttgart, Bibliothek des Instituts für Auslandbeziehungen, D-70173
___Trier, Stadtbibliothek, D-16845
___Tübingen, Bibliothek Stiftung Preussischer Kulturbestiz, D-72001
___Tübingen, Universitätsbibliothek, D-72016
___Überlingen, Leopold-Sophien-Bibliothek, D-88641
___Ulm, Stadtbibliothek, D-04741
___Weimar, Thüringische Landesbibliothek, D-99423
___Wiesbaden, Hessische Landesbibliothek, D-65185
___Wolfenbüttel, Herzog-August-Bibliothek, D-38304
___Worms, Stadtbibliothek, D-67547
___Wuppertal, Stadtbibliothek, D-42103

___Würzburg, Universitätsbibliothek, D-97074
___Zweibrücken, Bibliotheca Bipontina, D-66461
___Zwickau, Ratschulbibliothek, D-04886

   If your quest for German libraries is regionally oriented, you will find the following regional check-list useful:
___For Baden, see Freiburg im Breisgau, Heidelberg, Karlsruhe, Speyer, Stuttgart
___For Bayern, see Ansbach, Amberg, Aschaffenburg, Augsburg, Bamberg, Bayreuth, Coburg, Donauworth, Ingolstadt, Lindau, München, Nürnberg, Passau, Regensburg, Würzburg
___For Berlin, see Berlin
___For Brandenburg, see Berlin, Potsdam
___For Braunschweig, see Wolfenbüttel
___For Bremen, see Bremen
___For Easternmost Germany, see Düsseldorf, Hannover, Herne, Marburg, Münster
___For Emigration Library, see Stuttgart (Auslandsbeziehungen)
___For Hamburg, see Hamburg
___For Hessen, see Darmstadt, Frankfurt, Fulda, Giessen, Kassel, Marburg, Wiesbaden
___For Lippe, see Detmold
___For Mecklenburg, see Kiel, Lübeck, Rostock, Schwerin
___For Niedersachsen, see Braunschweig, Göttingen, Hannover, Hildesheim, Lüneburg
___For Oldenburg, see Oldenburg
___For Pfalz, see Speyer, Stuttgart, Trier
___For Pommern, see Greifswald, Kiel, Rostock, Schwerin
___For Rheinland, see Duisburg, Düsseldorf, Karlsruhe, Koblenz, Köln, Mainz, Mönchengladbach, Speyer, Wiesbaden
___For Saarland, see Saarbrücken, Trier
___For Sachsen, see Chemnitz, Dresden, Leipzig, Zwickau
___For Sachsen-Anhalt, see Dessau, Halle, Magdeburg
___For Schleswig-Holstein, see Hamburg, Kiel, Lübeck
___For Thüringen, see Gotha, Jena, Weimar
___For Westfalen, see Detmold, Dortmund, Münster
___For Württemberg, see Karlsruhe, Konstanz, Stuttgart, Tübingen, Ulm

   For libraries in France (Elsass, Lothringen) and Poland (Ostpreussen, Westpreussen, Pommern, Schlesien, Posen) which may be of assistance to you, the following may be consulted:
___Paris, Bibliothéque du Ministère des Affaires Etrangère, F-75007

___Paris-Vincennes, Bibliothéque du Service Historique de l'Armee de
      Terre, F-94300
___Colmar, Bibliothéque de la Ville de Colmar, F-68000
___Le Havre, Bibliothéque Municipale, F-76600
___Metz, Bibliothéque Municipale, F-57000
___Metz Cedex, Bibliothéque Universitaire, F-57045
___Mulhouse Cedex, Bibliothéque de l'Université de Haute Alsace,
      Section Lettres, F-68090
___Nancy Cedex, Bibliothéque Municipale, F-54042
___Nancy, Bibliothéque Interuniversitaire, Section Lettres, F-54000
___Strasbourg Cedex, Bibliothéque Nationale et Universitaire, F-67070
___Gdansk(Danzig), Biblioteka Gdańska PAN, PL-8D-858
___Katowice(Kattowitz), Biblioteka Slaska, PL-4D-956
___Poznan(Posen), Biblioteka Poznanskiego Towarzystwa Przyjacol Nauk,
      PL-61-725
___Poznan(Posen), Miejska Biblioteka Publiczna im E. Raczynskiego w
      Poznaniu, PL-6D-967
___Sopot, Biblioteka Główna Uniwersytetu Gdanskiego, PL-81-824
___Szczecin(Stettin), Wojewódzka i Miejska Biblioteka Publiczna w
      Szczecinie, PL-7D-952
___Torun, Biblioteka Uniwersytecka w Toruniu, PL-87-100
___Torun, Wojewódzka Biblioteka Publiczna i Ksiaznica Miejska im.
      Kopernika w Toruniu, PL-87-100
___Warszawa(Warsaw), Biblioteka Narodowa, PL-0D-973
___Warszawa(Warsaw), Biblioteka Publiczna m. st. Warszawy, PL-0D-950
___Warszawa(Warsaw), Biblioteka Uniwersytecka w Warszawie, PL-0D-
      927
___Wroclaw(Breslau), Biblioteka Uniwersytecka we Wroclawie, PL-5D-
      076

6. US libraries	6. US Bibliotheken
6. US Bibliotheken	6. US Bibliotheken

There are in the United States a number of very large genealogical libraries and a number of large general libraries which have good collections of German materials. Among those which you might use to try to obtain the numerous published volumes which have been mentioned in previous chapters are the following:
___Family History Library of the Genealogical Society of UT, 35 North
      West Temple St., Salt lake City, UT 84150. German collection

described in J. Cerny and W. Elliott, THE LIBRARY, Ancestry Publishing, Salt Lake City, UT, 1988.

___Public Library of Fort Wayne and Allen County, 301 West Wayne St., Fort Wayne, IN 46802. See K. B. Cavanaugh, A GENEALOGIST'S GUIDE TO THE FT. WAYNE, IN LIBRARY, The Author, Ft. Wayne, IN, 1980.

___NY Public Library, 5th Avenue and 42nd Sts., New York, NY 10022-1939. See NY Public Library, DICTIONARY CATALOG OF THE LOCAL HISTORY AND GENEALOGY DIVISION, Hall, Boston, MA, 1974. And SUPPLEMENTS since.

___Library of Congress, 1st and 2nd Sts. at East Capitol St. and Independence Ave., Washington, DC 20540.

___Western Reserve Historical Society Library, 10825 East Blvd., Cleveland, OH 44106.

___Detroit Public Library, Burton Historical Collection, 5201 Woodward Ave., Detroit, MI 48202.

___Newberry Library, 60 West Walton St., Chicago, IL 60610. See P. T. Sinko, GUIDE TO LOCAL AND FAMILY HISTORY AT THE NEWBERRY LIBRARY, Ancestry Publishing, Salt Lake City, UT, 1987.

___State Historical Society of WI Library, 816 State St., Madison, WI 53703. See J. P. Danky, GENEALOGICAL RESEARCH, AN INTRODUCTON TO THE RESOURCES OF THE STATE HISTORICAL SOCIETY OF WI, The Society, Madison, WI, 1986.

___Dallas Public Library, 1515 Young St., Dallas, TX 75201.

___Sutro Library, 480 Winston Dr., San Francisco, CA 94132. See G. E. Strong and G. F. Kurutz, LOCAL HISTORY AND GENEALOGICAL RESOURCES OF THE CA STATE LIBRARY AND ITS SUTRO BRANCH, CA State Library Foundation, Sacramento, CA, 1983.

___Public Library of Cincinnati and Hamilton County, 800 Vine St., Cincinnati, OH 45202-2071.

___Library of the German Genealogical Society of America, 1420 N. Clarement Blvd., No. 207E, Claremont, CA 91711.

___Harvard University Library, Cambridge, MA 02138.

___Yale University Library, New Haven, Ct 06520.

___University of IL Library, Urbana, IL 61801.

___University of CA-Berkeley Library, Berkeley, CA 94720.

___University of MI Library, Ann Arbor, MI 48109.

___University of Texas Library, Austin, TX 78712.

___University of CA-Los Angeles Library, Los Angeles, CA 90024.

226

___Stanford University Library, Stanford, CA 94305.
___University of MN Library, Minneapolis, MN 55455.
___University of KS Library, Lawrence, KS 66045.

CHAPTER 6
(KAPITEL 6)
THE GERMAN LANGUAGE
(DIE DEUTSCHE SPRACHE)

1. German words	1. Deutsche Wörter
1. **Deutsche Wörter**	*1. Deutsche Wörter*

The German language is really not a very difficult one because it has a strong kinship to English, and because it draws numerous words from Latin and Greek, both of which English draws from. Most Americans already know a sizable number of German words, and there are many, many more which you can easily make out. Just take a look at the following list and you will see for yourself.

Achtung	Diagramm	hier	Name
Adresse	Direktor	Hotel	Natur
alt	Drogist	Idee	Nummer
Amerika	enden	informieren	Onkel
Apfel	fallen	Intelligenz	Orange
Apparat	finden	Juli	Paar
attraktiv	Fisch	kalt	Papier
August	Frankfurter	Kamel	Park
Auto	freundlich	Karotte	Polen
Autobahn	Fuss	Katze	Polizei
Ball	Garten	Kindergarten	Postkarte
Bank	Gast	kolonial	Pumpernickel
beginnen	geographisch	kommen	Qualität
besser	Gesundheit	korrekt	Restaurant
Bett	Glas	Land	Ring
Bier	Glockenspiel	lang	rund
Biographie	Gras	Licht	Salat
blau	Gruppe	Limonade	Sauerbraten
Blitzkrieg	gut	Magistrat	Sauerkraut
Bratwurst	Haar	Mann	Schiff
braun	halb	Maus	Schokolade
bringen	Hand	Methodist	Schule
Bruder	hart	Minute	Schweden
Butter	Haus	Musik	senden
Delikatessen	helfen	Mutter	singen

Sohn	Tabak	Verboten	Wienerschnitzel
Sommer	Tee	voll	Wind
Spinat	Telefon	warm	Winter
Staat	Temperatur	waschen	Wort
Suppe	Vater	Wiener	Zucker

This chapter is meant to show you that you can acquire sufficient facility in German to make out entries in German books and records. You do not need to study the intricacies of German grammar or syntax. Basically, what you will need to do is to make yourself acquainted with German words. And you particularly need to know those relating to genealogical matters. These can practically all be looked up in a German-English/English-German dictionary and/or in the detailed listing of such genealogically-pertinent words in a later section of this chapter. Only two things are actually required: (a) a good German-English/English-German dictionary, and (b) a book on German handwriting.

To begin with, you should not spend too much money on the dictionary. There are several very good paperback ones which are recommended. They generally have between 80 and 100 thousand entries. Any one of them will do nicely.

___J. C. Traupman, THE BANTAM NEW COLLEGE GERMAN & ENGLISH DICTIONARY, Bantam Books, New York, NY, latest issue.

___HARPER-COLLINS GERMAN-ENGLISH, ENGLISH-GERMAN DICTIONARY, Collins, New York, NY, latest issue.

___HARRAP'S CONCISE ENGLISH-GERMAN, GERMAN-ENGLISH DICTIONARY, Prentice-Hall, New York, NY

Then, it would serve you well if you will acquire both of the following little paperback books. The first one deals with the special German handwriting that was used in most genealogical records up to about 1920/30. This writing is quite different than that used today in English. However, by reading this first book and by reading and using the second book, you will have little trouble teaching yourself how to read the old German records on your forebears. The second book is a workbook which will give you very valuable practice in writing the old German script so that you can recognize genealogically-related words and your progenitors' names in the handwritten records.

___E. M. Bentz, IF I CAN, YOU CAN DECIPHER GERMANIC RECORDS, E. M. Bentz, 13139, Old West Avenue, San Diego, CA 92129, latest printing.

___E. Reichmann, editor, WITTER'S GERMAN-ENGLISH WRITING AND READING PRIMER (Witter's Deutsch-Englische Schreib- und Lese-Fibel), NCSA Literatur, Green Valley, Nashville, IN 46204, 1987 reprint of the 1881 edition.

If you find that you really want to go into considerable detail with regard to German research, then you may want to purchase one of the larger dictionaries. These have around 165 to 240 thousand entries:

___H. Messinger, LANGENSCHEIDT NEW COLLEGE GERMAN DICTIONARY, GERMAN-ENGLISH, ENGLISH-GERMAN, Langenscheidt, Maspeth, NY, latest edition.

___CASSELL GERMAN DICTIONARY, GERMAN-ENGLISH, ENGLISH-GERMAN, Macmillan, New York, NY, latest edition.

___HARPER-COLLINS GERMAN-ENGLISH, ENGLISH-GERMAN DICTIONARY, Collins, New York, Ny, latest issue.

___OXFORD-DUDEN GERMAN DICTIONARY, GERMAN-ENGLISH, ENGLISH-GERMAN, Oxford University Press, New York, NY, latest edition.

It is not actually necessary to do research, but if you wish to instruct yourself in the German language, you may do so quite readily by using one of the following simple introductory books:

___P. Weis, LEARN GERMAN, Barrons, New York, NY, latest edition.

___BERLITZ GERMAN SELF TEACHER, Perigee, New York, NY, latest edition.

A marvelous innovation for genealogical researchers has recently come on the market. These are some IBM-compatible computer programs which will automatically translate English-to-German and German-to-English. They are exceptionally easy to use. All you do is type in the English that you wish to have translated, then press two keys, and the translation is made for you. It is the same for German-to-English. These computer programs are:

___Atech Microtac Software, GERMAN ASSISTANT FOR TRANSLATION FROM ENGLISH TO GERMAN, available from George K. Schweitzer, 407 Ascot Court, Knoxville, TN 37923-5807 for $125 postpaid.

___Atech Microtac Software, GERMAN ASSISTANT FOR TRANSLATION FROM GERMAN TO ENGLISH, available from George K. Schweitzer, 407 Ascot Court, Knoxville, TN 37923-5807 for $125 postpaid.

___Globalink Software, GTS-BASIC TRANSLATION FROM ENGLISH TO GERMAN, available from George K. Schweitzer, 407 Ascot

Court, Knoxville, TN 37923-5807 for $589 postpaid. A much more capable program.

___Globalink Software, GTS-BASIC TRANSLATION FROM GER-MAN TO ENGLISH, available from George K. Schweitzer, 407 Ascot Court, Knoxville, TN 37923-5807 for $589 postpaid. A much more capable program.

Finally, if you need to use an exceptionally adequate dictionary, you may find the following valuable. You can use it in large university libraries, or you may purchase a copy. However, it is quite expensive, and you should make the outlay only if you are intensely serious about German research.

___LANGENSCHEIDT NEW MONET-SANDERS ENCYCLOPEDIC DICTIONARY, GERMAN-ENGLISH, 2 volumes, ENGLISH-GERMAN, 2 volumes, Langenscheidt Publishers, Maspeth, NY, latest edition.

And if you are stuck on very old or very obscure German words, you will need to look the word up in the following detailed set of German Word Books, then look up their definitions in your German-to-English dictionary.

___G. Drosdowski, DUDEN, DAS GROSSE WÖRTERBUCH DER DEUTSCHEN SPRACHE, Dudenverlag, Mannheim, Deutsch-land, 1976, 6 Bände (6 volumes).

2. German print and script	2. Druck und Schrift in Deutsch
2. Deutsche Druck und Schrift	*(handwritten script)*

The German language has been printed in two major types of characters: Gothic (old) and Roman (modern). The Roman characters are the same as are used in printing the English language, and they have been used for German since about 1940. Prior to 1940, however, most of the printed material in the German language appeared in the Gothic type. The capital letters, the lower case letters, and the numerals in this type are presented on the next seven pages as Tables 1a, 1b, 1c, 2a, 2b, 3a, and 3b. Glance through these tables just to get a bit of an idea of this old German printed type.

In general, after a little practice, you will have no difficulty reading this old script (Gothic). As you prepare to do this practice, if you pay attention to several items you will be able to markedly speed up your

Table 1a.
German Type and Script

ROMAN TYPE	GERMAN TYPE	GERMAN SCRIPT
A a	𝔄 a	
B b	𝔅 b	
C c	ℭ c	
D d	𝔇 d	
E e	𝔈 e	
F f	𝔉 f	
G g	𝔊 g	
H h	ℌ h	
I i	ℑ i	
J j	ℑ i	
K k	𝔎 k	
L l	𝔏 l	
M m	𝔐 m	

Table 1b.
German Type and Script

ROMAN TYPE	GERMAN TYPE	GERMAN SCRIPT
N n	𝔑 𝔫	
O o	𝔒 𝔬	
P p	𝔓 𝔭	
Q q	𝔔 q	
R r	𝔑 r	
S s	𝔖 ſ ß	
T t	𝔗 t	
U u	𝔘 u	
V v	𝔙 v	
W w	𝔚 w	
X x	𝔛 x	
Y y	𝔜 y	
Z z	ℨ ʒ	

Table 1c.
German Type and Script

Ä ä Ä ä *Ä ä* Ö ö Ö ö *Ö ö*

Ü ü Ü ü *Ü ü*

ch	ch		ss	ff	
sch	ſch		ß, sz, ss	ß	
ck	ck		st	ſt	

tz	tz	
ph	ph	

Table 2a.
German Type and Script

Fraktur		Antiqua		Schreibschrift	
𝔄	a	A	a	𝒜	a
𝔅	b	B	b	ℬ	b
ℭ	c	C	c	ℒ	c
𝔇	d	D	d	𝒟	d
𝔈	e	E	e	ℰ	n
𝔉	f	F	f	ℱ	f
𝔊	g	G	g	𝒢	g
ℌ	h	H	h	ℋ	h
ℑ	i	I	i	ℐ	i
𝔍	j	J	j	𝒥	j
𝔎	k	K	k	𝒦	k
𝔏	l	L	l	ℒ	l
𝔐	m	M	m	ℳ	m
𝔑	n	N	n	𝒩	n
𝔒	o	O	o	𝒪	o
𝔓	p	P	p	𝒫	p
𝔔	q	Q	q	𝒬	q
𝔑	r	R	r	ℛ	r
𝔖	ſ, s	S	s	𝒮	s

Table 2b.
German Type and Script

Type		Roman		Script	
𝔗	t	T	t		
𝔘	u	U	u		
𝔙	v	V	v		
𝔚	w	W	w		
𝔛	x	X	x		
𝔜	y	Y	y		
ℨ	z	Z	z		
Ӓ	ä	Ä	ä	(e=sound)	
Ö	ö	Ö	ö	(e=sound)	
Ü	ü	Ü	ü	(i=sound)	
Ch	ch	Ch	ch		
	ck		ck		
Pf	pf	Pf	pf		
Ph	ph (f)	Ph	ph		
Sch	sch	Sch	sch		
Sp	sp (shp²)	Sp	sp		
	ſſ		ss		
St	st (sht¹)	St	st		
	ß		sz		
	tz		tz		

Table 3a.
German Type and Script

German type.	German script.	German type.	German script.
A a	*A a*	N n	*N n*
B b	*B b*	O o	*O o*
C c	*C c*	P p	*P p*
D d	*D d*	Q q	*Q q*
E e	*E e*	R r	*R r*
F f	*F f*	S ſ s	*S s*
G g	*G g*	T t	*T t*
H h	*H h*	U u	*U u*
I i	*I i*	V v	*V v*
J j	*J j*	W w	*W w*
K k	*K k*	X x	*X x*
L l	*L l*	Y y	*Y y*
M m	*M m*	Z z	*Z z*

Table 3b.
German Type and Script

Äe ä Ä $\ddot{A}$ $\ddot{a}$ ß β

Oe ö Ö $\ddot{O}$ $\ddot{o}$ ck

Ue ü U $\ddot{U}$ $\ddot{u}$ Sch sch

Äu $\ddot{A}u$ Sch sch }

Distinguish carefully between
capitals B and V,
capitals C and E,
capitals N and R,
capitals O and Q,
lower case f and s,
lower case n and u,
lower case r and x.

The German capitals I and J
are about the same.
When followed by a vowel,
it is J.
When followed by a consonant,
it is I.

The regular form of lower case s
is used at the end of a word or syllable.
A single s within a word or syllable
is represented as the s that looks like f.
Be sure to distinguish them.
When a double ss occurs at the end of a
word or syllable,
it is written as ß.

learning process. Pay particular attention to the capital letters that differ considerably from the type that you know: E, G, I, K, S, V. Notice also that I and J are exactly the same or very similar. Carefully inspect the A, O, and U with two dots over them. These dots are known as an umlaut and they alter the nature of the letter to produce a different letter.

Now observe the lower case letters which deviate from modern printing: k, and one form of s. Notice that one form of s resembles f very closely except for the absence of the right side of the crossbar. The form of s which looks like a modern s is used at the end of a word or a syllable, and the other form is used everywhere else. There are also some special combinations of letters. The first of these is the double-s (ss) which looks very much like a Greek beta ( ). This form of double-s is used at the end of a word or the root of a compound word. Otherwise, double-s is simply written as ss. Also take a careful look at the interesting form of tz. Finally, notice the umlaut on the lower-case letters a, o, and u, which as in the case of capitals, makes them over into different letters.

The handwriting that you will find in German records of all types before about 1940 is usually in Gothic (old German) script. It is not nearly so easy to read as the Gothic print, which we discussed just above. The standard Gothic way of writing the characters is also presented in Tables 1a, 1b, 1c, 2a, 2b, 3a, and 3b. Please look back at them. You will also find them on the next page in two slightly different forms. They are presented there as Table 4.

In order to learn this old script, which you absolutely must know if you are going to personally read old records, you need to actually write it. The easiest approach is to put all your German surnames into this writing. Then try your name and the full names of your parents and grandparents. Then put 30 or 40 of the German words in the previous section into this writing. Following this, you should practice making letters and writing words using the following little book:
___E. Reichmann, editor, WITTER'S GERMAN-ENGLISH WRITING AND READING PRIMER (Witter's Deutsch-Englische Schreib- und Lese-Fibel), NCSA Literatur, Green Valley, Nashville, IN 46204, 1987 reprint of the 1881 edition.
Be sure and perform all the exercises, that is, copy all the examples on pages 5-30. This will put you in excellent shape to make fruitful use of the following book:

Table 4.
German
Script

Table 4.
German
Script

___E. M. Bentz, IF I CAN, YOU CAN DECIPHER GERMANIC
RECORDS, E. M. Bentz, 13139, Old West Avenue, San Diego,
CA 92129, latest printing.

This volume will take you through many German genealogical words.
These will be words that you will encounter again and again in your
reading of records. And by the time you have copied out 100 or so of
them, you will find yourself reading the old script with remarkable facility.

Unfortunately, however, many German records are not written in
a careful reproduction of the standard script. As you can imagine, the
actual writing varied with the time period and sometimes with the area of
the country. As you well know from reading the writing of your friends,
the written language also varies from person to person. In the next few
pages (Tables 5a, 5b, and 5c) are presented some of the major variations
that you are likely to encounter.

Now, let's talk a bit as to exactly how you can handle this
situation. What you need to do is to take the document that you are
attempting to read and construct an alphabetical table of the way the
writer writes each capital letter and each lower-case letter. This can be
done by paying attention to:

1) the letters that generally extend above the line (b, d, k, l, t),
2) the letters that generally extend below the line (g, j, p, q, x, y,
z),
3) the letters that extend both above and below the line (f, h, s),
4) letters resembling modern letters (b, f, i, j, l, o, z),
5) given names which are well known (such as Johann, Heinrich,
Karl, Katharine, Marie, and Anna),
6) small words which occur frequently (such as und, von, am, zu,
ist, bei, mit, ein, aus, er, sie, Sie, ihr), and
7) words you expect to be used (such as birth = Geburt, born =
geboren, baptism = Taufe, marriage ceremony =
Trauung, death = Tod, burial = Begräbnis or Beerdigung,
many other such terms given in the next section).

Table 5a. German Script Variations

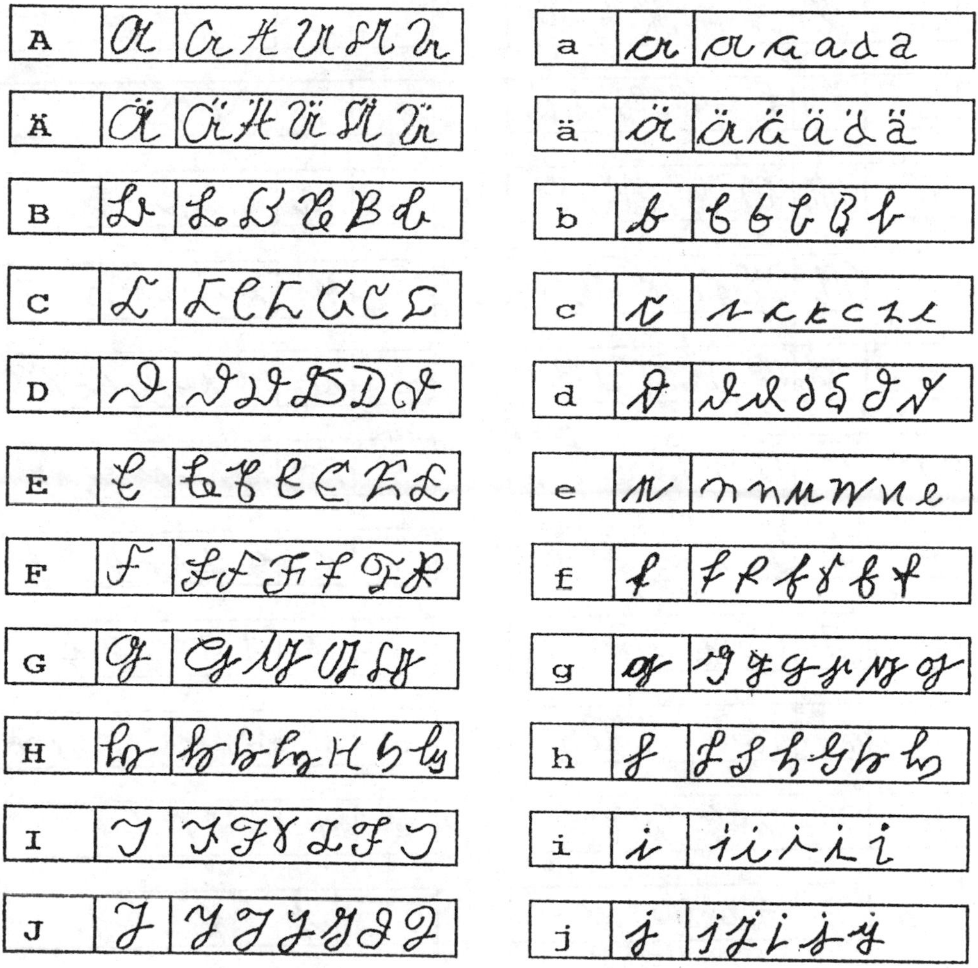

Table 5b. German Script Variations

K		k	
L		l	
M		m	
N		n	
O		o	
ö		ö	
P		p	
Q		q	
R		r	
S		s	
-s		ss	

Table 5c. German Script Variations

T					
U					
Ü					
V					
W					
X					
Y					
Z					
ch					
ck					
st					

t					
u					
ü					
v					
w					
x					
y					
z					
sch					
ß					
ph					

3. German terminology	3. Deutsche Terminologie

| **3. Deutsche Terminologie** | 3. *Deutsche Terminologie* |

There are many German terms that will be useful to you as you go about reading old German printed materials and old German manuscript (handwritten) records. The types of terms which will be treated in this section include: family relationships, genealogical terms, genealogical symbols, abbreviations, illness which were the causes of death, occupations, titles, and numbers. We will begin with terms for family <u>relationships</u>. An alphabetical list of some of the most important of these follows. Scan through it briefly now and then remember it when you are working with German materials.

adoptiert: adopted
Ahn(en): ancestor(s)
Altere: senior
angenommenes Kind: adopted child
Base: female cousin
Blutverwandtschapt: blood
      kinship
Braut: bride
Bräutigam: bridegroom
Brautkind: premarital child
Bruder: brother
Ehefrau: wife
ehelich: legitimate
Ehemann: husband
Ehepaar: married couple
Eltern: parents
Enkel: grandson
Enkelin: granddaughter
Erbe: heir
Familie: family
Findling: foundling
Frau: wife
Fräulein: unmarried female
Gatte: husband
Gattin: wife
Gemahl: spouse
Generation: generation

geschieden: divorced
Geschwister: siblings
getrennt: separated
Gevatter: godfather
Gevatterin: godmother
Grosseltern: grandparents
Grossmutter: grandmother
Grossvater: grandfather
Hurenkind: illegimate child
Junge: boy
Jüngere: junior
Jungfer: virgin
Jungfrau: virgin
Junggeselle: bachelor
Jüngling: bachelor
Kind(er): child(ren)
Knabe: boy
Kusin: male cousin
Kusine: female cousin
Mädchen: girl
Mutter: mother
Nebenfrau: concubine
Neffe: nephew
Nichte: niece
Oheim: uncle
Onkel: uncle
Pate: godfather

Paten: godparents
Patenkind: godchild
Patin: godmother
Plegesohn: foster son
Plegetochter: foster daughter
Schwager: brother-in-law
Schwägerin: sister-in-law
Schwester: sister
Schwiegermutter: mother-in-law
Schwiegervater: father-in-law
Sohn: son
Söhner: daughter-in-law
Stiefkind: stepchild
Stiefmutter: stepmother
Stiefvater: stepfather
Tante: aunt
Taufpate: godfather
Taufpaten: godparents
Taufpatin: godmother
Taufzeuge: godfather
Taufzeugin: godmother
Tochter: daughter

unbekannt: unknown
unehelich: illegitimate
unverheiratet: unmarried
Ureltern: ancestors
Urenkel: great grandson
Urenkelin: great granddaughter
Urgrosseltern: great grandparents
Urgrossmutter: great grandmother
Urgrossvater: great grandfather
Vater: father
verheiratet: married
verlobt: engaged
vermählt: married
verwandt: related
verwitwet: widowed
Vetter: male cousein
Vorfahr(en): ancestors
Vorkind(er): stepchild(ren)
Waise: orphan
Witwe: widow
Witwer: widower

Another very useful list of German terms consists of words which are particularly genealogical in their nature. The German language has many compound words in it. These are words such as Kirchenbücher (church books) which are made up by putting together two or more simpler words. In this case, the words are Kirche (church) and books (Bücher). An example of three words (actually four) put together is Abendmahlgästelisten, which is a compound of Abendmahl (communion), Gäste (attendees), and Listen (lists). The word for communion is a combination of Abend (evening) and Mahl (meal). In the following listing of genealogically-oriented words, you will not find many compound words. The reason is that you will be able without much trouble to see the individual words which make them up. Therefore, we have listed the simple words and prefixes which go into the compound words. For example, you will not find Kirchenbücher, Kirchenlisten, Kirchenverzeichnisse, Kirchenurkunde. Instead you will find the simpler words that make them up: Kirche, Bücher, Listen, Verzeichnisse, and Urkunde. This will not only keep the list a little shorter, it will facilitate your acquaintance with the language.

Abendmahl: communion
absterben: die
Adressbuch: city directory
Ahnentafel: ancestor chart
Akte(n): record(s)
Almosen: welfare
Alter: age
Amt: office
Anzeige: notice
Archiv: archive
Armen: poor
aufbieten: publish banns
Aufgeboten: marriage banns
ausgestorben: line died out
auswandern: to emigrate
Auswanderung: emigration
Band(Bände): volume(s)
Baptisten: Baptists
Beerdigung: burial
Begräbnis: burial
Berg: mountain
Beruf: occupation
bestatten: bury
Bestattungs: burial
Bevölkerungsliste: population
    lists
Bezirk: district
Bistum: diocese
Brief: letter
Brüdergemeinde: Moravians
Bruderschaft: brotherhood
Buch(-ü-er): book(s)
Burg: fortress
Bürger: citizen
Busse: penance
Chroniken: chronicles
Datum: date
Dorf: village
ebenda: the same place
Ehe: marriage
Ehebrecher: adulterer
einbürgern: naturalize

Einnahme(n): receipt(s)
einwandern: immigrate
Einwanderung: immigration
Einwilligung: consent
Einwohner; resident
ejusdem: the same
Entbindung: delivery
Erbe: heir
Erbschaft: legacy
evangelisch: Protestant
Familie: family
Filiale: branch church
Flecken: hamlet
Fluss: river
Forschung: research
freie Verbindung: common-law
    marriage
Friedhof: cemetery
Fürstentum: principality
Garnison: military garrison
Gäste: attendees
geboren: born
Gebühren: fee
Geburt: birth
gefallen: fallen in battle
Geistliche: clergyman
Geld: money
Gemeinde: community
Gemeinde: parish
genannt: known as
Gericht: court
Geschichte(n): history(ies)
Geschlect: family lineage
Gesellen: journeymen
gestorben: died
getauft: baptized
getraut: married
Gilde: guild
Glockenbücher: bell tolling books
Grab: grave
Grafschaft: area ruled by a Count
Grund: land

Gut: estate
Hausbücher: house books (all
  owners of a house)
Hebamme: midwife
Heimat: home
Heirat: marriage
Herkunft: origin
Herzogtum: duchy
hiesiger Ort: of this place
Hochschule: Institute
Hochzeit: wedding
Hof: farmstead
Hugenotten: Huguenots
Innung: guild
Katholicher: Catholic
katholisch: Catholic (adj)
kinderlos: childless
Kirche: church
Kirchensprengel: diocese
Kirchhof: church cemetery
Kommunikanten: communicants
Kommunion: communion
Konfirmation: confirmation
konfirmiert: confirmed
Kopfzahl: census
kopuliert: married
Krankheit: illness
Kreis: county
Lagerbücher: military levy books
Land: state
Landgericht: district court
Lebensdokumente: vital records
ledig: single
Lehrling: apprentice
Leichen: funeral
Leichenpredigten: funeral sermons
letzter Wille: last will
Liste(n): list(s)
lutherisch: Lutheran
Mädchenname: maiden name
Mannzahl: census
Matrikel: enrollment

Meister: master
melden: to register
mennonitisch: Mennonite
Methoden: Methodists
minderjährig: underage
Mitgleider: members
Musterungslisten: military lists
nachgelassen: surviving
Nachlass: legacy/estate
Nachlassgerichte: probate courts
Name: name
Niederkunft: delivery
noch lebende: still living
Nottaufe: emergency baptism
Oberlandesgericht: high court
Ort: place
Ortsippenbücher: locality lineage
  books
Ortslexika: gazetteers
Pfarr: parish
Pfarrer: minister
Polizei: police
Predigt: sermon
Proklamationen: banns
protestantisch: Protestant
Protokolle: official records
Quelle(n): source(s)
Ranglisten: military lists
reformiert: Reformed
Register: register(s)
Sammlung: collection
Schein(e): certificate(s)
Seelenregister: person register
Seite: page
selbe: same
Selbstmord: suicide
Sippen: family lineage
Staat: state
Stadt: city
Stammbaum: family tree
Stammrolle: military rosters
Stand: occupation

Standesamt: civil registry
Sterbe: death
Sterbefall: cause of death
sterben: die
Steuer: tax
Taufe: baptism
Testament: will
Tod: death
Todesursache: cause of death
Totenbücher: death books
Totengeläutbücher: death bell
 tolling books
totgeboren: stillborn
Trauung: wedding
ungefähr: about, circa
Universität: University
Urkunde: document(s)
Ursache: cause
Verein: society
Verlobung: engagement

Verlobungsanzeige: banns
verstorben: deceased
Verzeichnis(se): index(es)
Volkszählung: census
volljährig: of legal age
Vormund: guardian
Vornamen: first name
Weiler: hamlet
Wiedertäufer: Anabaptist
Wohnort: residence
Zehntregister: tithe register
Zeitschrift(en): periodical(s)
Zeitung(en): newspaper(s)
Zeuge: witness
Zeugnis: certificate
Zivilstandsregister: vital records
 registers
Zuname: surname
Zunft: guild
Zweitschriften: transcripts

In many of the handwritten German records you will find some very interesting <u>symbols</u> which have genealogical significance. The most important ones of these are as follows. We will give you the meaning in both English and German.

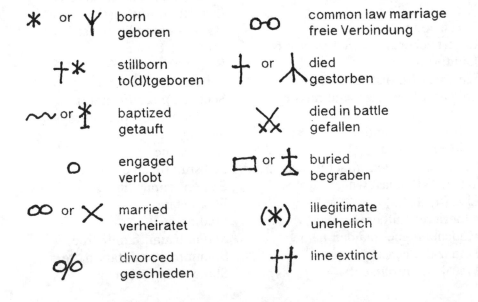

You will run into numerous <u>abbreviations</u> as you make your way through various German documents. These are the most common. They will be accompanied by both their German and English meanings.

a.(aus): from
a.d.h.(aus dem Hause): out of the house
ad.(adoptiert): adopted
Art.(Artikel): article
B.(Bruder): brother
b.v.(beide von): both from
Bd.(Band): volume
Bde.(Bände): volumes
Bev.(Bevölkerung): population
Bez.(Bezirk): district
bm.(Burgermeister): mayor
C.(copuliert): married
d.A.(der Altere): the older
d.B.(durch Boten): by messenger
d.H.(dem Herrn): to the gentle-men
d.J.(der Jüngere): the younger
d.l.J.(des laufenden Jahres): of the current year
eh.(eigenhändig): written by one's own hand
ehel.(ehelich): legitimate
err.(errechnet): approximated
ev.(evangelisch): Protestant
evang.(evangelisch): Protestant
Fl.(Fräulein): unmarried woman
Fr.(Frau): married woman
geb.(geboren): born
ged.(gedachter): assumed
gesch.(geschieden): divorced
gest.(gestorben): died
get.(getauft): baptized
getr.(getraut): married
gl.N.(gleichen Names): of the same name

H.(Herr): mister/sir
i.A.(im Auftrag): in charge
i.R.(im Ruhestand): retired
i.V.(in Vertretung): acting for
Jgfr.(Jungfrau): maiden
Jh.(Jahrhundert): century
K.B.(Kirchenbücher): church books
k.H.(kurzer Hand): without hesitation
Kath.(Katholisch): catholic
Kr.(Kreis): district
led.(ledig): single
Luth.(lutherisch): Lutheran
m.(mit): with
M.(Mutter): mother
männl.(männlich):masculine
Menn.(mennonitisch): Mennonite
N.S.(Nachschrift): postscript
Nr.(Nummer): number
o.V.(ohne Vorgang): without re-cord
Pfr.(Pfarrer): pastor
Qtg.(Quittung): receipt
Ref.(reformiert): Reformed
S.(Seite): page
s.(siehe): see
S.(Sohn): son
S.d.(Sohn des/der); son of
S.v.(Sohn von): son of
samt.(mitsamt): together with
Schw.(Schwester): sister
Slg.(Sammlung): collection
T.(Tochter): daughter
T.d.(Tochter des/der): daughter of
tf.(bctreffend): concerning

Tg.(Tagebuch): day book
u.(und): and
u.d.(und des/der): and of
V.(Vater): father
v.(von): from
v.J.(vorigen Jahres): of the
previous year
v.M.(vorigen Monats): of the
previous month
verh.(verheiratet): married
verh.(verheiratet): married

verl.(verlobt): engaged
verw.(verwitwet): widowed
Verz.(Verzeichnis): index
w.o.(wie oben): as above
weil.(weiland): deceased
wiebl.(weiblich): feminine
wwe.(Witwe): widow
wwer.(Witwer): widower
z.B.(zum Bericht): reportedly
Ztg.(Zeitung): newspaper

When you are reading death records, you will often come across words describing the illness which was the cause of death. A list of some of the more common ones will now be given. In some cases, the identification of an illness with its modern equivalent is not too certain, because descriptions of illnesses in previous centuries were not analytical or precise.

Abszess: abscess
Abtreibung: abortion
Abzehrung: consumption
Altersschwäche: old age
Anfall: stroke
Angina: angina
Asthma: asthma
Auszehrung: consumption
Bandwurm: tapeworm
Beulenpest: bubonic plague
Blattern: smallpox
Blätterrose: shingles
Blutfluss: hemorrhage
Blutgang: hemorrhage
Blutlauf: hemorrhage
Blutsturz: hemorrhage
Blutvergiftung: blood poisoning
Bräune: tonsilitis, diptheria
Brechruhr: cholera
Brustkrämpfe: breast spasms
Brustwassersucht: dropsy
Cholera: cholera
Diptherie: diptheria

Durchfall: diarrhea
Eiterbeule: abscess
Entkräftung: exhaustion
Epilepsie: epilepsy
Ertränkung: drowning
Fallsucht: epilepsy
Fäule: cancer
Faulfieber: putrid fever
Fehlgeburt: miscarriage
Fieber: fever
Fleckenkrankheit: scabs
Fleckfieber: spotted fever
Flecktyphus: typhus
Flussfieber: rheumatic fever
Gehirnschlag: apoplexy
Gelbsucht: jaundice
Geschwulst: swelling
Gicht: gout
Gliederstopfung: apoplexy
Gürtelrose: shingles
Halsentzündung: throat infection
Halsschwindsucht: throat consumption

Häule: croup
Herzschlag: heart attack
Hirnenzündung: brain infection
Husten: coughing
Influenza: influenza
Keist: asthma
Keuchhusten: whooping cough
Kindbettfieber: childbed fever
Kinderpocken: chicken pox
Knochenfrass: caries
Knochenkrebs: bone cancer
Kolic: colic
Kopfwassersucht: hydrocephalus
Krämfe: cramps, convulsions
Krätze: scabies
Krebs: cancer
Kropf: goiter
Krupp: croup
Lungenentzündung: pneumonia
Lungenschwindsucht: consumption
Lungensucht: consumption
Lustfeuche: syphillis
Magenkatarrh: gastritis
Mandelbräune: tonsillitis
Masern: measles
Milzverhärtung: anthrax
Nervenfieber: nervous fever
Nesselwurm: tapeworm
Pest: plague

Pocken: smallpox
Rachenbräune: diptheria
Räude: dry scab
Rheuma: rheumatism
Röteln: red measles
Ruhr: dysentary
Samenfluss: gonorrhea
Scharlachfieber: scarlet fever
Schlagenfall: stroke
Schlagfluss: apoplexy
Schleimfieber: typhus
Schwäche: debilitation
Schwämme: fungus
Schwindsucht: consumption
Stickfluss: suffocation
Stickhusten: whooping cough
Syphillis: syphillis
Tobsucht: raving madness
Tuberkulose: tuberculosis
Typhus: typhus
Unterleibstyphus: typhoid
Vergiftung: poisoning
Wasserkopf: hydrocephalus
Wassersucht: dropsy
Windpocken: chickenpox
Wochenbettfieber: childbed fever
Würmer: worms
Ziegenpeter: mumps
Zuchung: cramps, spasms

Another mini-dictionary that may be of help to you is a listing of some of the more common occupations. You are likely to run across these in church records, civil records, city records, and guild records.

Ackermann: farmer
Aderlasser: barber surgeon
Amman: magistrate
Amtmann: magistrate
Amtsknecht: servant
Amtsverwalter: administrator
Anbauer: peasant
Anstreicher: painter

Anwalt: lawyer
Apotheker: pharmacist
Arbeiter: worker
Armer: beggar
Arzt: physician
Aufseher: supervisor
Bäcker: baker
Bader: barber

Bamutter: midwife
Barbier: barber
Bartscherer: barber
Bauer: farmer
Baumeister: builder
Baumgärtner: orchardman
Bergmann: miner
Besenbinder: broom maker
Bettler: beggar
Bierbrauer: brewer
Bleicher; bleacher
Bote: messenger
Böttcher: cooper
Brauer: brewer
Brettschneider: sawyer
Brückenzöllner: bridge toll
collector
Buchdrucker: printer
Büchsenmacher: gunsmith
Bürgermeister: mayor
Bürstenmacher: brushmaker
Büttel: jailer
Büttner: cooper
Chirurg: surgeon
Dachdecker: thatcher
Diener: man servant
Dienerin: woman servant
Dienstbote: house servant
Dienstmädchen: servant girl
Doktor: educated man
Drechsler: thresher
Drucker: printer
Einlieger: farm worker
Eisengieer: foundryman
Eisenschmied: blacksmith
Erzgräber: miner
Fabinder: cooper
Fährmann: ferryman
Färber: dyer
Feldhüter: field watchman
Feldmesser: surveyor
Fischer: fisherman

Fischhändler: fish merchant
Flaschenmacher: bottle maker
Fleischer: butcher
Fuhrmann: wagoner
Gängler: peddler
Gärtner: gardener
Gastwirt: innkeeper
Geistlicher: clergyman
Geldeinnehmer: money agent
Gemüsegärtner: vegetable
gardener
Gemüsehändler: grocer
Gerber: tanner
Gerichtsbeisitzer: judge
Gerichtsschreiber: court clerk
Geschäftsmann: businessman
Gewürzhändler: spicer, grocer
Giesser: foundryman
Glasarbeiter: glassmaker
Glaser: glazier
Glöcknerküster: bell ringer
Goldschmied: goldsmith
Grobschmied: blacksmith
Grützler: grain miller
Gürtler: belt maker
Gütler: tenant farmer
Häcker: vine grower
Hammerschmied: blacksmith
Händler: dealer, merchant
Handschuhmacher: glove maker
Handwerker: craftsman
Haubenmacher: milliner
Hausdiener; house servant
Hausierer: peddler
Hebamme: midwife
Heizer: stoker
Hemdenmacher: shirt maker
Heuerling: day laborer
Hirt: shepherd, herdsman
Hofmuttersmann: cow breeder
Holzhändler: lumberman
Holzhauer: wood cutter

Honighändler: honey merchant
Hopfenbauer: hops grower
Hüfner: farmer
Hufschmied: blacksmith
Hure: prostitute
Hutmacher: hatmaker
Imker: beekeeper
Jäger: hunter
Kalkbrenner: lime burner
Kammerdiener: butler
Kannengiesser: pewter worker
Käsehändler: cheese merchant
Kaufmann: merchant
Kellner: waiter
Kerkermeister: jailer
Kerzenzieher: candlemaker
Kessler: boilermaker, tinker
Kettenschmied: chain maker
Kindermädchen: childrens' nurse
Kistenmacher: cabinet maker
Klempner: plumber
Knecht: servant
Knopfmacher: button maker
Koch: cook
Köhler: charcoal maker
Korbmacher: basket maker
Kötter: small farmer
Krämer: peddler, shopkeeper
Krankenschwester: nurse
Kruger: innkeeper
Kuchenbäcker: confectioner
Küfer: cooper
Kuhhirt: cowherder
Künstler: skilled worker
Kunsttischler: cabinet maker
Kupferschmied: coppersmith
Kürschner: furrier
Küster: sexton
Landmesser: surveyor
Lastträger: porter
Lederhändler: leather merchant
Lehrer: teacher

Leichenbediener: undertaker
Leinenweber: linen weaver
Lodenmacher: wool cloth weaver
Magd: female servant
Maler: artist
Mälzer: malt miller
Maurer: mason
Mehlhändler: flour merchant
Meier: overseer
Messerschmied: cutler
Messingsschmied: brass worker
Metzger: butcher
Milchhändler: milkman
Milchviehzüchter: cow breeder
Möbeltischler: furniture maker
Müller: miller
Musiker: musician
Nabenschmied: wheelwright
Nachtwächter: night watchman
Nadelmacher: needle maker
Nagelschmied: nail maker
Näherin: dressmaker
Notar: notary
Obstverkäufer: fruit dealer
Ochsenknecht: cowherder
Ohlenmacher: potter
Papierhändler: paper merchant
Papiermacher: paper maker
Pedell: servant
Pfandnehmer: pawnbroker
Pfannenschmied: pot/pan maker
Pfarrer: pastor, priest
Pfefferhändler: pepper merchant
Pferdeknecht: stable worker
Pfieffenmacher: pipe maker
Pflasterer: paver
Pflugschmied: plowsmith
Pförtner: porter
Pottaschbrenner: potash burner
Prediger: preacher
Priester: priest
Putzfrau: cleaning woman

Putzhändler: milliner
Rademacher: wheelwright
Rechenmeister: accountant
Rechtsanwalt: attorney
Reepschläger: rope maker
Richter: judge
Riemenschneider: harness maker
Sackmacher: sack maker
Säger: sawyer
Salpetersieder: saltpeter boiler
Salzhändler: salt merchant
Sattler; saddle maker
Schäfer: sheepherder
Schafhirt: sheepherder
Schiffbauer: shipbuilder
Schiffer: sailor
Schiffzimmerman: ship carpenter
Schindelmacher: shingle maker
Schlosser: locksmith
Schmelzer: caster
Schmied: blacksmith
Schneider: tailor
Schreiber: clerk
Schreiner: cabinet maker
Schuhmacher: shoemaker
Schüler: student
Schultheiss: village mayor
Schuster: shoemaker
Schweinehirt: swineherder
Seeman: seaman
Seidenkrämer: silk merchant
Seidenwirker: silk worker
Seifensieder: soap maker
Seiler: rope maker
Silberschmied: silversmith
Spangenmacher: brass worker
Spiegelmacher: mirror maker
Stadtschreiber: city clerk
Stallknecht: stable worker

Steinbrecher: quarryman
Steinhauer: stone cutter
Steinmetz: stone cutter
Steuereinnehmer: tax collector
Strumpfweber: stocking weaver
Taglöhner: day worker
Teppichweber: rug weaver
Tierarzt: veterinarian
Tischler: cabinet maker
Töpfer: potter
Torwächter: gatekeeper
Totengräber: gravedigger
Tuchhändler: cloth merchant
Tuchmacher: cloth maker
Uhrmacher: clockmaker
Verkäufer: salesman
Viehhändler: cattle trader
Viehhirt: cattle herder
Wächter: watchman
Waffenschmied: weapon maker
Wagner: cart maker
Wassermüller: water miller
Weber: weaver
Wehmutter: midwife
Weinbauer: grape grower
Weinhändler: wine merchant
Wirt: innkeeper
Wollweber: wool weaver
Wurstmacher: sausage maker
Zahnarzt: dentist
Zeidler: beekeeper
Zeugkrämer: cloth merchant
Ziegelbrenner: brick maker
Ziegeldecker: roofer (tile)
Ziegler: brick maker
Zimmermann: carpenter
Zöllner: toll collector
Zuckerbäcker: confectioner
Zwirnmacher: thread/string maker

Another item that you may run into is <u>titles</u>. Germans have been quite title-conscious throughout much of their history, and it will be useful for you to see some of the more prevalent ones. They follow.

Anwalt: lawyer
Bischof: bishop
Dechanat: dean
Dekan: dean
Doktor: learned person
Erzbischof: archbishop
Erzherzog: archduke
Erzherzogin: archduchess
Feldwebel: sergeant
Freiherr: baron
Freiherrin: baroness
Fürst: prince
Fürstin: princess
General: general
Graf: count
Gräfin: countess
Grossherzog: grand duke
Grossherzogin: grand duchess
Hauptmann: captain
Herzog: duke
Herzogin: duchess
Kaiser: emporer
Kaiserin: empress

Kaplan: chaplain
König: king
Königin: queen
Kronprinz: crown prince
Lehrer: male teacher
Lehrerin: female teacher
Leutnant: lieutenant
Magister: teacher
Major: major
Oberpfarrer: rector
Oberst: colonel
Pfalzgraf: count palatine
Pfarrer: pastor
Prinz: prince
Prinzessin: princess
Probst: dean
Professor: professor
Rechtsanwalt: lawyer
Rektor: dean
Richter: judge
Schultheiss: village mayor
Unteroffizier: corporal

Another item that will be of considerable use to you is a brief listing of German <u>numbers</u>. You will constantly be running across them as you work your way through various German genealogical records. In the following list the German word for a number is given first, then if the number is a cardinal number, the written form is shown, or if the number is an ordinal number, the written form is shown with a -st, -nd, -rd, or -th after it. Examples of cardinal numbers are one, two, three, and four; examples of ordinal numbers are first, second, third, and fourth. In German, a period after a number means it is an ordinal (1.= 1st, 2. = 2nd, 3. = 3rd, 4. = 4th, and 31.= 31st).

acht 8
achte 8th
achtzehn 18
achtzehnte 18th
achtzig 80
achtzigste 80th
drei 3
dreissig 30
dreissigste 30th

dreizehn 13	neun 9	siebzig 70
dreizehnte 13th	neunte 9th	siebzigste 70th
dritte 3rd	neunzehn 19	vier 4
eins 1	neunzehnte 19th	vierte 4thvierzehn 14
elf 11	neunzig 90	vierzehnte 14th
elfte 11th	neunzigste 90th	vierzig 40
erste 1st	sechs 6	vierzigste 40th
fünf 5	sechste 6th	zehn 10
fünfte 5th	sechszehn 16	zehnte 10th
fünfzehn 15	sechszehnte 16th	zwanzig 20
fünfzehnte 15th	sechszig 60	zwanzigste 20th
fünfzig 50	sechszigste 60th	zwei 2
fünfzigste 50th	sieben 7	zweite 2nd
hundert 100	siebte 7thsiebzehn	zwölf 12
hundertste 100th	siebzehnte	zwölfte 12th

In reference to numbers, please note that in German, the way they write 21 is one-and-twenty (einundzwanzig), or 36 is six-and-thirty (sechsunddreissig), or 78 is eight-and-seventy (achtundsiebzig). Likewise, the 21st is written one-and-twentieth (einundzwanzigste), 36th is written six-and-thirtieth (sechsunddreissigste), and 78 is written eight-and-seventieth (achtundsiebzigste). Therefore, when you see a word like zweiundfünfzig, you read it two-and-fifty or 52. And when you see vierhundertneunundsechzig, read it as four hundred nine-and-sixty, or 469.

A more extensive work on German terminology is:
___W. Ribbe und E. Henning, TASCHENBUCH FÜR FAMILIEN-GESCHICHTSFORSCHUNG, Verlag Degener, Neustadt/Aisch, Deutschland, 1990.
And an excellent detailed work on old German handwriting is:
___P. A. Grun, LESESCHLÜSSEL ZU UNSERER ALTEN SCHRIFT, C. A. Starke Verlag, Limburg/Lahn, Deutschland, 1984.
Abbreviations are treated extensively in:
___P. A. Grun, SCHLÜSSEL ZU ALTEN UND NEUEN ABKÜRZUNGEN, C. A. Starke Verlag, Limburg/Lahn, Deutschland, 1966.

4. Latin terminology	4. Lateinische Terminologie
4. Lateinische Terminologie	*4. Lateinische Terminologie*

When you go back into the older church records, you will find that they begin to be in combined German and Latin, and very early on, Latin tends to predominate. The Latin language persisted much later in Catholic records, so it will be necessary for you to own a Latin dictionary. A very good inexpensive paperback one is:

___D. P. Simpson, CASSELL'S LATIN-ENGLISH [ENGLISH-LATIN] DICTIONARY, Macmillan Publishing Co., New York, NY, latest edition. Over 35,000 entries.

If your work turns out to be extensive, then you will need a more detailed dictionary. This one is recommended:

___D. P. Simpson, CASSELL'S LATIN DICTIONARY, LATIN-ENGLISH, ENGLISH-LATIN, Macmillan Publishing Co., New York, NY, latest edition. Over 85,000 entries.

For detailed work, two works written German are essential. You will need to use them to look up Latin words, then to look up the meanings which are given in your German dictionary.

___F. Verdenhalven, FAMILIENKUNDLICHES WÖRTERBUCH, Verlag Degener, Neustadt/Aisch, Deutschland, 1969.

___W. Weidler, P. A. Grun, und K. D..Lampe, LATEIN FÜR DEN SIPPENFORSCHER, Verlag C. A. Starke, Görlitz, Deutschland, 1939.

In general, Latin language handwriting is in a script called Latin or Roman, and it usually resembles modern handwriting sufficiently that you will be able to make your way through it. However, remember that writing differs from individual to individual, so you may have to go through the process of constructing an alphabetical key for each scribe. In the following sections some of the more prevalent words that you will encounter are listed. Details for constructing an alphabetical key for an individual scribe have been discussed previously.

In the following sections some of the more prevalent words that you will encounter are listed. A very important aspect of the Latin language must now be noted. Latin employs an extraordinary number of endings for various words. Because of this, what is important is the so-called root of the word. This is the part of the word that appears before the endings. For example, the root nat- carries many different endings, all relating to birth: natio (a being born), nationes (a being born), nativus (born), nativa (born), nativum (born), natu (by birth), naturalis (produced by birth), natura (birth), natus (born), nata (born), natum (born), natus (son), nata (daughter). Care must be exercised because the roots of certain words resemble each other greatly. But, what you must bear in mind is that when a word is given in the list below, it may take several different endings, even though they may not all be listed. This is complicated, unfortunately, by the fact that the Latin in many church documents is not necessarily good Latin; it can take some peculiar forms, and can be spelled in some odd ways. This, of course, varies with the scribe.

The first category of words embraces those words which may in general be referred to as <u>genealogical</u> terms:

abortio: miscarriage
abortivum: premature birth
abortus: miscarriage
aetas: age
aetatis: age
alias: also known as
anche: grandfather
anno: in the year
avi: ancestors
avia: grandmother
avunculus: mother's brother
avus: grandfather
baptizatio: baptize
baptizatus: baptized
caelebs: bachelor, unmarried
casualia: church taxes
civis: male citizen
civissa: female citizen
civitas: city inhabitants
coemeterium: cemetery
coenam: communion

cognomen: family name
collateralis: wife
commater: godmother
compater: godfather
confirmatio: confirmation
conjugatis: married
conjunx: married person
connubium: marriage
decedere: die
decessit: died
decessus: death
defunctus: dead
denunciatio: banns
discidium: divorce
divortium: divorce
domicilium: domicile
domus: house
ducatus: duchy
ducissa: duchess
dux: duke
ecclesia: church

ejusdem: same (month)

eodem: same (day)

epitaphium: grave inscription

exitus: death

ex legitimo thoro: legitimate

familia: family

fidejussor: godparent

filia: daughter

filius: son

frater: brother

funeralia: funeral

funus: funeral

gener: son-in-law

genetrix: mother

germana: sister

germanus: brother

glos: sister-in-law

humare: bury

humatio: burial

illegitimus: illegitmate

incola: inhabitant

infans: small child

innuptus: unmarried

intestatus: without a will

junior: younger

liberi: children

majoritas: legal aged

marita: wife

maritus: husband

mater: mother

materna: godmother

matrimonium: marriage

matrina: godmother

monitiones: banns

mors: death

mortua: dead

mortualia: fee for burial

mortuus: dead

nata: born

natalis: birth place

nativitas: birth

naturalis: illegitimate

natus: born

necrologium: death book

nepos: grandson

neptis: granddaughter

nomen: name

nomina: names

nothus: illegimate

nupta: married

nuptara: bride

nuptiae: marriage

nuptias celebrare: marry

nupturus: bridegroom

obiit: dead

obire: die

obitus: die

orbitus: orphan

origo: origin

pagus: village

parens: parent

parentes: parents

parochia: parish

partus: childbirth

pastor: pastor

pater: father

paternus: godfather

patrina: godmother

patrinus: godfather

patruus: father's brother

posthumus: born after father's death

proavia: greatgrandmother

proavus: greatgrandfather

proclamatio: banns

progenitor: ancestor

pronepos: greatgrandson

proneptis: greatgranddaughter

provisor puerorum; guardian

puella: girl

puellus: boy

puer: boy

pueri: children

quondam: died

relicta: widow
relictus: widower
religio: religion
renatus: baptized, reborn
repudium: divorce
scortatio: adultery
scortator: adulterer
selig: dead
senior: senior
sepelira: bury
sepulcrum: grave
sepultura: burial
sepultus: buried
socer: father-in-law
socrus: mother-in-law
soror: sister
sponsor: godparent
sponsus: betrothed

spurius: illegimate
stuprum: adultery
susceptor: godfather
susceptrix: godmother
tinctus: dipped, baptized
tumulatus: grave mound
tutor: guardian
uxor: wife
vicus: village
vidus: widow
viduus: widower
vir: husband, man
virgo: unmarried girl
virtuosus: honorable
vita: life
vota secunda: second marriage
vulgo quaestitus: illegimate

A second list of useful material consists of Latin <u>abbreviations</u> which often occur genealogical records.

a.c. of the current year
a.Chr. before Christ
a.Chr.n. before Christ's birth
A.D. after Christ
a.e. in the named year
a.f. future years
a.m. before noon
a.p. in the previous year
a.pr. in the previous year
a.r.s. year of recuperation
a.st. Old Style dating
A.V. lived -- years
ai.el. of the previous year
ao. in the year
B.A.L. has lived 50 years
b.m. blessed memories
BX has lived
C.A.M. cause of death
C.M. cause of death
c.t. approximately

C.V. with wife
ca. about
CIB. citizen
civ. citizen
civ. citizen
cler. clergyman
COJUG. spouse
conj. wife
cop. married
cr. current
CT citizenship
CV citizenship
CVS wife
d. datum
d.a. the stated year
D.A. died in the year
d.d. under the date of
D.IN.P. died in peace
d.l. in the stated place
Dct. decree

DD days
DE on the day
den. died
des. designated
DETI the dead
DF the dead
dioc. diocese
dom. Sunday
Dt. paid
e.a. of the same year
e.o. officially
eccl. church
ed. published
EG sick
ej.a. of the same year
em. retired
eod.q.s. same day as above
EXTM according to the will
f. son/daughter
F. has lived
f.c. son of a citizen
fa. daughter
fasc. document
FF sons/brothers
ff. godparent
fil. son/daughter
FIX has lived
FL son/daughter
fl. son/daughter
FLA daughter
fr. father
fr. brother
FRA brother
FRS brothers
FS brothers
G. godfather
gen. father
h. hour
h.a. in this year
h.l. in this place
H.L.S.E. here lies buried
h.m. in this month

H.S.E. here is buried
h.t. in this time
HO.PO. afternoon hour
HR heir
HRD heirs
HS heirs
incl. inclusive
it. item
jun. junior
juv. youth
l. legitimate
l.c. at the stated place
l.p.s.m. legitimate by a subsequent
       marriage
L.S. burial place
m.c. current month
m.m.pr. in my own hand
m.n. New Style dating
m.n. recent custom
M.p. previous month
m.s. usual custom
m.v. old custom
mp. in one's own hand
n. born
N. note
N.N. name unknown
n.St. New Style dating
nat. born
NB. note well
Nep. grandson
o. died
ob. died
p. parents
P. pastor/father
p.a. per year
p.c.d. by a copy of a decree
p.Chr.n. after Christ's birth
p.d. after the date
p.e. for example
p.h.l. pastor this parish
P.L. local pastor
p.m. after death

p.m.s. by subsequent marriage
P.prim. Chief Pastor
p.r.s. read, approved, signed
p.rel. by an earlier report
par. parents
pat. godparents
patr. godparents
PD. yesterday
pp. pauper
PP. Catholic clergyman
ppa. by authority
PR parents
pr.pr. approximately
Q.M.O. the deceased
qu. questionable
r.f. surviving daughter
r.k. Roman Catholic
rel. surviving spouse
ren. baptized
S. son
s.a. without the year
s.a.e.l. without year and place
s.d. without date
S.D. on the day
s.l.r. with the right of return
s.v. if I may say so
s.v.r. with desire for return
SAE. century
SCL century
SEC. century
sen. senior
sep. buried
seq. following

sp. illegimate
sq. following
ss. signed
st.n. New Style dating
st.v. Old Style dating
stud. student
susc. sponsor
t. died/ended
t. witness
T. daughter/witness
t.a. according to the record
t.p. with full name
TP. time
tt. witnesses
TT. will
u.i. as below
u.o. as above
ult. last day of month
uts. as above
ux. wife
v. turn page
V.A.L. lived 50 years
V.E.L.R. widow and children
V.s.p. see next page
VC wife
vdt has seen
vid. see
VID. widow
VIX.A.FE.C. lived almost 100 years
vix.an. lived -- years
we. widow
wr. widower

Another listing of Latin words which will prove of use to you in reading the old records will now be set out. This is a list of <u>occupations</u>.

abacistus: accountant
aes fosser: copper miner
agricola: farmer
agrimensor: surveyor
albator: bleacher

ampularius: bottle maker
ancilla: female servant
apiarius: beekeeper
apothecarius: pharmicist
argentarius: banker

armarium fabricant: cabinet maker
artifex: craftsman
barbarius: barber
burgensis: citizen
calculator: accountant
calx urerer: lime burner
carnarius: butcher
carpentarius: wagon maker
carpenter: lignarius
carrucarius: wagoner
catopticus: mirror maker
caupo: shop or innkeeper
cementarius: mason
cerdo: tanner
cerevisiarius: brewer
charta mercator: paper dealer
chirurgus: surgeon
cingularius: belt maker
cistarus: box maker
civis: citizen
cocus: male cook
collector: tax collector
colonus: farmer
companarius: sexton
conlegium sodalitas: guild
consiliarius: mayor
coqua: female cook
cordarius: rope maker
corium: leather worker
crumenarius: sackmaker
crustularius: confectioner
cuparius: cooper
curare: stableman
dimida agricola: sharecropper
discipulus: student
doktor: learned man
domare pastor: cowherder
duca: duchess
dux: duke
ephipparius: saddlemaker
exactor: tax collector
faber: skilled worker

famella: female servant
famellus: male servant
familas: male servant
fartor: poultry farmer
ferrarius: blacksmith
ferreus mercator; iron merchant
ferreus conditor: iron foundryman
figulus: potter
fructus venditor: fruit seller
glutinator: bookbinder
grandduca: grand duchess
grandux: grand duke
horologiarius: clockmaker
hortulanus: gardener
hospes: innkeeper
impressor: printer
incola: inhabitant
indusiarius: shirt maker
infector: dyer
inquilinus: tenant
judex: judge
jurisconsultus: lawyer
laborius: laborer
laneus texer: wool weaver
lapicida: stone cutter
lapidarius: quarry worker
later fabricant: brickmaker
lignator: woodcutter
linifex: linen weaver
ludimagister: schoolmaster
macellarius: butcher
macellarius: butcher
magister civum: mayor
magister: male teacher
magistra: female teacher
magistratus: magistrate
marinarius: sailor
medicus: physician
mendicus: beggar
mercator: merchant
metallicus: miner
minutor: barber-surgeon

naupegas: shipbuilder
nauta: seaman
navita: seaman
negotiator: business man
nutrix: nurse
obstetrix: midwife
olitor: grocer
ollarius: potmaker
operarius: worker
oris pastor: sheepherder
papyriacus: paper maker
pastor: pastor
pauper: poorman
pecus mercator: cattle trader
pelzer: furrier
pharmacopola: pharmicist
pictor: painter
piper mercator: pepper merchant
piscator: fisherman
pistor: baker
portarius: gatekeeper
portitor: ferryman
sacellanus: chaplain
salinator: salt trader
sartor: tailor

scriba: notary
servus: small farmer
servus: serf
sponsor: godparent
stabularis: stableman
stannarius: pewter worker
supellex fabricant: furniture maker
sus pastor: swineherder
sutor: shoemaker
tector: thatcher
textilis mercator: textile merchant
textor: weaver
tinctor: dyer
tonsor: barber
tritor: thresher
urbs scriba: city clerk
venditor: salesman
venditor: peddler
vespillo: corpse bearer
vestiarius: tailor
vicus praefectus: village mayor
viego: cooper
vigilarius: watchman
vinum mercator: wine merchant
vitriarius: glazier

The next set of Latin words will provide you with a listing of illnesses which are often cited in church records as the causes of death.

abortio: miscarriage
abscessus: abscess
asthmaticus: asthsma
cancer: cancer
consumptio: consumption
contagium: infection
dysenteria: dysentary
febris: fever
fungus: fungus
haemorrhoia: hemorrhage
hernia: hernia
hydropisus: fluid accumulation

inflammatio pectus: inflammed
    chest
insania: madness
morbilli: measles
morbus: disease
pestilentia: plague
pestis: plague
pleuritis: pluerisy
proflurium: diarrhea
pulmoneus: lung disease
putris febris: putrid fever
spasmus: convulsion

stomach morbus: stomach disease
suffocatio: suffocation
tumor: swelling

tussis: a cough
typhus: typhus
ulcus: sore, ulcer

5. Dates and time	5. Datums– und Zeitangaben
5. Datums– und Zeitangaben	5. [handwritten]

The German fashion for <u>writing</u> <u>dates</u> differs from that usually practiced in this country. We write month/day/year, that is, December 5, 1924, or Dec 5, 1924, or 12/5/1924, or 12/5/24, or 12-5-1924, or 12-5-24. In German the practice is to write day/month/year, that is, 5 December 1924, or 5 Dec 1924, or 5/12/1924, or 5/12/24, or 5/12/1924, or 5/12/24. It is important to recognize this so that you will understand what is meant when you see 5/12/1924 in a German record. It does not mean May 12, 1924; it means 5 December 1924. It would be good if all dates had been recorded with the month spelled out (December) or abbreviated (Dec). Then no confusion would ensue. But, unfortunately, such is not always the case. So remember that 9-2-1957 means 9 February 1957, not September 2, 1957.

The next thing to remember is the German designations for <u>times</u>, hours, mornings, evenings, days, and months. In German, the words you will need to read time are the numbers (presented previously) and the terms that follow:

Abend: evening
gestern: yesterday
halb: half
Minuten: minutes
Mittag: noon

Mitternacht: midnight
Morgen: morning
nach: after
Nachmittag: afternoon
Stunde(n): hour(s)

Uhr: o'clock
Viertel: quarter
vor: before
Vormittag: forenoon

Now, if you will look at the following times and their translations, you will see how times may be read when they appear in records:

ein Uhr: one o'clock
zehn Uhr: ten o'clock
halb drei: half way to three (half hour before three)
halb neun: half way to nine (half hour before nine)
ein Viertel nach vier: a quarter after four
drei Viertel nach sieben: three quarters after seven

ein Viertel vor elf: a quarter before eleven
drei Viertel vor zwei: three quarters before two
zehn Minuten vor fünf: ten minutes before five
dreiundzwanzig Minuten nach sechs: 23 minutes after six
acht Uhr fünfzehn: eight fifteen (8:15)
zwolf Uhr sechsundvierzig: twelve forty-six (12:46)
achtzehn Minuten nach sieben am Morgen: 18 minutes after seven
    in the morning (7:18 am)
elf Uhr vierunddriessig am Abend: eleven thirty-four in the
    evening (11:34 pm)

The names of the <u>days</u>, then the months and seasons in German are now given. Included are some of the older designations which you may run across in the records of the 16th and 17th centuries. First, the days:

Aftermontag: Dienstag
Aftersonntag: Monday
Dienstag: Tuesday
dies dominica (Lat): Sunday
dies Jovis (Lat): Thursday
dies lunae (Lat): Monday
dies Martis (Lat): Tuesday
dies Mercurii (Lat): Wednesday
dies quarta (Lat): Wednesday
dies Saturni (Lat): Saturday
dies soli (Lat): Sunday
dies Veneris (Lat): Friday
Donnerstag: Thursday
Dornstag: Thursday
Eritag: Tuesday
feria quinta (Lat): Thursday
feria secunda (Lat): Monday
feria septima: Saturday
feria sexta (Lat): Friday

feria tertia (Lat): Tuesday
Freitag: Friday
Godenstag: Wednesday
Gudenstag: Wednesday
guter Tag: Monday
Laterntag: Saturday
Mantag: Monday
mitticher: Wednesday
Mittwoch: Wednesday
Montag: Monday
Sabbat: Saturday
Samstag: Saturday
Satertag: Saturday
Sinstag: Tuesday
Sonnabend: Saturday
Sonntag: Sunday
Wodenstag: Wednesday
Zinstag: Tuesday

Symbols were also often used for the days, the most prevalent ones being the following:

Sunday ☉   Monday ☽

Tuesday ♂   Wednesday ☿

Thursday ♃   Friday ♀

Saturday ♄

During part of the time that portions of the western section of Germany were under strong domination of the French Revolutionary Government, namely, 1792-1805, the French Empire used a different calendar. This calendar had 12 months with 30 days each plus an extra 5 days (or in leap year 6 days) which were attached to the end of the year. The months bore the following names: Vendemiaire (began Sep 22-24), Brumaire (began 22-24 Oct), Frimaire (began nov 21-23), Nivose (began 21-23 Dec), Pluviose (began 20-22 Jan), Ventose (began 19-21 Feb), Germinal (began 21-22 Mar), Florcal (began 20-21 Apr), Prairal (began 20-21 May), Messidor (began 19-20 Jun), Thermidor (began 19-20 Jul), and Fructidor (began 18-19 Aug). The extra days were added on to Fructidor, which means they occurred in late September.

Now, the list of weeks, months, and seasons will be presented.

7ber: September
7bris: September
8ber: October
8bris: October
9ber: November
9bris: November
10ber: December
10bris: December
April: April
Aprilis(Lat): April
August: August
Augustus(Lat): August
Brachet: June
Brachmond: June
Christmond:Dezember
Dezember: December
Eismond: January
Erntemond: August
Ernting: August
Feber: February

Februar: February
Februarius(Lat): February
Frühling: spring
Gilbhard: October
Hartung: January
Heilmond: December
Herbst: fall
Herbstmond: September
Heuert: July
Heumond: July
Hornung: February
Ianuarius(Lat): January
Iulius(Lat): July
Iunius(Lat): June
Jahr: year
Jahrhundert: century
Jahrzehnt: decade
Jänner: January
Januar: January

Juli: July
Julmond: Dezember
Juni: June
Lenzing: March
Lenzmond: March
Mai: May
Maien: May
Maius(Lat): May
Martius(Lat): March
März: March
Monat: month
Nebelmond: November
Nebelung: November
November: November
Oktober: October
Ostermond: April
Scheiding: September
September: September

Sommer: summer	Wintermond: Nov-	Woche(n): week(s)
Weinmond: October	ember	Wonnemond: May
Winter: winter		

Next, we need to take up with you the very important matter of the calendar. This is very important because a major calendar change was made in 1582, but not all areas adopted the change immediately. Many did so later, a few much later. By 1582, the Julian calendar had lost 10 days with regard to the seasons of the year. This was because the Julian calendar was based on the year being exactly 365.25 days (365 and a fourth of a day) long. The beginning of spring (vernal equinox) had actually moved from 21 March to 11 March, which was wrong. This occurred because the length of the year is actually only 365.2422 days. The Old Style (OS) Julian calendar provided for the extra quarter of a day by having a leap year every fourth year. During medieval times and in Christian nations, New Year's Day under the Old Style (OS) Julian calendar was celebrated on 25 March.

In 1582, Pope Gregory XIII corrected the past error by declaring that the day following 05 October 1582 be 15 October 1582. He also declared that century years not divisible evenly by 400 be eliminated as leap years. This meant that 1600 would be counted as a leap year, 1700, 1800, and 1900 would not, and that 2000 would. This revised calendar was called the New Style (NS) Gregorian calendar. It also adopted 01 January as New Year's Day. The Gregorian (NS) calendar was accepted by the Catholic areas of Germany quite soon (1583-1585), but many Protestant areas adopted it only later (1600-1700). The dates on which the New Style (NS) Gregorian calendar were introduced in some German areas are as follows:

Aachen: 11 Jan 1583
Augsburg: 16 Oct 1583
Baden: 27 Nov 1583
Bayern: 16 October 1583
Bohemia: 17 Jan 1584
Brandenburg: 15 Nov 1699
Breisgau: 24 Oct 1583
Cleve: 28 Nov 1583
Danzig: 1582
Deutschland(Cath): 1583-5
Deutschland(Evang): 1600-76
Eichstätt: 16 Nov 1583

Elsass(Öst): 24 Oct 1583
Freiburg: 12 Jan 1584
Friesland: 12 Jan 1701
Hessen: 15 Nov 1699
Hildesheim: 26 Mar 1631
Jülich-Berg: 13 Nov 1583
Köln: 14 Nov 1583
Lothringen: 20 Dec 1582
Mainz: 22 Nov 1583
Minden: 1630
Mühlhausen: 31 Oct 1583
Neuburg(Pfalz): 24 Dec 1615

Nürnberg: 03 Oct 1699

Osnabruck: 1624

Paderborn: 27 Jun 1584

Passau: Feb 1583

Pfalz(Rhein): 03 Oct 1699

Preussen: 02 Sep 1612

Regensburg: 16 Oct 1583

Sachsen: 15 Nov 1699

Schlesien: 23 Jan 1584

Siebenbürgen: 25 Dec 1590

Strassburg: 01 Mar 1682

Trier: 15 Oct 1583

Ulm: 03 Oct 1699

Unterwalden: Jun 1584

Westfalen: 12 Jul 1584

Würzburg: 15 Nov 1583

German researchers have to pay careful attention to the Old Style-New Style dates because Scotland did not adopt the New Style until 1600, and the remainder of Great Britain did not put it into complete effect until 03-14 September 1752. This means that the American colonies, being British, did not completely switch over until 03-14 September 1752. By this time, the two calendars (NS and OS) were 11 days out of phase, so 11 days had to be skipped. Hence, coordinating German dates and American colonial dates between 1582 and 1752 must be done with care. Remember that the new year did not start until 25 March under the Old Style (OS). To keep this clear, British and American dates between 01 January and 25 March should be double-dated. The Old Style year is generally shown first and the New Style year second. For example, you write 11 March 1716/1717, which means 11 March (Old Style using a 25 March New Year = 1716)/(New Style using a 01 January New Year = 1717). Of course, in Germany, they would be writing the date 22 March 1717, because they had both changed New Year's Day and added the extra days.

Not only did the German people employ the secular calendar which has just been discussed, the churches, both Catholic and Evangelical, used the ecclesiastical or church year. This calendar is based on two major events: Christmas (December 25) and Easter (determined by the solar-lunar cycles). The year begins with the First Sunday in Advent which occurs four Sundays before Christmas. The period (season) before Christmas is known as Advent. After Christmas, there is the season of Christmas (2 Sundays), then Epiphany (1-6 Sundays), then the season of Lent (40 days including 6 Sundays). Next comes the Easter season (7 Sundays), and this is followed by the Trinity Season (22-27 Sundays).

The church year with its major feast days is spelled out in detail for you here, with the German designations given first and the English following in parentheses. The days listed without asterisks are movable, that is, they depend on the day on which Christmas falls and on the date of Easter. The days listed with asterisks are immovable, that is, they always fall on the same date.

<u>Advents (Advent)</u> = 4 Sundays
      Adventssonntag (1st Sun in Advent): 4th Sun before Christmas
      ***Andreas (St. Andrew): 30 Nov
      (2nd Sun in Advent): 3rd Sun before Christmas
      (3rd Sun in Advent): 2nd Sun before Christmas
      ***Thomas (St. Thomas): 21 Dec
      (4th Sun in Advent): ist Sun before Christmas
      ***Weihnachts (Christmas): 25 Dec
<u>Weihnachts (Christmas)</u> = 2 Sundays
      ***Stephanus (St. Stephen): 26 Dec
      (1st Sun after Xmas)
      ***Johannes (St. John): 27 Dec
      ***Unschuldige Kindlein (Holy Innocents): 28 Dec
      (2nd Sun after Xmas)
      ***Beschneidung Christi (Circumcision of Our Lord): 01 Jan
<u>Epiphanie/Erscheinung (Epiphany)</u> = 1-to-6 Sundays
      ***Epiphanie (Epiphany): 06 Jan
      Septuagesima (Septuagesima Sun): 9th Sun before Easter
      Sexagesima (Sexagesima Sun): 8th Sun before Easter
      Quinquasgesima (Quinquagesima Sun): 7th Sun before Easter
      ***Pauli Bekehrung/Conversio (Conversion of St.Paul): 25 Jan
      ***Praesentatio Domini Nostrum (Presentation of Our Lord): 02
          Feb
      ***Matthias (St. Matthias): 24 Feb
<u>Fastenzeit (Lent)</u> = 40 days + 6 days of Holy Week
      Aschermittwoch (Ash Wednesday): 46 days before Easter
      I Invocavit (1st Sun in Lent): 6th Sun before Easter
      II Reminiscere (2nd Sun in Lent): 5th Sun before Easter
      III Oculi (3rd Sun in Lent): 4th Sun before Easter
      IV Laetare (4th Sun in Lent): 3rd Sun before Easter
      V Passionssonntag (5th Sun in Lent): 2nd Sun before Easter
      VI Palmsonntag (6th Sun in Lent): 1st Sun before Easter
      Karwoche (Holy Week): Montag (Monday)
                   Dienstag (Tuesday)
                   Mittwoch (Wednesday)
                   Gründonnerstag (Maundy Thursday)
                   Karfreitag (Good Friday)
                   Samstag (Easter Eve)
<u>Osternzeit (Easter)</u>: 8 Sundays

Ostern (Easter Sunday): See listing below for date in any given
    year
***Berkündigung Maria (Annunciation): 25 Mar
I Quasi Modo Geniti (2nd Sun of Easter): 1st Sun after Easter
II Misericordia (3rd Sun of Easter): 2nd Sun after Easter
III Jubilate (4th Sun of Easter): 3rd Sun after Easter
IV Cantate (5th Sun of Easter): 4th Sun after Easter
V Rogate/Vocem Juncunditatis (6th Sun of Easter): 5th Sun after
    Easter
Himmelfahrt Christi (Ascension Thu): 40 days after Easter
VI Exaudi (7th Sun of Easter): 6th Sun after Easter
***Marcus (St. Mark): 25 Apr
***Philippus und Jacobus (St. Philip and St. James): 01 May
Pfingsten (Pentecost/Whitsunday): 7th Sun or 50 days after Easter
<u>Trinititatis (Trinity)</u>: 22-to-27 Sundays
    (Trinity Sunday): 8th Sun after Easter
***Johannes der Täufer (St. John the Baptist): 24 Jun
***Petrus und Paulus (Sts. Peter and Paul): 29 Jun
***Heimsuchung Mariä (Visitation): 02 Jul
***Jacobus der Altere (St. James the Elder): 25 Jul
***Umgestaltung/Verklärung (Transfiguration of Our Lord): 06
    Aug
***Himmelfahrt Maria (Assumption of Mary): 15 Aug
***Bartholomäus (St. Bartholomew): 24 Aug
***Matthaeus (St. Matthew): 21 Sep
***Michael (St. Michael and All Angels): 29 Sep
***Lucas (St. Luke): 18 Oct
***Simeon und Judas (Sts. Simon and Jude): 28 Oct
***Reformations-Fest (Reformation Day-Protestant): 31 Oct
***Allerseelen/Allerheiligen (All Souls'/All Saints' Day): 01 Nov

The dates on which Easter fell during the period 1500-1900 will
now be set forth. Once you know that date, you can calculate the dates on
which each of the movable feasts listed above came. In this listing, M
stands for March, A stands for April, os stands for Old Style (Julian calendar), and ns stands for New Style (Gregorian calendar).
    1500(A19) 1501(A11) 1502(M27) 1503(A16) 1504(A07) 1505(M23)
1506(A12) 1507(A04) 1508(A23) 1509(A08) 1510(M31) 1511(A20)
1512(A11) 1513(M27) 1514(A16) 1515(A08) 1516(M23) 1517(A12)
1518(A04) 1519(A24) 1520(A08) 1521(M31) 1522(A20) 1523(A05)
1524(M27) 1525(A16) 1526(A01) 1527(A21) 1528(A12) 1529(M28)
1530(A17) 1531(A09) 1532(M31) 1533(A13) 1534(A05) 1535(M28)

1536(A16)   1537(A01)   1538(A21)   1539(A06)   1540(M28)   1541(A17)
1542(A09)   1543(M25)   1544(A13)   1545(A05)   1546(A25)   1547(A10)
1548(A01)   1549(A21)   1550(A06)   1551(M29)   1552(A17)   1553(A02)
1554(M25)   1555(A14)   1556(A05)   1557(A18)   1558(A10)   1559(M26)
1560(A14)   1561(A06)   1562(M29)   1563(A11)   1564(A02)   1565(A22)
1566(A14)   1567(M30)   1568(A18)   1569(A10)   1570(M26)   1571(A15)
1572(A06)   1573(M22)   1574(A11)   1575(A03)   1576(A22)   1577(A07)
1578(M30)   1579(A19)   1580(A03)   1581(M26)   1582(A13)   1583(osM27
nsA10)   1584(osA16 nsA01)   1585(osA11 nsA21)   1586(osA03 nsA06)
1587(osA16 nsM29)   1588(osA07 nsA17)   1589(osM30 nsA02)   1590(osA19
nsA22)   1591(osA04 nsA14)   1592(osM26 nsM29)   1593(osA15 nsA18)
1594(osM31 nsA10)   1595(osA20 nsM26)   1596(osA11 nsA14)   1597(osM27
nsA06)   1598(osA16 nsM22)   1599(osA08 nsA18)   1600(osM23 nsA02)
1601(osA12 nsA22)   1602(osA04 nsA07)   1603(osA24 nsM30)   1604(osA08
nsA18)   1605(osM31 nsA10)   1606(osA20 nsM26)   1607(osA05 nsA15)
1608(osM27 nsA06)   1609(osA16 nsA19)   1610(osA08 nsA11)   1611(osM24
nsA03)   1612(osA12 nsA22)   1613(osA04 nsA07)   1614(osA24 nsM30)
1615(osA09 nsA19)   1616(osM31 nsA03)   1617(osA20 nsA19)   1618(osA05
nsA15)   1619(osM28 nsM31)   1620(osA16 nsA19)   1621(osA01 nsA11)
1622(osA21 nsM27)   1623(osA13 nsA16)   1624(osM28 nsA07)   1625(osA17
nsM30)   1626(osA09 nsA12)   1627(osM25 nsA04)   1628(osA13 nsA23)
1629(osA05 nsA15)   1630(osM28 nsM31)   1631(osA10 nsA20)   1632(osA01
nsA11)   1633(osA21 nsM27)   1634(osA06 nsA16)   1635(osM29 nsM08)
1636(osA17 nsM23)   1637(osA09 nsA12)   1638(osM25 nsA04)   1639(osA14
nsA24)   1640(osA05 nsA08)   1641(osA25 nsM31)   1642(osA10 nsA20)
1643(osA02 nsA05)   1644(osA21 nsM27)   1645(osA06 nsA16)   1646(osM29
nsA01)   1647(osA18 nsA21)   1648(osA02 nsA12)   1649(osM25 nsA04)
1650(osA14 nsA17)   1651(osM30 nsA09)   1652(osA18 nsM31)   1653(osA10
nsA13)   1654(osM26 nsA05)   1655(osA15 nsM28)   1656(osA06 nsA16)
1657(osM29 nsA01)   1658(osA11 nsA21)   1659(osA03 nsA13)   1660(osA22
nsM28)   1661(osA14 nsA17)   1662(osM30 nsA09)   1663(osA19 nsM25)
1664(osA10 nsA13)   1665(osM26 nsA05)   1666(osA15 nsA25)   1667(osA07
nsA10)   1668(osM22 nsA01)   1669(osA11 nsA21)
1670(osA03 nsA06)   1671(osA23 nsM29)   1672(osA07 nsA17)   1673(osM30
nsA02)   1674(osA19 nsM25)   1675(osA04 nsA14)   1676(osM26 nsA05)
1677(osA15 nsA18)   1678(osM31 nsA10)   1679(osA20 nsA02)   1680(osA11
nsA21)   1681(osA03 nsA06)   1682(osA16 nsM29)   1683(osA08 nsA18)
1684(osM30 nsA02)   1685(osA19 nsA22)   1686(osA04 nsA14)   1687(osM27
nsM30)   1688(osA15 nsA18)   1689(osM31 nsA10)   1690(osA20 nsM26)
1691(osA12 nsA15)   1692(osM27 nsA06)   1693(osA16 nsM22)   1694(osA08
nsA11)   1695(osM24 nsA03)   1696(osA12 nsA22)   1697(osA04 nsA07)
1698(osA24 nsM30)   1699(osA09 nsA19)

1700(osM31 nsA11) 1701(osA20 nsM27) 1702(osA05 nsA16) 1703(osM28 nsA08) 1704(osA16 nsM23) 1705(osA08 nsA02) 1706(osM24 nsA04) 1707(osA13 nsA24) 1708(osA04 nsA08) 1709(osA04 nsM31) 1710(osA09 nsA20) 1711(osA01 nsA05) 1712(osA20 nsM27) 1713(osA05 nsA16) 1714(osM28 nsA01) 1715(osA17 nsA21) 1716(osA01 nsA12) 1717(osA21 nsM28) 1718(osA13 nsA17) 1719(osM29 nsA09) 1720(osA17 nsM31) 1721(osA09 nsA13) 1722(osM25 nsA05) 1723(osA14 nsM28) 1724(osA05 nsM16) 1725(osM28 nsA01) 1726(osA10 nsA21) 1727(osA02 nsA13) 1728(osA21 nsM28) 1729(osA06 nsA17)

1730(osM29 nsA09) 1731(osA18 nsM25) 1732(osA09 nsA13) 1733(osM25 nsA05) 1734(osA14 nsA25) 1735(osA06 nsA10) 1736(osA25 nsA01) 1737(osA10 nsA21) 1738(osA02 nsA06) 1739(osA22 nsM29) 1740(osA06 nsA17) 1741(osM29 nsA02) 1742(osA18 nsM25) 1743(osA03 nsA14) 1744(osM25 nsA05) 1745(osA14 nsA18) 1746(osM30 nsA10) 1747(osA19 nsA02) 1748(osA10 nsA14) 1749(osM26 nsA06) 1750(osA15 nsM29) 1751(osA07 nsA11) 1752(osM29 nsA02) 1753(osA11 nsA22) 1753(A22) 1754(A14) 1755(M30) 1756(A18) 1757(A10) 1758(M26) 1759(M26) 1760(A06) 1761(M22) 1762(A11) 1763(A03) 1764(A22) 1765(A07) 1766(M30) 1767(A19) 1768(A03) 1769(M26) 1770(A15) 1771(M31) 1772(A19) 1773(A11) 1774(A03) 1775(A16) 1776(A07) 1777(M30) 1778(A19) 1779(A04) 1780(M26) 1781(A15) 1782(M31) 1783(A20) 1784(A11) 1785(M27) 1786(A16) 1787(A08) 1788(M23) 1789(A12) 1790(A04) 1791(A24) 1792(A08) 1793(M31) 1794(A20) 1795(A05) 1796(M27) 1797(A16) 1798(A08) 1799(M24) 1800(A13) 1801(A05) 1802(A18) 1803(A10) 1804(A01) 1805(A14) 1806(A06) 1807(M29) 1808(A17) 1809(A02) 1810(A22) 1811(A14) 1812(M29) 1813(A18) 1814(A10) 1815(M26) 1816(A14) 1817(A06) 1818(M22) 1819(A11) 1820(A02) 1821(A22) 1822(A07) 1823(M30) 1824(A18) 1825(A03) 1826(M26) 1827(A15) 1828(A06) 1829(A19) 1830(A11) 1831(A03) 1832(A22) 1833(A07) 1834(M30) 1835(A19) 1836(A03) 1837(M26) 1838(A15) 1839(M31) 1840(A19) 1841(A11) 1842(M27) 1843(A16) 1844(A07) 1845(M23) 1846(A12) 1847(A04) 1848(A23) 1849(A08) 1850(M31) 1851(A20) 1852(A11) 1853(M27) 1854(A16) 1855(A08) 1856(M23) 1857(A12) 1858(A04) 1859(A24) 1860(A08) 1861(M31) 1862(A20) 1863(A05) 1864(M27) 1865(A16) 1866(A01) 1867(A21) 1868(A12) 1869(M28) 1870(A17) 1871(A09) 1872(M31) 1873(A13) 1874(A05) 1875(M28) 1876(A16) 1877(A01) 1878(A21) 1879(A13) 1880(M28) 1881(A17) 1882(A09) 1883(M25) 1884(A13) 1885(A05) 1886(A25) 1887(A10) 1888(A01) 1889(A21) 1890(A06) 1891(M29) 1892(A17) 1893(A02) 1894(M25) 1895(A14) 1896(A05) 1897(A18) 1898(A10) 1899(A02) 1900(A15)

Another feature of the church year is numerous festivals and holy days named in honor of saints and events in the lives of Jesus, Mary, Jesus' associates, the apostles, and the saints. In fact, every day of the year celebrates at least one such occasion. On many days, there are numerous commemorations. You may sometimes find dates in church records, particularly Catholic ones, given in terms of these festivals and memorial days. A very thorough listing of them is presented in:

___W. Ribbe and E. Henning, TASCHENBUCH FÜR FAMILIEN-GESCHICHTSFORSCHUNG, Verlag Degener, Neustadt/Aisch, Deutschland, 1980, pages 318-327.

6. Names	6. Namen
6. Namen	6. Namen

The present practice of naming in Western countries generally involves one or more given names and a family name. The given name(s) is(are) often called the Christian name(s) and the family name is designated the last name or the surname. Practically all names have a meaning which was derived from some historical circumstance. During the height of the Roman Empire, many persons used three names (praenomen = given name, nomen = local clan, cognomen = family), and some added a fourth (agnomen). After the Roman Empire fell, the use of last names was not widely practiced, as had been the case before the Empire. Family names began to be used in the northern part of Italy late in the 900s. The nobility used them to establish the family line by letting the names be inherited, and to set themselves above the commoners. By about 1200, the practice was widely spread, with many of the common people adopting last names. The increase of commerce, travel, and communication also called for the necessity of distinguishing among the many persons with the same first name. These growing interconnections among people caused the spread of the practice from Italy to other nations in the West, including the Germanic areas. Here, again, the nobility lead the way, those in the larger trade centers following, then the ordinary people. Finally, an inherited last name was made the law.

By the second half of the 1100s in the southern Germanic areas, hereditary surnames are beginning to appear. They moved steadily northward and by about 1600, the use of them was widespread. However, many people, especially in the north, continued to change their surnames from one generation to the next. The practice of changing persisted longest in

Lippe, Ostfriesland, and Schleswig-Holstein. Between 1670 and 1800, laws requiring an inherited surname were passed by the various German states and principalities.

The surnames of German-speaking peoples took their origins from many different sources:
1. Father's given name became a surname (patronymics).
   Hans --> Hansen
2. Mother's given name became a surname (metronymics).
   Maria --> Marien
3. Occupations became surnames. Zimmerman = carpenter.
4. Topographic places of origin became surnames. Wald = forest.
5. Regions, cities, towns of origin became surnames.
   Bremer = from Bremen.
6. Physical characteristics became surnames. Weiss = white.
7. Personal characteristics became surnames.
   Freundlich = friendly
8. Items that people were associated with became surnames.
   Vogel = bird
9. Farm names became surnames. Sonnefeld = sunny field

Each of these will now be discussed in a little detail.

Father's first name. Early practice in the Germanic areas was for people to bear only first names. However, as the population increased and commerce and transportation facilitated contact among larger and larger numbers of people, it became necessary to distinguish among persons bearing the same first name. For example, there might be two young men named Heinrich in an area. And when the name Heinrich was used, someone would ask: Which Heinrich? The answer would come back: Heinrich, Hans' son. Or the answer: Heinrich, Jakob's son. This could develop into them being called Heinrich Hanson and Heinrich Jakobson. Thus, last name development had occurred. There were also other suffixes (endings) which were used to identify sons: -sen, -s, -ing, -er. In many cases, the father's first name was simply added to the son's first name, so as to give Andreas Friedrich or Heinrich Adam. In addition, local dialects led to the use of many variants of names. For instance, Heinrich could appear as Heindrich, Heinreich, Hendrich, Hindrick, Hendrik, Henrych, Jennrich, and Hinnerk. Diminutives could also be used (little Heinrich): Heinel, Heynel, Heinlein, Heindl, Heintze, Heinz, Heinecke, Heinemann.

One of the most confusing aspects of surnaming is the use of non-hereditary patronymics. The last name of the son would be derived from the first name of the father, with the practice carrying on from generation to generation. The result is that the last name would change with each generation. For example, consider these:

Grandfather's name:	Anders Petersen
Father's name:	Nicol Andersen
Son's name:	Paul Nicolsen
Grandson's name:	Jorgen Paulsen
Great grandson's name:	Michel Jorgensen

This, of course, can and often does lead to considerable research difficulty. The practice of changing the last name with each generation was fairly common in northern and northwestern Germany in the early years. It persisted in Ostfriesland (adjacent to Holland) until about 1811, and in Schleswig-Holstein (adjacent to Denmark) until the period 1830-1850. What must be done is to locate records which form the bridge between the generations: birth, christening, marriage, and death. The major clue is usually the age, because once that is established, the year of birth can be identified. This narrows the record search to about a year, and often permits the child to be recognized.

Mother's first name. Last names also originated from the mother's first name, but this is not nearly as common as from the father's. An example is the last name Marien, which could be derived from the German Maria. It is often difficult to assign the origin of a name to a female, because many female names are derived from male names: Paula, Bertha, Johanna, Andrea.

Occupation. An easy way to distinguish between two persons named Wilhelm was to call one Wilhelm the shoemaker and the other Wilhelm the shepherd. In other words, occupations became important sources of surnames. Some examples are: Schreiber(writer), Kaufmann (merchant), Koch(cook), Steinmetz(stone mason), Fechter(swordsman), Hühner(poultryman), Obstler(fruit seller), Kalkbrenner(lime burner), and Fassbinder(cooper).

Topographic places of origin. Home locations were also means of identifying individuals with the same first names. Hence, such last names as the following arose: Ecke(corner), Grünwald(green woods),

Bach(brook), Hintermauer(behind the wall), Hohfelde(high field), Niedertal(lower valley), and Ingensand(in the sand).

Towns and regions. The towns and regions from which persons came also served to identify them and to provide names which were passed on to succeeding generations. Examples are: Bremer(from Bremen), Lindauer(from Lindau), Magdeburger(from Magdeburg), Adenauer(from Adenau), Dornhaim(from Dornheim), Schwaben(from Swabia), Unger(from Hungary).

Physical characteristics. Identification of people could often be made on the basis of outstanding physical characteristics. Therefore, such surnames as these came about: Kurz(short), Grau(gray hair), Kraus(curly), Grosskopf(large head), Kleinfuss(small foot).

Personal characteristics. Not only did physical characteristics often assist in differentiating persons, so did personal characteristics. This will be obvious from these examples: Denker(from denken, to think), Wilbold-(from Wille or determination), Ehrhardt(from Ehre or honor), Gottschalk-(from Gott which implies piety), Höflich(polite), Fröhlich(cheerful), Tausendteufel(a thousand devils).

Items people were associated with. Numerous names of this sort can be readily found. A few examples to give you the idea are as follows: Bär(bear), Stern(star), Eber(boar), Kupfer(copper), Rothfuchs(red fox), Zwiebel (onion), Rettich(radish), Fettmilch(rich milk), Ziegenspeck(goat bacon).

Farm names. A practice in some Germanic areas was for people to take the name of the farm on which they lived. Names of farms were often the names of people who had once lived on them, or they were descriptive names of the land. These farm names tended to persist, even though the owners of the farm changed. When a new owner purchased or went to live on the farm, he would change his name to the farm name. This practice produces difficulties similar to those presented by patronymic naming, which was discussed above. Sometimes church records, particularly confirmation records, will give both the old and the new names when changes of this sort occur.

There is a practice in Germany which must not be overlooked. Sometimes a suffix -in will be added to a daughter's last name. This practice simply denotes a female. In other words, the son of Johann

Roder would be Jakob Roder, but the daughter would be Anna Roderin.
You must be alert to this possibility to avoid the confusion that Roder and
Roderin in such a case are two distinct surnames.

German-American names. It is important to consider what
happened to German names when the people arrived here in the colonies
or the USA. Basically, three things occurred:
1) The name remained unaltered: Zimmerman
2) The name was altered to a more-English sort of spelling, which
        usually corresponded to how it sounded to English
        speakers: Simmerman
3) The name was translated: Carpenter.
Names were often unaltered when a German immigrant entered into a
German community, or when a German immigrant was well enough
educated to insist on the proper spelling. On the other hand, names were
altered when a German melded into the English-speaking society. One or
more of the special sounds of the German language were transformed into
rough English approximations. Some of the pronunciation clues that
might help you to understand these alterations are:

a is pronounced as in father or in what
        Angler --became--> Onkler
e is pronounced as in eight or in get
        Edel --became--> Aidell
i is pronounced as in machine or in wind
        Isselmann --became--> Easelman
o is pronounced as in obey or in often
        Odenthal --became--> Ohdendal
u is pronounced as oo in root or in foot
        Ummen --became--> Ooman
ie is pronounced as in brief
        Hiereth --became--> Hearett
ei is pronounced as i in white
        Meicha --became--> Micah
eu is pronounced as oy in boy
        Geuder --became--> Goidair
au is pronounced as ou in house
        Tauber --became--> Toubear
ä is pronounced as e in bed
        Abersold --became--> Ebersolt
ö is pronounced as er in kernel
        Kögel --became--> Caregull

ü is said by rounding your lips to say oo, but then saying ee instead
    Nüss --became--> Neese
ch is pronounced as h in hue
    Hachspiel --became--> Hockspeal
d at the end of a word of syllable is pronounced as t as in hint
    Glied --became--> Gliet --became--> Gleet
g at the end of a word or syllable is pronounced as ck in check
    Montag --became--> Moantack
j is pronounced as y in yes
    Jäger --became--> Yeager
s as the first letter in a word is pronounced as z
    Solger --became--> Zolgare
sch is pronounced as sh in fish
    Schüssler --became--> Shisler
th is pronounced as t
    Thurmann --became--> Tourman
v is pronounced as f in fish
    Vorster --became--> Farster
w is pronounced as v in vote
    Wepner --became--> Vaipner
z is pronounced as ts in hats
    Zingl --became--> Single

It is also well to remember that the letters in the following groups sound somewhat similar. They are therefore often found to be substituted for each other when names are altered.

(b--p--f--v)
    Bern--Pern--Fern--Vern

(d--t)
    Düttler--Tüttler

With regard to translations of surnames, you should use a good English-to-German dictionary to look up the German equivalents of English names which you suspect may have been originally German. For example, you will find that:

Smith could have been Schmidt.
Miller could have been Müller.
Taylor could have been Schneider.
Shoemaker could have been Schuhmacher.
Tanner could have been Gerber.
White could have been Weiss.
Short could have been Kurz.
Bean could have been Bohne.

Flowers could have been Blumen.
Bell could have been Klingel.

Among the better reference books for going into detail on names
are the following:

___H. Bahlow, DEUTSCHES NAMENLEXIKON, Suhrkanp, München,
Deutschland, 1972.

---J. K. Brechenmacher, ETYMOLOGISCHES WÖRTERBUCH DER
DEUTSCHEN FAMILIENNAMEN, Starke Verlag,
Limburg/Lahn, Deutschland, 1957, 2 Bände (2 volumes).

___A. Heintze und P. Cascorbi, DIE DEUTSCHEN FAMILIENNAMEN,
Buchhandlung des Waisenhauses, Berlin, Deutschland, 1933.

___G. F. Jones, GERMAN-AMERICAN NAMES, Genealogical Publish-
ing Company, Baltimore, MD, 1990.

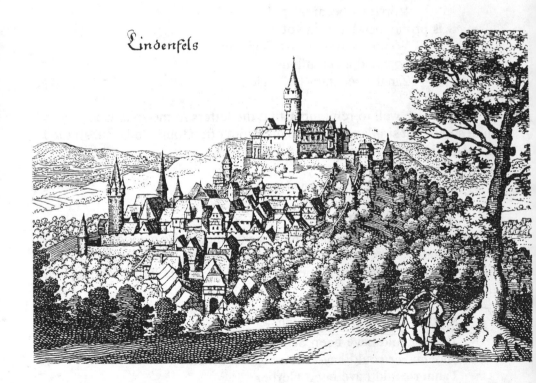

Lindenfels

Books by George K. Schweitzer

CIVIL WAR GENEALOGY. A 78-paged book of 316 sources for tracing your Civil War ancestor. Chapters include [I]: The Civil War, [II]: The Archives, [III]: National Publications, [IV]: State Publications, [V]: Local Sources, [VI]: Military Unit Histories, [VII]: Civil War Events.

GEORGIA GENEALOGICAL RESEARCH. A 242-paged book containing 1303 sources for tracing your GA ancestor along with detailed instructions. Chapters include [I]: GA Background, [II]: Types of Records, [III]: Record Locations, [IV]: Research Procedure and County Listings (detailed listing of records available for each of the 159 GA counties).

GERMAN GENEALOGICAL RESEARCH. A 280-paged book containing 1984 sources for tracing your German ancestor along with detailed instructions. Chapters include [I]: German Background, [II]: Germans to America, [III]: Bridging the Atlantic, [IV]: Types of German Records, [V]: German Record Repositories, [VI]: The German Language.

HANDBOOK OF GENEALOGICAL SOURCES. A 217-paged book describing all major and many minor sources of genealogical information with precise and detailed instructions for obtaining data from them. 129 sections going from adoptions, archives, atlases---down through gazetteers, group theory, guardianships---to War of 1812, ward maps, wills, and WPA records.

KENTUCKY GENEALOGICAL RESEARCH. A 170-paged book containing 1191 sources for tracing your KY ancestor along with detailed instructions. Chapters include [I]: KY Background, [II]: Types of Records, [III]: Record Locations, [IV]: Research Procedure and County Listings (detailed listing of records available for each of the 120 KY counties).

MARYLAND GENEALOGICAL RESEARCH. A 208-paged book containing 1176 sources for tracing your MD ancestor along with detailed instructions. Chapters include [I]: MD Background, [II]: Types of Records, {III]: Record Locations, [IV]: Research Procedure and County Listings (detailed listing of records available for each of the 23 MD counties and for Baltimore City).

MASSACHUSETTS GENEALOGICAL RESEARCH. A 279-paged book containing 1709 sources for tracing your MA ancestor along with detailed instructions. Chapters include [I]: MA Background, [II]: Types of records, [III]: Record Locations, [IV]: Research Procedure and County-Town-City Listings (detailed listing of records available for each of the 14 MA counties and the 351 cities-towns).

NEW YORK GENEALOGICAL RESEARCH. A 240-paged book containing 1426 sources for tracing your NY ancestor along with detailed instructions. Chapters include [I]: NY Background, [II]; Types of Records, [III]: Record Locations, [IV]: Research Procedure and NY City Record Listings (detailed listing of records available for the 5 counties of NY City), [V]: Record Listings for Other Counties (detailed listing of records available for each of the other 57 NY counties.)

NORTH CAROLINA GENEALOGICAL RESEARCH. A 172-paged book containing 1233 sources for tracing your NC ancestor along with detailed instructions. Chapters include I: NC Background, II: Types of Records, III: Record Locations, IV: Research Procedure and County Listings (detailed listing of records available for each of the 100 NC counties).

OHIO GENEALOGICAL RESEARCH, A 212-paged book containing 1241 sources for tracing your OH ancestor along with detailed instructions. Chapters include [I]: NC Background, [II]: Types of Records, [III]: Record Locations, [IV]: Research Procedure and County Listings (detailed listing of records available for each of the 100 NC counties).

PENNSYLVANIA GENEALOGICAL RESEARCH. A 225-paged book containing 1309 sources for tracing your PA ancestor along with detailed instructions. Chapters include I: PA Background, II: Types of Records, III: Record Locations, IV: Research Procedure and County Listings (detailed listing of records available for each of the 67 PA counties).

REVOLUTIONARY WAR GENEALOGY. A 110-paged book containing 407 sources for tracing your Revolutionary War ancestor. Chapters include I: Revolutionary War History, II: The Archives, III: National Publications, IV: State Publications, V: Local Sources, VI: Military Unit Histories, VII: Sites and Museums.

SOUTH CAROLINA GENEALOGICAL RESEARCH. A 190-paged book containing 1107 sources for tracing your SC ancestor along with detailed instructions. Chapters include I: SC Background, II: Types of Records, III: Record Locations, IV: Research Procedure and County Listings (detailed listing of records available for each of the 47 SC counties and districts).

TENNESSEE GENEALOGICAL RESEARCH. A 136-paged book containing 1073 sources for tracing your TN ancestor along with detailed instructions. Chapters include I: TN Background, II: Types of Records, III: Record Locations, IV: Research Procedure and County Listings (detailed listing of records available for each of the 96 TN counties).

VIRGINIA GENEALOGICAL RESEARCH. A 216-paged book containing 1273 sources for tracing your VA ancestor along with detailed instructions. Chapters include I: VA Background, II: Types of Records, III: Record Locations, IV: Research Procedure and County Listings (detailed listing of records available for each of the 100 VA counties and 41 major cities).

WAR OF 1812 GENEALOGY. A 75-paged book of 289 sources for tracing your War of 1812 ancestor. Chapters include I: History of the War, II: Service Records, III: Bounty Land and Pension Records, IV: National and State Publications, V: Local Sources, VI: Military Unit Histories, VII: Sites and Events.

All of the above books may be ordered from Dr. George K. Schweitzer at the address given on the title page. Or send a long SASE for a FREE descriptive leaflet on the books.